A New Model of Capital Asset Prices

James W. Kolari · Wei Liu · Jianhua Z. Huang

A New Model of Capital Asset Prices

Theory and Evidence

palgrave
macmillan

James W. Kolari
Department of Finance
Mays Business School
Texas A&M University
College Station, TX, USA

Wei Liu
USAA Bank
San Antonio, TX, USA

Jianhua Z. Huang
Department of Statistics
Texas A&M University
College Station, TX, USA

ISBN 978-3-030-65196-1 ISBN 978-3-030-65197-8 (eBook)
https://doi.org/10.1007/978-3-030-65197-8

This Palgrave Macmillan imprint is published by the registered company Springer Nature Switzerland AG
The registered company address is: Gewerbestrasse 11, 6330 Cham, Switzerland

To my wife Karie and son Wes
—James W. Kolari

To my wife Na and daughters Ashley and Chelsea
—Wei Liu

To my wife Lan and sons Tian-shu and Tian-da
—Jianhua Z. Huang

Preface

This book proposes a new capital asset pricing model dubbed the *ZCAPM* that consistently outperforms existing popular models in empirical tests using U.S. stock returns. The ZCAPM's dominance of established multifactor models in out-of-sample cross-sectional tests—the gold standard in comparative tests—is remarkable. We believe that the ZCAPM represents the next step in the evolution of asset pricing models. Consequently, this book is intended for academics and finance professionals that employ these models in their research activities. Finance Ph.D. students and professors can apply our ZCAPM to asset pricing problems. And, finance professionals, including portfolio managers, securities traders, and quants, can utilize the ZCAPM in their investment activities.

Early chapters in the book establish the theoretical foundation for the ZCAPM by mathematically deriving a special case of Fischer Black's renowned *zero-beta CAPM*. Black's model is a more general form of the famed *Capital Asset Pricing Model* (*CAPM*) by Nobel Laureate William Sharpe. Both models depend heavily on the mean-variance investment parabola of Nobel Laureate Harry Markowitz. In later chapters we document extensive empirical evidence supporting the ZCAPM based on more than 50 years of U.S. stock return data, many different samples of stocks, and comparisons to several popular multifactor models. These substantive tests using stock return data show that the ZCAPM is the premier asset pricing model in terms of surpassing the significance of other models in commonly used cross-sectional tests used to validate models. Also, we demonstrate practical applications of the ZCAPM in the areas of momentum investing and diversified portfolio formation with superior return/risk performance.

As a backstory, in summers from 2002 to 2017, James Kolari taught a graduate international finance seminar at the Hanken School of Economics in Vaasa, Finland. A long-time puzzle in financial economics is the very small impact of exchange rate movements on stock returns as measured by asset pricing models. After reviewing this vast literature, he began to suspect that problems in asset pricing models may be complicit in the puzzle. In the 1970s, researchers observed that stock return data only weakly supported the lauded CAPM. Motivated by this evidence, Black proposed the zero-beta CAPM to help reconcile CAPM theory and stock return evidence. However, he did not provide empirical proxies for the two efficient and inefficient (zero-beta) portfolios in his model.

In a series of 1990 papers, Eugene Fama and Kenneth French argued that things were worse than previously believed. The beloved CAPM was dead. They accumulated evidence that the CAPM's hypothesized relation between beta risk associated with proxy market portfolio returns and the cross-section of average U.S. stock returns did not hold. Due to this failure, to better fit stock return data, they proposed a three-factor model that augmented the CAPM's market portfolio factor with size and value factors. Responding to the Fama and French studies, Black criticized their three-factor model because: (1) it was developed by means of data snooping, and (2) there was little or no theoretical foundation. He continued to believe that, despite growing evidence to the contrary, the CAPM was valid. What if Black was right?

The biography *Fischer Black and the Revolutionary Idea of Finance* by Perry Mehrling (John Wiley & Sons, Inc.) was published in 2005. As recounted there, after working at the University of Chicago and Massachusetts Institute of Technology, Black took a job at Goldman Sachs in 1984 and worked there until he died in 1995. Always in the relentless pursuit of solutions to finance puzzles, as the first quant at Goldman Sachs, he worked one day a week on independent research. Over these years, he likely continued to develop his zero-beta CAPM ideas. Was it possible that he found an alternative form that bridged the gap between pure theory and practical investment in the real world?

In summer 2010 Kolari met Wei Liu, at the time a Ph.D. finance student at Texas A&M University. Liu had previously earned a Ph.D. in physics from Texas A&M and published numerous scientific papers.

Together, they set out to rediscover what Fischer Black may have learned about the zero-beta CAPM but did not publish due to proprietary research at Goldman Sachs. Their main goal was to find an alternative form of the zero-beta CAPM that could be readily estimated. Given Black's criticism of Fama and French's three-factor model, they focused on building a model based on the theoretical tenets of the CAPM and related zero-beta CAPM. In this regard, Liu's previous physics training was instrumental in using random matrix theory to better understand the asymptotic behavior of the minumum-variance investment parabola. By 2011 they had derived a special case of Black's zero-beta CAPM dubbed the *ZCAPM* that contained readily available asset pricing factors—namely, average market returns and the cross-sectional return dispersion of all assets' returns.

Excited about this new theoretical model with measurable factors, they began experimenting with different empirical approaches to estimate the theoretical ZCAPM. After some initial failures, empirical methods were adapted to take into account positive and negative effects of return dispersion on asset returns. Early tests of these methods corroborated the theoretical ZCAPM. However, these empirical tests relied on fitting regression models that use the response variable to define a signal variable indicating the sign of the effect of return dispersion. Soon thereafter, they met with Jianhua Huang, a statistics professor at Texas A&M University, who recommended a reformulation named the *empirical ZCAPM* that treats the unobservable sign as a latent or hidden variable and employs the expectation–maximization (EM) algorithm for the estimation of parameters. Importantly, this maximum likelihood approach enables the estimation of the probability that returns are positively versus negatively affected by movements in the return dispersion factor. A major refinement, the EM approach to estimating the empirical ZCAPM computes regression parameters, estimates the probability of positive or negative return dispersion effects, substantially boosts the goodness-of-fit of the model, and provides a statistically well-founded empirical methodology.

With both the theoretical and empirical ZCAPM in hand, we wrote a research paper using U.S. stock returns and submitted it to finance conferences. In 2012 our paper won the Best Paper in Investments Award at the largest finance conference in the world sponsored by the Financial Management Association. An attendee invited by us to the conference from the Teachers Retirement System of Texas (TRS) proposed that we set up an investment company and work privately with them on research and development (R&D) for pension fund management. An agreement was made to not publish our work in any manner, including the internet, academic journals, books, etc. From 2012 to 2015 we worked privately with TRS and Texas A&M University, which deepened our applied knowledge of the ZCAPM. During this time, Liu managed the investment company, conducted paper trading experiments, and actively rebalanced an R&D pension fund. Unfortunately, due to changes in management at TRS, our relationship was ended.

After closing our investment firm, we continued to develop the ZCAPM. Our research gradually grew beyond the normal bounds of published papers in academic journals with page length and other restrictions. For this reason, we opted to publish our ZCAPM research in a book. By presenting the theoretical derivation of the ZCAPM from the zero-beta CAPM, a weight of empirical evidence about the ZCAPM and its outperformance compared to other popular models, and useful applications to investment practices, we hope to blunt the natural skepticism that confronts any new and novel model with strong asset pricing claims.

To develop the ZCAPM we benefited greatly from previous work by Black on the zero-beta CAPM. As already mentioned, our ZCAPM is a special case of the zero-beta CAPM that takes on a new functional form with measurable factors. More precisely, the ZCAPM is comprised of *beta risk* associated with average market returns (i.e., CRSP index, S&P 500 index, or other general market indexes) and *zeta risk* related to the cross-sectional standard deviation of all stocks' returns in the market (i.e., return dispersion). Notice that beta risk in the ZCAPM is associated with average market returns rather than the theoretical market portfolio in the CAPM. Together, beta and zeta risks in the ZCAPM serve as a proxy for Sharpe's beta risk as proposed by the CAPM.

Another novel aspect of our ZCAPM model is taking into account positive and negative sensitivity of asset returns to return dispersion movements over time. To estimate the probability of these opposite forces, a mixture model comprised of two factor models is specified. No previous asset pricing models utilize a mixture model to our knowledge. As we will show, return dispersion is a powerful market factor that helps to explain stock returns but must be modeled as in our empirical ZCAPM to fully capture its dual positive and negative nature and be consistent with the theoretical ZCAPM.

Readers are encouraged to conduct empirical tests using our Matlab and R computer programs.

- Matlab codes used in our cross-sectional tests of the empirical ZCAPM are provided at the end of this book. Matlab is licensed software that combines a desktop environment with a programming language for matrix and array mathematics.
- R programs for estimating and testing the empirical ZCAPM are available on GitHub (https://github.com/zcapm). R is a free software environment for statistical computing and graphics. It compiles and runs on a wide variety of UNIX platforms, Windows, and MacOS. Readers can find our Matlab and Python codes at the GitHub website also.

We should note that our R programs execute at a faster speed than the Matlab and Python programs. We challenge readers to use our software and prove for themselves the superior efficacy of the ZCAPM.

College Station, USA — James W. Kolari
San Antonio, USA — Wei Liu
College Station, USA — Jianhua Z. Huang

Acknowledgments

The authors gratefully acknowledge financial support from the Center for International Studies, Mays Business School, Texas A&M University as well as support from both the Hanken School of Economics and the University of Vaasa in Vaasa, Finland.

Helpful comments about our asset pricing model have been received from participants at the Midwest Finance Association 2012 meetings in New Orleans, Louisiana, the Multinational Finance Society 2012 conference in Krakow, Poland, the Financial Management Association 2012 conference in Atlanta, Georgia, and the Southern Finance Association 2020 conference in Palm Springs, California (virtual format). We are grateful to have been awarded the Best Paper in Investments at the Financial Management Association conference. Also, we are thankful for financial support and real world experience gained from work with the Teachers Retirement System of Texas and Texas A&M University.

Many people at academic institutions and investment firms have shared useful comments with us over the years, including Ali Anari, Will Armstrong, Ihsan Badshah, Geert Bekaert, Grant Birdwell, Saurabh Biswas, Jaap Bos, Yong Chen, Gjergji Cici, Brett Cornwell, Lammertjan Dam, Huaizhang Deng, Bilal Ertuk, Wayne Ferson, Paige Fields, Tristan Fitzgerald, Markus Franke, Wesley Gray, Klaus Grobys, Yao Han, Britt Harris, Tim Jones, Hagen Kim, Johan Knif, Sudhir Krishnamurthi, Anestis Ladas, Scott Lee, Qi Li, Yutong Li, Kelly Newhall, Chris Pann, Francisco Penaranda, Ralitsa Petkova, Mike Pia, Seppo Pynnönen, Liqian

Ren, Kyle Rusconi, Katharina Schüller, William Smith, Mikhail Sokolov, Sorin Sorescu, Ty Sorrel, Jene Tebeaux, Ahmet Tuncez, David Veal, Jack Vogel, Ivo Welch, Mark Westerfield, Jian Yang, Nan Yang, Christopher Yost-Bremm, Jun Zhang, Zhao Xin, Tony van Zijl, Yangru Wu, Zhaodong Zhong, and Yuzhao Zhang.

We are thankful for the assistance of Ph.D. students at Texas A&M University. Yao Han (finance) provided assistance with cross-sectional statistical tests. Zhao Tang Luo (statistics) wrote the initial R codes to conduct replication exercises to check our Matlab codes. Huiling Liao (statistics) further developed R codes, composed the R package, and assisted with additional tests. Jacob Atnip (finance) read through the mauscript and helped with final editing.

Finally, we would like to express our gratitude to Executive Editor Tula Weis at Palgrave Macmillan for her willingness to work with us and make this book possible. Also, Project Coordinator Ashwini Elango was instrumental in manuscript preparation and production. An anonymous referee provided useful comments.

Contents

Part IV Empirical Evidence

Part V Applications of the ZCAPM

Part VI Conclusion

About the Authors

Professor James W. Kolari is the JP Morgan Chase Professor of Finance and Academic Director of the Commercial Banking Program in the Department of Finance at Texas A&M University. After earning a Ph.D. in Finance from Arizona Station University in 1980, he has taught financial institutions and markets classes and been active in international education, consulting, and executive education. In 1986 he was a Fulbright Scholar at the University of Helsinki and Bank of Finland. He has served as a Visiting Scholar at the Federal Reserve Bank of Chicago, Senior Research Fellow at the Swedish School of Business and Economics (Hanken), Finland, and Faculty Fellow with the Mortgage Bankers Association of America, in addition to being a consultant to the U.S. Small Business Administration, American Bankers Association, Independent Bankers Association of America, and numerous banks and other organizations. With over 100 articles published in refereed journals, numerous other papers and monographs, and over 15 co-authored books, he ranks in the top 1–2% of finance scholars in the United States. His papers have appeared in domestic and international journals, including the *Journal of Finance*, *Journal of Business*, *Review of Financial Studies*, *Review of Economics and Statistics*, *Journal of Money, Credit and Banking*, *Journal of Banking and Finance*, *Journal of Economic Dynamics and Control*, *Journal of Financial Research*, *Real Estate Economics*, *Journal of International Money and Finance*, and *Scandanavian Journal of Economics*. Papers in Russian, Finnish, Dutch, Italian, Spanish, and Chinese have appeared outside of the United States. He is a co-author of leading college textbooks in commercial banking, introductory business, and global business courses.

Dr. Wei Liu received his first Ph.D. in Physics in 2004 from Texas A&M University. His research focused on particle physics theory. After working as a postdoc for a few years, he changed his career path and earned a second Ph.D. in Finance in 2013 from Texas A&M University with an emphasis on asset pricing. From 2013 to 2016, he served as the manager and part owner of a small investment company. Developing asset pricing models based on statistical analysis, he created U.S. equity investment strategies to manage $100 million for the Teachers Retirement System of Texas. Subsequently, in 2017 he joined IberiaBank Corporation in Birmingham, Alabama as a senior analyst building and documenting risk models. Internal risk models for the bank as well analyses for regulatory agencies were implemented. In 2018 he returned to Texas working for USAA Bank in San Antonio as a senior quantitative analyst with duties designing and implementing models for bank stress testing, loss forecasts, allowance for loan and lease losses, and credit risk management analysis. Recently, Dr. Liu has been engaged with various marketing issues at the bank.

Professor Jianhua Z. Huang is Professor of Statistics and Arseven/Mitchell Chair in Astronomical Statistics in the Department of Statistics at Texas A&M University. He received his B.A. in Probability and Statistics (1989) at Beijing University, M.A. in Probability and Statistics (1992) at Beijing University, and Ph.D. in Statistics (1997) at University of California at Berkeley. His areas of expertise are in statistical machine learning, computational statistics, statistical methods for big data sets, nonparametric and semi-parametric statistical modeling and inference, functional data analysis, spatial data analysis, application of statistics in business, social and natural sciences and engineering. He has supervised 21 Ph.D. students and published over 100 refereed papers. He is a Fellow of American Statistical Association, Fellow of Institute of Mathematical Statistics, and Elected Member of International Statistical Institute. Additionally, he has served on the editorial board of *Chemometrics and Intelligent Laboratory System*, *Journal of American Statistical Association*, *Journal of Multivariate Analysis*, and *STAT*.

List of Figures

List of Tables

PART I

Introduction

CHAPTER 1

Asset Pricing Evolution

Abstract Based on the groundbreaking work by Markowitz (1959) on the mean-variance investment parabola and concept of diversification, the renowned *Capital Asset Pricing Model* (CAPM) of Sharpe (1964) and others proposed an equilibrium pricing framework that became the main branch of a new field of finance literature known as *asset pricing*. Black (1972) extended their analyses to develop a more general asset pricing model named the *zero-beta CAPM*. After reviewing these foundational asset pricing models, the present book derives a special case of the zero-beta CAPM dubbed the *ZCAPM*. This theoretical derivation is crucial to the specification of the empirical ZCAPM, which we use to estimate the ZCAPM using U.S. stock returns. By contrast, popular multifactor models dominating the asset pricing literature nowadays have little or no theoretical justification; instead, they use empirical tests to search for possible asset pricing factors. Following Fama and French (1992, 1993, 1995, 1996), who have argued that the CAPM is dead due to its empirical failure, multifactor models typically employ long/short portfolios formed from different firm characteristics. With no connection to the general equilibrium framework of the CAPM, the growing number of multifactors and resultant shopping mall of contender models have evolved into a separate branch in the evolutionary tree of asset pricing. Based on over 50 years of U.S. stock returns, we compare our empirical ZCAPM to popular multifactor models. As we will see, extensive empirical tests not only support the ZCAPM but consistently dominate those of other models. In view of these exceptional

J. W. Kolari et al., *A New Model of Capital Asset Prices*,
https://doi.org/10.1007/978-3-030-65197-8_1

results, we subsequently apply the ZCAPM to practical investment problems, including the momentum mystery as well as construction of diversified, high-performing portfolios. Taken as a whole, we believe that the theoretical and empirical ZCAPM presented in this book represent the next evolutionary step in asset pricing. As we will see, the ZCAPM not only revives the CAPM but grafts multifactor models onto the original main branch of asset pricing.

Keywords Asset pricing · CAPM · Cross-sectional return dispersion · Cross-sectional tests · Fischer Black · Harry Markowitz · Investment parabola · Market factor · Multifactor models · Portfolio analysis · Return dispersion · Securities investment · Stock market · Richard Roll · William Sharpe · ZCAPM · Zero-beta CAPM

1.1 Origins of the CAPM

Numerous authors are credited with inventing the renowned *Capital Asset Pricing Model* (CAPM), including Treynor (1961, 1962), Sharpe (1964), Lintner (1965), Mossin (1966), and Black (1972).[1] Among these authors, Professor William Sharpe was awarded the Nobel Prize in Economics in 1990 for his general equilibrium theory of capital asset prices in financial markets. From the 1960s to 1980s, the CAPM and its companion models[2] established themselves as the main branch of a new field of financial studies—namely, *asset pricing*.

As a Ph.D. student attending the University of California at Los Angeles (UCLA), Sharpe worked closely with Professor Harry Markowitz, who later shared the Nobel Prize with him along with Professor Merton Miller. Markowitz (1959) is renowned for the concept of diversification, wherein the total risk of two or more assets (as measured by their return variances) can be less than the sum of their individual risks due to less than perfect correlation of their returns. In two-dimensional return and risk space, assuming

[1] See also the continuous time version of the CAPM known as the *intertemporal CAPM* by Merton (1973).

[2] See the consumption CAPM (CCAPM) of Lucas (1978) and Breeden (1979), conditional CAPM of Ferson and Harvey (1991, 1996), production-based asset pricing model (PAPM) of Cochrane (1991), and international CAPM of Stulz (1981, 1995).

risk-averse investors, he proposed that the investment opportunity set of all risky assets is outlined by a *mean-variance parabola*.

Figure 1.1 shows a picture of Markowitz's investment parabola. Asset returns for stocks, bonds, commodities, real estate, etc., are measured on the Y-axis, and the variances (or standard deviations) of returns are on the X-axis. For example, we could compute the one-month return for all stocks in the stock market and plot them in the graph against the variance of daily returns in the month. The investment parabola is based on the returns and variances of assets computed in some time period, such as a day, month, year, etc. All assets are plotted within the boundaries of the parabola.

Markowitz showed that diversified portfolios can be constructed with lower total risk than individual assets. The outer boundary of the investment parabola in Fig. 1.1 shows the infinite number of minimum variance portfolios that can be created from individual assets. The global minimum variance portfolio is labeled *G* in the diagram. Portfolio *G* lies at the left-most point (or vertex) on the axis of symmetry of the parabola that divides it equally into upper and lower regions. Diversified portfolios with returns

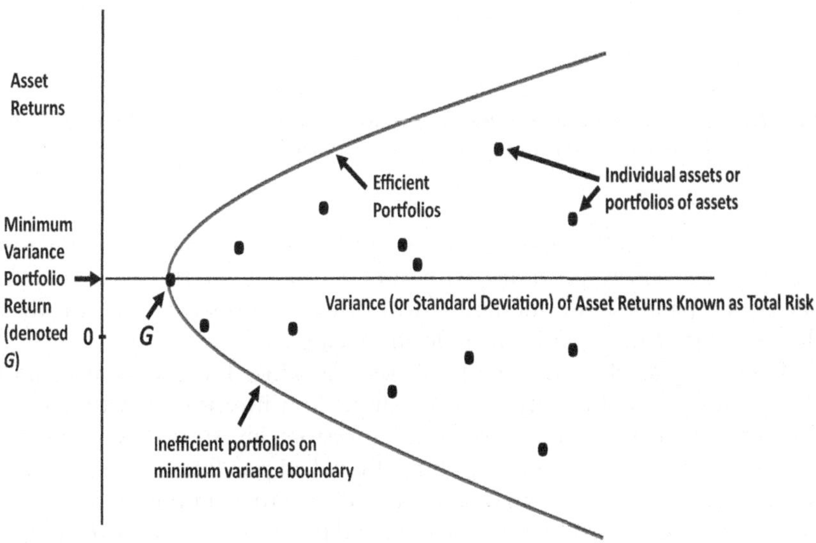

Fig. 1.1 The Markowitz mean-variance investment parabola showing the relationship between the returns and risks of assets

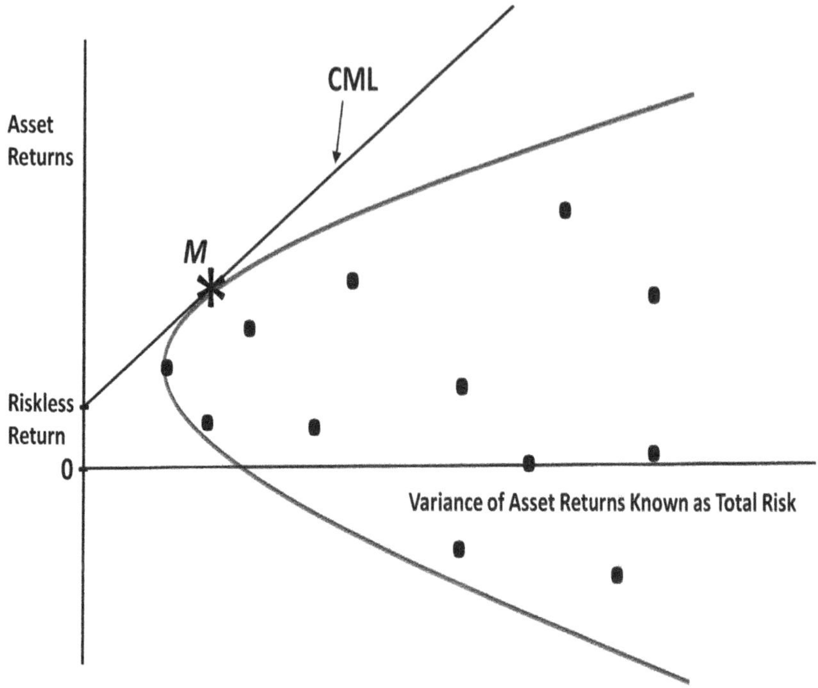

Fig. 1.2 The Capital Market Line (CML) locates risky market portfolio *M* as the tangent point on the ray from the riskless asset to the investment parabola

greater than *G* on the upper boundary of the parabola lie on the ***efficient frontier***. Conversely, portfolios with returns below *G* on the lower boundary of the parabola are inefficient with lower returns per unit risk than diversified portfolios along the efficient frontier.

Extending Markowitz's work, Sharpe introduced a riskless asset into the investment opportunity set that changes how investors view the mean-variance parabola. Assuming risk-averse investors, investors now seek some combination of the riskless asset and a diversified portfolio on the efficient frontier. As illustrated in Fig. 1.2, Sharpe argued that, among risky portfolios on the efficient frontier, investors would prefer the portfolio *M* marked with an asterisk.[3] If the investor picks any other diversified portfolio on the efficient frontier, the resultant combination would be less efficient in the sense of providing lower return/risk. The optimal portfolio offering the highest return/risk results is represented by the tangent point of the line extending from the riskless rate of return to the parabola. This unique portfolio was named the ***market portfolio*** by Sharpe.

In theory, the market portfolio M contains all assets in the market. All investors are assumed to hold this portfolio regardless of their risk preferences (known as the *separation theorem*). The combination of the riskless asset and portfolio M form the Capital Market Line (CML) drawn in Fig. 1.2 as a straight line connecting these two points. The CML shows the possible return/risk combinations of investing in these two assets. If investors can borrow at the riskless rate and buy M, they can move up the CML above M.

Given the mean-variance parabola, riskless rate, market portfolio M, and related CML, Sharpe's CAPM can be derived as shown in the next chapter. The CAPM posits that the major market force affecting all assets over time is the market portfolio M. When the expected return of the general market increases, most individual assets' expected returns tend to increase, and vice versa for decreases in the general market. This market force was named *systematic risk* by Sharpe. The amount of systematic risk for an individual asset is measured by its ***beta*** (β), which captures the sensitivity of its expected returns to changes in market portfolio returns. In theory, higher (lower) betas are associated with higher (lower) expected returns of assets. In the real world, β is estimated as the regression coefficient of an asset's rate of return over time with respect to a proxy market portfolio's rate of return. Asset returns should be closely and linearly related to beta risk.

1.2 The CAPM Controversy

Unfortunately, since its inception, the CAPM has been under attack due to weak empirical evidence. In the 1990s, after repeated tests of the relationship between stock returns and beta (β) using stock market indexes to proxy the theoretical market portfolio, Professors Eugene Fama and Kenneth French (1992, 1993, 1995, 1996) concluded that the CAPM did not fit the

[3] Tobin (1958) showed that a tangent point between a borrowing and lending rate and the opportunity set of risky assets identified an optimal portfolio of risky assets.

empirical evidence. For the population of U.S. stocks over a long period of time exceeding 25 years, higher (lower) betas did not translate into higher (lower) average returns. Due to the empirical failure of the CAPM, Fama and French declared the CAPM *dead*. In its place they proposed alternative three-, five-, and six-factor models that add zero-investment factors to the CAPM—namely, size, book-to-market equity (value), profit, capital investment, and momentum.[4] Each factor is a long/short portfolio (e.g., long small stocks and short large stocks for the size factor).

While their zero-investment factors have some significance in empirical tests and are popular among academics and practitioners alike, they have no connection to the theoretical framework of general equilibrium pricing per Sharpe's CAPM. Contrarily, they are empirically chosen due to their significance in asset pricing tests using U.S. stock returns. For these reasons, we refer to them as *ad hoc* models.[5] Incredibly, as researchers adopted the long/short factor construction methods of Fama and French, a plethora of so-called *multifactors* counting into the hundreds flooded the finance literature. Contending *multifactor models* now battle for survival of the fittest in a process of empirical selection along this new evolutionary branch of asset pricing.

1.3 The Roll Critique

In the real world, it is far from clear how to construct and buy the CAPM's market portfolio M. One way to do this is to estimate the investment parabola using the population of stock returns. However, estimating the parabola from thousands of stock returns turns out to be impossible due to statistical problems in computing both expected asset returns and the inverse covariance matrix of these returns. It is not surprising that, using optimal weights based on the return/risk framework of Markowitz, studies have documented poor out-of-sample performance of diversified portfolios. Many authors have attempted to resolve the estimation problems of computing efficient portfolios, but the out-of-sample results continue to be disappointing. For these reasons, we cannot reliably draw the investment parabola to find M. According to Richard Roll (1977), ambigu-

[4] See also Fama and French (2015, 2018, 2020).

[5] Fama and French (1993, p. 7) recognized that some readers might view their factors as ad hoc; however, they argued that size, value, and other factors are related to economic fundamentals.

ity surrounding market portfolio M is a major drawback of the CAPM. If investors cannot find M, then the CAPM cannot be implemented by investors or tested by researchers.

1.4 The Zero-Beta CAPM Alternative

As covered in more detail in forthcoming Chapter 2, Fischer Black (1972) attempted to solve the problem of locating a single market portfolio by developing a more general form of the CAPM. He argued that the market portfolio can be located by finding any two minimum variance portfolios on the investment parabola boundary. If the two portfolios are orthogonal (or uncorrelated) with one another, they can be used in place of the market portfolio M in the CAPM. One portfolio lies on the efficient frontier and the other on the lower inefficient boundary, which he referred to as the *zero-beta portfolio* due to its zero correlation with the efficient portfolio. The combination of these two portfolios can be used to obtain M. According to Black, there are two market factors affecting asset returns: (1) an efficient portfolio return and (2) and its inefficient zero-beta portfolio return. There are an infinite number of efficient/inefficient portfolio pairs possible in Black's *zero-beta CAPM*. Also, in Black's alternative CAPM, it is not necessary to assume that investors can borrow and lend at the riskless rate to locate market portfolio M.

Of course, Roll's criticism of the CAPM's market portfolio M applies equally to Black's efficient and inefficient portfolios in the zero-beta CAPM. Sharpe (1973) pointed out that the zero-beta portfolio is not on the efficient frontier of Markowitz, is not directly identifiable, and has no empirical counterpart. How can we form these models' portfolios in the real world? The theoretical portfolio ideas underpinning the CAPM and zero-beta CAPM are compelling, but it is unclear how to implement them in the real world. The problem is that we need proxies for minimum variance portfolios on the investment parabola that are readily estimable from measurable asset returns and risks. Herein lies the major motivation for our ZCAPM and this book.

1.5 ZCAPM Solution

Based on earlier work by the authors in Liu et al. (2012, 2020) and Liu (2013), Chapter 3 mathematically derives a new model of capital asset pricing dubbed the *ZCAPM*. The ZCAPM is developed from Black's zero-beta

CAPM but contains return and risk variables that are easily measured with available market data. In the present book, we concentrate our discussion and later empirical analyses on U.S. stocks, but the reader can extend the same principles to other asset classes (e.g., bonds, commodities, real estate, etc.) The first risk factor is the average return of all stocks in the stock market. This average market return is commonly reported in the financial press on a daily basis. Everyday examples of general stock market indexes are the S&P 500 index, Russell 2000 index, etc. The Center for Security Prices (CRSP) database provided by the University of Chicago offers a very broad index including all U.S. common stocks. The CRSP index is commonly used in academic asset pricing studies. The second risk factor is the cross-sectional standard deviation of all stocks' returns. This factor is not generally reported on a daily basis in the financial press but can be readily computed by simply calculating the standard deviation of returns across all stocks trading on a given day in the stock market. Hereafter we denote this total return dispersion measure as *RD*. Both of these risk factors are available on a daily basis in the stock market.

Since some researchers have used *RD* in an asset pricing model, there is precedent in the literature for this risk factor. However, unlike these authors, our ZCAPM is theoretically grounded in the same general equilibrium framework as Black and Sharpe. As such, Markowitz's investment parabola plays a central role in our ZCAPM. Contributing to Markowitz's work on the investment parabola, we derive two new results in Chapter 3 that were previously unknown: (1) the average market return lies on the axis of symmetry of the parabola at an interior location and (2) the width of the investment parabola is determined in large part by *RD*. In Chapter 4 we confirm the latter result using Markowitz's mathematical treatment of the mean-variance parabola. Note that, given the parabola's width is shaped by return dispersion, we can logically infer that the average market return lies approximately on its axis of symmetry (i.e., the mean lies in the middle of a distribution of values).

Using these new insights about the investment parabola, and departing from previous models containing *RD*, our ZCAPM decomposes *RD* into positive and negative risk effects at any time t (e.g., daily positive and negative sensitivity to *RD*). We hypothesize that *RD* can have opposite effects on stocks depending on the sign of their sensitivity to *RD*. Given beta risk related to average stock market returns, an asset with positive (negative) sensitivity to *RD* is posited to experience higher (lower) returns as *RD* increases over time, and vice versa as *RD* decreases over time. As shown in later empirical analyses, the ZCAPM substantially boosts the significance and explanatory power of *RD* as an asset pricing factor in out-of-sample tests of the relation between the cross section of average stock returns and *RD* loadings.

To intuitively understand the dual volatility effects of *RD*, Chapter 3 locates two orthogonal efficient and inefficient portfolios in the spirit of Black's zero-beta CAPM with equal time-series variances. Denoted I^* and ZI^*, respectively, these two unique portfolios can be reached by geometrically moving horizontally along the axis of symmetry of the investment parabola (defined by the average market return) and then vertically up or down within the parabola (whose width is shaped by *RD*). This geometry is very different from Sharpe's CAPM, in which the investor utilizes the tangent line (CML) connecting the riskless rate to the risky efficient frontier to find market portfolio M. Of course, in the real world, nobody actually does this kind of CAPM calculus. Investor behavior is instead more akin to the ZCAPM in terms of investing in a general market index representing the average returns of assets and then seeking more efficient portfolios which can be achieved by taking into account other risk factors in the market.

This investor behavior is consistent with multifactor models incorporating different zero-investment risk factors also. Regarding these models, the average market return is supplemented with various long/short factors proposed by Fama and French and others. The proposed multifactors themselves are rough measures of return dispersion—namely, high return portfolios minus low return portfolios. Over extended periods of time, these long/short factors tend to have positive returns. However, because they can become negative in some periods, their ability to capture return dispersion is diminished at times. In the ZCAPM, rather than use these proxies for return dispersion that capture different slices of the total dispersion, we utilize total return dispersion itself. Unlike long/short multifactors, total return dispersion is always positive, never *crashes* (e.g., negative momentum returns), and affects all stocks regardless of their firm characteristics. Consistent with Sharpe's notion of a systematic risk factor, *RD* is pervasive and persistent in its effects on assets in the market.

In the ZCAPM, the average market return factor captures changes in the level of the investment parabola from day-to-day, and the *RD* factor captures daily changes in the width of the parabola. Even if the average market return does not change from one day to the next (i.e., the axis of symmetry does not move), a change in *RD* can move asset returns up and down. In this case, as *RD* increases (decreases), assets in the upper region of the investment parabola will experience increasing (decreasing) returns, and assets in the lower region of the parabola will experience decreasing (increasing) returns.

To empirically measure opposite *RD* market forces inherent in the investment parabola, Chapter 4 specifies a novel regression model that incorporates *beta risk* (β_i) associated with average market returns and *zeta risk* (Z_i) related to market *RD*. Unlike previous models containing an *RD* factor, our *empirical ZCAPM* introduces a signal variable $D_{it} = +1, -1$ to denote positive and negative sensitivity, respectively, of the *i*th asset to changes in *RD* at time *t*. The sign of the zeta risk coefficient Z_i is determined by D_{it}. If $D_{it} = +1$, the stock reacts positively (negatively) to an increase (decrease) in *RD*, whereas $D_{it} = -1$ indicates that the stock is negatively (positively) sensitive to an increase (decrease) in *RD*.

One problem in implementing the above signal approach is that D_{it} is a latent or unobserved variable. A priori, we do not know whether an asset is positively or negatively sensitive to changes in the width of the parabola as measured by return dispersion. To estimate the probability of this latent (or hidden) variable, we utilize the well-known expectation–maximization (EM) algorithm by Dempster et al. (1977). The EM algorithm is used to estimate the statistical parameters in the empirical ZCAPM, including the probability p_i $(1 - p)$ that D_{it} equals $+1$ (-1) for the *i*th asset. Using probability parameter p_i, the zeta risk coefficient is redefined as $Z_i^* = Z_i(2p_i - 1)$.

While the application of the EM algorithm for the maximum likelihood estimation of regression parameters is fairly widespread in the hard sciences, it is not familiar to most finance students, academics, and professionals. Even so, it is increasingly being applied in financial research (e.g., see Wu (1983), Kon (1984), Rudd (1991), Asquith et al. (1998), McLachlan and Krishnan (2008), Harvey and Liu (2016), Chen et al. (2017), and others). In statistical terms, our empirical ZCAPM is a mixture model with two components, wherein each component is a two-factor model. One two-factor model has a beta risk factor and positive zeta risk factor. The other two-factor model has a beta risk factor and negative zeta risk factor. Which two-factor model to use is determined by the EM estimation of the probability p_i that $D_{it} = +1$ and probability $1 - p_i$ that $D_{it} = -1$. To our knowledge, no previous asset pricing models employ a probabilistic mixture model to specify an asset pricing model.

As already mentioned, it is important to recognize that our beta risk is different from beta risk in the CAPM. Beta risk in the CAPM arises from market portfolio M that lies on the efficient frontier. By contrast, beta risk in our ZCAPM comes about due to the average market return of the entire stock market that lies somewhere along the axis of symmetry of the investment parabola. Also, departing from the CML of Sharpe, we do not locate *M* by drawing a tangent line to the efficient frontier. Instead, we move horizontally along the axis of symmetry and then vertically up and down (at a given time-series variance) to locate an efficient portfolio and its counterpart zero-beta portfolio on the lower boundary of the parabola. These two unique portfolios with equal time-series variance (denoted as I^* and ZI^*) can be used to locate *M* and together represent a special case of Black's zero-beta CAPM.

Based on U.S. stock returns spanning over 50 years, Chapters 5–7 present empirical evidence to support the ZCAPM. Chapter 5 describes our stock return data, standard Fama and MacBeth (1973) cross-sectional tests, and different popular asset pricing models. Using portfolios sorted by estimated beta and zeta coefficients (viz., β^* and Z^*) in the empirical ZCAPM, we provide descriptive statistics for their one-month-ahead average returns. This preliminary evidence suggests that, while average returns do not increase as beta risk increases, they do increase as zeta risk increases. The positive relation between one-month-ahead returns and zeta risk is most conspicuous when using equal-weighted (as opposed to value-weighted) portfolio returns.

Chapter 6 begins by conducting cross-sectional Fama and MacBeth tests to evaluate the traditional model used by previous researchers that incorporates an *RD* asset pricing factor. However, our results do not support this traditional model, which motivates the ZCAPM as an alternative way to model *RD*. Using the empirical ZCAPM, graphical analyses demonstrate a close relation between the cross section of one-month-ahead (out-of-sample) average stock returns and estimated zeta risk coefficients Z^*. Further graphical analyses illustrate a close relation between one-month-ahead realized returns and one-month-ahead predicted returns by the ZCAPM. In this first piece of evidence documenting the dominance of the ZCAPM over other existing models, our realized/predicted return graphs indicate that the ZCAPM outperforms other popular asset pricing models in general and by a large margin when test assets contain industry portfolios in particular.

Chapter 7 shows that, in virtually all cross-sectional tests, the empirical ZCAPM repeatedly dominates all other models and factors. Out-of-sample Fama and MacBeth tests for a variety of portfolios show that zeta risk loadings Z^* estimated via the EM algorithm are consistently significant at a high level. By comparison, familiar multifactors in the Fama and French (1992, 1993, 1995) three-factor model, Carhart (1997) four-factor model, and Fama and French (2015, 2018) five- and six-factor models are less significant and priced in some but not all test assets.[6] For a variety of different test assets, including portfolios sorted on size, book-to-market, profit, capital investment, beta and zeta risk coefficients, and industries, out-of-sample cross-sectional tests with one-month-ahead stock returns indicate that the market price of zeta risk associated with *RD* has t-values in the range of approximately 3–6. Importantly, these out-of-sample t-statistic results for zeta risk loadings surpass the $t = 3.0$ and $t = 3.4$ hurdle rates recently established by Harvey et al. (2015) and Chordia et al. (2020), respectively, for the significance of asset pricing factors. In stark contrast, cross-sectional t-values associated with popular multifactors, including size, value, momentum, profit, and capital investment loadings in the three-, four-, five-, and six-factor models, do not pass the 3.0 hurdle rate in different test asset portfolios in almost all cases.

In addition to high statistical significance in cross-sectional tests, estimated risk premiums associated with zeta risk are economically substantial—for example, ranging from approximately 0.30–0.50% per month per unit estimated zeta coefficient. Compelling evidence for the ZCAPM is that R^2 values are relatively high compared to other models. Estimated R^2 values for the empirical ZCAPM range from approximately 70% to as high as 98%. At near 100% goodness-of-fit in some tests of stock portfolios, there is little or no room for other significant factors. Some skeptics may view these results as "too good to be true." However, confirming our findings, further comparative results show that the ZCAPM repeatedly outperforms popular three-, four-, five-, and six-factor models in terms of predicting one-month-ahead stock returns, especially for industry portfolios. Regarding the latter industry portfolios, when they are included in the test assets, the other models break down for the most part. Only the ZCAPM appears to be able to price these exogenous stock portfolios in out-of-sample analyses. This industry portfolio evidence highlights the superior performance of the empirical ZCAPM compared to other models.

[6] Because these models are the most often cited and used empirical asset pricing models in academic research studies, we compare our ZCAPM results to them. In our applied work with the Teachers Retirement System of Texas (TRS), practitioners frequently utilized these models also.

We conduct numerous robustness checks with split subsample periods and different test assets based on microcap and larger size market capitalization portfolios, profit and capital investment portfolios, and the largest 500 individual stocks by market capitalization. Also, out-of-sample periods greater than one month are tested. Overall, we find that *RD* is the only factor consistently priced in the cross section of average stock returns with *t*-values that exceed the hurdle rate of 3 in many test assets.

Lastly, we test recently proposed four-factor models by Hou et al. (2015) and Stambaugh and Yuan (2017) and find that their factors are generally significant across different test assets but have *t*-values less than the 3 threshold. Also, like the Fama and French models, the ZCAPM consistently outperforms these four-factor models across a variety of test asset portfolios, especially when industry portfolios are included in the test assets. Altogether, these and other empirical results lead us to conclude that:

1. zeta risk associated with return dispersion is a salient asset pricing factor; and
2. the empirical ZCAPM explains most of the cross-sectional variation in stock returns.

Simply put, the ZCAPM is a better asset pricing model than other popular models available in the finance literature. This observation is not conjecture or a trick due to using methods that might favor our model over other models. The empirical evidence in this book validates our ZCAPM as the premier asset pricing model relative to existing popular models using standard cross-sectional tests found in almost all empirical tests of different models proposed by researchers over almost 50 years. Interestingly, because our ZCAPM is built upon the CAPM and zero-beta CAPM, our results imply that the foundational mean-variance asset pricing framework of these models represents a good depiction of investor behavior in the stock market. In turn, the CAPM and alternative zero-beta CAPM are not dead but instead reborn in the form of the ZCAPM.

Chapters 8 and 9 apply the ZCAPM to the practice of securities investment. Here we move from ZCAPM invention and testing in previous chapters to ZCAPM innovation with respect to securities portfolios. Chapter 8 attempts to tackle the long-standing mystery of what explains momentum trading profits. Seminal work by Jegadeesh and Titman (2001) has shown that buying (long position) previous winner stocks and selling (short position) loser stocks earns as much as 1.50% per month on average over time.

Many studies confirm generous momentum profits for stocks, bonds, currencies, and commodities. A major controversy surrounds the explanation of these abnormal profits. Behaviorists argue that market psychology helps to explain these unexpectedly high profits. Other authors point to risk-based, rational market explanations for the gains. Here we hypothesize that a large portion of momentum profits arise rationally from market risk associated with cross-sectional market volatility.

It is well known that momentum profits are not explained by systematic risk arising from the market factor but no previous studies consider their relation to systematic risk stemming from cross-sectional market volatility. Momentum itself is a measure of return dispersion that takes the difference between stocks with very high and very low returns (i.e., two ends of the cross-sectional distribution of returns) in a one-year formation period. Using the empirical ZCAPM, we form zero-investment portfolios that are long (short) stocks with positive (negative) sensitivity to *RD* as measured by zeta risk coefficients in a one-year estimation period. Long/short portfolio returns for both momentum portfolios and zeta risk portfolios are computed in the next out-of-sample month. Hence, rather than forming long/short portfolios based on past return levels, we form these portfolios using past zeta risk levels. Cross-sectional test results show that momentum and return dispersion factor loadings are similarly priced in test assets sorted on both momentum and zeta risk. Zero-investment portfolio returns based on zeta risk in the post-formation month are comparable to momentum portfolio returns but clearly outperform zero-investment size, value, profit, and capital investment portfolio returns. Nonetheless, high risk return dispersion portfolios outperformed momentum portfolios, especially hybrid portfolios combining return dispersion and momentum portfolios. Importantly, regression analyses demonstrate that zero-investment momentum returns are very significantly related to zero-investment, return dispersion returns with higher t-statistics and adjusted R^2 values compared to other factors. We conclude that momentum profits are closely related to zeta risk associated with return dispersion.

Chapter 9 extends our momentum findings by utilizing the empirical ZCAPM to create diversified aggregate portfolios that combine the CRSP stock index with zero-investment portfolios sensitive to *RD*. The latter long/short zeta risk portfolios have different levels of zeta risk in absolute value terms. We find that the resultant aggregate portfolios outperform the CRSP index, for they lie on a frontier located well above this index. Also, we employ the ZCAPM to build a proxy minimum variance portfolio (denoted g) that is used in place of the CRSP index. Combining proxy portfolio g with different long/short zeta risk portfolios enables the creation of even more efficient aggregate portfolios than those based on CRSP plus zeta risk portfolios. Strikingly, setting the standard deviation of returns equal to the CRSP index, an aggregate portfolio with a much higher average monthly return can be achieved of approximately 1.75% compared to 0.88% for the CRSP index, or approximately a 100% improvement in performance! Additionally, higher risk aggregate portfolios earn as much as 3.30% per month on average over our 54-year sample period. These and other results confirm the influence of cross-sectional *RD* on aggregate stock portfolio performance.

We form long only aggregate portfolios in Chapter 9 also. These portfolios combine either the CRSP index or proxy portfolio g with long only zeta risk portfolios. Again our aggregate portfolios outperform the CRSP index. For example, by combining proxy portfolio g and a long/short zeta risk portfolio to form an aggregate portfolio with approximately the same total risk as the CRSP index, we earn 1.24% per month. Robustness analyses of zero-investment portfolios formed using the estimated beta coefficients of popular size, value, and momentum factors show that these factors are not useful in constructing relatively high-performing aggregate portfolios. We conclude that return dispersion enables the construction of superior investment portfolios. An important implication of our findings is that investors can benefit from ZCAPM-based investment portfolios, particularly institutional investors such as mutual funds, pension funds, insurance companies, commercial banks, hedge funds, etc., that manage diversified portfolios for clients.

Finally, Chapter 10 reviews the evolution of asset pricing, including the origin of the CAPM, alternative zero-beta CAPM, other CAPM-related models, multifactor models, and our ZCAPM. Because factors constructed from zero-investment (long/short) portfolios are themselves coarse measures of return dispersion, multifactor models are related to the ZCAPM and thereby the CAPM. Hence, all asset pricing models are fundamentally linked to the market portfolio. Echoing Professor Milton Friedman's famous Keynesian phrase: "We are all Sharpians now."

1.6 Summary

In this book we propose and test a new capital asset pricing model. Based on the famous CAPM by Sharpe (1964) and others as well as the more general zero-beta CAPM by Black (1972), we derive a special case of the zero-beta CAPM dubbed the *ZCAPM*. Our new model contains two factors: (1) average market returns associated with beta risk and (2) cross-sectional return dispersion (*RD*) related to zeta risk. The latter zeta risk is unique in the sense that assets can have either positive or negative sensitivity to *RD*. A useful analogy is sailing a ship on a windy day. The tidal current (average market return) of the sea pulls the ship in a direction, while surface waves (market volatility) continuously rock the ship up and down.

Unlike many multifactor models that are so popular these days, the theoretical ZCAPM is based on portfolio theory and equilibrium asset pricing principles created by Markowitz, Sharpe, Black, and others. To estimate the ZCAPM in the real world, we specify a novel empirical ZCAPM containing a signal variable to capture positive versus negative sensitivity to *RD*. The well-established expectation–maximization (EM) algorithm is used to obtain maximum likelihood estimates of model parameters, including the probability of positive and negative *RD* sensitivity. In this regard, we break new ground in asset pricing by using a probabilistic mixture model to specify the empirical ZCAPM. Based on U.S. stock returns over more than 50 years, we document extensive evidence that not only strongly supports the empirical ZCAPM but dominates other popular models in virtually all tests. Subsequently, we apply the ZCAPM to practical investment problems that further support our new capital asset pricing model. The plan for forthcoming chapters is as follows:

Chapter 2 formally derives the famed CAPM, derives the more general zero-beta CAPM, and discusses popular multifactor models.

Chapter 3 mathematically derives the theoretical ZCAPM as a special case of the zero-beta CAPM.

Chapter 4 specifies the empirical ZCAPM and describes the estimation of its statistical parameters using the expectation–maximization (EM) algorithm.

Chapter 5 discusses our stock return data, empirical test methods, descriptive statistics, and some preliminary evidence on the ZCAPM.

Chapter 6 presents tests of the traditional model that incorporates return dispersion as a factor as well as out-of-sample graphical evidence that compares the ZCAPM to other popular asset pricing models.
Chapter 7 reports extensive out-of-sample, cross-sectional tests that strongly support the ZCAPM with comparisons to other asset pricing models plus numerous robustness checks.
Chapter 8 applies the ZCAPM to the momentum factor to help explain this long-standing anomaly in financial markets.
Chapter 9 applies the ZCAPM to the construction of zero-investment zeta risk portfolios as well as diversified, high-performing investment portfolios.
Chapter 10 contains a synopsis of the evolution of asset pricing and the ZCAPM with discussion of future research as well as dualistic philosophy.

In closing, at the end of this book, we provide a Compendium containing the Matlab programs used to estimate the empirical ZCAPM and perform cross-sectional tests in this book. Also, R programs for these analyses can be downloaded from GitHub (https://github.com/zcapm). Advantages of the latter programs are: (1) R is free software available on the internet and (2) R runs faster in estimating the empirical ZCAPM. We encourage readers to use our software, replicate our results, and conduct new empirical analyses.

Bibliography

Asquith, D., Jones, J., & Kieschnick, R. (1998). Evidence on price stabilization and underpricing in early IPO returns. *Journal of Finance, 53*, 1759–1773.
Black, F. (1972). Capital market equilibrium with restricted borrowing. *Journal of Business, 45*, 444–454.
Black, F. (1993). Beta and return. *Journal of Portfolio Management, 20*, 8–18.
Black, F., Jensen, M. C., & Scholes, M. (1972). The capital asset pricing model: Some empirical tests. In M. C. Jensen (Ed.), *Studies in the theory of capital markets*. New York, NY: Praeger.
Breeden, N. D. (1979). An intertemporal asset pricing model with stochastic consumption and investment opportunities. *Journal of Financial Economics, 7*, 265–296.
Carhart, M. M. (1997). On persistence in mutual fund performance. *Journal of Finance, 52*, 57–82.

Chen, Y., Cli, M., & Zhao, H. (2017). Hedge funds: The good, the bad, and the lucky. *Journal of Financial and Quantitative Analysis 52*, 1081–1109.
Chordia, T., Goyal, A., & Saretto, A. (2020). Anomalies and false rejections. *Review of Financial Studies, 33*, 2134–2179.
Cochrane, J. H. (1991). Production-based asset pricing and the link between stock returns and economic fluctuations. *Journal of Finance, 46*, 209–237.
Dempster, A. P., Laird, N. M., & Rubin, D. B. (1977). Maximum likelihood from incomplete data via the EM algorithm. *Journal of the Royal Statistical Society, 39*, 1–38.
Fama, E. F., & French, K. R. (1992). The cross-section of expected stock returns. *Journal of Finance, 47*, 427–465.
Fama, E. F., & French, K. R. (1993). The cross-section of expected returns. *Journal of Financial Economics, 33*, 3–56.
Fama, E. F., & French, K. R. (1995). Size and book-to-market factors in earnings and returns. *Journal of Finance, 50*, 131–156.
Fama, E. F., & French, K. R. (2015). A five-factor asset pricing model. *Journal of Financial Economics, 116*, 1–22.
Fama, E. F., & French, K. R. (1996). The CAPM is wanted, dead or alive. *Journal of Finance, 51*, 1947–1958.
Fama, E. F., & French, K. R. (2018). Choosing factors. *Journal of Financial Economics, 128*, 234–252.
Fama, E. F., & French, K. R. (2020). Comparing cross-section and time-series factor models. *Review of Financial Studies, 33*, 1892–1926.
Fama, E. F., & MacBeth, J. D. (1973). Risk, return, and equilibrium: Empirical tests. *Journal of Political Economy, 81*, 607–636.
Ferson, W. E., & Harvey, C. R. (1991). The variation of economic risk premiums. *Journal of Political Economy, 99*, 385–415.
Ferson, W. E., & Harvey, C. R. (1996). *Conditioning variables and the cross-section of stock returns* (Working Paper). Duke University.
Harvey, C. R., & Liu, Y. (2016). *Rethinking performance evaluation* (Working Paper No. 22134). National Bureau of Economic Research, Cambridge, MA.
Harvey, C. R., Liu, Y., & Zhu, H. (2015). and the cross-section of expected returns. *Review of Financial Studies, 29*, 5–68.
Hou, K., Xue, C., & Zhang, L. (2015). Digesting anomalies: An investment approach. *Review of Financial Studies, 28*, 650–705.
Jegadeesh, N., & Titman, S. (2001). Profitability of momentum strategies: An evaluation of alternative explanations. *Journal of Finance, 56*, 699–720.
Kon, S. (1984). Models of stock returns: a comparison. *Journal of Finance, 39*, 147–165.
Lintner, J. (1965). The valuation of risk assets and the selection of risky investments in stock portfolios and capital budgets. *Review of Economics and Statistics, 47*, 13–37.

Liu, W. (2013). *A new asset pricing model based on the zero-beta CAPM: Theory and evidence* (Doctoral dissertation). Texas A&M University.

Liu, W., Kolari, J. W., & Huang, J. Z. (2012, October). *A new asset pricing model based on the zero-beta CAPM.* Presentation at the annual meetings of the Financial Management Association, Atlanta, GA.

Liu, W., Kolari, J. W., & Huang, J. Z. (2020, October). *Return dispersion and the cross-section of stock returns.* Presentation at the annual meetings of the Southern Finance Association, Palm Springs, CA.

Lucas, R. E. (1978). Asset prices in an exchange economy. *Econometrica, 46*, 1429–1445.

Markowitz, H. M. (1959). *Portfolio selection: Efficient diversification of investments.* New York, NY: Wiley.

McLachlan, G. J., & Krishnan, T. (2008). *The EM algorithm and extensions* (2nd ed.). New York, NY: Wiley.

Merton, R. C. (1973). An intertemporal capital asset pricing model. *Econometrica, 41*, 867–887.

Mossin, J. (1966). Equilibrium in a capital asset market. *Econometrica, 34*, 768–783.

Roll, R. (1977). A critique of the asset pricing theory's tests, Part I: On past and potential future testability of the theory. *Journal of Financial Economics, 4*, 129–176.

Rudd, P. (1991). Extensions of estimation methods using the EM algorithm. *Journal of Econometrics, 49*, 305–341.

Sharpe, W. F. (1964). Capital asset prices: A theory of market equilibrium under conditions of risk. *Journal of Finance, 19*, 425–442.

Sharpe, W. F. (1973). *The capital asset pricing model: Traditional and "zero-beta" versions.* Presented at the Midwest Finance Association Conference.

Stambaugh, R. F., & Yuan, Y. (2017). Mispricing factors. *Review of Financial Studies, 30*, 1270–1315.

Stulz, R. M. (1981). A model of international asset pricing. *Journal of Financial Economics, 9*, 383–406.

Stulz, R. M. (1995). International portfolio choice and asset pricing: An integrative survey. In R. A. Jarrow, V. Maksimovic, & W. T. Ziemba (Eds.), *Handbooks in operations research and management science* (Vol. 9, Chapter 6, pp. 201–223). Amsterdam, North-Holland: Elsevier.

Treynor, J. L. (1961). *Market value, time, and risk* (Unpublished manuscript).

Tobin, J. (1958). Liquidity preference as behavior towards risk. *Review of Economic Studies, 25*, 65–86.

Treynor, J. L. (1962). *Toward a theory of market value of risky assets* (Unpublished manuscript).

Wu, J. (1983). On the convergence properties of the EM algorithm. *Annals of Statistics, 11*, 95–103.

PART II

Theoretical ZCAPM

CHAPTER 2

Capital Asset Pricing Models

Abstract This chapter distinguishes between two main branches of asset pricing: (1) general equilibrium models and (2) multifactor models. We begin by reviewing the pathbreaking work by Sharpe (1964) and others, who utilized equilibrium pricing conditions in the mean-variance return world of Markowitz (1959) to derive the theoretical CAPM. Its market model form is used in empirical tests to regress excess stock returns on excess market returns (proxied by general market index returns minus Treasury bill rates) and thereby estimate beta risk coefficients. Early tests of the market model found a weaker relation between U.S. stock returns and beta than expected by the CAPM. In an attempt to overcome empirical issues in early CAPM tests, Black (1972) proposed the zero-beta CAPM as a more general form. Here we review his mathematical derivation of the zero-beta CAPM. As we will see, both of these famous models are grounded in similar portfolio theory and general equilibrium conditions. The remainder of the chapter covers various multifactor models with little or theoretical foundation but empirical support. In a series of papers, Fama and French (1992, 1993, 1995, 1996) presented convincing empirical evidence that the market model did not work for U.S. stock returns over many years and therefore declared the CAPM *dead*. They subsequently proposed a three-factor model that augmented the market model's general market index with size and value multifactors, which provided a better fit to U.S. stock return data. We also discuss the following extensions of the three-factor model: Carhart's (1997) four-factor model (adding a momentum factor),

J. W. Kolari et al., *A New Model of Capital Asset Prices*,
https://doi.org/10.1007/978-3-030-65197-8_2

and Fama and French's (2015) five-factor model (adding profit and capital investment factors). Lastly, we overview the Hou et al. (2015) q-factor model, Stambaugh and Yuan's (2017) mispricing four-factor model, Fama and French's (2018, 2020) six-factor model adding momentum to their five-factor model, and other recent model developments.

Keywords Asset pricing · CAPM · Cross-sectional tests · Equilibrium pricing · Fama and French models · Fischer Black · Investment parabola · Market model · Multifactor models · Return dispersion · Stock market · William Sharpe · Valuation · ZCAPM · Zero-beta CAPM

2.1 General Equilibrium Versus Multifactor Models

The renowned capital asset pricing model (CAPM) of Sharpe (1964) and others was a breakthrough achievement due to the establishment of general equilibrium conditions that govern risk and return in financial markets. This theoretical foundation was built upon previous Nobel Prize winning work by Markowitz (1959) on diversification and the resultant mean-variance efficient investment parabola. A more general form of the CAPM was developed by Black (1972). These models have sturdy theoretical foundations that should be considered a prerequisite for any asset pricing model. Because the present book builds upon these general equilibrium models by deriving a special case of the zero-beta CAPM dubbed the *ZCAPM*, in this chapter we formally derive the CAPM and zero-beta CAPM.

Also, we review several multifactor models using various zero-investment factors that have gained widespread acceptance in the wake of the CAPM's empirical failure. These models have three problems:

1. They are not derived from general equilibrium conditions common to the CAPM, zero-beta CAPM, and other derivative CAPM forms[1] but rather fitted to stock return data.

[1] See the consumption CAPM (CCAPM) of Lucas (1978) and Breeden (1979), intertemporal CAPM (ICAPM) of Merton (1973), conditional CAPM of Ferson and Harvey (1991, 1996), and production-based asset pricing model (PAPM) of Cochrane (1991), and international CAPM of Stulz (1981, 1995).

2. Multifactors in these models are proliferating into the hundreds as observed by Cochrane (2011).
3. The shopping mall of contender models is growing.

These problems are creating considerable confusion in asset pricing. What is the theoretical justification for each model? Which factors are most significant? Are some models better than others? Are different models specific to different sets of stock return data?

Our ZCAPM resolves these problems by proposing a parsimonious model based on portfolio theory and general equilibrium conditions with two readily measurable factors: (1) average market returns and (2) return dispersion. Using these two factors, Chapter 4 specifies the empirical ZCAPM for estimation purposes. Chapters 5–7 show that zeta risk associated with return dispersion in the empirical ZCAPM is more significant than popular multifactors and that the empirical ZCAPM explains most of the cross section of average U.S. stock returns. According to extensive tests discussed in these chapters, the empirical ZCAPM supplants multifactor models and their zero-investment factors.

2.2 CAPM

The stochastic discount factor (SDF) is the focal variable that links asset prices to their future cash flows (see Cochrane 2005; Ferson 2019). The SDF is a linear function of general market returns in the now-famous Capital Asset Pricing Model (CAPM) of Treynor (1961, 1962), Sharpe (1964), Lintner (1965), and Mossin (1966). In 1990 William Sharpe was awarded the Nobel Prize in Economics for the CAPM. Importantly, the CAPM is built upon earlier work by Harry Markowitz (1959), with whom he shared the Nobel Prize along with Merton Miller.

Figure 1.2 in the previous chapter showed that the market portfolio M in the CAPM is the mean-variance efficient portfolio located at the tangent point between Sharpe's Capital Market Line (CML) and Markowitz's mean-variance investment parabola. In market equilibrium, prices of assets adjust until all assets are held by investors. The market portfolio M is a strictly theoretical construct that represents a value-weighted index of all assets with weights equal to the ratio of the market value of each asset to the market value of all assets.

The CAPM assumes the following equilibrium conditions: (1) perfectly competitive capital markets exist for assets (i.e., no transactions costs, no taxes, and investors are price-takers); (2) investors have homogeneous expectations concerning the probability distributions of future returns on risky assets; (3) investors choose portfolios that maximize their expected utility of wealth; (4) investors are risk averse with quadratic utility functions, have a common planning horizon, and can borrow and lend at the riskless rate; and (5) the market portfolio M is formed from long positions in assets. Because short selling is quite common among publicly traded stocks in the market, the last assumption of only long positions in the market portfolio is unrealistic. As we will see, Black (1972) later relaxed this assumption.

2.2.1 *Formal Derivation of the CAPM*

Investors on the CML in Fig. 1.2 can hold portfolio C composed of the riskless asset f and market portfolio M. This combination of assets yields the following expected rate of return:

$$E(\widetilde{R}_C) = yR_f + (1 - y)E(\widetilde{R}_M), \tag{2.1}$$

where y is the percent invested in the riskless asset with constant rate of return, and $(1 - y)$ percent is held in M. Investors can also form a portfolio by combining some risky asset i with M. In this case the expected rate of return is:

$$E(\widetilde{R}_C) = yE(\widetilde{R}_i) + (1 - y)E(\widetilde{R}_M). \tag{2.2}$$

The standard deviation of the portfolio in Eq. (2.2) is:

$$\sigma(\widetilde{R}_C) = [y^2\sigma^2(\widetilde{R}_i) + (1 - y)^2\sigma^2(\widetilde{R}_M) + 2y(1 - y)\,\mathrm{cov}(\widetilde{R}_i, \widetilde{R}_M)]^{1/2}, \tag{2.3}$$

where $\mathrm{cov}(\widetilde{R}_i, \widetilde{R}_M)$ denotes the covariance between asset i and M returns.

Next we derive the slope of the efficient frontier. Referring to Eq. (2.2), we know that $dE(\widetilde{R}_C)/dy = E(\widetilde{R}_i) - E(\widetilde{R}_M)$. And, using Eq. (2.3), we have $d\sigma(\widetilde{R}_C)/dy = [y\sigma^2(\widetilde{R}_i) - \sigma^2(\widetilde{R}_M) + y\sigma^2(\widetilde{R}_M) + \mathrm{cov}(\widetilde{R}_i, \widetilde{R}_M) - 2y\,\mathrm{cov}(\widetilde{R}_i, \widetilde{R}_M)]/\sigma(\widetilde{R}_C)$. Hence, the change in portfolio C returns per unit change in total risk, or the slope of the CML, at the market portfolio with $y = 0$ is:

$$\frac{dE(\widetilde{R}_C)}{d\sigma(\widetilde{R}_C)} = \frac{[E(\widetilde{R}_i) - E(\widetilde{R}_M)]}{[-\sigma^2(\widetilde{R}_M) + \mathrm{cov}(\widetilde{R}_i, \widetilde{R}_M)]/\sigma(\widetilde{R}_M)}. \tag{2.4}$$

The slope of the CML in Fig. 1.2 is easily seen to be $[E(\widetilde{R}_m) - R_f]/\sigma(\widetilde{R}_M)$. Setting the slope of the CML equal to the slope of the efficient frontier at the market portfolio M with $y = 0$, we have:

$$\frac{[E(\widetilde{R}_M) - R_f]}{\sigma(\widetilde{R}_M)} = \frac{[E(\widetilde{R}_i) - E(\widetilde{R}_M)]}{[-\sigma^2(\widetilde{R}_M) + \operatorname{cov}(\widetilde{R}_i, \widetilde{R}_M)]/\sigma(\widetilde{R}_M)}. \tag{2.5}$$

After rearranging terms, we obtain:

$$E(\widetilde{R}_i) = R_f + [E(\widetilde{R}_M) - R_f]\frac{\operatorname{cov}(\widetilde{R}_i, \widetilde{R}_M)}{\sigma^2(\widetilde{R}_M)}. \tag{2.6}$$

Simplifying notation by setting $\operatorname{cov}(\widetilde{R}_i, \widetilde{R}_M)]/\sigma^2(\widetilde{R}_M) = \beta_i$, the familiar form of the CAPM is specified:

$$E(\widetilde{R}_i) = R_f + \beta_i[E(\widetilde{R}_M) - R_f], \tag{2.7}$$

where β_i (viz., beta) is the all-important measure of systematic risk related to general market movements by market portfolio M. Note that the beta of M equals 1. This benchmark risk value implies that beta greater (less) than one indicates higher (lower) market risk relative to the overall market.

The main takeaway of the CAPM is that, as beta increases, regardless of investor risk preferences, a linear relation between expected return and risk is hypothesized. This relation is depicted by the Security Market Line (SML) in Fig. 2.1. The SML gives the equilibrium risk-adjusted pricing for assets. Because investors can diversify away some part of total risk, only beta risk is relevant to pricing (i.e., systematic risk related to the market portfolio). Total risk contains systematic (priced) risk and unsystematic (diversified) risk. Assets above (below) the SML in Fig. 2.1 have returns that are too high (low) and therefore are overpriced (underpriced) with respect to equilibrium returns per unit beta risk.

Practically speaking, the CAPM has powerful implications. For example, per the discussion above, investors can evaluate whether an asset is earning a rate of return that is appropriate for its risk and buy (sell) assets that are underpriced (overpriced). Additionally, if you estimated betas for individual stocks and then sorted them into portfolios with low to high betas, the high beta portfolios should earn higher returns than the low beta portfolios in the future. This fundamental insight from the CAPM would be valuable to any investor seeking to not only control risk in their stock portfolio but earn fair returns per unit risk. Given beta for a stock, managers within

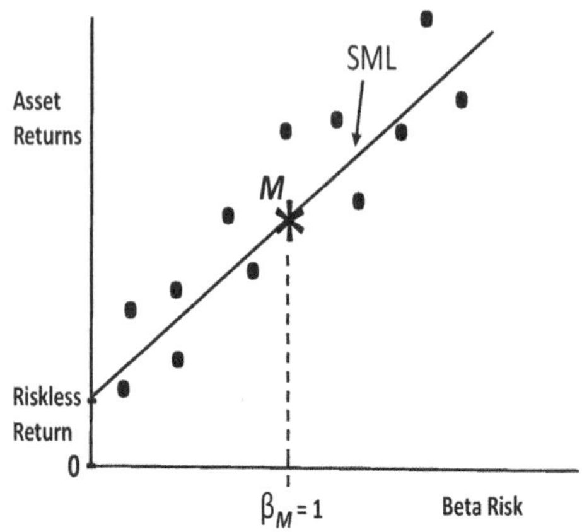

Fig. 2.1 The Security Market Line (SML) of the Capital Asset Pricing Model (CAPM) shows the relationship between asset returns and beta risk

firms could estimate the cost of equity and cost of capital (i.e., the cost of capital is the weighted costs of debt and equity capital). Moreover, portfolio managers in mutual funds, pension funds, and other institutional investors could apply beta to determine whether or not they are outperforming the market (i.e., a positive alpha is earned). Many other applications of the CAPM are possible. It is no wonder that a Nobel Prize was awarded to Professor Sharpe in recognition of the CAPM's substantial contributions to investment theory and practice.

2.2.2 *CAPM Market Model*

As originally proposed by Markowitz (1959) and further developed by Sharpe (1963) and Fama (1968), empirical tests of the CAPM use the so-called *market model* in excess return form:

$$R_{it} - R_{ft} = \alpha_i + \beta_i(R_{mt} - R_{ft}), \tag{2.8}$$

where R_{it} is the realized rate of return on stock i in time period t (e.g., daily or monthly), R_{ft} is the government bond interest rate, and R_{mt} is the realized average rate of return on the stock market as a whole.[2] Notice that we use the lower case notation m here in recognition of the fact that

[2] For further elaboration of the market model, see Black et al. (1972).

the market portfolio M cannot be observed. In U.S. stock market studies, different proxies for M are used, including (for example) the S&P 500 index and CRSP index of all U.S. stocks constructed and distributed by the Center for Research and Security Prices at the University of Chicago. The excess return $R_{mt} - R_{ft}$ represents the market premium over the riskless government bond rate (e.g., Treasury bill rate). Stock risk premiums $R_{it} - R_{ft}$ are regressed on market risk premiums $R_{mt} - R_{ft}$ using ordinary least squares (OLS) regression methods.

According to CAPM theory, α_i in the market model should equal zero. Jensen (1968) inferred that α_i allows researchers to test the CAPM. If so-called *Jensen's alpha* is greater than zero, then either the market is not efficient as assumed or a missing factor exists beyond the general market proxy used to estimate market portfolio M.[3] As noted in Chapter 1, Roll (1977) has argued that the CAPM cannot be tested without accurate estimates of M. The *Roll critique* is often cited as a serious bias in empirical tests of the CAPM. If M is unknown, how can investors hold this portfolio? If they do not hold M, how can the CAPM be used to price assets in markets?

Of course, in the real world, stocks do not lie exactly on the SML. Some stocks will be randomly located above or below the SML. For this reason, the market model is modified as follows:

$$R_{it} - R_{ft} = \alpha_i + \beta_i(R_{mt} - R_{ft}) + e_{it}, \tag{2.9}$$

where e_{it} is a random error (with mean zero and constant variance) to account for scatter around the SML.

Early tests of the market model by Black et al. (1972) rejected the CAPM. Based on U.S. stock returns in the period 1931–1961, time-series regressions of excess returns revealed that high (low) beta stocks had significant negative (positive) intercepts. The authors were careful to note that estimates of beta for individual assets suffer from substantial measurement error that can bias cross-sectional tests of the relation between their rates of return and betas. They therefore established the prevailing methodology of using portfolios in beta tests (see also Blume 1970; Friend and Blume 1970). Positive and negative measurement errors tend to cancel out in portfolios. Of course, a drawback of portfolios is their smaller range of

[3] One possible missing factor is that investment managers have special skills in utilizing market information to outperform other market participants.

beta values than individual stocks, which works against the ability to detect significant return/beta relations. Indeed, random portfolios may well have portfolios close to 1, or the proxy market index beta. Partially offsetting this issue, researchers sort individual stocks by their estimated betas and then form portfolios with betas ranked from low to high.

Numerous authors, including Douglas (1969), Friend and Blume (1970), Miller and Scholes (1972), Fama and MacBeth (1973), Stambaugh (1982), Gibbons and Shanken (1983), and others, have confirmed that the relation between average returns and beta is flatter than predicted by the CAPM with a positive intercept. Low beta stocks have too high returns, and high beta stocks have too low returns. Among these studies, Fama and MacBeth (1973) proposed an innovation that has become standard practice in cross-sectional tests:

1. In the first step, time-series regressions are estimated to obtain beta coefficients in an estimation window (e.g., five years of monthly returns or one year of daily returns).
2. In the second step, cross-sectional regressions are estimated based on regressing one-month-ahead returns on betas from the first step, which provides coefficient estimates of the risk premiums associated with beta loadings.

This two-step process is rolled forward one month at a time and repeated to the end of the sample period. A time series of risk premium estimates (i.e., the coefficients in second step cross-sectional regressions) is generated for each beta risk. Subsequently, a t-test of these time-series estimates is computed to determine if the average risk premium over time is significantly different from zero. This rolling Fama and MacBeth procedure eliminates correlation between residuals in cross-sectional regressions that can bias average risk premium t-tests. By contrast, if cross-sectional regressions are performed within sample (i.e., portfolios returns in each month in the sample period are regressed on average beta estimates for the entire period), a correction is needed to adjust the standard errors in the t-statistic.[4]

Despite lackluster evidence in favor of the CAPM in early studies, the CAPM became the workhorse for asset pricing in academic research and practitioner circles over the next 30 years. No serious contenders existed

[4] See Cochrane (2005, Chapter 12) for discussion of the Shanken (1992) correction.

to challenge its central role in asset pricing. Even though some published evidence that general market indexes used in empirical tests were efficient portfolios, the Roll critique suggests that empirical evidence against the CAPM implies that market index proxies are inefficient. That is, commonly used general market indexes in CAPM tests lie somewhere in the interior of the investment parabola, not on the efficient frontier.

2.3 Zero-Beta CAPM

Black (1972) attempted to reconcile CAPM theory with early contradictory evidence by proposing a more general form that did not assume that investors can borrow at a riskless rate. Earlier joint work by Black et al. (1972) led him to believe that diversified portfolio returns and betas were better explained by the following model:

$$E(\widetilde{R}_i) = E(\widetilde{R}_{ZM}) + \beta_{i,M}[E(\widetilde{R}_M) - E(\widetilde{R}_{ZM})], \quad (2.10)$$

where $E(\widetilde{R}_{ZM})$ is the expected return of the zero-beta portfolio ZM that has zero correlation with market portfolio M (i.e., they are orthogonal portfolios), and other notation is as before. Portfolio M lies on the superior, positively sloped boundary of the Markowitz minimum variance investment parabola, i.e., efficient frontier. Portfolio ZM lies on the inferior, negatively sloped boundary of the parabola. Assuming $\widetilde{R}_{ZM} > R_f$, portfolios with low betas less than one will earn higher returns than predicted by the CAPM, and high beta portfolios more than one will earn lower returns than the CAPM contends. These relations are consistent with early CAPM evidence discussed above.

In view of this empirical insight, Black derived a more general form of the CAPM with no riskless asset. Upon doing so, he specified the following zero-beta CAPM:

$$E(\widetilde{R}_i) = E(\widetilde{R}_{ZI}) + \beta_{i,I}[E(\widetilde{R}_I) - E(\widetilde{R}_{ZI})], \quad (2.11)$$

where $E(\widetilde{R}_I)$ and $E(\widetilde{R}_{ZI})$ are the expected returns of orthogonal portfolios I and ZI that lie on the efficient frontier and inferior boundary of the parabola, respectively, and $\beta_{i,I}$ is the sensitivity or beta risk of asset i's return with respect to efficient portfolio I's return. The excess return $E(\widetilde{R}_I) - E(\widetilde{R}_{ZI})$ equals the return on a zero-investment portfolio that is long efficient portfolio I and short zero-beta portfolio ZI (rather than riskless rate R_f as in the CAPM). Now $E(\widetilde{R}_{ZI})$ is the borrowing rate.

Assuming further that the riskless asset exists but cannot be shorted (i.e., no borrowing at this rate), Black restated the zero-beta CAPM as a two-factor model:

$$E(\widetilde{R}_i) - R_f = \beta_{i,I}[E(\widetilde{R}_I) - R_f] + \beta_{i,ZI}[E(\widetilde{R}_{ZI}) - R_f], \tag{2.12}$$

where $\beta_{i,I}$ and $\beta_{i,ZI}$ represent the sensitivities or beta risks of asset i with respect to efficient portfolio I and zero-beta portfolio ZI, respectively.

The zero-beta CAPM postulates that identification of the market portfolio M, which is defined in the CAPM as the tangent portfolio with respect to a ray from the riskless rate to the efficient frontier, is not a necessary condition for testing the CAPM. Any orthogonal pair of minimum variance index portfolios I and ZI on the minimum variance parabola is sufficient to construct M. Among all efficient risky portfolios, the true market portfolio is the one composed of the weighted sum of all individuals' portfolios. In this regard, the zero-beta CAPM allows both long and short positions in assets to construct portfolios I and ZI, in contrast to the CAPM's restriction that only long positions can be used in M (i.e., a value-weighted index of all assets[5]) and that short positions (borrowing) are only allowed in the riskless asset. As shown by Roll (1977, 1980), there is nothing unique about the market portfolio in the context of the zero-beta CAPM, which can be replaced by any market index that is an efficient portfolio plus its zero-beta portfolio counterpart.

Studies by Pulley (1981), Kallberg and Ziemba (1983), Levy (1983), Kroll et al. (1984), Green and Hollifield (1992), Jagannathan and Ma (2003), Levy and Ritov (2010), and others have found that sizeable short positions are needed to obtain the most efficient minimum variance parabola. As such, the common real world practice of shorting assets tends to favor the theoretical assumptions of the zero-beta CAPM. Consistent with the Roll critique discussed earlier, Fama (1976), Roll (1977), Ross (1977), and Kandel (1984) have asserted that mean-variance efficiency of the market portfolio is a necessary condition for testing the linear relation between expected asset returns and single factor (market) returns.

[5] See Roll (1977) and Levy (1983, 2007).

2.3.1 *Formal Derivation of the Zero-Beta CAPM*

Here we review Black's derivation of the zero-beta CAPM by starting with the standard mean-variance portfolio problem. Given the expected returns and matrix of covariances of returns for n assets, we find the minimum variance parabola based on the set of optimal asset weights that minimizes the return variance for each feasible portfolio expected return. Following Markowitz (1959), we minimize the portfolio's variance subject to the constraints that it's expected return equals $E(\widetilde{R}_I)$ and constituent asset weights sum to one:

$$\underset{\omega}{\text{Min}}\frac{1}{2}\omega'\Sigma\omega + \eta[E(\widetilde{R}_I) - \omega'E(\widetilde{R})] + \kappa(1 - \omega'e), \tag{2.13}$$

where ω is the weights vector (with dimension $n \times 1$), e is a vector of ones (with dimension $n \times 1$), $E(\widetilde{R}) = [E(\widetilde{R}_1), E(\widetilde{R}_2), \ldots, E(\widetilde{R}_n)]'$ is the expected one-period return vector for n assets (with dimension $n \times 1$), and Σ is the covariance matrix for n assets (with dimension $n \times n$). The first order conditions with respect to ω, η, and κ give

$$\begin{aligned} \Sigma\omega - \eta E(\widetilde{R}) - \kappa e &= 0 \\ E(\widetilde{R}_I) - \omega' E(\widetilde{R}) &= 0 \\ 1 - \omega' e &= 0. \end{aligned} \tag{2.14}$$

Solving for the optimal weights ω^*, we get

$$\begin{aligned} \omega^* &= \frac{B - AE(\widetilde{R})}{BC - A^2}\Sigma^{-1}e + \frac{CE(\widetilde{R}) - A}{BC - A^2}\Sigma^{-1}E(\widetilde{R}_I) \\ &\equiv \phi + \psi E(\widetilde{R}_I), \end{aligned} \tag{2.15}$$

where

$$\begin{aligned} A &\equiv E(\widetilde{R})'\Sigma^{-1}e \\ B &\equiv E(\widetilde{R})'\Sigma^{-1}E(\widetilde{R}) \\ C &\equiv e'\Sigma^{-1}e \end{aligned} \tag{2.16}$$

are known scalars, and

$$\phi \equiv \frac{B\Sigma^{-1}e - A\Sigma^{-1}E(\widetilde{R})}{BC - A^2}$$
$$\psi \equiv \frac{C\Sigma^{-1}E(\widetilde{R}) - A\Sigma^{-1}e}{BC - A^2} \tag{2.17}$$

are known $n \times 1$ vectors. From these equations, the familiar definition of the variance of efficient portfolio I is

$$\sigma_I^2 = \frac{1}{C} + \frac{C\left[E(\widetilde{R}_I) - \frac{A}{C}\right]^2}{BC - A^2}. \tag{2.18}$$

According to the CAPM, in return-standard-deviation space, the equation of the line through the tangent point $[E(\widetilde{R}_M), \sigma_M]$ (i.e., market portfolio M) is

$$E(\widetilde{R}_{ZI}) - E(\widetilde{R}_M) = \frac{BC - A^2}{C[E(\widetilde{R}_M) - \frac{A}{C}]}\sigma_M(\sigma_{ZI} - \sigma_M), \tag{2.19}$$

where $\frac{BC-A^2}{C[E(\widetilde{R}_M)-\frac{A}{C}]}\sigma_M$ is the slope of the line (see Merton 1972, p. 1856). Substituting the riskless rate R_f for $E(\widetilde{R}_{ZI})$ to obtain the highest (most efficient) slope of the CML, we can set $\sigma_{ZI} = 0$. Consistent with our earlier derivation in Subsect. 2.2.1, the slope of the CML becomes $[E(\widetilde{R}_M) - R_f]/\sigma(\widetilde{R}_M)$.

Departing from the CAPM, previous papers by Roll (1980), Kandel (1984, 1986), and others (e.g., see van Zijl 1987) have geometrically derived the properties of Black's zero-beta CAPM in return-variance space. Here we follow Roll's (1980) geometry as shown in Fig. 2.2. In return-variance space, given some market index I on the efficient frontier, a ray extending from this portfolio down through the global minimum variance portfolio G to the Y-axis gives the expected return on the zero-beta index $E(\widetilde{R}_{ZI})$.[6] Using this reference point for the zero-beta return, the portfolio ZI can be horizontally located on the inferior (inefficient) portion of the minimum variance parabola. According to Black, an infinite number of pairs of minimum variance portfolios I and ZI can be identified in this way.

[6] See also an earlier paper by Roll (1977, p. 142, footnote 8) in which he discusses this geometry in mean-variance space.

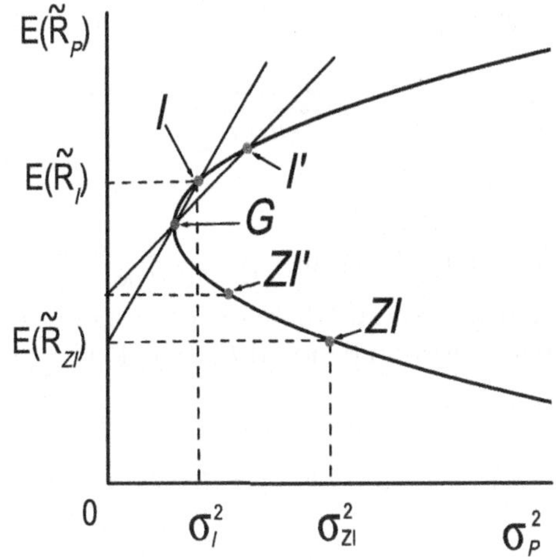

Fig. 2.2 The geometry of the zero-beta CAPM using Roll's approach locates pairs of efficient frontier and inefficient zero-beta portfolios

According to Black, the expected return on an arbitrary risky asset portfolio P can be specified in terms of the expected returns on efficient portfolio I and its zero-beta portfolio counterpart ZI. To see this, we define the covariance between the returns of portfolios I and P as:

$$\operatorname{cov}(\widetilde{R}_I, \widetilde{R}_P) = (\omega^{I'})\Sigma\omega^P = [\phi + \psi E(\widetilde{R}_I)]'\Sigma\omega^P. \tag{2.20}$$

This covariance term can be written in terms of A, B, and C as follows:

$$\begin{aligned}
&= \left(\frac{B\Sigma^{-1}e - A\Sigma^{-1}E(\widetilde{R})}{BC - A^2} + \frac{C\Sigma^{-1}E(\widetilde{R}) - A\Sigma^{-1}e}{BC - A^2}E(\widetilde{R}_I)\right)' \Sigma\omega^P \\
&= \frac{Be'\Sigma^{-1}\Sigma\omega^P - AE(\widetilde{R})'\Sigma^{-1}\Sigma\omega^P}{BC - A^2} + \frac{CE(\widetilde{R}_I)E(\widetilde{R})'\Sigma^{-1}\Sigma\omega^P - AE(\widetilde{R}_I)e'\Sigma^{-1}\Sigma\omega^P}{BC - A^2} \\
&= \frac{B - AE(\widetilde{R}_P) + CE(\widetilde{R}_I)E(\widetilde{R}_P) - AE(\widetilde{R}_I)}{BC - A^2}.
\end{aligned} \tag{2.21}$$

Solving for $E(\widetilde{R}_P)$, we get:

$$\begin{aligned}
E(\widetilde{R}_P) &= \frac{AE(\widetilde{R}_I) - B}{CE(\widetilde{R}_I) - A} + \operatorname{cov}(\widetilde{R}_I, \widetilde{R}_P)\left(\frac{BC - A^2}{CE(\widetilde{R}_I) - A}\right) \\
&= \frac{A}{C} - \frac{BC - A^2}{C^2E(\widetilde{R}_I) - \frac{A}{C}} + \operatorname{cov}(\widetilde{R}_I, \widetilde{R}_P)\frac{\sigma_I^2}{\sigma_I^2}\left(\frac{BC - A^2}{CE(\widetilde{R}_I) - A}\right),
\end{aligned} \tag{2.22}$$

where $\sigma_I^2 = \frac{1}{C} + \frac{C[E(\widetilde{R}_I)-\frac{A}{C}]^2}{BC-A^2}$. Expanding Eq. (2.22), we have

$$E(\widetilde{R}_P) = \frac{A}{C} - \frac{BC-A^2}{C^2[E(\widetilde{R}_I)-\frac{A}{C}]} + \frac{\text{cov}(\widetilde{R}_I,\widetilde{R}_P)}{\sigma_I^2}\left(E(\widetilde{R}_I) - \frac{A}{C} + \frac{BC-A^2}{C^2[E(\widetilde{R}_I)-\frac{A}{C}]}\right). \tag{2.23}$$

The portfolio return $\frac{A}{C} - \frac{BC-A^2}{C^2[E(\widetilde{R}_I)-\frac{A}{C}]}$ is orthogonal to efficient portfolio return $E(\widetilde{R}_I)$ and therefore corresponds to the expected return on the zero-beta portfolio denoted $E(\widetilde{R}_{ZI})$. This result can be seen by observing that

$$(\omega^{ZI'})\Sigma\omega^I = [\phi + \psi E(\widetilde{R}_{ZI})]'\Sigma[\phi + \psi E(\widetilde{R}_I)] = 0 \tag{2.24}$$

$$B - AE(\widetilde{R}_{ZI}) + CE(\widetilde{R}_I)E(\widetilde{R}_{ZI}) - AE(\widetilde{R}_I) = 0 \tag{2.25}$$

$$E(\widetilde{R}_{ZI}) = \frac{AE(\widetilde{R}_I) - B}{CE(\widetilde{R}_I) - A} = \frac{A}{C} - \frac{BC-A^2}{C^2[E(\widetilde{R}_I)-\frac{A}{C}]}. \tag{2.26}$$

Rewriting Eq. (2.23), we obtain:

$$E(\widetilde{R}_P) = E(\widetilde{R}_{ZI}) + \beta_P[E(\widetilde{R}_I) - E(\widetilde{R}_{ZI})], \tag{2.27}$$

which is the same as Black's zero-beta CAPM defined earlier in Eq. (2.11).

Numerous authors have tested for the existence of the zero-beta CAPM. Gibbons (1982) derived likelihood ratio tests (LRT) of zero-beta portfolio returns in the absence of a riskless asset that rejects the zero-beta CAPM in three out of four subperiods. By contrast, Jobson and Korkie (1982) found that, after adjustment for excess skewness in the sample chi-squared statistic, the zero-beta CAPM was rejected in only one of these four subperiods. Stambaugh (1982) provided further evidence of significant zero-beta parameter estimates for U.S. stocks.[7] In forthcoming chapters, we extend these previous studies by: (1) deriving a new zero-beta CAPM geometry; (2) developing an alternative form of the zero-beta CAPM dubbed the ZCAPM; and (3) conducting asset pricing tests of the ZCAPM.

[7] Kandel (1984) derived an LRT without requiring iteration, Shanken (1985) generalized the test to a multifactor model and showed that the CRSP equal-weighted index was inefficient, and Zhou (1991) proposed an equivalent eigenvalue test (see also Shanken 1986).

2.4 Multifactor Models

In the 1990s empirical tests by Eugene Fama, Kenneth French, and others confirmed the failure of the CAPM. Subsequently, Fama and French (1992, 1993, 1995) proposed *multifactor models* that augment the CAPM market factor with zero-investment, long/short factors that improve explanatory power and drive down alphas in time-series regression models. In a survey article, Fama and French (2004) discussed the logic of the CAPM, reviewed many empirical studies on the failure of the CAPM, and described their proposed multifactor models. As summarized there, consistent with Tobin's (1958) separation theorem, the CAPM's Security Market Line (SML) embodies the efficient set of portfolio combinations of M and the riskless asset. The beta for each asset is proportional to its risk contribution to the market portfolio. Also, the CAPM assumes unrestricted borrowing and lending at the riskless rate. In this regard, Fama and French recognized that all models make unrealistic assumptions. They argued that it was the job of empirical tests to validate models based on real-world data.

Using more than 25 years of U.S. stock return data, Fama and French (1992) showed that little or no relation exists between average returns and betas among beta-sorted portfolios.[8] By contrast, two firm characteristics—namely, market capitalization (or size) and book-to-market (B/M) equity (or value)—were significantly related to average stock returns in cross-sectional tests. Small stocks tended to earn higher average returns than big stocks over time. Also, value firms with high B/M ratios had higher average returns than growth stocks with low B/M ratios. These findings led the authors to conclude that, unlike CAPM beta, size and B/M help to explain the cross section of average stock returns.

2.4.1 *Three-Factor Model*

Fama and French (1993) deepened their analyses of size and B/M by constructing factors based on these firm characteristics. They formed zero-investment portfolios of small and big stocks and then defined a *size factor* that equals small stocks' returns (long position) minus big stocks' returns (short) in each month or day over time. Similarly, a *value* factor was defined

[8] Other studies by Lakonishok and Shapiro (1984, 1986), He and Ng (1994), Davis (1994), Miles and Timmermann (1996) and others found little or no return/beta relation also.

as high B/M stocks' returns minus low B/M stocks' returns. In combination with the market factor, these characteristic portfolios were used to specify a three-factor model. Since their size and value factors are not linked or tied to the theoretical development of the CAPM, we refer to them as *ad hoc* in nature.

Interestingly, the size and value factors are theoretically related to the ZCAPM proposed in this book. Both of these characteristic portfolios measure some part of total return dispersion. That is, they are cross-sectional dispersion measures that capture different aspects of the cross-sectional standard deviation of returns. In forthcoming Chapter 3, we will see that return dispersion defines the width or span of the mean-variance investment parabola, a previously unrecognized property of Markowitz's investment parabola. Based on this portfolio theory, our ZCAPM incorporates market return dispersion as a key asset pricing factor. Not surprisingly, our empirical ZCAPM tests in Chapters 6 and 7 show that the size and value factors are explained by zeta risk associated with return dispersion.

Returning to Fama and French, the authors added their new size and value multifactors to the CAPM market portfolio proxy factor to specify the following three-factor model:

$$R_{it} - R_{ft} = \alpha_i + \beta_{i,m}(R_{mt} - R_{ft}) + \beta_{i,S}SMB_t + \beta_{i,V}HML_t + e_{it}, \quad (2.28)$$

where SMB and HML denote the size and value factors, respectively, and loadings $\beta_{i,S}$ and $\beta_{i,V}$ estimate the sensitivity of excess returns of the ith stock or stock portfolio to these factors. In the 1963–1991 period, Fama and French estimated the average market premium to be 0.43% per month (or about 5% per year) compared to 0.29% and 0.40% per month (or 3.5% and 4.8% per year) for the size and value factors, respectively. Sorts of stocks into their beta loadings on size and value factors revealed that, unlike CAPM beta sorts, returns significantly differed across low and high betas. Further analyses of corporate bonds were included in their study, but we focus here on the stock results.

A major finding was that Jensen's alpha (i.e., α_i) in the Fama and French three-factor model was near zero and normally insignificant for 25 portfolios sorted on size and B/M firm characteristics. This result is striking in that estimated alphas for the CAPM market model or the size and value factors by themselves are relatively large and significant. A joint test that the alphas of test asset portfolios equal zero developed earlier by Gibbons et al. (GRS) (1989) corroborated these results. Thus, augmenting the market factor with size and value factors eliminated mispricing for the most part. In a later study, consistent with the Roll critique, they inferred that tests of the CAPM failed due to bad proxies for the market portfolio and concluded that "... valid tests of the CAPM await the coming of *M*" (Fama and French (1996, p. 1956).

As already mentioned, a shortcoming of Fama and French's three-factor model is that there is not much theoretical support for the size and value factors. Previous researchers—for example, Basu (1977), Statman (1980), Banz (1981), Lakonishok and Shapiro (1984, 1986), Rosenberg et al. (1985), Bhandari (1988), among others—reported evidence that firm characteristics are related to stock returns. The size and value factors were chosen due to their relatively high relation to returns compared to other firm-specific traits (e.g., earnings/price ratios, leverage ratios, etc.). However, Black (1993) contended that Fama and French's size and value factors were the result of data mining. He argued that, since the Banz (1981) study, no size effect was evident in the Fama and French (1992) results. In his words, "Lack of theory is a tipoff: watch out for data mining!" (Black 1993, p. 75).

Taking issue with Fama and French's rejection of the CAPM, Kothari et al. (1995) found that beta is more strongly related to portfolio returns using quarterly and annual returns to estimate betas than monthly returns. However, as Fama and French (1996) showed, empirical tests continued to support size and value factors in terms of helping to explain average stock returns.[9]

Another potential problem in Fama and French's tests is endogeneity due to the use of size and value sorted portfolios to test size and value factors. Due to this endogeneity issue, Lewellen et al. (2010), Daniel and Titman (2012), and others have recommended expanding the set of test assets to include combined portfolios that correlate less strongly with proposed factors. They suggested that industry portfolios are a particularly good choice for test assets due to being largely exogenous to various factors.

Despite the above criticisms, because the size and value ***mimicking portfolios*** based on investable long/short positions provide a simple way to define stock return factors, many researchers subsequently utilized this innovation to construct other multifactors. Alternative multifactors are generally developed from various anomalies in stock returns related to past

[9] See also Fama and French (1998), who showed that the three-factor model outperforms the CAPM market model in international tests.

returns, profit, capital investment, credit risk, term premiums, dividend yields, etc. A rich seedbed for anomalies is stock trading strategies that seek to earn abnormal profits not explained by risk. Trading schemes are ubiquitous among stock investors.

2.4.2 Four-Factor Model

One of the oldest market trading strategies is momentum. Stocks that were losers (winners) in the recent past tend to continue losing (winning) in the near future. To study mutual funds' performance over time, Carhart (1997) modified the three-factor model by incorporating a momentum factor. His four-factor model is:

$$R_{it} - R_{ft} = \alpha_i + \beta_{i,m}(R_{mt} - R_{ft}) + \beta_{i,S}SMB_t + \beta_{i,V}HML_t + \beta_{i,MOM}MOM_t + e_{it}, \tag{2.29}$$

where MOM_t is a zero-investment factor equal to high past return stock returns minus low past stock returns (i.e., the previous one-year period can be used to classify stocks into high- and low-decile portfolios in terms of returns). The momentum factor has been proven by many authors to be significant in cross-sectional tests.

Similar to the size and value factors, a glaring issue is the lack of theory underlying the momentum factor. In the context of our ZCAPM proposed in Chapter 3, it is another return-dispersion-based factor and therefore is related to zeta risk associated with market return dispersion. In Chapter 8 we document evidence that corroborates a close relationship between momentum and zeta risk.

2.4.3 Five-Factor Model

Another paper by Fama and French (1995) linked the B/M, operating profit, and capital investment characteristics of firms. High B/M (value) firms are associated with low profit and investment, and vice versa for low B/M firms.[10] Taking advantage of these relationships, Fama and French (2015) proposed a five-factor model:

$$\begin{aligned} R_{it} - R_{ft} = \alpha_i + \beta_{i,m}(R_{mt} - R_{ft}) + \beta_{i,S}SMB_t + \beta_{i,V}HML_t + \\ \beta_{i,R}RMW_t + \beta_{i,C}CMA_t + e_{it}, \end{aligned} \tag{2.30}$$

[10] See also Novy-Marx (2013) on the profit premium.

where RMW_t is the robust profit minus weak profit factor, and CMA_t is the conservative minus aggressive capital investment factor. The multifactors in this model are created by means of four sorts: two size groups, two B/M groups, two operating profit groups, and two capital investment groups. The intersection of these sorts provides 16 value-weighted portfolios in each month over time. As an example, the size factor is long the eight small size portfolios minus the eight big portfolios. The value, profit, and investment factors are similarly constructed.[11]

In the sample period 1963–2013, the historical average risk premiums per month for these multifactors based on 2 × 2 × 2 × 2 sorts were: $R_m - R_f = 0.50\%$, $SMB = 0.30\%$, $HML = 0.30\%$, $RMW = 0.25\%$, and $CMA = 0.14\%$. Average intercepts were generally lower for the five-factor model compared to the three-factor model. Also, the five-factor model outperformed the three-factor model in terms of cross-sectional variance of returns left unexplained. Finally, comparative tests showed that *HML* is redundant. Most of the value factor is captured by the other four factors, especially the profit and investment factors. Hence, a more parsimonious four-factor model is:

$$R_{it} - R_{ft} = \alpha_i + \beta_{i,m}(R_m - R_{ft}) + \beta_{i,S}SMB_t + \beta_{i,R}RMW_t + \beta_{i,C}CMA_t + e_{it}. \quad (2.31)$$

Like other multifactors, we consider *RMW* and *CMA* to be return-dispersion-based factors and, as such, related to the ZCAPM.

Recently, Fama and French (2020) proposed modified versions of their five-factor model in which the multifactors are replaced by long/short mimicking portfolios estimated from a cross-sectional regression. For example, in one version of their new model, they regress test asset portfolio returns in month t on lagged firm characteristic values at time $t-1$ (i.e., market capitalization, book-to-market equity (B/M) ratio, profit, and capital investment). This cross-sectional regression is much different than the traditional Fama–MacBeth second step cross-sectional regressions of month t returns on the beta factor loadings obtained from Eq. (2.30). As Ferson (2019, p. 223) has observed, the estimated coefficients (or λ_ks) in this cross-sectional regression are long/short portfolios (e.g., long high B/M stock returns and short low B/M stock returns). Given this fact, they insert these mimicking portfolios as the factors in time-series regression Eq. (2.30). And, to allow for time-varying risk, they proposed another form of

[11] Other sorting procedures and resultant factors are tested in their study also.

this model by replacing the beta loadings with the lagged firm characteristic values. Based on various tests of the intercepts (pricing errors) of the time-series models (e.g., GRS tests), they found that both of these five-factor models improve upon their previous multifactor models. All of their intercept tests are in-sample, and no out-of-sample cross-sectional tests are provided. Also, like their earlier multifactors in Eq. (2.30), their new long/short mimicking portfolios derived from cross-sectional regressions are return-dispersion-based factors.

2.4.4 Other Multifactor Models

Closely related to the Fama and French five-factor model, Hou et al. (2015) proposed a four-factor model containing the following factors: (1) market ($R_m - R_f$), (2) equity market capitalization (ME), (3) investment to assets ratio (IA), and (4) return on equity (ROE). Because their model is grounded in production q-theory, they referred to it as the q-factor model. Empirical tests in the 1972–2012 period showed that the q-factor model explained many different anomalies in stock returns, including momentum (e.g., price and industry momentum), value versus growth, capital investment, profitability, intangibles (e.g., R&D, corporate governance, etc.), and trading frictions (e.g., illiquidity, idiosyncratic volatility, short-term reversal, etc.). Of almost 80 anomalies, about one-half had insignificant average returns, which was attributed in many cases to the influence of microcaps on portfolio stock returns. Compared to other popular models, the q-model outperformed Fama and French's three-factor model as well as Carhart's four-factor model in terms of explaining stock return anomalies.

More recently, Stambaugh and Yuan (2017) created a four-factor model with market ($R_m - R_f$), size (SMB), management ($MGMT$), and performance ($PERF$) factors. Their management and performance mispricing factors are developed from stocks' rankings with respect to a number of well-known anomalies. They separated 11 anomalies into two clusters and used these clustered anomalies to compute two zero-investment portfolios as factors. Taking into account over 80 anomalies in the sample period 1967–2013, their four-factor model outperformed the five-factor model of Fama and French (2015) as well as a four-factor model of Hou et al. (2015). Other tests supported their model also. Hence, they concluded that mispricing factors can help explain expected returns.

Barillas and Shanken (2018) tested different configurations of models using various factors in studies by Asness and Frazzini (2013), Fama and French (2015), and Hou et al. (2015). Based on novel tests of relative performance, a five-factor model incorporating market, size, value, profit, investment, and momentum factors outperformed other possible juxtapositions of factors based on different in-sample and out-of-sample tests. However, tests using different portfolios raised some doubts about this model. In the same year Fama and French (2018) published a similar multifactor model by adding momentum to their five-factor model to create a six-factor model. Also, Hou et al. (2018) incorporated a growth factor in the *q*-factor model. Departing from these papers, Lettau and Pelger (2020) developed a model with five latent asset pricing factors using Principal Component Analysis (PCA) methods (see also Lettau and Pelger 2020).[12]

Intense work continues on multifactor models. The battle pits competing models against one another in the quest for the most significant factors and best asset pricing model. Fama and French (2015) single out small stocks as the greatest challenge to asset pricing models. In forthcoming Chapter 7 we show that the ZCAPM does an excellent job of pricing small stock portfolios that exceeds other models.

Another serious challenge for asset pricing models is theoretical. According to Merton's (1973) intertemporal CAPM (ICAPM), risk premiums associated with a number of state variables are not captured by the market factor. Fama and French (2015) have conjectured that size, value, profit, and investment factors capture exposures to these unknown state variables. But what if essential state variables can be directly estimated (rather than proxied) using readily available market information? In the next chapter, we show that the ZCAPM is a special case of Black's zero-beta CAPM and derive a simple specification from the mean-variance investment parabola. Two state variables emerge that can be estimated from market information: the mean return of all stock returns and their cross-sectional standard deviation. No guessing is required about the possible factors that might be related to some undefined latent state variables. As we document in Chapter 6, the ZCAPM's two state variables explain a large share of average stock returns in the cross section. Also, the ZCAPM repeatedly

[12] This statistical approach to finding factors has precedent in previous factor analytic studies by Chamberlain and Rothschild (1983), Connor and Korajczyk (1986), and others. See also earlier work by Chen et al. (1986) on models containing various state variables as factors, including unanticipated changes (or innovations) in the term premium, default premium, growth rate of industrial production, and inflation.

outperforms other models on a consistent basis across different test asset portfolios, time periods, and out-of-sample periods.

2.5 Summary

Asset pricing models can be classified into two branches: (1) general equilibrium models and (2) multifactor models. Using the Markowitz (1959) mean-variance return paradigm and general equilibrium conditions, we derived Sharpe's (1964) pathbreaking capital asset pricing model (CAPM). Unfortunately, early empirical evidence based on stock market returns did not support Sharpe's (1964) CAPM market model. Studies found that the slope of the Security Market Line (SML) relating stock returns to betas was flatter with a higher intercept than predicted by the CAPM. Later evidence by Fama and French (1992, 1993, 1995) documented that the SML is essentially flat for all practical purposes. Hence, higher beta portfolios do not earn higher average returns than low beta portfolios. Black (1972) proposed the zero-beta CAPM to help reconcile CAPM theory with evidence. A flatter relation between returns and betas is predicted by his model. Unfortunately, both the CAPM and zero-beta CAPM have problems in terms of computing the aggregate portfolios in their models. Commonly used general market indexes are poor proxies for the market portfolio M in the CAPM. Also, it is not clear how to construct mean-variance efficient portfolios I and their zero-beta portfolio counterparts ZI in the zero-beta CAPM.

Fama and French (1992, 1993, 1995) introduced multifactor models as a new branch of asset pricing. Because these models are not derived under general equilibrium conditions as in the CAPM but instead are data-driven, we refer to these atheoretical forms as multifactor models. Multifactors are zero-investment portfolios with long/short positions in a particular firm characteristic or stock return anomaly. Compared to the CAPM market model, Fama and French's three-factor model, including market, size, and value factors, tended to lower Jensen alpha estimates and increased explanatory power of average stock returns. Carhart (1997) added a momentum factor to create a four-factor model. Fama and French (2015) expanded their three-factor model to a five-factor model by including profit and capital investment factors. However, they dropped the value factor due to redundancy with respect to the other factors. Closely related to this four-factor model, Hou et al. (2015) proposed a q-factor model with similar factors. Stambaugh and Yuan (2017) advanced another four-factor model with market, size, and two mispricing management and performance factors. Fama and French (2018, 2020) augmented their five-factor model with a momentum factor to propose a six-factor model. And, Lettau and Pelger (2020) have extended previous work on latent asset pricing factors based on Principal Components Analysis (PCA).

According to Cochrane (2011), the growing number of multifactors proposed by researchers to address various return anomalies has created a *factor zoo*. Which factors should researchers and practitioners use in their asset pricing models? Which combinations of factors are recommended? With so many multifactors numbering in the hundreds based on various stock return anomalies, asset pricing faces serious problems. In his Presidential Address, Cochrane opined, "... the world would be much simpler if betas on only a few factors, important in the covariance matrix of returns, accounted for a larger number of mean characteristics" (Cochrane 2011, p. 1061). In a similar vein, Fama and French (1995) raised the question, "What are the underlying economic state variables that produce variation in earnings and returns related to size and BE/ME ... and so explain the risk premiums associated with size and BE/ME?".

We believe that the ZCAPM offers a parsimonious asset pricing model that addresses these concerns. It consists of two state variables—namely, average market returns and their cross-sectional standard deviation—that are derived from Markowitz's portfolio theory and general equilibrium conditions using Black's zero-beta CAPM. Empirical tests show that beta and zeta risks associated with these two factors are powerful explanatory risk metrics of average stock returns in the cross section. Also, per Fama and French's query above, they well explain size and BE/ME risk premiums, in addition to risk premiums for a wide variety of test asset portfolios and individual stocks. As discussed in forthcoming Chapters 6–8, popular multifactors constructed as zero-investment long/short portfolio returns are explained almost completely by zeta risk associated with total market return dispersion in the empirical ZCAPM.

Bibliography

Asness, C., & Frazzini, A. (2013). The devil in HML's details. *Journal of Portfolio Management, 39*, 49–68.

Banz, R. W. (1981). The relationship between return and market value of common stocks. *Journal of Financial Economics, 9*, 3–18.

Barillas, F., & Shanken, J. (2018). Comparing asset pricing models. *Journal of Finance*, 715–754.

Basu, S. (1977). Investment performance of common stocks in relation to their price-earnings ratios: A test of the efficient market hypothesis. *Journal of Finance, 12*, 129–156.

Bhandari, L. C. (1988). Debt/equity ratio and expected common stock returns: Empirical evidence. *Journal of Finance, 43*, 507–528.

Black, F. (1972). Capital market equilibrium with restricted borrowing. *Journal of Business, 45*, 444–454.

Black, F. (1993). Beta and return. *Journal of Portfolio Management, 20*, 8–18.

Black, F., Jensen, M. C., & Scholes, M. (1972). The capital asset pricing model: Some empirical tests. In M. C. Jensen (Ed.), *Studies in the theory of capital markets*. New York, NY: Praeger.

Blume, M. (1970). Portfolio theory: A step towards its practical application. *Journal of Business, 43*, 152–174.

Breeden, N. D. (1979). An intertemporal asset pricing model with stochastic consumption and investment opportunities. *Journal of Financial Economics, 7*, 265–296.

Carhart, M. M. (1997). On persistence in mutual fund performance. *Journal of Finance, 52*, 57–82.

Chamberlain, G., & Rothschild, M. (1983). Arbitrage, factor structure, and mean-variance analysis on large asset markets. *Econometrica, 51*, 1281–1304.

Chen, N., Roll, R., & Ross, S. A. (1986). Economic forces and the stock market. *Journal of Business, 59*, 383–404.

Cochrane, J. H. (1991). Production-based asset pricing and the link between stock returns and economic fluctuations. *Journal of Finance, 46*, 209–237.

Cochrane, J. H. (2005). *Asset Pricing* (Revised ed.). Princeton, NJ: Princeton University Press.

Cochrane, J. H. (2011). Presidential address: Discount rates. *Journal of Finance, 56*, 1047–1108.

Connor, G., & Korajczyk, R. A. (1986). Performance measurement with the arbitrage pricing theory: A new framework for analysis. *Journal of Financial Economics, 15*, 373–394.

Daniel, K., & Titman, S. (2012). Testing factor-model explanations of market anomalies. *Critical Finance Review, 1*, 103–139.

Davis, J. (1994). The cross-section of realized stock returns: The pre-Compustat evidence. *Journal of Finance, 49*, 1579–1593.

Douglas, G. W. (1969). Risk in the equity markets: An empirical appraisal of market efficiency. *Yale Economic Essays, 9*, 3–45.

Fama, E. F. (1968). Risk, return, and equilibrium: Some clarifying comments. *Journal of Finance, 23*, 29–40.

Fama, E. F. (1976). *Foundations of finance*. New York, NY: Basic Books.

Fama, E. F., & French, K. R. (1992). The cross-section of expected stock returns. *Journal of Finance, 47*, 427–465.
Fama, E. F., & French, K. R. (1993). The cross-section of expected returns. *Journal of Financial Economics, 33*, 3–56.
Fama, E. F., & French, K. R. (1995). Size and book-to-market factors in earnings and returns. *Journal of Finance, 50*, 131–156.
Fama, E. F., & French, K. R. (1996). Multifactor explanations of asset pricing anomalies. *Journal of Finance, 51*, 55–84.
Fama, E. F., & French, K. R. (1998). Value versus growth: The international evidence. *Journal of Finance, 53*, 1975–1999.
Fama, E. F., & French, K. R. (2004). The Capital Asset Pricing Model: Theory and evidence. *Journal of Economic Perspectives, 18*, 25–46.
Fama, E. F., & French, K. R. (2015). A five-factor asset pricing model. *Journal of Financial Economics, 116*, 1–22.
Fama, E. F., & French, K. R. (2018). Choosing factors. *Journal of Financial Economics, 128*, 234–252.
Fama, E. F., & French, K. R. (2020). Comparing cross-section and time-series factor models. *Review of Financial Studies, 33*, 1892–1926.
Fama, E. F., & MacBeth, J. D. (1973). Risk, return, and equilibrium: Empirical tests. *Journal of Political Economy, 81*, 607–636.
Ferson, W. E. (2019). *Empirical Asset Pricing: Models and Methods*. Cambridge, MA: The MIT Press.
Ferson, W. E., & Harvey, C. R. (1991). The variation of economic risk premiums. *Journal of Political Economy, 99*, 385–415.
Ferson, W. E., & Harvey, C. R. (1996). *Conditioning variables and the cross-section of stock returns* (Working Paper). Duke University.
Friend, I., & Blume, M. (1970). Measurement of portfolio performance under uncertainty. *American Economic Review, 60*, 607–636.
Gibbons, M. R. (1982). Multivariate tests of financial models: A new approach. *Journal of Financial Economics, 10*, 3–27.
Gibbons, M. R., Ross, S. A., & Shanken, J. (1989). A test of the efficiency of a given portfolio. *Econometrica, 57*, 1121–1152.
Gibbons, M. R., & Shanken, J. (1983). *A test of the Sharpe-Lintner CAPM* (Working Paper). University of California, Berkeley, CA.
Green, R. C., & Hollifield, B. (1992). When will mean-variance efficient portfolios be well diversified? *Journal of Finance, 47*, 1785–1809.
He, J., & Ng, L. K. (1994). Economic forces, fundamental variables and equity returns. *Journal of Business, 67*, 599–639.
Hou, K., Mo, H., Xue, C., & Zhang, L. (2018). q^5 (Working Paper). Ohio State University.
Hou, K., Xue, C., & Zhang, L. (2015). Digesting anomalies: An investment approach. *Review of Financial Studies, 28*, 650–705.

Jagannathan, R., & Ma, T. (2003). Risk reduction in large portfolios: A role for portfolio weight constraints. *Journal of Finance, 58*, 1651–1684.
Jensen, M. C. (1968). The performance of mutual funds in the period 1945–1964. *Journal of Finance, 23*, 389–416.
Jobson, J. D., & Korkie, B. (1982). Potential performance and tests of portfolio efficiency. *Journal of Financial Economics, 10*, 433–465.
Kallberg, J. G., & Ziemba, W. T. (1983). Comparison of alternative utility functions in portfolio selection problems. *Management Science, 29*, 1257–1276.
Kandel, S. (1984). The likelihood ratio test statistic of mean-variance efficiency without a riskless asset. *Journal of Financial Economics, 13*, 575–592.
Kandel, S. (1986). The geometry of the maximum likelihood estimator of the zero-beta return. *Journal of Finance, 41*, 339–346.
Kothari, S. P., Shanken, J., & Sloan, R. G. (1995). Another look at the cross-section of expected stock returns. *Journal of Finance, 50*, 185–224.
Kroll, Y., Levy, H., & Markowitz, H. (1984). Mean-variance versus direct utility maximization. *Journal of Finance, 39*, 47–61.
Lakonishok, J., & Shleifer, A. (1984). Stock returns, beta, variance and size: An empirical analysis. *Financial Analysts Journal, 40*, 36–41.
Lakonishok, J., & Shapiro, A. C. (1986). Systematic risk, total risk and size as determinants of stock market returns. *Journal of Banking and Finance, 10*, 115–132.
Lettau, M., & Pelger, M. (2020). Factors that fit the time series and cross-section of stock returns. *Review of Financial Studies, 33*, 2274–2325.
Levy, H. (1983). The capital asset pricing model: Theory and empiricism. *Economic Journal, 93*, 145–165.
Levy, M. (2007). Conditions for a CAPM equilibrium with positive prices. *Journal of Economic Theory, 137*, 404–415.
Levy, M., & Ritov, Y. (2010). Mean-variance efficient portfolios with many assets: 50% short. *Quantitative Finance, 10*, 1–11.
Lewellen, J., Nagel, S., & Shanken, J. A. (2010). A skeptical appraisal of asset pricing tests. *Journal of Financial Economics, 96*, 175–194.
Lintner, J. (1965). The valuation of risk assets and the selection of risky investments in stock portfolios and capital budgets. *Review of Economics and Statistics, 47*, 13–37.
Lucas, R. E. (1978). Asset prices in an exchange economy. *Econometrica, 46*, 1429–1445.
Markowitz, H. M. (1959). *Portfolio Selection: Efficient Diversification of Investments.* New York, NY: John Wiley & Sons.
Merton, R. C. (1972). An analytical derivation of the efficient portfolio frontier. *Journal of Financial and Quantitative Finance, 7*, 1851–1872.
Merton, R. C. (1973). An intertemporal capital asset pricing model. *Econometrica, 41*, 867–887.

Miles, D., & Timmermann, A. (1996). Variation in expected stock returns: Evidence on the pricing of equities from a cross-section of UK companies. *Economica, 63*, 369–382.
Miller, M., & Scholes, M. (1972). Rates of return in relation to risk: A reexamination of some recent findings. In M. C. Jensen (Ed.), *Studies in the theory of capital markets* (pp. 47–78). New York, NY: Praeger.
Modigliani, F., & Miller, M. H. (1963). Corporation income taxes and the cost of capital: A correction. *American Economic Review, 53*, 433–443.
Mossin, J. (1966). Equilibrium in a capital asset market. *Econometrica, 34*, 768–783.
Novy-Marx, R. (2013). The other side of value: The gross profitability premium. *Journal of Financial Economics, 108*, 1–28.
Pulley, L. B. (1981). General mean-variance approximation to expected utility for short holding periods. *Journal of Financial and Quantitative Analysis, 16*, 361–373.
Roll, R. (1977). A critique of the asset pricing theory's tests, Part I: On past and potential future testability of the theory. *Journal of Financial Economics, 4*, 129–176.
Roll, R. (1980). Orthogonal portfolios. *Journal of Financial and Quantitative Analysis, 15*, 1005–1012.
Rosenberg, B., Reid, K., & Lanstein, R. (1985). Persuasive evidence of market inefficiency. *Journal of Portfolio Management, 11*, 9–17.
Ross, S. A. (1977). The capital asset pricing model (CAPM), short sale restrictions and related issues. *Journal of Finance, 32*, 177–183.
Shanken, J. (1985). Multivariate tests of the zero-beta CAPM. *Journal of Financial Economics, 14*, 327–348.
Shanken, J. (1986). Testing portfolio efficiency when the zero-beta rate is unknown: A note. *Journal of Finance, 41*, 269–276.
Shanken, J. (1992). On the estimation of beta pricing models. *Review of Financial Studies, 5*, 1–34.
Sharpe, W. F. (1963). A simplified model for portfolio analysis. *Management Science, 9*, 277–293.
Sharpe, W. F. (1964). Capital asset prices: A theory of market equilibrium under conditions of risk. *Journal of Finance, 19*, 425–442.
Stambaugh, R. F. (1982). On the exclusion of assets from tests of the the two-parameter model. *Journal of Financial Economics, 10*, 237–268.
Stambaugh, R. F., & Yuan, Y. (2017). Mispricing factors. *Review of Financial Studies, 30*, 1270–1315.
Statman, D. (1980). Book values and stock returns. *The Chicago MBA: A Journal of Selected Papers, 4*, 25–45.
Stulz, R. M. (1981). A model of international asset pricing. *Journal of Financial Economics, 9*, 383–406.

Stulz, R. M. (1995). International portfolio choice and asset pricing: An integrative survey. In R. A. Jarrow, V. Maksimovic, & W. T. Ziemba (Eds.), *Handbooks in operations research and management science* (Vol. 9, Chapter 6, pp. 201–223). Amsterdam, North-Holland: Elsevier.

Tobin, J. (1958). Liquidity preference as behavior toward risk. *Review of Economic Studies*, *4*, 65–86.

Treynor, J. L. (1961). *Market value, time, and risk* (Unpublished manuscript).

Treynor, J. L. (1962). *Toward a theory of market value of risky assets* (Unpublished manuscript).

van Zilj, T. (1987). Risk decomposition: Variance or standard deviation - A reexamination and extension. *Journal of Financial and Quantitative Analysis*, *22*, 237–247.

Zhou, G. (1991). Small sample tests of portfolio efficiency. *Journal of Financial Economics*, *30*, 165–191.

CHAPTER 3

Theoretical Form of the ZCAPM

Abstract This chapter mathematically derives the theoretical ZCAPM. To do this, we employ the geometry of the mean-variance investment parabola to show that a new CAPM (dubbed the ZCAPM) can be developed as a special case of Black's (1972) zero-beta CAPM. As discussed in the previous chapter, Black's zero-beta CAPM posits that an infinite number of pairs of efficient index I and orthogonal inefficient ZI portfolios on the investment parabola are possible. Each pair of portfolios can be used to proxy the market portfolio M. Here we show that the ZCAPM is based on two orthogonal portfolios denoted I^* and ZI^* on the parabola that have the same variance of returns. Given these two unique portfolios, we utilize random matrix theory mathematics to derive expressions for their expected returns. The resultant ZCAPM is an alternative but equivalent form of Black's zero-beta CAPM. Unlike other CAPM models, the market factors in the ZCAPM can be readily estimated using daily market returns for assets. In applications to stocks (for example), the ZCAPM requires only the mean and cross-sectional standard deviation (return dispersion) of daily returns for all stocks in the market. These values can be easily computed. In the ZCAPM, sensitivities of an individual stock or portfolio to average stock market returns and market return dispersion are measures of beta risk and zeta risk, respectively. Unlike other models that incorporate return dispersion as an asset pricing factor, zeta risk captures both positive and negative sensitivity to return dispersion on any day t. These contrary forces of cross-sectional market volatility risk are a distinctive feature of the ZCAPM

J. W. Kolari et al., *A New Model of Capital Asset Prices*,
https://doi.org/10.1007/978-3-030-65197-8_3

due to its close connection to the mean-variance investment parabola. In our theoretical derivation of the ZCAPM, we rely heavily on Markowitz's (1959) mean-variance investment parabola and Black's (1972) zero-beta CAPM, which itself is a more general form of the Sharpe's (1964) CAPM. Hence, our ZCAPM stands on the shoulders of these classical finance theories by famous authors that were awarded the Nobel Prize in Economics. In this regard, we are most indebted to Fischer Black, who passed away before receiving Nobel recognition. We duly, albeit posthumously, celebrate his valuable insights that made possible our ZCAPM.

Keywords Asset pricing · Beta risk · Cross-sectional return dispersion · efficient frontier · Efficient portfolio · Fischer Black · Harry Markowitz · Mean-variance investment parabola · Random matrix theory · Return dispersion · Securities investment · Stock market · Theoretical ZCAPM · Valuation · ZCAPM · Zero-beta CAPM. Zero-beta portfolio · Zeta risk

3.1 Special Case of the Zero-Beta CAPM: The ZCAPM

As reviewed in Chapter 2, Roll (1980) provided a geometric approach for locating Black's (1972) zero-beta portfolio ZI that is orthogonal to index portfolio I lying on the efficient frontier of the investment parabola. Using his approach, an infinite number of pairs of I and ZI portfolios are possible. Here we provide a new geometric approach for identifying portfolios I and ZI, which naturally leads to the location of two unique portfolios denoted I^* and ZI^* with equal return variances. These two portfolios represent a special case of the zero-beta CAPM named the ZCAPM.

Given Markowitz's (1959) return-variance framework, we propose a simple geometric approach that begins by choosing any portfolio X on the minimum variance investment parabola. As shown in Fig. 3.1, two rays extending from a chosen intercept $E(\widetilde{R}_X)$ to tangent points on the superior and inferior curves of the symmetric, minimum variance parabola yield the portfolios I and ZI, respectively. We obtain the following equations for these two tangent lines[1]:

[1] These equations can be reduced to the simple expression $E(\widetilde{R}_{ZI}) = [B - AE(\widetilde{R}_I)]/[A - CE(\widetilde{R}_I)]$, from which it follows by Roll (1977), Corollary 3, that I and ZI are orthogonal.

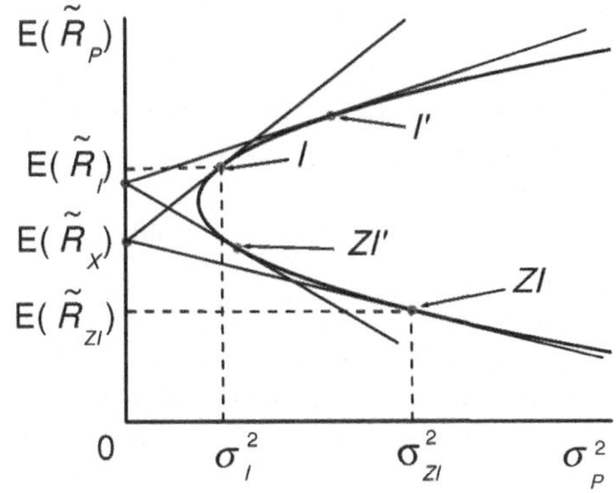

Fig. 3.1 New geometric approach to identify orthogonal zero-beta CAPM portfolios ZI and ZI' with respect to efficient portfolios I and I', respectively, on the mean-variance investment parabola

$$E(\widetilde{R}_{ZI}) - \frac{(BC - A^2)}{2C[E(\widetilde{R}_{ZI}) - \frac{A}{C}]}\left(\frac{1}{C} + \frac{C\left[E(\widetilde{R}_{ZI}) - \frac{A}{C}\right]^2}{BC - A^2}\right)$$

$$= E(\widetilde{R}_I) - \frac{(BC - A^2)}{2C[E(\widetilde{R}_I) - \frac{A}{C}]}\left(\frac{1}{C} + \frac{C\left[E(\widetilde{R}_I) - \frac{A}{C}\right]^2}{BC - A^2}\right), \tag{3.1}$$

where A, B, and C are defined (as in Eq. 2.16 of Chapter 2) in the familiar form

$$\begin{aligned} A &\equiv E(\widetilde{R})'\Sigma^{-1}e \\ B &\equiv E(\widetilde{R})'\Sigma^{-1}E(\widetilde{R}) \\ C &\equiv e'\Sigma^{-1}e, \end{aligned} \tag{3.2}$$

with $E(\widetilde{R}) = [E(\widetilde{R}_1), E(\widetilde{R}_2), \cdots, E(\widetilde{R}_n)]'$ the expected one-period return vector for n assets (with dimension $n \times 1$), Σ the covariance matrix for n assets (with dimension $n \times n$), and e a vector of ones (with dimension $n \times 1$).

3.1.1 *Proof of Equivalence of Geometric Approaches*

We want to show that Eq. (3.1) gives the same pair of efficient portfolio *I* and orthogonal portfolio *ZI* as obtained by Roll (1980). To simplify the notation, using the general formula for a parabola, we can write

$$\sigma_P^2 = a[E(\widetilde{R}_P) - b]^2 + c, \tag{3.3}$$

where a, b, and c are functions of A, B, and C (e.g., b is the expected return on the global minimum variance portfolio, and c is its variance). For any given portfolio I at position $[E(\widetilde{R}_I), \sigma_I^2]$, according to Roll's approach, the equation of the line passing through portfolios I and G is

$$E(\widetilde{R}_P) - E(\widetilde{R}_I) = \frac{E(\widetilde{R}_I) - b}{\sigma_I^2 - c}(\sigma_P^2 - \sigma_I^2). \tag{3.4}$$

The expected return on portfolio *ZI* that is orthogonal to portfolio *I* is the intercept of the above equation, or

$$\begin{aligned} E(\widetilde{R}_{ZI}) &= E(\widetilde{R}_I) - \frac{E(\widetilde{R}_I) - b}{\sigma_I^2 - c} \times \sigma_I^2 \\ &= E(\widetilde{R}_I) - \frac{E(\widetilde{R}_I) - b}{a[E(\widetilde{R}_I) - b]^2}\{a[E(\widetilde{R}_I) - b]^2 + c\} \\ &= b - \frac{c}{a[E(\widetilde{R}_I) - b]}. \end{aligned} \tag{3.5}$$

Substituting $E(\widetilde{R}_{ZI})$ from Eq. (3.5) into Eq. (3.3), we get the variance of portfolio *ZI*, or

$$\sigma_{ZI}^2 = \frac{c^2}{a[E(\widetilde{R}_I) - b]^2} + c. \tag{3.6}$$

To prove our approach, we use the same orthogonal portfolios *I* and *ZI* as in Roll's approach above. The equation of one tangent line through portfolio *I* and some intercept at $E(\widetilde{R}_X)$ is

$$E(\widetilde{R}_P) - E(\widetilde{R}_I) = \frac{1}{2a[E(\widetilde{R}_I) - b]}(\sigma_P^2 - \sigma_I^2), \tag{3.7}$$

where $\partial E(\widetilde{R}_I)/\partial\sigma_I^2$ equals $1/2a[E(\widetilde{R}_I) - b]$. The intercept of this line is

$$E(\widetilde{R}_X) = E(\widetilde{R}_I) - \frac{a[E(\widetilde{R}_I) - b]^2 + c}{2a[E(\widetilde{R}_I) - b]}$$
$$= \frac{E(\widetilde{R}_I) + b}{2} - \frac{c}{2a[E(\widetilde{R}_I) - b]}. \tag{3.8}$$

Next, we draw a second tangent line from Roll's portfolio *ZI* on the parabola to some intercept at $E(\widetilde{R}_{X'})$ defined as

$$E(\widetilde{R}_P) - E(\widetilde{R}_{ZI}) = \frac{1}{2a[E(\widetilde{R}_{ZI}) - b]}(\sigma_P^2 - \sigma_{ZI}^2). \tag{3.9}$$

We want to show that the intercepts of the two tangent lines above are the same. Substituting Eqs. (3.5) and (3.6) into Eq. (3.9) and setting $\sigma_P^2 = 0$, the intercept for Eq. (3.9) is

$$E(\widetilde{R}_{X'}) = b - \frac{c}{a[E(\widetilde{R}_I) - b]} - \frac{\sigma_{ZI}^2}{2a[E(\widetilde{R}_{ZI}) - b]}$$
$$= b - \frac{c}{a[E(\widetilde{R}_I) - b]} + \frac{[E(\widetilde{R}_I) - b]}{2c} \times \left(\frac{c^2}{a[E(\widetilde{R}_I) - b]^2} + c\right)$$
$$= b - \frac{c}{a[E(\widetilde{R}_I) - b]} + \frac{c}{2a[E(\widetilde{R}_I) - b]} + \frac{E(\widetilde{R}_I) - b}{2}$$
$$= \frac{E(\widetilde{R}_I) + b}{2} - \frac{c}{2a[E(\widetilde{R}_I) - b]} = E(\widetilde{R}_X). \tag{3.10}$$

Hence, tangents from orthogonal portfolios *I* and *ZI* on the minimum variance parabola have the same intercept. As such, our approach gives the same pair of orthogonal *I* and *ZI* portfolios as Roll (1980).

3.1.2 Locating Unique ZCAPM Portfolios I^* and ZI^*

Based on our new geometry, it is natural to extend two rays from the expected return on the minimum variance portfolio *G*, or $E(\widetilde{R}_G)$, to tangent points on the minimum variance parabola denoted I^* and ZI^*. Upon doing so, the above equations conveniently yield the following known solutions for the expected returns of orthogonal portfolios on the parabola (see proof in Appendix A)[2]:

$$E(\widetilde{R}_{I^*}) = \frac{A}{C} + \sqrt{\frac{BC - A^2}{C^2}}$$

$$E(\widetilde{R}_{ZI^*}) = \frac{A}{C} - \sqrt{\frac{BC - A^2}{C^2}}. \tag{3.11}$$

Because $\frac{A}{C}$ is well known to equal the expected return on the global minimum variance efficient portfolio G, portfolio X can only be G. Setting the return variances of portfolios I^* and ZI^* equal to one another, these two equations can be identified via geometry by Roll (1980) as well as Merton (1972).[3] However, the choice of these two particular portfolios is much less obvious using their approach. We refer to this special case of the zero-beta CAPM as the ZCAPM due to its use of the global minimum variance portfolio G to identify unique portfolios I^* and ZI^*. Figure 3.2 illustrates our geometry based on the portfolios G, I^*, and ZI^*.[4]

The expected return expressions in Eq. (3.11) for portfolios I^* and ZI^* are important due to the fact that testing the zero-beta CAPM does not require an exclusive pair of market index M and companion zero-beta index ZM. To see this, assume that the *true* market and zero-beta portfolios are M and ZM. Based on Black's zero-beta CAPM as specified in Eq. (2.11) in Chapter 2, assuming no riskless rate, we have

[2] For another proof, see Francis and Kim (2013, Chapter 7, Appendix). As a check, upon substituting the values for $E(\widetilde{R}_{I^*})$ and $E(\widetilde{R}_{ZI^*})$ from Eq. (3.11) into Eq. (3.1), both sides of Eq. (3.1) reduce to the equivalent value A/C. Also, substituting these values into the orthogonal condition reduces to zero.

[3] After Merton's work on efficient portfolio frontiers, it became standard practice to use a $[E(\widetilde{R}_P), \sigma_P]$ space approach to derive tangent portfolios. As Merton shows, when the intercept is set at $E(\widetilde{R}_G)$, then upper and lower asymptotes are obtained between rays from this intercept and the efficient *hyperbola*. For any other intercept, only one tangent point to the efficient frontier can be derived. By contrast, using a $[E(\widetilde{R}_P), \sigma_P^2]$ space approach, for any given intercept, two tangent points on the minimum variance *parabola* can be obtained.

[4] The formulas in Eq. (3.11) can be derived from Fig. 3.2 also. By similar triangles, we know that $\sigma_G^2 : \sigma_{ZI^*}^2 = 1 : 2$, such that $\sigma_{ZI^*}^2 = 2/C$. Substituting this result into Eq. (2.18) in the previous chapter yields Eq. (3.11).

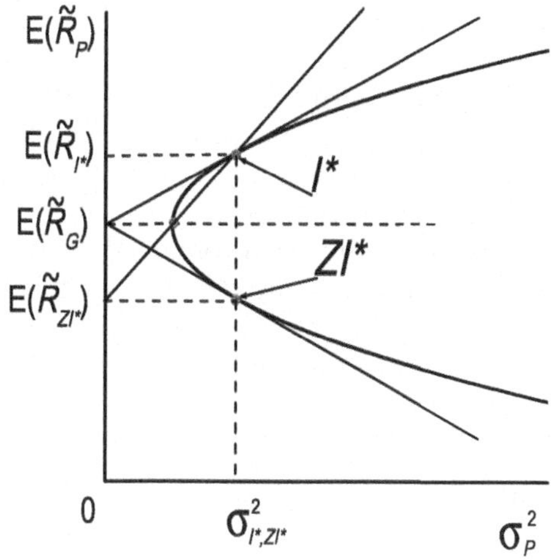

Fig. 3.2 Roll and new geometric approaches are shown to locate two unique ZCAPM orthogonal portfolios I^* and ZI^* on the mean-variance investment parabola with equal return variance or total risk

$$E(\widetilde{R}_I) = \beta_{I,M} E(\widetilde{R}_M) + (1 - \beta_{I,M}) E(\widetilde{R}_{ZM})$$
$$E(\widetilde{R}_{ZI}) = \beta_{ZI,M} E(\widetilde{R}_M) + (1 - \beta_{ZI,M}) E(\widetilde{R}_{ZM}), \tag{3.12}$$

where $\beta_{I,M}$ and $\beta_{ZI,M}$ are beta risks of portfolios I and ZI associated with market portfolio M, respectively. Upon solving these equations using a latent variable approach applied in conditional asset pricing (see Gibbons and Ferson 1985; Ferson and Locke 1998), we get

$$E(\widetilde{R}_M) = \frac{1 - \beta_{ZI,M}}{\beta_{I,M} - \beta_{ZI,M}} E(\widetilde{R}_I) - \frac{1 - \beta_{I,M}}{\beta_{I,M} - \beta_{ZI,M}} E(\widetilde{R}_{ZI})$$
$$E(\widetilde{R}_{ZM}) = \frac{\beta_{ZI,M}}{\beta_{ZI,M} - \beta_{I,M}} E(\widetilde{R}_I) - \frac{\beta_{I,M}}{\beta_{ZI,M} - \beta_{I,M}} E(\widetilde{R}_{ZI}). \tag{3.13}$$

Hence, using Eqs. (3.12) and (3.13) above, we can alternatively write Black's zero-beta CAPM for the ith asset as:

$$\begin{aligned} E(\widetilde{R}_i) &= \beta_{i,M} E(\widetilde{R}_M) + (1 - \beta_{i,M}) E(\widetilde{R}_{ZM}) \\ &= \frac{\beta_{i,M} - \beta_{ZI,M}}{\beta_{I,M} - \beta_{ZI,M}} E(\widetilde{R}_I) + \frac{\beta_{I,M} - \beta_{i,M}}{\beta_{I,M} - \beta_{ZI,M}} E(\widetilde{R}_{ZI}) \\ &= \frac{\beta_{i,M} - \beta_{ZI,M}}{\beta_{I,M} - \beta_{ZI,M}} E(\widetilde{R}_I) + \left(1 - \frac{\beta_{i,M} - \beta_{ZI,M}}{\beta_{I,M} - \beta_{ZI,M}}\right) E(\widetilde{R}_{ZI}) \\ &\equiv \beta_{i,I} E(\widetilde{R}_I) + (1 - \beta_{i,I}) E(\widetilde{R}_{ZI}), \end{aligned} \tag{3.14}$$

where $\beta_{i,I} \equiv (\beta_{i,M} - \beta_{ZI,M})/(\beta_{I,M} - \beta_{ZI,M})$. Confirming Roll (1977, 1980), Eq. (3.14) shows that it is not necessary to identify the true market and zero-beta portfolios M and ZM when testing the zero-beta CAPM. If any pair of portfolios I and ZI on the minimum variance parabola can be identified, an equivalent zero-beta CAPM can be specified.[5]

Similar results can be obtained for the zero-beta CAPM when a riskless asset exists. Given any efficient portfolio K comprised of some weights of orthogonal market and zero-beta portfolios M and ZM plus the riskless asset, we can write the zero-beta CAPM as

$$E(\widetilde{R}_K) = w_M E(\widetilde{R}_M) + w_{ZM} E(\widetilde{R}_{ZM}) + w_f R_f \tag{3.15}$$

with

$$w_M + w_{ZM} + w_f = 1. \tag{3.16}$$

Substituting Eq. (3.13) into Eq. (3.15), we get

$$\begin{aligned} E(\widetilde{R}_K) &= \frac{w_M(1 - \beta_{ZI,M}) - w_{ZM}\beta_{ZI,M}}{\beta_{I,M} - \beta_{ZI,M}} E(\widetilde{R}_I) \\ &\quad + \frac{w_M(\beta_{I,M} - 1) + w_{ZM}\beta_{I,M}}{\beta_{I,M} - \beta_{ZI,M}} E(\widetilde{R}_{ZI}) + w_f R_f \\ &\equiv w_I E(\widetilde{R}_I) + w_{ZI} E(\widetilde{R}_{ZI}) + w_f R_f \end{aligned} \tag{3.17}$$

with $w_I \equiv \frac{w_M(1-\beta_{ZI,M})-w_{ZM}\beta_{ZI,M}}{\beta_{I,M}-\beta_{ZI,M}}$ and $w_{ZI} \equiv \frac{w_M(\beta_{I,M}-1)+w_{ZM}\beta_{I,M}}{\beta_{I,M}-\beta_{ZI,M}}$, such that $w_I + w_{ZI} + w_f = 1$ still holds. It should be noted that, under the CAPM setup, efficient portfolios lie along the tangent line connecting R_f and M; hence, w_{ZM} must be zero in Eq. (3.15) to make portfolio K efficient. Consequently, a unique pair of coefficients w_I and w_{ZI} in Eq. (3.17) satisfies $w_I E(\widetilde{R}_I) + w_{ZI} E(\widetilde{R}_{ZI}) = (1 - w_f) E(\widetilde{R}_M)$. It is easy to see that: (1) if $E(\widetilde{R}_I) > E(\widetilde{R}_M)$, then $w_I > 0$ and $w_{ZI} > 0$; and (2) if $E(\widetilde{R}_I) < E(\widetilde{R}_M)$, then $w_I > 0$ and $w_{ZI} < 0$.

Using Eq. (3.15), it is worthwhile noting that the variance of portfolio K for portfolios M and ZM is:

$$\sigma_K^2 = w_M^2 \sigma_M^2 + w_{MZ}^2 \sigma_{ZM}^2. \tag{3.18}$$

[5] See Wheatley (1989) for discussion of untestable distributional assumptions in latent variable tests of mean-variance CAPM models with unobservable benchmark returns.

According to Black (1972, pp. 453–454), starting with the incorrect assumption that $R_f > E(\widetilde{R}_{MZ})$, if we increase w_f and decrease w_{MZ} by the same amount, the variance of portfolio K will decrease but its return will increase. These results contradict the fact that portfolio K is efficient. As such, Black infers that $E(\widetilde{R}_{ZM})$ must be larger than R_f.[6]

3.2 Expected Returns of Portfolios I^* and ZI^*

The above geometric analyses identify two orthogonal portfolios—namely, efficient index I^* and zero-beta index ZI^*—that are unique to the ZCAPM. We next derive mathematical expressions for the expected returns of these portfolios on the investment parabola.

Previous studies have found that theoretical predictions from random matrix theory about the correlation (covariance) structure of stock prices agree with empirical data for U.S. common stock prices.[7] Consequently, evidence generally supports the use of random matrix theory to derive the asymptotic behavior of the minimum variance investment parabola for stocks. In practice, it is almost impossible to calculate the real values of parabola parameters A, B, and C with so many stocks. One problem is that the empirical estimation of the covariance matrix Σ is not well justified due to the fact that its elements are time-dependent unobservable quantities. Another problem is that, for large samples, gathering sufficient observations to invert the covariance matrix is very difficult (e.g., a matrix dimensioned for 5,000 assets requires more than 5,000 observations for each asset to avoid singularity). Especially for large dimension matrices, random matrix theory provides a powerful tool to extract their statistical properties and

[6] See Roll (1977, pp. 141–142) for a graphical analysis.

[7] See Laloux et al. (1999), Plerou et al. (1999), and Rosenow et al. (2000), who documented that U.S. stock prices have a large random component plus a small nonrandom component. Laloux et al. (1999) found that 94% of the total number of eigenvalues of the correlation matrix of S&P 500 stocks fall within the predicted range from random matrix theory. Similar results are found in favor of random matrix predictions by Plerou et al. (1999) and Rosenow et al. (2000), who showed that the correlation coefficient matrix for returns of the largest 1,000 U.S. stocks shares universal properties with the Gaussian Orthogonal Ensemble (GOE) of random matrices. This inference is confirmed by Plerou et al. (1999) in two independent tests of nearest-neighbor spacing and next-nearest-neighbor spacing of the obtained eigenvalues of the underlying correlation coefficient matrix, respectively. Agreement between the empirical data and GOE prediction is consistent with extensive evidence in favor of the random walk hypothesis (e.g., see Cootner 1964; Fama 1965; Kendall and Hill 1953; Malkiel 1973; Lo and MacKinlay 1988, and others).

has been applied in many fields, including different applied sciences (e.g., see seminal work by Wigner 1955) as well as multivariate statistical analyses (e.g., see Johnstone 2001; Wishart 1928, and others).

3.2.1 *Derivation of Investment Parabola Parameters Based on Random Matrix Theory*

Given that each element of the covariance matrix of asset returns is random from some distribution with a finite second moment, our main goal is to find the basic statistical properties of a large dimension matrix, in particular the distribution of eigenvalues of the matrix. More specifically, we seek to derive the asymptotic behavior of investment parabola parameters A, B, and C for large samples of assets to find their respective limit values. These quantities are needed to estimate converging values for the expected returns and variances of the ZCAPM portfolios I^* and ZI^*.[8]

We assume that stock returns have joint normal distributions[9]:

$$\widetilde{R}_i \sim N(\mu_i, \sigma_i^2), i = 1, \cdots, n.$$

The resulting covariance matrix can be written as

$$\begin{aligned} \Sigma &= E[(\widetilde{R}_i - \overline{R}_i)(\widetilde{R}_j - \overline{R}_j)] \\ &\equiv D\mathbb{C}D, \end{aligned} \tag{3.19}$$

with any correlation coefficient of $\mathbb{C}$ sharing the universal properties of the Gaussian orthogonal ensemble of random matrices and only containing a small nonrandom component,[10] and

$$D = diag(\sigma_1, \sigma_2, \cdots, \sigma_n) = \begin{vmatrix} \sigma_1 & 0 & 0 & \cdots & 0 \\ 0 & \sigma_2 & 0 & \cdots & 0 \\ \vdots & \vdots & \ddots & \vdots & \vdots \\ 0 & \cdots & 0 & 0 & \sigma_n \end{vmatrix}. \tag{3.20}$$

[8] See Liu (2013) and Liu et al. (2012).

[9] In the long run, stock returns are log normal distributed, but in the short run (say monthly) the normal distribution is a reasonable assumption.

[10] Laloux et al. (1999), Plerou et al. (1999), and Rosenow et al. (2000) have shown that matrix $\mathbb{C}$ has a large random component, which is consistent with random matrix prediction, and a small nonrandom component related to the collective movement of the market.

Because $\mathbb{C}$ is symmetric, nonsingular, and diagonalizable, the covariance matrix Σ is positive definite. For any given matrix $\mathbb{C}$, we can always find a real unitary matrix U such that $U'\mathbb{C}U = \lambda(\mathbb{C}) \equiv diag(\lambda_1(\mathbb{C}), \lambda_2(\mathbb{C}), \cdots, \lambda_n(\mathbb{C}))$ with $\lambda_i(\mathbb{C})$ being the ith eigenvalue of matrix $\mathbb{C}$.[11]

Appendix B at the end of this chapter solves for the asymptotic properties of $C = e'\Sigma^{-1}e$ in Eq. (3.2). An interesting inference from our results is that the variance of the minimum portfolio vanishes as n goes to infinity, such that the parabola collapses. This outcome is not surprising, as the minimum variance portfolio is diversified in terms of both idiosyncratic and systematic risks. When the number of assets goes to infinity, all of the idiosyncratic volatilities can be diversified away, which is obvious from the equal-weighted summation of n iid normal distributed random variables. At the same time, all systematic risks can be diversified away too. The reason is that we have an infinite number of systematic risk factors available based on our assumption that the market is 5% nonrandom (i.e., the number of risk factors of $0.05n$ will go to infinity as n approaches infinity). Thus, the variance of the minimum portfolio will go to zero when n goes to infinity, i.e., theoretically all the risks can be diversified away when n goes to infinity, and the frontier will collapse.

However, this large sample limit is not relevant in the real world. Our markets contain assets in the thousands, not billions or more, which is far below any reasonable large sample limit. In the real world the number of risk factors is not extremely large. Consequently, they will play an important role in pricing assets and their contributions cannot be diversified away. Our ZCAPM is based on theoretical results from the more realistic limited sample assumption.

When n is large but finite, we cannot ignore the contributions from the terms capturing deviations from the predictions of random matrix theory. In this case, using the equations in Appendix B and notation defined therein, we have

$$
\begin{aligned}
C &\approx \left(\frac{1}{\overline{\sigma_{ave}}^2} + \sigma_\sigma^2\right)\frac{n}{2\pi}F(\lambda_{min}, \lambda_{max}) + \frac{1}{\overline{\sigma_{ave}}^2}\frac{\theta n}{L} \\
&= \left[\frac{1}{\overline{\sigma_{ave}}^2}\left(\frac{F(\lambda_{min}, \lambda_{max})}{2\pi} + \frac{\theta}{L}\right) + \frac{\sigma_\sigma^2 F(\lambda_{min}, \lambda_{max})}{2\pi}\right]n, \qquad (3.21)
\end{aligned}
$$

[11] The unitary matrix has the following properties: $UU' = U'U = I$, where $U' = U^{-1}$.

and the values for A and B can be obtained as follows:

$$A \approx \left(\frac{E(\widetilde{R}_a)}{\overline{\sigma_{ave}}^2} + E(\widetilde{R}_a)\sigma_\sigma^2\right)\frac{nF(\lambda_{min}, \lambda_{max})}{2\pi} + \frac{E(\widetilde{R}_a)}{\overline{\sigma_{ave}}^2}\frac{\theta n}{L}$$
$$= \left[\frac{1}{\overline{\sigma_{ave}}^2}\left(\frac{F(\lambda_{min}, \lambda_{max})}{2\pi} + \frac{\theta}{L}\right) + \frac{\sigma_\sigma^2 F(\lambda_{min}, \lambda_{max})}{2\pi}\right]E(\widetilde{R}_a)n \quad (3.22)$$

$$B \approx \left[E(\widetilde{R}_a)^2 + \sigma(\widetilde{R}_a)^2\right]\left(\frac{1}{\overline{\sigma_{ave}}^2} + \sigma_\sigma^2\right)\frac{nF(\lambda_{min}, \lambda_{max})}{2\pi} + \frac{E(\widetilde{R}_a)^2}{\overline{\sigma_{ave}}^2}\frac{\theta n}{L}$$
$$= \left[\frac{1}{\overline{\sigma_{ave}}^2}\left(\frac{F(\lambda_{min}, \lambda_{max})}{2\pi} + \frac{\theta}{L}\right) + \frac{\sigma_\sigma^2 F(\lambda_{min}, \lambda_{max})}{2\pi}\right]E(\widetilde{R}_a)^2 n$$
$$+ \left(\frac{1}{\overline{\sigma_{ave}}^2} + \sigma_\sigma^2\right)\frac{F(\lambda_{min}, \lambda_{max})}{2\pi}\sigma(\widetilde{R}_a)^2 n. \quad (3.23)$$

3.2.2 *Random Matrix Approximations of Expected Returns for I^* and ZI^**

Based on these estimated values for A, B, and C from random matrix theory, we can calculate the expected returns for portfolios I^* and ZI^*. From Eqs. (3.21) to (3.23), we can easily obtain the approximations for the ratios of A/C and B/C as

$$\frac{A}{C} \approx E(\widetilde{R}_a) \quad (3.24)$$
$$\frac{B}{C} \approx E(\widetilde{R}_a)^2 + f^2(\theta)\sigma_a^2, \quad (3.25)$$

where $E(\widetilde{R}_a)$ is the expected return of all assets' returns, $\sigma_a^2 \equiv \sigma(\widetilde{R}_a)^2$ is the cross-sectional variance of all assets' returns, and

$$f(\theta) \equiv \sqrt{\frac{\left(\frac{1}{\overline{\sigma_{ave}}^2} + \sigma_\sigma^2\right)\frac{F(\lambda_{min}, \lambda_{max})}{2\pi}}{\frac{1}{\overline{\sigma_{ave}}^2}\left(\frac{F(\lambda_{min}, \lambda_{max})}{2\pi} + \frac{\theta}{L}\right) + \frac{\sigma_\sigma^2 F(\lambda_{min}, \lambda_{max})}{2\pi}}}. \quad (3.26)$$

Now the expected returns for portfolios I^* and ZI^* can be simply solved as

$$\begin{aligned} E(\widetilde{R}_{I^*}) &= \frac{A}{C} + \sqrt{\frac{BC - A^2}{C^2}} \\ &= \frac{A}{C} + \sqrt{\frac{B}{C} - \left(\frac{A}{C}\right)^2} \\ &\approx E(\widetilde{R}_a) + f(\theta)\sigma_a \end{aligned} \tag{3.27}$$

$$\begin{aligned} E(\widetilde{R}_{ZI^*}) &= \frac{A}{C} - \sqrt{\frac{BC - A^2}{C^2}} \\ &\approx E(\widetilde{R}_a) - f(\theta)\sigma_a, \end{aligned} \tag{3.28}$$

and their variances are

$$\begin{aligned} \sigma^2_{I^*} &= \frac{1}{C} + \frac{C\left[E(\widetilde{R}_{I^*}) - \frac{A}{C}\right]^2}{BC - A^2} = \frac{2}{C} = \sigma^2_{ZI^*} \\ &\approx \frac{2}{\left[\frac{1}{\overline{\sigma_{ave}}^2}\left(\frac{F(\lambda_{min}, \lambda_{max})}{2\pi} + \frac{\theta}{L}\right) + \frac{\sigma^2_{\sigma}F(\lambda_{min}, \lambda_{max})}{2\pi}\right]n}. \end{aligned} \tag{3.29}$$

Equations (3.27) and (3.28) indicate that the expected returns of the two orthogonal portfolios I^* and ZI^* on the mean-variance parabola can be located by taking into account positive versus negative sensitivity to return dispersion σ_a.

In the above equations, $E(\widetilde{R}_a)$ is the average return on n population assets in the market (hereafter *portfolio a*), σ^2_a is the cross-sectional variance of n assets' returns (or return dispersion), and $\frac{1}{\overline{\sigma_{ave}}}$ and σ^2_{σ} are (as mathematically defined in Eqs. (B3.4) and (B3.5) in the Appendix) the expected value and variance, respectively, of the inverse standard deviation of assets. The limit values of these quantities enable estimates of the expected returns and variances of the I^* and ZI^* portfolios. The term $0 < f(\theta) < 1$ captures the nonrandom component of asset prices ranging from 0 to 1 (i.e., total nonrandomness to total randomness). The expected returns $E(\widetilde{R}_{I^*})$ and $E(\widetilde{R}_{ZI^*})$ in these equations incorporate only the random portion of market volatility. Because it is likely that $f(\theta)$ is near 1 due to the fact that previously cited studies by Laloux et al. (1999), Plerou et al. (1999), and Rosenow et al. (2000) have confirmed that stock prices have large random and relatively small nonrandom components, we set $f(\theta) = 1$ in Eqs. (3.27) and (3.28) as reasonably close approximations of their expected returns.

Recalling from Subsect. 3.1.2 that $\frac{A}{C} = E(\widetilde{R}_G)$, a new finding from Eqs. (3.21) and (3.22) is that $\frac{A}{C}$ in large samples approximately converges to the average (or mean) return for the n population assets in the market. We denote this average market return as $E(\widetilde{R}_a)$ in Eqs. (3.27) and (3.28). Given that $E(\widetilde{R}_G) \approx E(\widetilde{R}_a)$, such that portfolio a lies somewhere on the axis of symmetry that splits the parabola into two halves, the equal-weighted market return is unlikely to be a reasonable proxy for the market portfolio M, as it represents an estimate of $E(\widetilde{R}_a)$ and therefore $E(\widetilde{R}_G)$. Of course, the expected return on the market portfolio M should lie a considerable distance above the axis of symmetry at $E(\widetilde{R}_G)$. Likewise, if value-weighted returns are used to construct portfolios on the efficient frontier, the same problem arises, as the value-weighted average return for n assets again has the property that $E(\widetilde{R}_G) \approx E(\widetilde{R}_a)$. Since equal- and value-weighted market index returns have standard deviations greater than σ_G,[12] the upshot of these findings is that previous empirical tests of the CAPM and zero-beta CAPM using an equal-weighted or value-weighted market index poorly proxy the expected return on market portfolio M, which is considerably higher than the expected returns on these commonly used average market indexes.

Consistent with this theoretical result, most empirical studies have found that commonly used market proxies are inefficient (but do not specify their location on the parabola's axis of symmetry).[13] According to the Roll (1977) critique discussed in Chapter 2, empirical tests of the CAPM are flawed due to potentially bad estimates of M. Of course, using a proxy for

[12] This inference follows from the fact that portfolios G and a have the same expected return but portfolio G at the vertex of the minimum variance parabola lies to the left of portfolio a on the axis of symmetry.

[13] See Ross (1980), Gibbons (1982), Jobson and Korkie (1982), Shanken (1985), Kandel and Stambaugh (1987), Gibbons et al. (1989), MacKinlay and Richardson (1991), and Zhou (1993). As discussed earlier, it is well known that efficient portfolios must include short positions, not only long positions as in market indices. Nonetheless, Levy and Roll (2010) have reported evidence that market indices are mean-variance efficient; however, Brière et al. (2011) overturned this finding using a new vertical distance test assuming that all assets are risky.

M with expected return approximately equal to the central tendency of the minimum variance parabola, or $E(\widetilde{R}_G)$, and standard deviation σ_a greater than σ_G would lead to lower slopes for the Capital Market Line (CML) and Security Market Line (SML) than predicted by theory. In turn, tests of the CAPM based on equal- or value-weighted market indices would be biased against its existence. This propensity to reject the CAPM is exactly what happened. As discussed in Chapter 2, studies repeatedly found either weak evidence or no evidence to support the CAPM using proxy market indexes that measure average market returns.

Another new theoretical result revealed by Eqs. (3.27) and (3.28) is that the span of the minimum variance parabola is defined in large part by the cross-sectional standard deviation of all assets' returns denoted σ_a. In line with these equations, as cross-sectional market volatility increases (decreases), the span of the parabola widens (narrows). Of course, simple logic would say that, if the width of the parabola is determined in large part by return dispersion, the average market return lies approximately on its axis of symmetry in the middle of the cross-sectional distribution of returns. Thus, two salient state variables that help to explain changes in the level and shape of the parabola over time are average market returns and their cross-sectional standard deviation, respectively. Assets lying within the parabola are impacted by changes (innovations) in these market forces. As average market returns and their cross-sectional standard deviation change over time, assets' returns will be differentially affected due to their respective sensitivities to movements in these fundamental state variables.

As a visual aid, Fig. 3.3 diagrams the movement over time of the investment parabola. The variance of returns on the X-axis is a time-series variance (e.g., the variance of minute-by-minute returns for each asset in one day), whereas return dispersion is a cross-sectional variance (e.g., the variance of daily returns across all n assets on a particular day). Changes in the level and shape of the investment parabola are determined by movements in the average return of all assets in the market denoted $E(\widetilde{R}_a)$ and cross-sectional return dispersion of all assets' returns denoted σ_a. Assets within the parabola are impacted by these changes over time. For example, the graph shows how the expected return on the ith asset (marked with an asterisk) is affected by movements in the parabola. From $t = 1$ to $t = 2$, the average market return does not change, but the return of asset i increases due to an increase in market return dispersion. By contrast, those assets below the average market return would experience decreasing returns. Hence, return dispersion

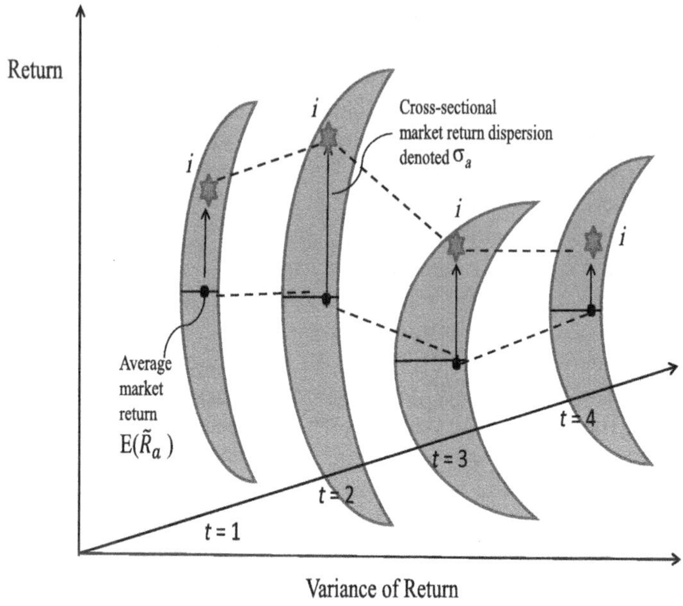

Fig. 3.3 The level and width of the investment parabola changes over time. The individual *i*th asset's return is affected by changes in both the level (average market returns) and width (cross-sectional market return dispersion) of the investment parabola

can positively or negatively affect asset returns depending on whether asset returns are greater or less than the average market return.

The main takeaway from Fig. 3.3 is that assets' returns are driven by shifts in the average market return and market return dispersion over time. Previous tests of the CAPM market model only take into account average market returns using general market indexes. Prior studies do not capture the dual opposing effects of return dispersion on asset returns. Casual inspection of Fig. 3.3 suggests that asset prices are driven by two market forces: (1) the average level of assets' returns and (2) the cross-sectional dispersion of assets' returns.

Equations (3.27) and (3.28) show that $E(\widetilde{R}_{I^*})$ and $E(\widetilde{R}_{ZI^*})$ can be computed by simply adding and subtracting σ_a from $E(\widetilde{R}_a)$, respectively. In effect, increasing cross-sectional market volatility tends to increase $E(\widetilde{R}_{I^*})$ but decrease $E(\widetilde{R}_{ZI^*})$ around the average market return $E(\widetilde{R}_a)$, all else the same. Thus, it is not necessary to estimate the covariance matrix to estimate $E(\widetilde{R}_{I^*})$ and $E(\widetilde{R}_{ZI^*})$, only the cross-sectional average return and standard deviation of returns for the n population assets in the market. Note also that, while the time-series variance of returns of portfolios I^* and ZI^* are equal to one another, or $\sigma^2_{I^*} = \sigma^2_{ZI^*}$, these time-series variances are very different from the cross-sectional variance of portfolio a, or σ^2_a.

It is important to note that cross-sectional return dispersion is widely recognized as a macroeconomic state variable nowadays. It has been linked to fundamental economic variables, including unemployment rates, economic uncertainty, economic restructuring, business cycles, market volatility caused by various macroeconomic shocks, and aggregate idiosyncratic risk. Research by Gomes et al. (2003) and Zhang (2005) has found an association between return dispersion, macroeconomic states, and stock returns. A number of authors have written on this subject, including Loungani et al. (1990), Christie and Huang (1994), Duee (2001), Connolly and Stivers (2003), Zhang (2006), Adrian and Rosenberg (2008), Chichernea et al. (2015), Choudhry et al. (2016), Demirer et al. (2019), among others. However, with respect to our findings above, no previous studies directly link return dispersion to the span or width of the investment parabola. Also, these studies do not theoretically link return dispersion to the zero-beta CAPM.

3.3 Expected Returns of Assets in the ZCAPM

We now have sufficient results to redefine the expected rate of return on assets in Black's zero-beta CAPM to specify our alternative ZCAPM form.

3.3.1 No Riskless Asset Exists

Assuming no riskless asset, Black's (1972) zero-beta CAPM expression was specified earlier in Eq. (3.14). By substituting the definitions for $E(\widetilde{R}_{I^*})$ and $E(\widetilde{R}_{ZI^*})$ in Eqs. (3.27) and (3.28) (where $f(\theta) = 1$ as discussed earlier) into this expression, we can rewrite the zero-beta CAPM in its special ZCAPM case for portfolios I^* and ZI^* as follows:

$$
\begin{aligned}
E(\widetilde{R}_i) &= \beta_{i,I^*}E(\widetilde{R}_{I^*}) + (1 - \beta_{i,I^*})E(\widetilde{R}_{ZI^*}) \\
&= E(\widetilde{R}_{ZI^*}) + \beta_{i,I^*}[E(\widetilde{R}_{I^*}) - E(\widetilde{R}_{ZI^*})] \\
&= E(\widetilde{R}_a) - \sigma_a + \beta_{i,I^*}\{[E(\widetilde{R}_a) + \sigma_a] - [E(\widetilde{R}_a) - \sigma_a]\} \\
&= E(\widetilde{R}_a) + (2\beta_{i,I^*} - 1)\sigma_a \\
E(\widetilde{R}_i) &= E(\widetilde{R}_a) + Z^*_{i,a}\sigma_a, \qquad (3.30)
\end{aligned}
$$

where the coefficient $Z^*_{i,a}$ captures positive and negative sensitivity of the ith asset to random market volatility associated with the cross-sectional dispersion of all assets' returns. We use the letter Z rather than β to differentiate this risk parameter from traded factors (i.e., RD is a nontraded factor) in addition to the asterisk superscript to recognize its connection to orthogonal portfolios I^* and ZI^* with opposite return dispersion sensitivities.

From our earlier ZCAPM geometry in Fig. 3.2, it is clear that Eq. (3.30) is an equivalent form of the zero-beta CAPM. The minimum variance parabola spans the investment opportunity set's distribution of returns, wherein $E(\widetilde{R}_a)$ represents an average return in the middle of this distribution that corresponds to the parabola's axis of symmetry, and σ_a captures the cross-sectional volatility of assets in the market around the average return, which is crucial to defining the return/risk space. As already mentioned, σ_a determines the curvature of the parabola. As σ_a increases (decreases), the distance between the superior and inferior frontiers of the parabola would increase (decrease). According to the ZCAPM, when $Z^*_{i,a} = 1$ or -1, then $E(\widetilde{R}_i)$ equals $E(\widetilde{R}_{I^*})$ or $E(\widetilde{R}_{ZI^*})$, respectively, which agrees with the geometry of the ZCAPM in Fig. 3.2. Rather than using the tangent lines from the expected return on the global minimum variance portfolio G to the minimum variance parabola to locate unique ZCAPM portfolios I^* and ZI^*, this analytical form of the ZCAPM locates these orthogonal, minimum variance portfolios by following a different geometric path—namely, horizontally along the expected return on market assets (equal to the expected return on G) and then vertically up or down by the cross-sectional standard deviation of market assets' returns.[14]

[14]The ZCAPM in Eq. (3.33) has some similarities to the three-moment CAPM of Kraus and Litzenberger (1976) and Friend and Westereld (1980) but is distinctly different in a number of ways. The three-moment CAPM contains the expected return on the market portfolio and squared market portfolio return in a two-factor asset pricing model extension of the CAPM. Corresponding market beta and gamma risk measures take into account the systematic standard deviation and systematic skewness, respectively, of the ith risky asset. However, in place of the market factor, the ZCAPM employs the average return on all assets

3.3.2 A Riskless Asset Exists

When we introduce the existence of a riskless asset, using $E(\widetilde{R}_{I^*})$ and $E(\widetilde{R}_{ZI^*})$ defined in Eqs. (3.27) and (3.28) (and again assuming $f(\theta) = 1$), the zero-beta CAPM in Eq. (3.17) can be rewritten as

$$\begin{aligned} E(\widetilde{R}_i) &= w_{I^*}E(\widetilde{R}_{I^*}) + w_{ZI^*}E(\widetilde{R}_{ZI^*}) + w_f R_f \\ &= w_{I^*}[E(\widetilde{R}_a) + \sigma_a] + w_{ZI^*}[E(\widetilde{R}_a) - \sigma_a] + w_f R_f \\ &= (w_{I^*} + w_{ZI^*})E(\widetilde{R}_a) + (w_{I^*} - w_{ZI^*})\sigma_a + w_f R_f, \end{aligned} \tag{3.31}$$

where there are now three orthogonal assets I^*, ZI^*, and f. Investors can have both long and short positions in these assets, but the sum of their weights must equal one. Here i can be any asset, including the riskless asset. The above equation can be rewritten in ZCAPM form as

$$E(\widetilde{R}_i) - R_f = (w_{I^*} + w_{ZI^*})[E(\widetilde{R}_a) - R_f] + (w_{I^*} - w_{ZI^*})\sigma_a \tag{3.32}$$

$$E(\widetilde{R}_i) - R_f = \beta_{i,a}[E(\widetilde{R}_a) - R_f] + Z^*_{i,a}\sigma_a, \tag{3.33}$$

where $\beta_{i,a} = w_{I^*} + w_{ZI^*}$ is beta risk measuring the sensitivity of the ith asset's excess returns to average market excess returns of all assets, and zeta risk coefficient $Z^*_{i,a} = w_{I^*} - w_{ZI^*}$ is a measure of the sensitivity of an asset's excess returns to the market return dispersion of all assets.[15] We use the notation $\beta_{i,a}$ to make clear that it is not a market beta associated with

in the market, not the expected return on the mean-variance efficient market portfolio. Also, rather than using the second moment of the market portfolio (i.e., the standard deviation of market portfolio returns), the ZCAPM employs the cross-sectional standard deviation of all assets in the market in a given period t, a much different measure of market volatility. Moreover, the ZCAPM posits dual opposite market volatility effects, rather than one-sided directional effects in the three-moment CAPM. A relatively large literature exists on the CAPM with higher-order co-movements, particularly skewness. In general, the empirical evidence is mixed with some evidence that investors pay a premium for positive co-skewness. See Sears and Wei (1985) and Högholm et al. (2011) for further discussion and references.

[15] If all funds are invested in either I^* or ZI^*, then $\beta_{I^*,a} = \beta_{ZI^*,a} = 1$. If all funds are invested in either I^* or ZI^*, then $Z^*_{I^*,a} = 1$ or $Z^*_{ZI^*,a} = 1$, respectively. With no riskless asset, Eq. (3.33) reduces to Eq. (3.30), as $\beta_{i,a} \equiv w_{I^*} + w_{ZI^*} = 1$. Also, if we restrict $w_f > 0$ (i.e., no borrowing at the riskless rate is allowed), then $\beta_{i,a} < 1$.

the market portfolio, or $\beta_{i,M}$ (denoted as simply β_i by Sharpe (1964) as reviewed in Chapter 2), but instead is related to average returns on the portfolio of n assets in the market. Consistent with arguments in Shanken (1987), and given that the true market portfolio can be constructed from any two portfolios on the parabola, the intuition of the two-factor ZCAPM model is that the factors (i.e., fundamental state variables) are multivariate proxies for the unobservable equilibrium market portfolio (see also Shanken and Weinstein 2006).

An interesting insight from the two-factor ZCAPM is that cross-sectional market return dispersion manifests opposing market forces that can positively or negatively impact asset returns at any given time t. To see this, suppose that the cross-sectional distribution of asset returns widens due to an increase in σ_a. All else the same, assets with returns less than the expected market return would experience decreasing returns, whereas assets with returns greater than the expected market return would have increasing returns. Conversely, if market return dispersion decreases rather than increases, then the former assets would experience increasing returns, and the latter assets decreasing returns.

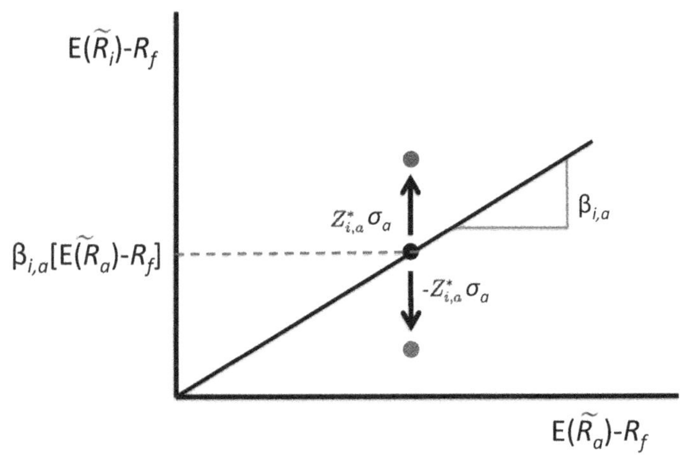

Fig. 3.4 Dual opposing market volatility effects are taken into account by the ZCAPM. Expected returns above and below beta-adjusted expected returns occur due to zeta risk related to positive and negative sensitivity to cross-sectional return dispersion (σ_a), respectively

Extending this simple intuition to the ZCAPM in Eq. (3.33), Fig. 3.4 shows that, given an asset's return exceeds its expected return defined by its beta risk (i.e., $\beta_{i,a}[E(\widetilde{R}_a) - R_f]$), if $Z^*_{i,a}$ is positive for the asset, increasing (decreasing) market return dispersion will tend to push up (down) its excess return. An opposite effect occurs if an asset's $Z^*_{i,a}$ coefficient is negative, as its excess return will tend to decrease (increase) in response to increased (decreased) market return dispersion. These dual contrary relationships imply that, as noted above, market return dispersion can have opposing effects on asset returns. In Chapter 9, we provide empirical evidence on this hypothesized relation by using estimated $Z^*_{i,a}$ coefficients to form portfolios that trace out the shape of an investment parabola using out-of-sample (one-month-ahead) returns.

Few theoretical asset pricing papers incorporate market volatility in a CAPM setting. Merton's (1973) intertemporal CAPM (ICAPM) posited that the prices of risk of discount-rate and cash-flow beta components should be equal and proportional, respectively, to the variance of market returns. Based on his model as well as earlier work by Campbell (1993, 1996), Chen (2003) took into account changes in the investment opportunity set using forecasts of time-varying expected market returns and time-varying market volatilities. In this general specification of the ICAPM, an asset's expected return is determined by risks related to market returns, changes in market return forecasts, and changes in market volatility forecasts.[16] Bansal et al. (2012) proposed a dynamic capital asset pricing model (DCAPM) that incorporates risks associated with cash flows, discount rates, and volatility. They found that both economic and return-based measures of volatility are highly persistent with respect to both consumption and equity returns. Also, volatility risks were useful in explaining risk premia for size and book-to-market sorted portfolios. Another study by Campbell et al. (2018) extended Campbell (1993) by incorporating stochastic volatility. Investors hedge against declines in expected stock returns and increases in the volatility of stock returns. Their ICAPM model has three dimensions

[16] Chen (2003) showed that, if there is a positive covariance between an asset's return and future market volatility, then an asset's return will decrease (i.e., investors confronted with increased uncertainty will reduce consumption and increase savings). However, empirical tests based on estimates of the VAR-GARCH model did not support forecasted market volatility as an explanatory factor in the cross section of stock returns.

of risk that are determined by the investor's coefficient of relative risk aversion. Empirical tests with different test asset portfolios demonstrated good explanatory power in the cross section of average stock returns and stable parameter estimates.

It is noteworthy that Merton's ICAPM, Bansal et al.'s DCAPM, Campbell et al.'s ICAPM extension, and related studies' models require identification of the market portfolio, which raises the Roll critique. By contrast, the ZCAPM in Eq. (3.33) only requires estimation of the average return on market assets and their cross-sectional standard deviation (as opposed to the standard deviation of the market portfolio's return). These less stringent requirements bode well for the ZCAPM in terms of its empirical testability. More importantly, the ZCAPM departs from these CAPM studies by using both *cross-sectional* (rather than time-series) market volatility and incorporating *positive and negative* market volatility effects on asset returns.

3.4 Summary

Black's (1972) zero-beta CAPM posited that an infinite number of efficient index *I* and orthogonal index *ZI* portfolios exist on the mean-variance investment parabola of Markowitz (1959). Any given pair of these portfolios can be used to construct the market portfolio *M* of the CAPM. Using new geometry different from Roll (1980), we showed that two orthogonal portfolios denoted I^* and ZI^* can be identified on the parabola with equal return variances. Applying random matrix theory mathematics, we derived estimates of the expected returns of portfolios I^* and ZI^*, which embody the general form of the ZCAPM. Two new insights about the mean-variance parabola emerged: (1) the average market return lies at an interior location on the axis of symmetry of the parabola and (2) the width of the parabola is determined by return dispersion in large part. This geometry forms the theoretical foundation of the ZCAPM.

Under realistic assumptions, we specified theoretical versions of the ZCAPM without and with a riskless asset. The resultant ZCAPM hypothesizes that the expected return of individual assets is a function of average market returns and return dispersion in the market. Sensitivity to these market factors is captured by beta risk and zeta risk, respectively. Beta risk (denoted $\beta_{i,a}$) in the ZCAPM differs from previous models such as the CAPM, as it is associated with average market returns rather than the return on the market portfolio. Additionally, zeta risk (denoted $Z^*_{i,a}$) is different from other models that incorporate a return dispersion factor, as it can have dual positive and negative return effects on assets at any given time t. This two-sided, opposite market volatility risk is a distinctive feature of the ZCAPM that arises by virtue of the mean-variance investment parabola with span determined by return dispersion. As we will see in the next chapter, cross-sectional volatility in the ZCAPM presents an intriguing challenge to empirically model.

Appendix A: Expected Returns for Portfolios I^* and ZI^*

Here we derive expressions for $E(\widetilde{R}^*_I)$ and $E(\widetilde{R}^*_{ZI})$ in Eq. (3.11). The familiar definition of the variance of any efficient portfolio I from Eq. (2.18) in Chapter 2 is

$$\sigma_I^2 = \frac{1}{C} + \frac{C\left[E(\widetilde{R}_I) - \frac{A}{C}\right]^2}{BC - A^2}. \tag{A3.1}$$

For the minimum variance portfolio G, substituting $E(\widetilde{R}_I) = E(\widetilde{R}_G) = \frac{A}{C}$, the above variance reduces to $1/C$. For efficient portfolio I^*, taking the derivative $\partial/\partial\sigma^2_{I^*}$ on both sides of the above equation and solving for the slope, we obtain

$$\frac{\partial E(\widetilde{R}_{I^*})}{\partial\sigma^2_{I^*}} = \frac{BC - A^2}{2C\left[E(\widetilde{R}_{I^*}) - \frac{A}{C}\right]}. \tag{A3.2}$$

The tangent line to point $(E(\widetilde{R}_{I^*}), \sigma^2_{I^*})$ intersects point $(\frac{A}{C}, 0)$. Given the slope relation

$$\frac{\partial E(\widetilde{R}_{I^*})}{\partial\sigma^2_{I^*}} = \frac{BC - A^2}{2C\left[E(\widetilde{R}_{I^*}) - \frac{A}{C}\right]} = \frac{E(\widetilde{R}_{I^*}) - \frac{A}{C}}{\sigma^2_{I^*}}, \tag{A3.3}$$

and replacing $\sigma^2_{I^*}$ with Eq. (A3.1), we get

$$\frac{BC - A^2}{2C\left[E(\widetilde{R}_{I^*}) - \frac{A}{C}\right]} = \frac{E(\widetilde{R}_{I^*}) - \frac{A}{C}}{\frac{1}{C} + \frac{C\left[E(\widetilde{R}_{I^*}) - \frac{A}{C}\right]^2}{BC - A^2}}. \tag{A3.4}$$

Now we can solve for $E(\widetilde{R}_{I^*})$ to obtain

$$E(\widetilde{R}_{I^*}) = \frac{A}{C} + \sqrt{\frac{BC - A^2}{C^2}}. \tag{A3.5}$$

By geometric symmetry, $E(\widetilde{R}_{ZI^*})$ is

$$E(\widetilde{R}_{ZI^*}) = \frac{A}{C} - \sqrt{\frac{BC - A^2}{C^2}}. \tag{A3.6}$$

Appendix B: Properties of Matrix C

This appendix solves for the asymptotic properties of $C = e'\Sigma^{-1}e$ in Eq. (3.2), which can be defined for n population assets as follows:

$$\begin{aligned}
C &= e'\Sigma^{-1}e \\
&= e'(D\mathbb{C}D)^{-1}e \\
&= e'D^{-1}\mathbb{C}^{-1}D^{-1}e \\
&= e'D^{-1}(UU'\mathbb{C}UU')^{-1}D^{-1}e \\
&= e'D^{-1}(U\,diag(\mathbb{C})U')^{-1}D^{-1}e \\
&= e'D^{-1}U(diag(\mathbb{C}))^{-1}U'D^{-1}e \\
&= (1/\sigma_1, 1/\sigma_2, \cdots, 1/\sigma_n)U(diag(\mathbb{C}))^{-1}U'(1/\sigma_1, 1/\sigma_2, \cdots, 1/\sigma_n)' \\
C &= RMC + NRMC
\end{aligned} \tag{B3.1}$$

with RMC = random matrix component, and $NRMC$ = nonrandom matrix component.

The *RMC* component can be simplified as follows:

$$
\begin{aligned}
RMC &= (1/\sigma_1, 1/\sigma_2, \cdots, 1/\sigma_n) U_{RMC} (diag(\mathbb{C}))^{-1}_{RMC} U'_{RMC} (1/\sigma_1, 1/\sigma_2, \cdots, 1/\sigma_n)' \\
&= \left(\sum_{i=1}^{n} \frac{u_{1i}}{\sigma_i}, \sum_{i=1}^{n} \frac{u_{2i}}{\sigma_i}, \cdots, \sum_{i=1}^{n} \frac{u_{ki}}{\sigma_i} \right) \\
&\quad \times [diag(\mathbb{C})]^{-1} \left(\sum_{i=1}^{n} \frac{u_{1i}}{\sigma_i}, \sum_{i=1}^{n} \frac{u_{2i}}{\sigma_i}, \cdots, \sum_{i=1}^{n} \frac{u_{ki}}{\sigma_i} \right)' \\
&= \sum_{j=1}^{k} \frac{\left(\sum_{i=1}^{n} \frac{u_{ji}}{\sigma_i} \right)^2}{\lambda_j(\mathbb{C})} \\
&\approx \sum_{j=1}^{k} \left(\sum_{i=1}^{n} \frac{u_{ji}}{\sigma_i} \right)^2 \left[\frac{1}{k} \sum_{j=1}^{k} \frac{1}{\lambda_j(\mathbb{C})} \right] \\
&\approx E\left[\sum_{j=1}^{k} \left(\sum_{i=1}^{n} \frac{u_{ji}}{\sigma_i} \right)^2 \right] E\left(\frac{1}{\lambda(\mathbb{C})} \right) \\
&= E\left[\sum_{j=1}^{k} \left(\sum_{i=1}^{n} \frac{u_{ji}}{\sigma_i} \right)^2 \right] \frac{Q}{2\pi q^2} \int_{\lambda_{min}}^{\lambda_{max}} \frac{\sqrt{(x-\lambda_{min})(\lambda_{max}-x)}}{x^2} dx \\
&\approx \left(\frac{1}{\overline{\sigma_{ave}}^2} + \sigma_\sigma^2 \right) \frac{kQ}{2\pi q^2} \int_{\lambda_{min}}^{\lambda_{max}} \frac{\sqrt{(x-\lambda_{min})(\lambda_{max}-x)}}{x^2} dx \\
&= \left(\frac{1}{\overline{\sigma_{ave}}^2} + \sigma_\sigma^2 \right) \frac{k}{2\pi} F(\lambda_{min}, \lambda_{max}) \qquad \text{(B3.2)}
\end{aligned}
$$

$$
RMC \approx \left(\frac{1}{\overline{\sigma_{ave}}^2} + \sigma_\sigma^2 \right) \frac{2n^{3/2}}{\pi} \text{ when } n \text{ is large,} \qquad \text{(B3.3)}
$$

where the dimension of matrix U_{RMC} is $n \times k$ (k is close to but less than n) and that of matrix $(diag(\mathbb{C}))^{-1}_{RMC}$ is $k \times k$, and the expected value of the inverse standard deviation and its standard deviation, respectively, are defined as

$$
\frac{1}{\overline{\sigma_{ave}}} = E\left(\frac{1}{\sigma} \right) \approx \frac{1}{n} \sum_{i=1}^{n} \frac{1}{\sigma_i}, \qquad \text{(B3.4)}
$$

$$\sigma_\sigma^2 = E\left(\frac{1}{\sigma} - \frac{1}{\overline{\sigma_{ave}}}\right)^2 \approx \frac{1}{n}\sum_{i=1}^{n}\left(\frac{1}{\sigma_i} - \frac{1}{\overline{\sigma_{ave}}}\right)^2, \tag{B3.5}$$

where the above constants Q and q in Eq. (B3.3) are related to λ_{min} and λ_{maz} via

$$\lambda_{min} = q^2(1 + 1/Q - 2\sqrt{1/Q})$$
$$\lambda_{max} = q^2(1 + 1/Q + 2\sqrt{1/Q}).$$

In deriving the first approximate equivalence in Eq. (B3.3), we utilize the independence between random variables u (elements of any column in unitary matrix U), σ (standard deviations of stocks), and $\lambda(\mathbb{C})$ (eigenvalues of matrix $\mathbb{C}$). In deriving the third approximate equivalence in Eq. (A3.3), we use the random matrix theory result that the components of any eigenvector of the random matrix follow the Gaussian distribution with mean zero and variance σ_{RMC}, i.e., $u_{ij} \sim N(0, \sigma_{RMC}^2)$. We also know from the unitary matrix property that, for any given eigenvector s, we have $\sum_{i=1}^{n} u_{si}^2 = 1$, which leads to $u_{si} \sim N(0, 1/n)$, i.e., $\sigma_{RMC} = 1/\sqrt{n}$. Hence, for any given j, we can obtain

$$E\left[\left(\sum_{i=1}^{n}\frac{u_{si}}{\sigma_i}\right)^2\right]$$
$$= E\left[\sum_{i=1}^{n}\frac{u_{si}^2}{\sigma_i^2}\right] + \text{cross terms (which are zeros from the independence condition)}$$
$$= n\left(\frac{1}{\overline{\sigma_{ave}}^2} + \sigma_\sigma^2\right)\left(0 + \frac{1}{n}\right)$$
$$= \frac{1}{\overline{\sigma_{ave}}^2} + \sigma_\sigma^2. \tag{B3.6}$$

Based on the findings of Laloux et al. (1999) and Plerou et al. (1999), components of the eigenvector (denoted as the Tth eigenvector) for the biggest eigenvalue (≈ 50) are almost equal weighted, such that all of its components (u_{Ti}) are almost equal to $1/\sqrt{n}$ (since $\sum_{i=1}^{n} u_{Ti}^2 = 1$ by the unitary matrix property). Consequently, the nonrandom matrix component *NRMC* can be written as

$$\begin{aligned} NRMC &= \left(\sum_{i=1}^{n}\frac{u_{Ti}}{\sigma_i}\right)\frac{1}{L}\left(\sum_{i=1}^{n}\frac{u_{Ti}}{\sigma_i}\right) + \text{a few small terms} \\ &= \frac{1}{\sqrt{n}}\left(\sum_{i=1}^{n}\frac{1}{\sigma_i}\right)\frac{1}{L}\frac{1}{\sqrt{n}}\left(\sum_{i=1}^{n}\frac{1}{\sigma_i}\right) + \text{a few small terms} \\ &\approx \frac{1}{\overline{\sigma_{ave}}^2}\frac{\sqrt{n}\times\sqrt{n}}{L} + \text{a few small terms} \\ NRMC &\equiv \frac{1}{\overline{\sigma_{ave}}^2}\frac{\theta n}{L}, \end{aligned} \tag{B3.7}$$

where we have defined a constant $\theta > 1$ to account for nonrandom contributions, and L is the largest nonrandom eigenvalue in the matrix $\mathbb{C}$. We see from these results that, when n is not too large ($\sim$1000), the contributions from random and nonrandom asset prices are comparable in evaluating C. However, when n is very large, the contribution of random noise dominates C. The variance of the minimum variance portfolio is given by $1/C$, which decreases as the number of assets n increases.

Similarly, we can derive the approximate form for A and B by replacing $(1/\sigma_1, 1/\sigma_2, \cdots, 1/\sigma_n)$ by $(E(\widetilde{R}_1)/\sigma_1, E(\widetilde{R}_2)/\sigma_2, \cdots, E(\widetilde{R}_n)/\sigma_n)$ in Eq. (B3.1). Following the steps in the Eq. (B3.2), the RMC form for A and B are given as

$$\begin{aligned} RMC_A &= E\left[\sum_{j=1}^{k}\left(\sum_{i=1}^{n}\frac{E(\widetilde{R}_i)u_{ji}}{\sigma_i}\right)\left(\sum_{i=1}^{n}\frac{u_{ji}}{\sigma_i}\right)\right]\frac{Q}{2\pi q^2}\int_{\lambda_{min}}^{\lambda_{max}}\frac{\sqrt{(x-\lambda_{min})(\lambda_{max}-x)}}{x^2}dx \\ RMC_B &= E\left[\sum_{j=1}^{k}\left(\sum_{i=1}^{n}\frac{E(\widetilde{R}_i)u_{ji}}{\sigma_i}\right)^2\right]\frac{Q}{2\pi q^2}\int_{\lambda_{min}}^{\lambda_{max}}\frac{\sqrt{(x-\lambda_{min})(\lambda_{max}-x)}}{x^2}dx. \end{aligned} \tag{B3.8}$$

By applying the assumption of independence between $E(\widetilde{R}_i)$ and σ_i ($i = 1, \cdots, n$), they can approximately be reduced as

$$RMC_A \approx \left(\frac{E(\widetilde{R}_a)}{\overline{\sigma_{ave}}^2} + E(\widetilde{R}_a)\sigma_\sigma^2\right)\frac{nF(\lambda_{min}, \lambda_{max})}{2\pi}$$

$$RMC_B \approx \left[E(\widetilde{R}_a)^2 + \sigma(\widetilde{R}_a)^2\right]\left(\frac{1}{\overline{\sigma_{ave}}^2} + \sigma_\sigma^2\right)\frac{nF(\lambda_{min}, \lambda_{max})}{2\pi}, \tag{B3.9}$$

where $E(\widetilde{R}_a)$ is the mean value of the expected returns of all assets, and $\sigma(\widetilde{R}_a)$ is the standard deviation of the expected returns of all assets.

The *NRMC* component for *A* and *B* can also be obtained following the steps in Eq. (B3.7), viz.,

$$NRMC_A = \left(\sum_{i=1}^{n}\frac{E(\widetilde{R}_i)u_{Ti}}{\sigma_i}\right)\frac{1}{L}\left(\sum_{i=1}^{n}\frac{u_{Ti}}{\sigma_i}\right) + \text{a few small terms}$$

$$= \frac{1}{\sqrt{n}}\left(\sum_{i=1}^{n}\frac{E(\widetilde{R}_i)}{\sigma_i}\right)\frac{1}{L}\frac{1}{\sqrt{n}}\left(\sum_{i=1}^{n}\frac{1}{\sigma_i}\right) + \text{a few small terms}$$

$$\approx \frac{1}{\overline{\sigma_{ave}}^2}\frac{E(\widetilde{R}_a)\sqrt{n} \times \sqrt{n}}{L} + \text{a few small terms}$$

$$NRMC_A \equiv \frac{E(\widetilde{R}_a)}{\overline{\sigma_{ave}}^2}\frac{\theta n}{L}$$

$$NRMC_B = \left(\sum_{i=1}^{n}\frac{E(\widetilde{R}_i)u_{Ti}}{\sigma_i}\right)\frac{1}{L}\left(\sum_{i=1}^{n}\frac{E(\widetilde{R}_i)u_{Ti}}{\sigma_i}\right) + \text{a few small terms}$$

$$= \frac{1}{\sqrt{n}}\left(\sum_{i=1}^{n}\frac{E(\widetilde{R}_i)}{\sigma_i}\right)\frac{1}{L}\frac{1}{\sqrt{n}}\left(\sum_{i=1}^{n}\frac{E(\widetilde{R}_i)}{\sigma_i}\right) + \text{a few small terms}$$

$$\approx \frac{1}{\overline{\sigma_{ave}}^2}\frac{E(\widetilde{R}_a)^2\sqrt{n} \times \sqrt{n}}{L} + \text{a few small terms}$$

$$NRMC_B \equiv \frac{E(\widetilde{R}_a)^2}{\overline{\sigma_{ave}}^2}\frac{\theta n}{L}, \tag{B3.10}$$

Finally, the approximate expressions for A and B are given as

$$
\begin{aligned}
A &\approx \left(\frac{E(\widetilde{R}_a)}{\overline{\sigma_{ave}}^2} + E(\widetilde{R}_a)\sigma_\sigma^2\right)\frac{nF(\lambda_{min}, \lambda_{max})}{2\pi} + \frac{E(\widetilde{R}_a)}{\overline{\sigma_{ave}}^2}\frac{\theta n}{L} \\
&= \left[\frac{1}{\overline{\sigma_{ave}}^2}\left(\frac{F(\lambda_{min}, \lambda_{max})}{2\pi} + \frac{\theta}{L}\right) + \frac{\sigma_\sigma^2 F(\lambda_{min}, \lambda_{max})}{2\pi}\right]E(\widetilde{R}_a)n \\
B &\approx \left[E(\widetilde{R}_a)^2 + \sigma(\widetilde{R}_a)^2\right]\left(\frac{1}{\overline{\sigma_{ave}}^2} + \sigma_\sigma^2\right)\frac{nF(\lambda_{min}, \lambda_{max})}{2\pi} + \frac{E(\widetilde{R}_a)^2}{\overline{\sigma_{ave}}^2}\frac{\theta n}{L} \\
&= \left[\frac{1}{\overline{\sigma_{ave}}^2}\left(\frac{F(\lambda_{min}, \lambda_{max})}{2\pi} + \frac{\theta}{L}\right) + \frac{\sigma_\sigma^2 F(\lambda_{min}, \lambda_{max})}{2\pi}\right]E(\widetilde{R}_a)^2 n \\
&\quad + \left(\frac{1}{\overline{\sigma_{ave}}^2} + \sigma_\sigma^2\right)\frac{F(\lambda_{min}, \lambda_{max})}{2\pi}\sigma(\widetilde{R}_a^2)n.
\end{aligned}
\tag{B3.11}
$$

Bibliography

Adrian, T., & Rosenberg, J. (2008). Stock returns and volatility: Pricing the short-run and long-run components of market risk. *Journal of Finance, 63*, 2997–3030.

Bansal, R., Kiku, D., Shaliastovich, I., & Yaron, A. (2012). *Volatility, the macroeconomy, and asset prices* (Working Paper). Duke University and University of Pennsylvania.

Black, F. (1972). Capital market equilibrium with restricted borrowing. *Journal of Business, 45*, 444–454.

Brière, M., Drut, B., Mignon, V., Oosterlink, K., & Szafarz, A. (2011). *Is the market portfolio efficient? A new test to revisit Roll (1977) versus Levy and Roll (2010) controversy* (Working Paper). Université Libre de Bruxelles.

Campbell, J. Y. (1993). Intertemporal asset pricing without consumption data. *American Economic Review, 83*, 487–512.

Campbell, J. Y. (1996). Understanding risk and return. *Journal of Political Economy, 104*, 298–345.

Campbell, J. Y., Giglio, S., Polk, C., & Turley, R. (2018). An intertemporal CAPM with stochastic volatility. *Journal of Financial Economics, 128*, 207–233.

Chen, J. (2003). *Intertemporal CAPM and the cross-section of stock returns* (Working Paper). University of Southern California.

Chichernea, D. C., Holder, A. D., & Petkevich, A. (2015). Does return dispersion explain the accrual and investment anomalies? *Journal of Accounting and Economics, 60*, 133–148.

Choudhry, T., Papadimitriou, F. I., & Shabi, S. (2016). Stock market volatility and business cycle: Evidence from linear and nonlinear causality tests. *Journal of Banking and Finance*, *66*, 89–101.

Christie, W., & Huang, R. (1994). The changing functional relation between stock returns and dividend yields. *Journal of Empirical Finance*, *1*, 161–191.

Connolly, R., & Stivers, C. (2003). Momentum and reversals in equity index returns during periods of abnormal turnover and return dispersion. *Journal of Finance*, *58*, 1521–1556.

Cootner, P. H. (1964). *The random character of stock market prices*. Cambridge, MA: MIT Press.

Demirer, R., Gupta, R., Zhihu, L., & Wing-Keung, W. (2019). Equity return dispersion and stock market volatility: Evidence from multivariate linear and nonlinear causality tests. *Sustainability*, *11*, 1–15.

Duffee, G. R. (2001). *Asymmetric cross-sectional dispersion in stock returns: Evidence and implications* (Working Paper). University of California at Berkeley, Berkeley, CA.

Fama, E. F. (1965). Random walks in stock market prices. *Financial Analysts Journal*, *21*, 55–59.

Ferson, W. E., & Locke, D. H. (1998). Estimating the cost of capital through time: Analysis of sources of error. *Management Science*, *44*, 485–500.

Francis, J. C., & Kim, D. (2013). *Modern portfolio theory: Foundations, analysis, and new developments*. Hoboken, NJ: John Wiley & Sons Inc.

Friend, I., & Westerfield, R. (1980). Co-skewness and capital asset pricing. *Journal of Finance*, *35*, 897–913.

Gibbons, M. R. (1982). Multivariate tests of financial models: A new approach. *Journal of Financial Economics*, *10*, 3–27.

Gibbons, M. R., & Ferson, W. E. (1985). Testing asset pricing models with changing expectations and an unobservable market portfolio. *Journal of Financial Economics*, *14*, 217–236.

Gibbons, M. R., Ross, S. A., & Shanken, J. (1989). A test of the efficiency of a given portfolio. *Econometrica*, *57*, 1121–1152.

Gomes, J., Kogan, L., & Zhang, L. (2003). Equilibrium cross section of returns. *Journal of Political Economy*, *111*, 693–732.

Högholm, K., Knif, J., Koutmos, G., & Pynnönen, S. (2011). *Distributional asymmetry of loadings on market co-moments* (Working Paper). Hanken, School of Economics, University of Vaasa, and Fairfield University.

Jobson, J. D., & Korkie, B. (1982). Potential performance and tests of portfolio efficiency. *Journal of Financial Economics*, *10*, 433–465.

Johnstone, I. M. (2001). On the distribution of the largest eigenvalue in principal components analysis. *The Annals of Statistics*, *29*, 295–327.

Kandel, S., & Stambaugh, R. F. (1987). On correlations and inferences about mean/variance efficiency. *Journal of Financial Economics*, *18*, 61–90.

Kendall, M. G., & Hill, B. A. (1953). The analysis of economic time-series-part I: Prices. *Journal of the Royal Statistical Society, 116*, 11–34.
Kraus, A., & Litzenberger, R. H. (1976). Skewness preference and the valuation of risk assets. *Journal of Finance, 31*, 1085–1100.
Laloux, L., Cizeau, P., Potters, M., & Bouchaud, J. P. (1999). Noise dressing of financial correlation matrices. *Physical Review Letters, 83*, 1467–1470.
Levy, M., & Roll, R. (2010). The market portfolio may be mean/variance efficient after all. *Review of Financial Studies, 23*, 2464–2491.
Liu, W. (2013). *A new asset pricing model based on the zero-beta CAPM: Theory and evidence* (Doctoral dissertation). Texas A&M University.
Liu, W., Kolari, J. W., & Huang, J. Z. (2012, October). *A new asset pricing model based on the zero-beta CAPM*. Atlanta, GA: Presentation at the annual meetings of the Financial Management Association.
Lo, A. W., & MacKinlay, A. C. (1988). Stock market prices do not follow random walks: Evidence from a simple specification test. *Review of Financial Studies, 1*, 41–66.
Loungani, P., Rush, M., & Tave, W. (1990). Stock market dispersion and unemployment. *Journal of Monetary Economics, 25*, 367–388.
MacKinlay, A. C., & Richardson, M. P. (1991). Using generalized method of moments to test mean/variance efficiency. *Journal of Finance, 46*, 511–527.
Malkiel, B. G. (1973). *A Random Walk Down Wall Street* (6th ed.). New York, NY: W. W. Norton & Company Inc.
Markowitz, H. M. (1959). *Portfolio selection: Efficient Diversification of Investments*. New York, NY: John Wiley & Sons.
Merton, R. C. (1972). An analytical derivation of the efficient portfolio frontier. *Journal of Financial and Quantitative Finance, 7*, 1851–1872.
Merton, R. C. (1973). An intertemporal capital asset pricing model. *Econometrica, 41*, 867–887.
Plerou, V., Gopikrishnan, P., Rosenow, B., Amaral, L. A. N., & Stanley, H. E. (1999). Universal and nonuniversal properties of cross correlations in financial time series. *Physical Review Letters, 83*, 1471–1474.
Pulley, L. B. (1981). General mean-variance approximation to expected utility for short holding periods. *Journal of Financial and Quantitative Analysis, 16*, 361–373.
Roll, R. (1977). A critique of the asset pricing theory's tests, part I: On past and potential future testability of the theory. *Journal of Financial Economics, 4*, 129–176.
Roll, R. (1980). Orthogonal portfolios. *Journal of Financial and Quantitative Analysis, 15*, 1005–1012.
Rosenow, B., Plerou, V., Gopikrishnan, P., Amaral, L. A. N., & Stanley, H. E. (2000). Application of random matrix theory to study cross-correlations of stock prices. *International Journal of Theoretical and Applied Finance, 3*, 399–403.

Ross, S. A. (1980). *A test of the efficiency of a given portfolio*. Paper prepared for the World Econometrics Meetings, Aix-en-Provence.
Sears, R. S., & Wei, K. C. J. (1985). Asset pricing, higher moments, and the market risk premium: A note. *Journal of Finance, 40*, 1251–1253.
Shanken, J. (1985). Multivariate tests of the zero-beta CAPM. *Journal of Financial Economics, 14*, 327–348.
Shanken, J. (1987). Multivariate proxies and asset pricing relations: Living with the Roll critique. *Journal of Financial Economics, 18*, 91–110.
Shanken, J., & Weinstein, M. I. (2006). Economic forces and the stock market revisited. *Journal of Empirical Finance, 13*, 129–144.
Sharpe, W. F. (1964). Capital asset prices: A theory of market equilibrium under conditions of risk. *Journal of Finance, 19*, 425–442.
Wheatley, S. M. (1989). A critique of latent variable tests of asset pricing models. *Journal of Financial Economics, 23*, 325–338.
Wigner, E. P. (1955). Characteristic vectors of bordered matrices with infinite dimensions. *Annals of Mathematics, 62*, 548–564.
Wishart, J. (1928). Generalized product moment distribution in samples. *Biometrika, 20A*, 32–52.
Zhang, L. (2005). The value premium. *Journal of Finance, 60*, 67–103.
Zhang, X. F. (2006). Information uncertainty and stock returns. *Journal of Finance, 61*, 105–136.
Zhou, G. (1981). Small sample tests of portfolio efficiency. *Journal of Financial Economics, 30*, 165–191.
Zhou, G. (1993). Asset pricing tests under alternative distributions. *Journal of Finance, 48*, 1927–1942.

PART III

Empirical ZCAPM

CHAPTER 4

Empirical Form of the ZCAPM

Abstract This chapter develops empirical models to estimate the theoretical ZCAPM. We review prior empirical studies that incorporate return dispersion (*RD*) in a traditional asset pricing model as well as research on asymmetric market risk. Departing from these studies, and confirming our random matrix results in Chapter 3, we use mean-variance mathematics in Markowitz to prove that the width of the mean-variance investment parabola is defined in large part by *RD*. This new result implies that the average market return lies on its axis of symmetry in the middle of the parabola. Using these insights about the mean-variance parabola, our empirical ZCAPM differs from traditional models in two ways: (1) beta risk is associated with average market returns rather than a proxy market portfolio and (2) zeta risk related to *RD* can be either positive or negative in sign. Unlike other asset pricing models, the empirical ZCAPM is a probabilistic mixture model with two components, each of which is a two-factor regression model with either positive or negative sensitivity to *RD*. To determine the sign of zeta risk related to *RD*, we estimate the empirical ZCAPM using the well-established expectation-maximization (EM) algorithm, which is an iterative method to find maximum likelihood estimates of statistical parameters. The EM algorithm assumes that, even though the sign of the zeta risk coefficient is unknown, the probability of a positive or negative sign can be estimated via latent information contained in observed data. We provide step-by-step instructions on how to estimate the ZCAPM with the EM algorithm.

J. W. Kolari et al., *A New Model of Capital Asset Prices*,
https://doi.org/10.1007/978-3-030-65197-8_4

Keywords Asset pricing · Asymmetric market risk · Beta risk · Empirical ZCAPM · Expectation-maximization (EM) algorithm · Investment parabola · Latent variable · Macroeconomic state variable · Maximum likelihood · Mean-variance investment parabola · Return dispersion · Signal variable · Stock market · Valuation · ZCAPM · Zero-beta CAPM · Zeta risk

4.1 Related Literature

The theoretical ZCAPM in Chapter 3 posits that expected returns are explained by beta risk associated with average market returns and zeta risk related to return dispersion (*RD*). The latter zeta risk can be positive or negative for different assets. As discussed there, many authors consider *RD* to be a macroeconomic state variable related to unemployment rates, economic uncertainty, business cycles, macroeconomic shocks, etc.[1]

In view of the consensus opinion that *RD* proxies marketwide risk, some studies have included this risk factor in asset pricing models.[2] For example, Jiang (2010) augmented a general market index with cross-sectional return dispersion in the U.S. stock market. He distinguished between cross-sectional return dispersion and time-series market volatility, which had little or no correlation with one another in many sample periods.[3] Testing 25 stock portfolios sorted on estimated CAPM betas and return dispersion betas, empirical tests indicated that beta coefficients (or loadings) associated with *RD* were significant in cross-sectional regressions. A closely related paper by Demirer and Jategaonkar (2013) repeated tests similar to Jiang and found that *RD* better explains the cross-section of average stock returns when market returns are relatively high. However, when market returns are low, *RD* was not significant.

[1] See Loungani et al. (1990), Christie and Huang (1994), Duffee (2001), Connolly and Stivers (2003), Gomes et al. (2003), Zhang (2006), Adrian and Rosenberg (2008), Chichernea et al. (2015), Choudhry et al. (2016), Demirer et al. (2019), and others.

[2] A related but different branch of literature incorporates time-series aggregate return volatility in asset pricing models as a marketwide risk factor. See Ang et al. (2006, 2009), Adrian and Rosenberg (2008), Jiang (2010), Da and Schaumburg (2011), Chang et al. (2013), Bansal et al. (2012), Farago and Tédongap (2015), and Bollerslev et al. (2018).

[3] However, some studies have found that return dispersion is correlated with future market volatility. See Stivers (2003) and Connolly and Stivers (2003).

Another paper by Garcia et al. (2014) augmented the Fama and French (1992, 1993, 1995) three-factor model with a return dispersion factor. Using equal-weighted returns for U.S. stock portfolios, *RD* proved to be a significant asset pricing factor. By contrast, tests using value-weighted returns did not corroborate their findings. Unlike Garcia et al., using value-weighted returns, Chichernea et al. (2015) similarly added *RD* to the three-factor model and found that it was signifiicant. The aforementioned studies obtained a positive relation between stock returns and *RD*. However, Verousis and Voukelators (2015) found a negative relation between U.S. stock returns and a zero-investment *RD* factor (i.e., long stocks with low sensitivity to return dispersion and short stocks with high sensitivity).[4]

In sum, previous empirical evidence on return dispersion as an asset pricing factor is mixed. *RD* was found to be both positively and negatively related to average stock returns as well as insignificant at times. ZCAPM theory helps to reconcile these mixed findings by explicitly taking into account the opposite impacts of *RD* on stock returns. Some stocks will experience increasing returns as *RD* increases, whereas others will exhibit decreasing returns, and vice versa for decreasing *RD*. In this chapter, we propose an empirical version of the ZCAPM that takes into account these dual opposing market effects of return dispersion on stock returns. Unlike previous models incorporating *RD*, our empirical ZCAPM is grounded in CAPM and zero-beta CAPM equilibrium conditions and mean-variance portfolio theory. Also, forthcoming chapters show that the ZCAPM substantially boosts the significance and explanatory power of *RD* in cross-sectional analyses of stock returns.

4.2 Asymmetric Market Risk

Some published studies take into account asymmetric market risk effects. Original work in this area by Ang et al. (2006) proposed asymmetric market beta risk. In other words, upside and downside beta risk could be different from one another or asymmetric in nature. They estimated downside and upside betas, denoted as β^- and β^+, for individual stocks. To do this, they added a dummy variable in the CAPM market model that equals -1 or $+1$ when the average daily market excess return is below or above the mean

[4] They interpreted this negative relationship to hedging behavior by investors.

market return in a sample year, respectively.[5] Their results using equally weighted portfolios indicated that high unconditional average stock returns are associated with high downside betas.[6] High upside betas did not exhibit any obvious relationship to average stock returns. They concluded that greater weight is placed by investors on downside risk than upside gains.[7]

More closely associated with our ZCAPM, some studies have investigated downside and upside volatility. Savage (2009) argued that, given volatility (or uncertainty) in the price of stock over time, a long investor faces the risk the stock will decline in value, whereas a short investor has the risk the stock's value will rise.[8] Similarly, Ambrosio and Kinniry (2008) recognized that downside and upside volatility have different risk implications to investors. They conjectured that, "A volatility measure should be able to distinguish between positive and negative volatility in order to take risk aversion into account" (2008, p. 5). With this in mind, they proposed that volatility can be measured with the percentage of days in a period that a stock index level increased versus decreased by equal or more than some threshold percentage. Lastly, a more recent study by Bollerslev et al. (2020) utilized a relative difference in semi-variance measure to proxy good and bad volatility, which they found strongly predicted cross-sectional returns. Using high-frequency intraday data, firms with high (low) good versus bad relative volatilities tended to have low (high) future returns. The authors noted that, similar to Breckenfelder and Tédongap (2012) and Farago and Tédongap (2015), investors appear to price downside volatility more significantly than upside volatility.

[5] An earlier study by Pettengill et al. (1995) documented positive and negative betas of stock portfolios when market returns are above and below the riskless rate, respectively. Hence, they inferred asymmetric beta effects conditional on up versus down markets.

[6] See also Jahankhani (1976) for estimates of downside betas for stocks.

[7] A recent study by Levi and Welch (2018) reexamined the question of asymmetric beta effects. Contrary to Ang et al.'s findings, all-days (plain) betas predicted downside betas better than downside betas themselves, and positive alphas associated with downside betas equaled those for plain betas. Interestingly, the positive relation between downside betas and rates of returns reversed using ex ante as opposed to ex post downside betas.

[8] Relatedly, Zhang (2006) investigated the effects of good and bad news on stocks of firms with high information uncertainty. He found that greater information uncertainty results in lower future stock returns after the announcement of bad news for a firm but higher future stock returns after good news. Numerous studies have found asymmetric stock price reactions to good and bad news (e.g., Brown et al. 1988; French et al. 1987; Haugen et al. 1991, and others). For further discussion, see Campbell and Hentschel (1992).

4.3 Asymmetric Market Risk and the ZCAPM

The above literature relies upon an empirical approach to modeling asymmetric market risk to better understand descriptive evidence in the stock market. By contrast, our ZCAPM approach posits asymmetric return dispersion effects based on the mean-variance parabola of Markowitz (1959) and general equilibrium theories by Sharpe (1964) and Black (1972) per the CAPM and zero-beta CAPM. In Chapter 3, using random matrix theory, we derived two new insights about the mean-variance parabola: (1) average market returns lie on the axis of symmetry and (2) return dispersion of all assets in the market determines the width of the parabola. As the span of the parabola widens due to increasing return dispersion, the expected returns of assets located above (below) the axis of symmetry tend to increase (decrease), all else the same. Again, the axis of symmetry is a horizontal line that divides the parabola into two congruent halves. Figure 3.3 provided a graphical illustration of the parabola moving over time.

Because these new insights about the investment parabola are crucial to understanding our ZCAPM, we next provide an alternative proof of the relation between cross-sectional return variance and the width of the investment parabola. If it is true that the parabola's width is determined by market return dispersion, it should be possible to obtain the same result using a different mathematical approach. Simple logic suggests that, given return dispersion largely defines the parabola's width, the average market return should approximately lie in the middle of the parabola on the axis of symmetry (i.e., the mean of a distribution of asset returns). We later in Chapter 9 document empirical evidence of this geometry by using U.S. stock returns. There we construct aggregate market indexes by means of the ZCAPM that are relatively efficient compared to the CRSP index and trace out the shape of a parabola. Consistent with our investment parabola theory, the CRSP index lies approximately on the axis of symmetry of the ZCAPM estimated parabola and, therefore, does not proxy an efficient market portfolio but rather the average market return.

Many readers may not be familiar with random matrix mathematics used in Chapter 3 to derive the above investment parabola results. For this reason we apply Markowitz's (1959) celebrated diversification principles to give further proof that the width of the parabola is determined by return dispersion. As reviewed in Chapter 3, the equation for the Markowitz efficient frontier is:

$$\sigma_P^2 = \frac{1}{c} + \frac{c(\bar{R}_P - \frac{a}{c})^2}{bc - a^2}, \tag{4.1}$$

where $a \equiv \bar{R}'\Sigma^{-1}e$, $b \equiv \bar{R}'\Sigma^{-1}\bar{R}$, $c \equiv e'\Sigma^{-1}e$ with e defined as an $n \times 1$ vector of ones, Σ is the covariance matrix, σ_P is the volatility of an efficient portfolio on the efficient frontier, and $\bar{R}_P$ is the expected return of the efficient portfolio.

To simplify matters, we assume three stocks comprise the market. Each stock is independent of the other stocks, such that the market has three risk factors. We denote expected asset returns as $\bar{R}' = (\bar{R}_1, \bar{R}_2, \bar{R}_3)$ with covariance matrix $diag(\sigma_1^2, \sigma_2^2, \sigma_3^2)$. To facilitate the derivation without sacrificing generality, we set $\sigma_1 = \sigma_2 = \sigma_3 = \sigma$. Under these starting conditions, we have:

$$\begin{aligned} c &= e'\Sigma^{-1}e = \frac{3}{\sigma^2} \\ a &= \bar{R}'\Sigma^{-1}e = \frac{\bar{R}_1 + \bar{R}_2 + \bar{R}_3}{\sigma^2} \\ b &= \bar{R}'\Sigma^{-1}\bar{R} = \frac{\bar{R}_1^2 + \bar{R}_2^2 + \bar{R}_3^2}{\sigma^2}. \end{aligned} \tag{4.2}$$

Based on these values, the denominator of Eq. (4.1) can be defined as:

$$\begin{aligned} bc - a^2 &= \frac{3(\bar{R}_1^2 + \bar{R}_2^2 + \bar{R}_3^2) - (\bar{R}_1 + \bar{R}_2 + \bar{R}_3)^2}{\sigma^4} \\ &= \frac{2(\bar{R}_1^2 + \bar{R}_2^2 + \bar{R}_3^2) - 2(\bar{R}_1\bar{R}_2 + \bar{R}_1\bar{R}_3 + \bar{R}_2 R_3)}{\sigma^4} \\ &= \frac{(\bar{R}_1 - \bar{R}_2)^2 + (\bar{R}_1 - \bar{R}_3)^2 + (\bar{R}_2 - \bar{R}_3)^2}{\sigma^4}. \end{aligned} \tag{4.3}$$

The cross-sectional variance σ_{CS}^2 is generally defined as:

$$\begin{aligned} \sigma_{CS}^2 &= \frac{[\bar{R}_1 - (\bar{R}_1 + \bar{R}_2 + \bar{R}_3)/3]^2 + [\bar{R}_2 - (\bar{R}_1 + \bar{R}_2 + \bar{R}_3)/3]^2 + [\bar{R}_3 - (\bar{R}_1 + \bar{R}_2 + \bar{R}_3)/3]^2}{3 - 1} \\ &= \frac{[(\bar{R}_1 - \bar{R}_2) + (\bar{R}_1 - \bar{R}_3)]^2 + [(\bar{R}_2 - \bar{R}_1) + (\bar{R}_2 - \bar{R}_3)]^2 + [(\bar{R}_3 - \bar{R}_1) + (\bar{R}_3 - \bar{R}_2)]^2}{18} \\ &= \frac{(\bar{R}_1 - \bar{R}_2)^2 + (\bar{R}_2 - \bar{R}_3)^2 + (\bar{R}_3 - \bar{R}_1)^2}{6}. \end{aligned} \tag{4.4}$$

Combining Eqs. (4.3) and (4.4), we obtain $bc - a^2 = 6\sigma_{CS}^2/\sigma^4$, such that Eq. (4.1) can be modified as:

$$\sigma_P^2 = \frac{\sigma^2}{3} + \frac{\sigma^2}{2\sigma_{CS}^2}(\bar{R}_P - (\bar{R}_1 + \bar{R}_2 + \bar{R}_3)/3)^2. \tag{4.5}$$

Using this equation, Fig. 4.1 diagrams the results. As shown there, as cross-sectional variance σ_{CS}^2 increases from 1 to 8, the width of the mean-variance

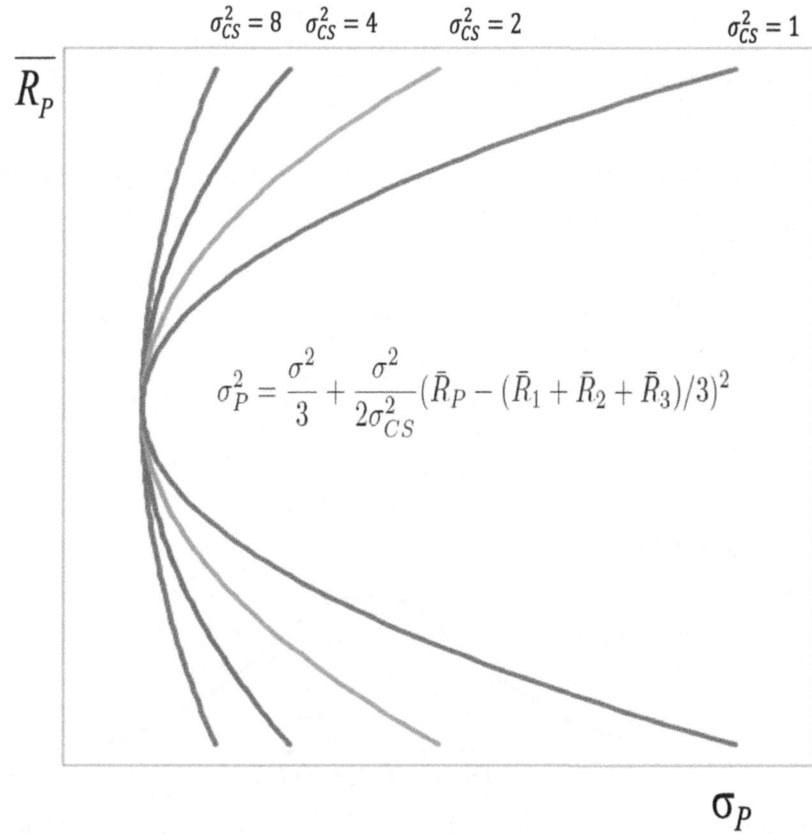

Fig. 4.1 Cross-sectional return variance (denoted σ_{CS}^2) directly affects the width of the mean-variance investment parabola

parabola becomes larger. It is clear that span of the parabola is largely determined by return dispersion. These results confirm our random matrix theory findings for the mean-variance parabola in Chapter 3.

Given this result, we illustrate the asymmetric effects of return dispersion on asset returns in Fig. 4.2. Panel A shows the cross-sectional distribution of expected returns for all assets at time $t = 1$. The cross-sectional standard deviation of all assets' expected returns denoted σ_{m1} (i.e., return dispersion) equals 1%. The locations in the distribution of expected returns for the market return in addition to assets A and B are denoted $E(R_{m1})$, $E(R_{A1})$, and $E(R_{B1})$, respectively. In Panel B at $t = 2$, the cross-sectional standard deviation of assets' expected returns increases to $\sigma_{m2} = 2\%$. This increase in return dispersion implies a wider investment parabola. Assuming that the mean market return does not change over time, or $E(R_{m1}) = E(R_{m2})$, we see that the:

(1) expected return of asset A increases from $E(R_{A1})$ at $t = 1$ to $E(R_{A2})$ at $t = 2$, and

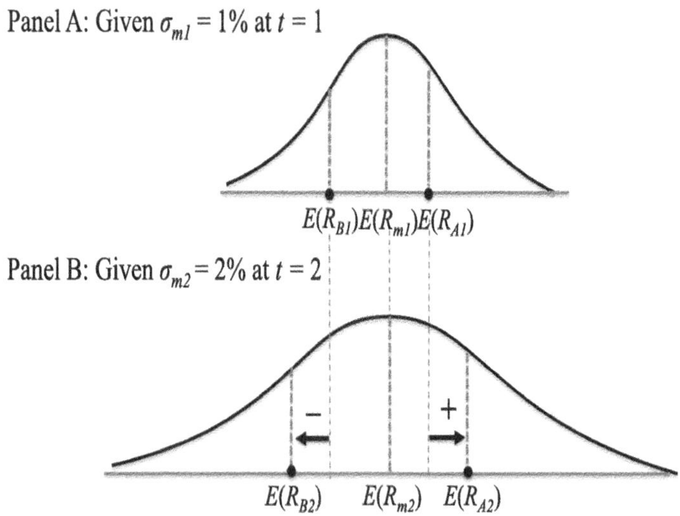

Fig. 4.2 Increasing return dispersion from time $t = 1$ to $t = 2$ ($\sigma_{m2} > \sigma_{m1}$) has asymmetric positive and negative effects on asset returns, as shown by increasing the return of asset A but decreasing the return of asset B

(2) expected return of asset B decreases from $E(R_{B1})$ at $t = 1$ to $E(R_{B2})$ at $t = 2$.

In sum, return dispersion can have dual opposing effects on the expected returns of different assets over time. Generally speaking, as return dispersion increases over time, assets with returns greater (less) than the average market return experience increasing (decreasing) returns. Conversely, if return dispersion decreases over time, the opposite return effects will occur—that is, assets with returns greater (less) than the average market return experience decreasing (increasing) returns.

4.4 Traditional Return Dispersion Models

Previous studies discussed earlier by Jiang (2010), Demirer and Jategaonkar (2013), Garcia et al. (2014), Chichernea et al. (2015), and Verousis and Voukelatos (2015) utilized *RD* as a risk factor by augmenting the market factor in the following ordinary least squares (OLS) regression model:

$$R_{it} - R_{ft} = \alpha_i + \beta_{i,m}(R_{mt} - R_{ft}) + Z_{i,m}\sigma_{mt} + u_{it}, \quad t = 1, \cdots, T, \qquad (4.6)$$

where $R_{it} - R_{ft}$ is the excess return of the *i*th stock or stock portfolio over the riskless rate R_{ft}, α_i is the mispricing term, $R_{mt} - R_{ft}$ is the excess market return, $\beta_{i,m}$ is the beta risk associated with proxy *m* for the theoretical market portfolio *M* of Sharpe (1964), σ_{mt} is return dispersion (*RD*) at time *t* based on the cross-sectional standard deviation of returns of assets in the market proxy portfolio, $Z_{i,m}$ is the zeta coefficient associated with *RD*, and $u_{it} \sim$ iid $N(0,\sigma_i^2)$. As noted in Chapter 3, because the *RD* factor is not a zero-investment portfolio (i.e., it is a nontraded factor), we designate its factor loading as *Z* rather than using β to distinguish it from other typical long/short factors. According to relation (4.6), stock returns depend on two risk premia—namely, a market risk premium associated with beta risk as in the static CAPM of Sharpe (1964), and an *RD* risk premium associated with zeta risk. As previously discussed, studies link *RD* to fundamental economic variables, business cycles, aggregate market volatility, firm-specific characteristics, and aggregate idiosyncratic volatility.

4.5 ZCAPM Approach to Return Dispersion

Consistent with asymmetric return dispersion effects, we propose a conditional multifactor representation of equilibrium expected returns.[9] Our state variables are the average stock market return and return dispersion (i.e., the first and second moments of the return distribution). Based on the theoretical form of the ZCAPM in Eq. (3.33) of Chapter 3, the expected return generating process for the ith asset at time t can be written as:

$$E(R_{it}) - R_{ft} = \beta_{i,a}[E(R_{at}) - R_{ft}] + Z^*_{i,a}\sigma_{at}, \tag{4.7}$$

where $E(R_{at})$ is the expected market return based on the average return of all assets (rather than a proxy m for the theoretical market portfolio M), beta risk coefficient $\beta_{i,a}$ measures sensitivity to expected excess market returns, σ_{at} is the cross-sectional standard deviation of all asset returns (or return dispersion denoted RD) at time t, zeta risk coefficient $Z^*_{i,a}$ measures positive or negative sensitivity to return dispersion, and other notation is as before. The asterisk superscript on the zeta risk coefficient indicates that it is theoretically related to orthogonal portfolios I^* and ZI^* on the mean-variance investment parabola. This pair of orthogonal portfolios is unique due to their equal return variances. Notably, the dual opposing impacts of RD on expected asset returns in the context of the parabola departs from the traditional model above.

The empirical challenge is determining the sign of the zeta risk coefficient in ZCAPM relation (4.7). In particular, we need to consider the possibility that the sign may change over time. To address this issue, we propose the following novel empirical model:

$$R_{it} - R_{ft} = \beta_{i,a}(R_{at} - R_{ft}) + Z_{i,a}D_{it}\sigma_{at} + u_{it}, \quad t = 1, \cdots, T \tag{4.8}$$

where $Z_{i,a} > 0$ is a fixed constant, D_{it} is a signal variable taking values $+1$ and -1 to indicate positive and negative RD effects, respectively, on the ith asset's returns at time t, $u_{it} \sim$ iid $N(0, \sigma_i^2)$, and other notation is as before. Because D_{it} is latent or unobservable, we assume that D_{it} are independent random variables with the following two-point distribution:

$$D_{it} = \begin{cases} +1 & \text{with probability } p_i \\ -1 & \text{with probability } 1 - p_i, \end{cases} \tag{4.9}$$

[9] This section is based on earlier work by Liu (2013) and Liu et al. (2012, 2020).

where p_i is the probability of a positive return dispersion effect, and $1 - p_i$ is the probability of a negative return dispersion effect. Signal variable observations D_{it} are assumed to be independent of u_{it}. We hereafter refer to Eq. (4.8) as the *empirical ZCAPM.*

Notice that our empirical ZCAPM does not contain mispricing term α_i in the traditional model (4.6). First, this exclusion can be justified by the fact that no mispricing term is contained in theoretical ZCAPM relation (4.7). Second, the mispricing term is typically included in empirical factor models to improve their fit to data. However, because evaluation of the empirical ZCAPM in forthcoming chapters is based on out-of-sample tests, improving in-sample data fitting is not necessary. Third, and last, we have found in real data applications that including a mispricing term in our empirical ZCAPM never improves the in-sample data fitting (in terms of decreasing residual variance in the regression model).

Let $\mathcal{T}_+ = \{t : 1 \leq t \leq T, D_{it} = +1\}$ and $\mathcal{T}_- = \{t : 1 \leq t \leq T, D_{it} = -1\}$ denote respective sets of time indices corresponding to positive and negative signs of the signal variable. The empirical ZCAPM Eqs. (4.8) and (4.9) can then be expanded into two equations as follows:

$$R_{it} - R_{ft} = \beta_{i,a}(R_{at} - R_{ft}) + Z_{i,a}\sigma_{at} + u_{it}, \quad t \in \mathcal{T}_+ \tag{4.10}$$

$$R_{it} - R_{ft} = \beta_{i,a}(R_{at} - R_{ft}) - Z_{i,a}\sigma_{at} + u_{it}, \quad t \in \mathcal{T}_-, \tag{4.11}$$

where Eq. (4.10) has probability p_i, and Eq. (4.11) has probability $1 - p_i$.

In terms of statistical jargon, our empirical ZCAPM is a probabilistic mixture model with two mixture components. Each of the components is itself a two-factor regression model as shown in Eqs. (4.10) and (4.11). The hidden dummy variable D_{it} with two-point distribution $D_{it} = +1$ (with probability p_i) and $D_{it} = -1$ (with probability $1 - p_i$) for the ith asset determines which regression model is operative. To the authors' knowledge, no previous studies propose a mixture asset pricing model.

The coefficient of *RD* in regression Eq. (4.10) is a random variable $Z_{i,a}D_{i,t}$, which may take two possible values $+Z_{i,a}$ or $-Z_{i,a}$, depending on the sign of the signal variable $D_{i,t}$. Notice that the signal variable has mean $E(D_{it}) = 2p_i - 1$ and variance $\text{Var}(D_{it}) = 4p_i(1 - p_i)$. We can separate out the mean from the random coefficient $Z_{i,a}D_{i,t}$ of σ_{at} to get

$$Z_{i,a}D_{i,t} = Z_{i,a}(2p_i - 1) + Z_{i,a}[D_{it} - (2p_i - 1)].$$

Therefore, denoting $Z^*_{i,a} = Z_{i,a}(2p_i - 1)$ and $u^*_{it} = Z_{i,a}[D_{it} - (2p_i - 1)]\sigma_{at} + u_{it}$, we can rewrite ZCAPM relation (4.8) as

$$R_{it} - R_{ft} = \beta_{i,a}(R_{at} - R_{ft}) + Z^*_{i,a}\sigma_{at} + u^*_{it}, \quad t = 1, \cdots, T. \tag{4.12}$$

Since the term $Z^*_{i,a}\sigma_{at}$ of Eq. (4.12) can be interpreted as the result of integrating out the probability distribution of the unobservable signal variable in the term $Z_{i,a}D_{it}\sigma_{at}$ of model (4.8), we refer to Eq. (4.12) as the ***marginal form*** of the empirical ZCAPM. The parameter $Z^*_{i,a}$ corresponds to the ***zeta risk loading*** in theoretical ZCAPM relation (4.7).

Depending on the probability p_i of signal variable D_{it} being +1 in-sample period $t = 1, \cdots, T$, the sign of the zeta risk loading $Z^*_{i,a}$ can be positive or negative. Specifically, if $p_i > 1/2$ (or $< 1/2$), then $Z^*_{i,a}$ has a positive (or negative) sign. Depending on its sign, $Z^*_{i,a}$ intuitively measures the average increase or decrease of asset returns in response to a one unit change in *RD*.

The marginal form of the empirical ZCAPM allows us to identify a major difference between the traditional approach to modeling return dispersion and our ZCAPM approach. While the variance of the error term u_{it} in traditional model (4.6) is constant, the variance of the error term u^*_{it} in our marginal ZCAPM model (4.12) depends on return dispersion as follows:

$$\text{Var}(u^*_{it}) = 4\,p_i(1 - p_i)\,Z^2_{i,a}\,\sigma^2_{at} + \text{Var}(u_{it}). \tag{4.13}$$

The heterogeneity of error variance as shown above is a prominent feature of our model separating it from factor models commonly used in asset pricing. Also, it implies that the traditional approach for modeling return dispersion in an asset pricing model is not valid.

Our empirical ZCAPM is very different from other factor models used in the asset pricing literature. ZCAPM relation (4.12) is based on a two-component mixture model wherein each component is a two-factor regression model. Also, the zeta risk loading $Z^*_{i,a}$ incorporates the mean of a two-point probability distribution of signal variables D_{it}. Two state variables represent the factors defined at any given time t in the ZCAPM: (1) the average return of all assets and (2) their cross-sectional return dispersion. By contrast, the Fama and French models and related multifactor models utilize firm characteristic portfolios (i.e., long/short zero-investment portfolios) as factors, whereas other models employ hidden (unknown) state variables as factors (e.g., Merton's [1973] ICAPM).[10]

4.6 Expectation-Maximization (EM) Algorithm for Estimating the Empirical ZCAPM

A standard statistical tool for parameter estimation is maximum likelihood, which maximizes the observed data likelihood to obtain estimates of the model parameters. The inclusion of latent, unobservable signal variables D_{it} in empirical ZCAPM Eq. (4.8) creates a challenge to the application of maximum likelihood methods. As we shall see below in Eq. (4.16), the observed data likelihood has a complicated form due to summation over the distribution of latent variables. Fortunately, the well-known Expectation-Maximization (EM) algorithm developed by Dempster et al. (1977) provides a solution to this issue.[11]

According to the general framework of the EM algorithm, the complete data is comprised of both observed data and unobserved data (i.e., latent variables). Because the complete data is not available, the latent variable distribution should be integrated out from the complete data likelihood to obtain the observed data likelihood. The EM algorithm avoids this integration step but still enables valid statistical inferences by iterating between an E-step and M-step until convergence is achieved. The E-step estimates the conditional expectation of the complete data log-likelihood conditional on the observed data and the current guess of the parameter values. The M-step maximizes the conditional expectation obtained from the E-step. Under regularity conditions, the EM algorithm converges to a stationary point of the likelihood equation (Wu 1983).

Readers unfamiliar with the EM algorithm are recommended to review papers that have utilized this econometric approach in finance studies. Some good examples in this regard are Kon (1984), Rudd (1991), Asquith et al. (1998), McLachlan and Krishnan (2008), Harvey and Liu (2016), Chen et al. (2017), and citations therein. Wikipedia gives a simple description of the EM algorithm.

[10] In defining factors, Daniel et al. (2020, p. 1928) carefully distinguished between zero-investment portfolios and state variables. They referred to Fama and French (1996, p. 57) and Cochrane (2005, p. 174) for further discussion.

[11] See also Jones and McLachlan (1990), McLachlan and Peel (2000), McLachlan and Krishnan (2008), among others.

For our empirical ZCAPM in Eqs. (4.8) and (4.12), we denote $\theta_i = (\beta_{i,a}, Z_{i,a}, \sigma_i^2, p_i)$ as the collection of model parameters for the ith asset. We denote the complete data set for the ith asset as $\{R_{it}, D_{it}\}$, the (incomplete) observed data set as $\{R_{it}\}$, and the unobservable latent data set as $\{D_{it}\}$. The complete data likelihood of the model is:

$$\mathcal{L}(\theta_i; \{R_{it}, D_{it}\}) = \prod_{t=1}^{T} P_{\theta_i}(R_{it}|D_{it})P_{\theta_i}(D_{it}), \tag{4.14}$$

where

$$\begin{aligned} P_{\theta_i}(D_{it}) &= p_i^{I(D_{it}=1)}(1-p_i)^{I(D_{it}=-1)}, \\ P_{\theta_i}(R_{it}|D_{it}) &= \frac{1}{\sqrt{2\pi\sigma_i^2}}\exp\left\{-\frac{\left(R_{it} - R_{ft} - \beta_{i,a}(R_{at} - R_{ft}) - Z_{i,a}D_{it}\sigma_{at}\right)^2}{2\sigma_i^2}\right\}. \end{aligned} \tag{4.15}$$

The method of maximum likelihood seeks to maximize the observed data likelihood for estimating the model parameters. The observed data likelihood of the model is

$$\mathcal{L}(\theta_i; \{R_{it}\}) = \sum_{D_{it}=\pm 1; t=1,\ldots,T} \mathcal{L}(\theta_i; \{R_{it}, D_{it}\}), \tag{4.16}$$

where the summation is over 2^T possible combinations of values for $\{D_{it}\}$. Since calculation of this summation is prohibitive even for moderate large T, direct maximization of Eq. (4.16) to obtain the maximum likelihood estimate is not computationally feasible.

The EM algorithm seeks to find the mixmum likelihood estimator by iteratively applying the following two steps until convergence:

Expectation step (E-step). Compute the expected value of the log complete data likelihood function conditional on the observed data, i.e., compute the expected log likelihood:

$$Q_i(\theta_i, \theta_i') = E_{\theta_i'}\left[\log \mathcal{L}(\theta_i; \{R_{it}, D_{it}\})|\{R_{it}\}\right], \tag{4.17}$$

where $\theta_i' = (\beta_{i,a}', Z_{i,a}', (\sigma_i')^2, p_i')$ is the current guess of the parameter vector θ_i.

Maximization step (M-step). Update the estimate of θ_i by solving the following optimization problem:

$$\operatorname*{Max}_{\theta_i} Q_i(\theta_i, \theta_i'). \tag{4.18}$$

Next, we work out details of these two steps. Using Eqs. (4.14) and (4.15), the log complete data likelihood can be written as

$$\log \mathcal{L}(\theta_i; \{R_{it}, D_{it}\}) = \sum_{t=1}^{T} \Bigg\{ [I(D_{it} = 1) \log p_i + I(D_{it} = -1) \log(1 - p_i)]$$

$$- \frac{1}{2} \log[2\pi\sigma_i^2] - \frac{1}{2\sigma_i^2}[R_{it} - R_{ft} - \beta_{i,a}(R_{at} - R_{ft}) - Z_{i,a}D_{it}\sigma_{at}]^2 \Bigg\}, \tag{4.19}$$

where $I(\cdot)$ denotes the indicator function. To compute the expected log likelihood in Eq. (4.17), we need to compute $\hat{p}_{it}(\theta_i') \equiv P_{\theta_i'}(D_{it} = 1|R_{it})$ and

$$\widehat{RSS}(\theta_i') \equiv E_{\theta_i'}\{[R_{it} - R_{ft} - \beta_{i,a}(R_{at} - R_{ft}) - Z_{i,a}D_{it}\sigma_{at}]^2 | R_{it}\}. \tag{4.20}$$

When θ_i' reaches values at the convergence of the EM algorithm, $\hat{p}_{it}$ estimates the probability of a positive return dispersion effect for the ith asset at time t.

Bayes' rule is applied to compute $\hat{p}_{it}(\theta_i') = P_{\theta_i'}(D_{it} = 1|R_{it})$:

$$\hat{p}_{it} = \frac{P_{\theta_i'}(R_{it}|D_{it} = 1) \cdot P_{\theta_i'}(D_{it} = 1)}{P_{\theta_i'}(R_{it}|D_{it} = 1) \cdot P_{\theta_i'}(D_{it} = 1) + P_{\theta_i'}(R_{it}|D_{it} = -1) \cdot P_{\theta_i'}(D_{it} = -1)}, \tag{4.21}$$

where

$$P_{\theta_i'}(D_{it} = 1) = p_i', \qquad P_{\theta_i'}(D_{it} = -1) = 1 - p_i' \tag{4.22}$$

$$P_{\theta_i'}(R_{it}|D_{it} = \pm 1) = \frac{1}{\sqrt{2\pi(\sigma_i')^2}} \exp\left\{ - \frac{(R_{it} - R_{ft} - \beta_{i,a}'(R_{at} - R_{ft}) \mp Z_{i,a}'\sigma_{at})^2}{2(\sigma_i')^2} \right\}. \tag{4.23}$$

It readily follows that

$$E_{\theta_i'}(I(D_{it} = 1)|R_{it}) = P_{\theta_i'}(D_{it} = 1|R_{it}) = \hat{p}_{it}(\theta_i'), \tag{4.24}$$

$$E_{\theta_i'}(I(D_{it} = -1)|R_{it}) = P_{\theta_i'}(D_{it} = -1|R_{it}) = 1 - \hat{p}_{it}(\theta_i'), \tag{4.25}$$

and

$$\hat{D}_{it} \equiv E_{\theta_i'}(D_{it}|R_{it}) = P_{\theta_i'}(D_{it} = 1|R_{it}) - P_{\theta_i'}(D_{it} = -1|R_{it}) = \hat{p}_{it} - (1 - \hat{p}_{it})$$

$$\hat{D}_{it} \equiv 2\hat{p}_{it} - 1. \tag{4.26}$$

On the other hand, using Eq. (4.26) and the fact that $D_{it}^2 = 1$, we have

$$\begin{aligned}
\widehat{RSS}(\theta_i') &= E_{\theta_i'}\{[R_{it} - R_{ft} - \beta_{i,a}(R_{at} - R_{ft})]^2 \\
&\quad - 2[R_{it} - R_{ft} - \beta_{i,a}(R_{at} - R_{ft})]Z_{i,a}D_{it}\sigma_{at} + Z_{i,a}^2 D_{it}^2 \sigma_{at}^2 | R_{it}\} \\
&= [R_{it} - R_{ft} - \beta_{i,a}(R_{at} - R_{ft})]^2 \\
&\quad - 2[R_{it} - R_{ft} - \beta_{i,a}(R_{at} - R_{ft})]Z_{i,a}\hat{D}_{it}\sigma_{at} + Z_{i,a}^2 \sigma_{at}^2 \\
&= [R_{it} - R_{ft} - \beta_{i,a}(R_{at} - R_{ft}) - Z_{i,a}\hat{D}_{it}\sigma_{at}]^2 + Z_{i,a}^2(1 - \hat{D}_{it}^2)\sigma_{at}^2.
\end{aligned} \tag{4.27}$$

Combining Eqs. (4.19) and (4.20) as well as Eqs. (4.24) to (4.27), we obtain

$$\begin{aligned}
Q_i(\theta_i, \theta_i') = \sum_{t=1}^{T} \Bigg\{ & [\hat{p}_{it}\log p_i + (1 - \hat{p}_{it})\log(1 - p_i)] - \frac{1}{2}\log[2\pi\sigma_i^2] \\
& - \frac{(R_{it} - R_{ft} - \beta_{i,a}(R_{at} - R_{ft}) - Z_{i,a}\hat{D}_{it}\sigma_{at})^2}{2\sigma_i^2} \\
& - \frac{Z_{i,a}^2(1 - \hat{D}_{it}^2)\sigma_{at}^2}{2\sigma_i^2} \Bigg\}.
\end{aligned} \tag{4.28}$$

This expression is the expected log likelihood from Eq. (4.17) needed in the E-step of the EM algorithm.

The M-step of the EM algorithm optimizes θ_i in the $Q_i(\theta_i, \theta_i')$ function where θ_i' is the current guess of θ_i. Inspection of expression $Q_i(\theta, \theta_i')$ in Eq. (4.28) indicates that the parameters $(\beta_{i,a}, Z_{i,a}, \sigma_i^2, p_i)$ are well-separated such that each parameter can be optimized with a closed-form solution when other parameters are fixed. This condition suggests the M-step of the EM algorithm can be implemented by iteratively optimizing the parameters. The simplicity of this iterative procedure is the main rationale for using the EM algorithm, as opposed to directly maximizing the observed data likelihood.

The steps of the whole EM algorithm are provided below.

(1) Initialize the set of parameters $\hat{\theta}_i^0 = (\hat{\beta}_{i,a}^0, \hat{Z}_{i,a}^0, (\hat{\sigma}_i^0)^2, \hat{p}_i^0)$ for the ith asset. First, estimate the simple OLS regression for the CAPM market model with no mispricing error:

$$R_{it} - R_{ft} = \beta_{i,a}(R_{at} - R_{ft}) + \epsilon_{it}, \quad t = 1, \cdots, T \tag{4.29}$$

and set $D_{it}^0 = +1$ when $\epsilon_{it} > 0$ or $D_{it}^0 = -1$ when $\epsilon_{it} < 0$ to compute the initial probability $\hat{p}_i^0 = \frac{1}{T}\sum_{t=1}^{T} I(D_{it}^0 = +1)$. Next, run the following regression:

$$R_{it} - R_{ft} = \beta_{i,a}(R_{at} - R_{ft}) + Z_{i,a}D_{it}^0\sigma_{at} + \varepsilon_{it}, \quad t = 1, \cdots, T \tag{4.30}$$

to obtain $\hat{\beta}_{i,a}^0$, $\hat{Z}_{i,a}^0$, and the initial variance $(\hat{\sigma}_i^0)^2 = \frac{1}{T}\sum_{t=1}^{T} \varepsilon_{it}^2$. Set these initials as the current estimates of the parameters; that is, set $\theta_i' = \hat{\theta}_i^0$.

(2) Compute:

$$\hat{p}_{it} = \frac{\eta_{it}^+ p_i'}{\eta_{it}^+ p_i' + \eta_{it}^-(1 - p_i')} \tag{4.31}$$

with

$$\eta_{it}^{\pm} = \exp\left\{-\frac{(R_{it} - R_{ft} - \beta_{i,a}'(R_{at} - R_{ft}) \mp Z_{i,a}'\sigma_{at})^2}{2(\sigma_i')^2}\right\}, \tag{4.32}$$

and $\hat{D}_{it} = 2\hat{p}_{it} - 1$.

(3) Solve the following linear equations to get updated estimates of $\hat{\beta}_{i,a}$ and $\hat{Z}_{i,a}$:

$$\left(\sum_{t=1}^{T}(R_{at} - R_{ft})^2\right)\beta_{i,a} + \left(\sum_{t=1}^{T}\hat{D}_{it}(R_{at} - R_{ft})\sigma_{at}\right)Z_{i,a} = \sum_{t=1}^{T}(R_{it} - R_{ft})(R_{at} - R_{ft}),$$
$$\left(\sum_{t=1}^{T}\hat{D}_{it}(R_{at} - R_{ft})\sigma_{at}\right)\beta_{i,a} + \left(\sum_{t=1}^{T}\sigma_{at}^2\right)Z_{i,a} = \sum_{t=1}^{T}\hat{D}_{it}(R_{it} - R_{ft})\sigma_i. \tag{4.33}$$

If $\hat{Z}_{i,a} < 0$, let $\hat{Z}_{i,a} \leftarrow -\hat{Z}_{i,a}$.

(4) Compute the updated variance:

$$\hat{\sigma}_i^2 = \frac{1}{T}\sum_{t=1}^{T}\{(R_{it} - R_{ft} - \hat{\beta}_{i,a}(R_{at} - R_{ft}) - \hat{Z}_{i,a}\hat{D}_{it}\sigma_{at})^2 + \hat{Z}_{i,a}^2(1 - \hat{D}_{it}^2)\sigma_{at}^2\}. \tag{4.34}$$

(5) Compute the updated probability:

$$\hat{p}_i = \frac{1}{T}\sum_{t=1}^{T}\hat{p}_{it}. \tag{4.35}$$

(6) Define the vector

$$\Delta\theta = \left(\frac{|\hat{\beta}_{i,a} - \beta'_{i,a}|}{|\beta'_{i,a}| + 1}, \frac{|\hat{Z}_{i,a} - Z'_{i,a}|}{|Z'_{i,a}| + 1}, \frac{|(\hat{\sigma}_i)^2 - (\sigma'_i)^2|}{|(\sigma'_i)^2| + 1}, \frac{|\hat{p}_i - p'_i|}{|p'_i| + 1} \right), \tag{4.36}$$

and declare convergence when $\text{Max}(\Delta\theta) < 0.1\%$. If convergence is not reached, update θ'_i to the recent values of $\hat{\theta}_i$ obtained from steps (3) to (5), and repeat steps (2) to (5).

4.7 Summary

In this chapter, we developed an empirical form of the theoretical ZCAPM derived in Chapter 3 that can be estimated with readily available market information. To further support random matrix theory in Chapter 3 that the span or width of the investment parabola is determined by the cross-sectional standard deviation of returns (or return dispersion) in the market, we provided another proof of this concept based on Markowitz's (1959) familiar equation for the efficient frontier. A simple numerical example showed that the parabola's width is directly related to return dispersion. Given this relationship, we graphically illustrated the asymmetric effects of return dispersion on asset returns. In response to increasing return dispersion in the market, assets with returns greater (less) than the average market return will tend to experience increasing (decreasing) returns, and vice versa for decreasing return dispersion. Of course, since the parabola's width is determined in large part by return dispersion in the market, the average market return must lie in the middle of the cross-sectional distribution of returns on the axis of symmetry of the parabola.

These new insights about the investment parabola fundamentally change the language of equilibrium asset pricing. Rather than seeking the tangent portfolio on the efficient frontier to find market portfolio M as in Sharpe's (1964) CAPM, efficient portfolios in our ZCAPM can be located by horizontally moving along the axis of symmetry using average market returns and then vertically up to the efficient frontier using positive return dispersion. Conversely, we can use negative return dispersion to move vertically down to the lower, inefficient boundary of the parabola. As Black (1972) proved, combining two orthogonal efficient and inefficient portfolios on the miniumum variance parabola can be used to locate market portfolio M. In forthcoming Chapter 9 we demonstrate this geometry by computing portfolios with out-of-sample returns and risks that trace out the shape of a parabola.

In terms of modeling return dispersion, we reviewed the traditional approach used by previous researchers to incorporate return dispersion in a two-factor asset pricing model. Excess stock returns are specified as a function of a general market index and the return dispersion of the stock market. This traditional model is empirically driven (or ad hoc in nature) with little or no underlying theoretical support.

By contrast, the ZCAPM is based on the mean-variance parabola of Markowitz (1959) and general equilibrium principles of Sharpe's (1964) CAPM and Black's (1972) zero-beta CAPM. Importantly, the theoretical ZCAPM proposes asymmetric return dispersion effects on assets, which is captured by *zeta risk*. In view of these dual opposing market forces, we proposed a novel empirical ZCAPM that uses an unobservable binary signal variable to capture positive and negative return dispersion effects on asset returns. In statistical terminology, our ZCAPM is a two-component mixture model, where each component of the mixture model is itself a two-factor regression model comprised of average market return and market return dispersion factors and respective beta risk and zeta risk coefficients.

Since the signal variable cannot be observed by investors and instead is a latent or hidden variable, we employ the expectation-maximization (EM) algorithm to estimate model parameters, including the probability that the signal variable is positive or negative. The EM algorithm is a common statistical methodology in the hard sciences, but only occasionally employed in finance studies. For this reason, we provided step-by-step instructions for estimating the empirical ZCAPM via the EM algorithm.

Readers interested in estimating the empirical ZCAPM can utilize the Matlab code in the Compendium at the end of this book. Also, R programs can be downloaded from GitHub (https://github.com/zcapm). Our R programs for the empirical ZCAPM run considerably faster than the Matlab programs.

Bibliography

Adrian, T., & Rosenberg, J. (2008). Stock returns and volatility: Pricing the short-run and long-run components of market risk. *Journal of Finance, 63*, 2997–3030.

Ambrosio, F. J., & Kinniry, F. M, Jr. (2008). *Stock Market Volatility Measures in Perspective, Investment Counseling and Research*. Valley Forge, PA: The Vanguard Group.

Ang, A., Chen, J., & Xing, Y. (2006). Downside risk. *Review of Financial Studies, 19*, 1191–1239.

Ang, A., Hodrick, R. J., Xing, Y., & Zhang, X. (2006). The cross-section of volatility and expected returns. *Journal of Finance, 61*, 259–299.

Ang, A., Hodrick, R. J., Xing, Y., & Zhang, X. (2009). High idiosyncratic volatility and low returns: International and further U.S. evidence. *Journal of Financial Economics, 91*, 1–23.

Asquith, D., Jones, J., & Kieschnick, R. (1998). Evidence on price stabilization and underpricing in early IPO returns. *Journal of Finance, 53*, 1759–1773.

Bansal, R., Kiku, D., Shaliastovich, I., & Yaron, A. (2012). *Volatility, the macroeconomy, and asset prices* (Working Paper). Duke University and University of Pennsylvania.

Black, F. (1972). Capital market equilibrium with restricted borrowing. *Journal of Business, 45*, 444–454.

Bollerslev, T., Hood, B., Huss, J., & Pedersen, L. H. (2018). Risk everywhere: Modeling and Managing Volatility. *Review of Financial Studies, 31*, 2729–2773.

Bollerslev, T., Li, S. Z., & Zhao, B. (2020). Good volatility, bad volatility, and the cross-section of stock returns. *Journal of Financial and Quantitative Analysis, 55*, 751–781.

Breckenfelder, H.-J., and R. Tédongap, 2012, Asymmetry matters: A high-frequency risk-reward trade-off, Working paper, Stockholm School of Economics.

Brown, K. C., Harlow, W. V., & Tinic, S. M. (1988). Risk aversion, uncertain information, and market efficiency. *Journal of Financial Economics, 22*, 355–385.

Campbell, J. Y., & Hentschel, L. (1992). No news is good news: An asymmetric model of changing volatility in stock returns. *Journal of Financial Economics, 31*, 281–318.

Carhart, M. M. (1997). On persistence in mutual fund performance. *Journal of Finance, 52*, 57–82.

Chang, Y., Christoffersen, P., & Jacobs, K. (2013). Market skewness risk and the cross-section of stock returns. *Journal of Financial Economics, 107*, 46–68.

Chen, Y., Cliff, M., & Zhao, H. (2017). Hedge funds: The good, the bad, and the lucky. *Journal of Financial and Quantitative Analysis, 52*, 1081–1109.

Chichernea, D. C., Holder, A. D., & Petkevich, A. (2015). Does return dispersion explain the accrual and investment anomalies? *Journal of Accounting and Economics, 60*, 133–148.

Choudhry, T., Papadimitriou, F. I., & Shabi, S. (2016). Stock market volatility and business cycle: Evidence from linear and nonlinear causality tests. *Journal of Banking and Finance, 66*, 89–101.

Christie, W., & Huang, R. (1994). The changing functional relation between stock returns and dividend yields. *Journal of Empirical Finance, 1*, 161–191.

Cochrane, J. H. (1996). A cross-sectional test of an investment-based asset pricing model. *Journal of Political Economy, 104*, 572–621.

Cochrane, J. H. (2005). *Asset Pricing* (Rev. ed.). Princeton, NJ: Princeton University Press.

Connolly, R., & Stivers, C. (2003). Momentum and reversals in equity index returns during periods of abnormal turnover and return dispersion. *Journal of Finance, 58*, 1521–1556.

Da, Z., & Schaumburg, E. (2011). *The pricing of volatility risk across asset classes* (Working Paper). University of Notre Dame and Federal Reserve Bank of New York.

Daniel, K., Mota, L., Rottke, S., & Santos, T. (2020). The cross-section of risk and returns. *Review of Financial Studies, 33*, 1927–1979.

Daniel, K., & Titman, S. (2012). Testing factor-model explanations of market anomalies. *Critical Finance Review, 1*, 103–139.

Demirer, R., Gupta, R., Zhihu, L., & Wing-Keung, W. (2019). Equity return dispersion and stock market volatility: Evidence from multivariate linear and nonlinear causality tests. *Sustainability, 11*, 1–15.

Demirer, R., & Jategaonkar, S. P. (2013). The conditional relation between dispersion and return. *Review of Financial Economics, 22*, 125–134.

Dempster, A. P., Laird, N. M., & Rubin, D. B. (1977). Maximum likelihood from incomplete data via the EM algorithm. *Journal of the Royal Statistical Society, 39*, 1–38.

Duffee, G. R. (2001). *Asymmetric cross-sectional dispersion in stock returns: Evidence and implications* (Working Paper). Berkeley: University of California at Berkeley.

Fama, E. F., & French, K. R. (1992). The cross-section of expected stock returns. *Journal of Finance, 47*, 427–465.

Fama, E. F., & French, K. R. (1993). The cross-section of expected returns. *Journal of Financial Economics, 33*, 3–56.

Fama, E. F., & French, K. R. (1995). Size and book-to-market factors in earnings and returns. *Journal of Finance, 50*, 131–156.

Fama, E. F., & French, K. R. (1996). Multifactor explanations of asset pricing anomalies. *Journal of Finance, 51*, 55–84.

Fama, E. F., & French, K. R. (2015). A five-factor asset pricing model. *Journal of Financial Economics, 116*, 1–22.

Fama, E. F., & French, K. R. (2018). Choosing factors. *Journal of Financial Economics, 128*, 234–252.
Fama, E. F., & MacBeth, J. D. (1973). Risk, return, and equilibrium: Empirical tests. *Journal of Political Economy, 81*, 607–636.
Farago, A., & Tédongap, R. (2015). *Downside risks and the cross-section of asset returns* (Working Paper). Stockholm School of Economics.
French, K. R., Schwert, G. W., & Stambaugh, R. F. (1987). Expected stock returns and volatility. *Journal of Financial Economics, 19*, 3–29.
Garcia, R., Mantilla-Garcia, D., & Martellini, L. (2014). A model-free measure of aggregate idiosyncratic volatility and the prediction of market returns. *Journal of Financial and Quantitative Analysis, 49*, 1133–1165.
Gomes, J., Kogan, L., & Zhang, L. (2003). Equilibrium cross section of returns. *Journal of Political Economy, 111*, 693–732.
Harvey, C. R., & Liu, Y. (2016). *Rethinking performance evaluation* (Working Paper No. 22134). Cambridge, MA: National Bureau of Economic Research.
Haugen, R. A., Talmer, E., & Torous, W. N. (1991). The effect of volatility changes on the level of stock prices and subsequent expected returns. *Journal of Finance, 46*, 985–1007.
Jahankhani, A. (1976). E-V and E-S capital asset pricing models: Some empirical tests. *Journal of Financial and Quantitative Analysis, 11*, 513–528.
Jiang, X. (2010). Return dispersion and expected returns. *Financial Markets and Portfolio Management, 24*, 107–135.
Jones, P. N., & McLachlan, G. J. (1990). Algorithm AS 254: Maximum likelihood estimation from grouped and truncated data with finite normal mixture models. *Applied Statistics, 39*, 273–282.
Kon, S. (1984). Models of stock returns: A comparison. *Journal of Finance, 39*, 147–165.
Levi, Y., & Welch, I. (2018). *Market-beta and downside risk* (Working Paper). University of Southern California and University of California at Los Angeles.
Lewellen, J., Nagel, S., & Shanken, J. A. (2010). A skeptical appraisal of asset pricing tests. *Journal of Financial Economics, 96*, 175–194.
Liu, W. (2013). *A new asset pricing model based on the zero-beta CAPM: Theory and Evidence* (Doctoral dissertation). Texas A&M University.
Liu, W., Kolari, J. W., & Huang, J. Z. (2012). *A new asset pricing model based on the zero-beta CAPM*. Atlanta, GA (October): Presentation at the annual meetings of the Financial Management Association.
Liu, W., Kolari, J. W., & Huang, J. Z. (2020). *Return dispersion and the cross-section of stock returns*. Palm Springs, CA (October): Presentation at the annual meetings of the Southern Finance Association.
Loughran, T., & Ritter, J. R. (2000). Uniformly least powerful tests of market efficiency. *Journal of Financial Economics, 55*, 361–389.

Loungani, P., Rush, M., & Tave, W. (1990). Stock market dispersion and unemployment. *Journal of Monetary Economics, 25*, 367–388.
Markowitz, H. M. (1959). *Portfolio Selection: Efficient Diversification of Investments*. New York, NY: John Wiley & Sons.
McLachlan, G., & Peel, D. (2000). *Finite Mixture Models*. New York, NY: Wiley-Interscience.
McLachlan, G. J., & Krishnan, T. (2008). *The EM Algorithm and Extensions* (2nd ed.). New York, NY: John Wiley & Sons.
Merton, R. C. (1973). An intertemporal capital asset pricing model. *Econometrica, 41*, 867–887.
Pettengill, G. N., Sundaram, S., & Mathur, I. (1995). The conditional relation between beta and returns. *Journal of Financial and Quantitative Analysis, 30*, 101–116.
Rudd, P. (1991). Extensions of estimation methods using the EM algorithm. *Journal of Econometrics, 49*, 305–341.
Savage, S. (2009). *The Flaw of Averages: Why We Underestimate Risk in the Face of Uncertainty*. Hoboken, NJ: John Wiley and Sons.
Sharpe, W. F. (1964). Capital asset prices: A theory of market equilibrium under conditions of risk. *Journal of Finance, 19*, 425–442.
Stivers, C. (2003). Firm-level return dispersion and the future volatility of aggregate stock market returns. *Journal of Financial Markets, 6*, 389–411.
Verousis, T., & Voukelators, N. (2015). *Cross-sectional dispersion an expected returns, 5th Annual Conference of the Financial Engineering and Banking Society*. France: Nantes.
Wu, J. (1983). On the convergence properties of the EM algorithm. *Annals of Statistics, 11*, 95–103.
Zhang, X. F. (2006). Information uncertainty and stock returns. *Journal of Finance, 61*, 105–136.

PART IV

Empirical Evidence

CHAPTER 5

Stock Return Data and Empirical Methods

Abstract This chapter gives methodological details of our sample data and empirical tests that will be used in forthcoming chapters. A large time series of common stock returns over 50 years is employed for all U.S. stocks in the CRSP database. Based on estimating the empirical ZCAPM, we provide preliminary evidence on the relation between out-of-sample (one-month-ahead) returns of stock portfolios sorted by estimated beta and zeta risks. Across different beta quintiles, equal-weighted portfolios reveal a strong relation between zeta risk and one-month-ahead stock returns. Consistent with previous studies on the empirical failure of the CAPM, no relation between beta risk and one-month-ahead stock returns is evident. Also, we review empirical test methods of asset pricing models using out-of-sample Fama and MacBeth (1973) cross-sectional regression analyses. A number of popular asset pricing models are specified that are used as benchmarks to evaluate our ZCAPM in forthcoming chapters. Finally, time-series and cross-sectional regression models for empirical ZCAPM analyses are specified.

Keywords Asset pricing, beta risk · CAPM · Carhart · Cross-sectional tests · Fama and MacBeth · Fama and French · Market price of risk · Multifactor models · Return dispersion · Securities investment · Stock market · Time-series regression model · ZCAPM · Zero-beta CAPM · Zeta risk

J. W. Kolari et al., *A New Model of Capital Asset Prices*,
https://doi.org/10.1007/978-3-030-65197-8_5

5.1 In-Sample Versus Out-of-Sample Tests

Researchers utilize both in-sample and out-of-sample tests of asset pricing models. In-sample tests are strictly ex post in the sense that all information (e.g., returns and beta risk) is observed by the researcher, investor, etc. For example, a 50-year period of U.S. stock returns could be used to estimate CAPM betas via the market model for each portfolio of stocks or individual stock. Subsequently, these betas can be related in-sample to the average returns of the portfolios over the entire sample period. This backward-looking approach gives a historical record of average beta and average returns over time.

By contrast, out-of-sample tests are closer to an investable strategy by a market participant. Information is observed in some period to estimate (for example) beta risk and, thereafter, returns in the next period are related to previously estimated betas. In effect, backward-looking risk measures are associated with forward-looking returns. According to Simin (2008, p. 356), out-of-sample test procedures in asset pricing analyses tend to reduce a number of evaluation problems, such as data snooping, inappropriate use of R^2 to measure predictability, and risk premium estimation issues. Moreover, Ferson et al. (2013) have concluded that the relative validity of different asset pricing models is best judged using out-of-sample tests. Out-of-sample tests clearly constitute a higher hurdle than in-sample tests in the evaluation of a prospective model. For these reasons, we emphasize out-of-sample tests that are more relevant to making investment decisions as well as judging different asset pricing models than in-sample tests.

For empirical ZCAPM cross-sectional tests in forthcoming chapters, we estimate beta and zeta coefficients in a 12-month period of time using daily returns, and then test whether realized returns in the next month are associated with the earlier estimated beta and zeta coefficients. If a strong association is found, we infer that the ZCAPM is a valid asset pricing model. Comparative analyses with respect to other popular asset pricing models are used to evaluate the relative efficacy of the ZCAPM. As we will see, the empirical ZCAPM consistently dominates other models in virtually all out-of-sample tests, in many cases by a large margin.

5.2 Sample Data

We downloaded daily and monthly value-weighted returns for U.S. common stocks from the Chicago Research in Security Prices (CRSP) database. Our sample period covers over a half century from July 1963 to December

2018, in which cross-sectional tests are conducted in the analysis period January 1965 to December 2018. We proxy mean market returns R_{at} and riskless returns R_{ft} using value-weighted CRSP index returns and U.S. Treasury bill rates, respectively, on day t. As discussed in Chapter 4, previous researchers estimate beta risk using the CRSP index to proxy market portfolio M returns in Sharpe's (1964) CAPM denoted as R_{mt}. In the ZCAPM, beta risk is also related to CRSP index, but this index is associated with average market returns R_{at} on the axis of symmetry of the mean-variance parabola, rather than proxy market portfolio returns R_{mt} in the CAPM.

Descriptive statistics for U.S. stock returns in our analysis period from January 1965 to December 2018 are reported in Table 5.1.[1] In Panel A we see that the average monthly return for the CRSP index is 0.88% compared to 0.38% for the Treasury bill, such that the average market risk premium is 0.50% per month. In Panel B we see that the daily average market return is 0.04% compared to 1.81% for the daily average cross-sectional standard deviation of returns (i.e., return dispersion denoted *RD*). Hence, on a daily basis, *RD* is quite large compared to mean market returns. Given their large differences in magnitude, it is not surprising that the correlation between these two ZCAPM factors is only 0.07. This low correlation suggests that they contain different market information.

Table 5.1 also reports the average monthly returns for Fama and French's (1992, 1993, 1995, 2015, 2018) size, value, momentum, profit, and capital investment factors downloaded from Kenneth French's website.[2] These factors have the following average monthly returns: SMB = 0.25%, HML = 0.32%, MOM = 0.67%, RMW = 0.26%, and CMA = 0.28%, respectively. Although these mean values are positive for all factors, they are negative in many months in our analysis period. By contrast, our return dispersion factor is always positive from day-to-day over time.

We employ a variety of different U.S. common stock portfolios in cross-sectional tests of the proposed empirical ZCAPM. Following many asset pricing studies, as originally constructed by Fama and French (1992), we utilize 25 size-B/M sorted portfolios. Also, we include 47 industry portfolios. In Subsect. 2.3.1 of Chapter 2, we noted that industry portfolios are recommended by Lewellen et al. (2010), Daniel and Titman (2012), and

[1] Our total sample period includes the year 1964 in which we estimate time-series regressions of different asset pricing models. In the analyses period, starting in January 1965, we conduct out-of-sample (one-month-ahead) cross-sectional regression analyses of the models.

[2] See https://mba.tuck.dartmouth.edu/pages/faculty/ken.french/data_library.

Table 5.1 Descriptive statistics for the analysis period January 1965 to December 2018

Panel A. Monthly data (percent)				
	Mean	Std dev	Min	Max
R_f	0.38	0.27	0	1.35
R_a	0.88	4.44	−22.64	16.61
SMB	0.25	3.06	−14.91	18.32
HML	0.32	2.83	−11.18	12.87
MOM	0.67	4.24	−34.39	18.36
RMW	0.26	2.19	−18.33	13.33
CMA	0.28	2.01	−6.86	9.56
Panel B. Daily data (percent)				
	Mean	Std dev	Min	Max
R_f	0.018	0.01	0	0.06
R_a	0.042	0.99	−17.41	11.35
$\sigma_a(RD)$	1.814	0.62	0.76	10.77
SMB	0.009	0.52	−11.17	6.08
HML	0.016	0.50	−4.22	4.83
MOM	0.031	0.71	−8.22	7.05
RMW	0.013	0.37	−2.92	4.40
CMA	0.014	0.37	−5.93	2.53

Average monthly returns (Panel A) and average daily returns (Panel B) are contained in this table. Variables are defined as follows (in percent terms): R_f (riskless rate) = U.S. Treasury bill return, R_a (average market return) = value-weighted CRSP common stock index return, σ_a (return dispersion denoted *RD*) = cross-sectional standard deviation of daily value-weighted returns for all CRSP common stocks, *SMB* (size factor) = small minus big firms' stock returns, *HML* (value factor) = high B/M minus low B/M firms' stock returns, *MOM* (momentum factor) = high past return stocks minus low past return stocks, *RMW* (profit factor) = robust operating profitability minus weak operating profitability returns, and *CMA* (capital investment factor) = conservative investment minus aggressive investment returns. With the exception of σ_m, which is computed using daily CRSP stock returns, data series are downloaded from Kenneth French's website for the period 1965 to 2018

others as exogenous test assets unrelated to proposed factors in asset pricing tests.[3] Daily and monthly returns for these portfolios are downloaded from French's website.

Another set of 25 portfolios is created by estimating the empirical ZCAPM specified in Eq. (4.12) in Chapter 4 and then forming 5 × 5 quintile sorts for all CRSP stocks' estimated beta and zeta coefficients (i.e., within each quintile rank of beta coefficients, quintile ranks of zeta coeffi-

[3] Lewellen et al. discerned that size-B/M sorted portfolios suffer from endogeneity problems when testing Fama and French's three-factor model containing size and B/M (value) factors.

cients are formed).[4] To do this, using the daily return series, we begin by estimating the empirical ZCAPM for the 6-month period from July 1963 to December 1963. Estimated parameter values are used to sort stocks into 25 beta-zeta sorted portfolios, and average value-weighted daily and monthly returns for these portfolios are computed in the next month January 1964. Daily returns for the entire 6-month estimation period and next month, as well as stock prices more than \$1, are required to include a stock in these portfolios. The process is repeated by rolling forward one month at a time to generate return series for the 25 beta-zeta sorted portfolios in the period from January 1964 to December 2018.

We provide descriptive statistics for these 25 beta-zeta risk portfolios in Tables 5.2 and 5.3 and related Figs. 5.1 and 5.2. Table 5.2 documents their one-month-ahead average value-weighted returns (Panel A), excess returns over the average one-month Treasury bill rate (Panel B), and standard deviation of monthly returns (Panel C) over the analysis period from January 1965 to December 2018.

In Panel A of Table 5.2, we see that average returns tend to be higher among high zeta risk (Z^*) portfolios compared to low zeta risk portfolios. The high β portfolios exhibit the strongest relation in this regard, as average returns increase from −0.09% per month for the low Z^* portfolio to 1.12% for the high Z^* portfolio. Figure 5.1 illustrates this strong relation between average returns and zeta risk among high β portfolios. One reason for this finding is that high β portfolios contain more small market capitalization stocks than other β portfolios. This inference is supported by the standard deviation of returns in Panel C. The high β portfolios have substantially higher standard deviations than the other lower beta risk portfolios. This high total risk can be attributed to their small size. Hence, we infer that other beta risk portfolios contain a greater mixture of small and large stocks, such that their value-weighted returns are skewed by larger stocks. In these portfolios it is difficult to see a clear pattern between average stock returns and zeta risk due to the confounding effects of large size on value-weighted returns.

[4] A set of 100 portfolios was created using 10 × 10 sorts on estimated beta and zeta coefficients, but the results were unchanged for the most part. Sorting stocks on factor loadings follows Black et al. (1972) and Fama and MacBeth (1973), who sort stocks into portfolios based on betas. Sorts on factor loadings should form portfolios that have a spread in average returns. Conversely, there are some potential criticisms of this approach to creating test assets, including data mining, invalid tests of market premiums, and spurious risk factor problems (see Lo and MacKinlay 1990; MacKinlay 1995; Ferson et al. 1999).

Table 5.2 Average out-of-sample, value-weighted monthly returns for 25 beta-zeta risk sorted portfolios in the period January 1965 to December 2018

Panel A. Average returns (percent)					
	Low Z^*	2	3	4	High Z^*
Low β	0.70	0.86	0.86	0.81	0.79
2	0.93	0.96	0.86	0.97	0.84
3	0.91	0.95	0.93	0.85	0.92
4	0.65	0.89	0.83	0.89	0.99
High β	−0.09	0.45	0.67	0.85	1.12
Panel B. Average excess returns (percent)					
	Low Z^*	2	3	4	High Z^*
Low β	0.31	0.47	0.48	0.43	0.41
2	0.55	0.57	0.48	0.58	0.45
3	0.52	0.57	0.55	0.46	0.54
4	0.27	0.51	0.45	0.50	0.60
High β	−0.48	0.06	0.29	0.47	0.73
Panel C. Standard deviation (percent)					
	Low Z^*	2	3	4	High Z^*
Low β	5.80	3.74	3.29	3.60	4.45
2	5.37	4.21	3.69	3.66	3.98
3	6.20	4.91	4.42	4.38	4.55
4	7.66	6.24	5.58	5.34	5.43
High β	10.09	8.34	7.59	7.34	7.95

This table reports the average value-weighted monthly returns (in percent) for 25 portfolios sorted on estimated beta and zeta coefficients in the ZCAPM. These coefficients are estimated in the prior 6-month period using daily returns. Out-of-sample returns are computed for each portfolio in the one-month-period ahead of the 6-month estimation period. The estimation period is rolled forward one month at a time and a monthly time series of returns for each portfolio is generated in the analysis period 1965 to 2018. Averages of these monthly times-series returns are computed (Panel A), in addition to their excess returns over the average one-month Treasury bill rate (Panel B), and the time-series standard deviation of monthly returns (Panel C)

To remove the influence of large stocks on portfolio returns, equal-weighted return results are reported in Table 5.3 and Figure 5.2. As shown in Table 5.3, now the positive relation between average returns and zeta risk is obvious across beta risk portfolios. In all rows with different beta (β) portfolios, not only for high β portfolios, average returns noticeably increase from low Z^* to high Z^* portfolios. Figure 5.2 clearly depicts the positive relation between average returns and zeta risk across different beta risk portfolios. We infer that, after removing the influence of size in average returns, a strong positive effect of zeta risk on stock returns is apparent.

Table 5.3 Average out-of-sample, equal-weighted monthly returns for 25 beta-zeta risk sorted portfolios in the period January 1965 to December 2018

Panel A. Average returns (percent)					
	Low Z*	2	3	4	High Z*
Low β	0.51	0.86	0.83	0.90	1.01
2	0.98	1.13	1.09	1.09	1.16
3	0.89	1.17	1.16	1.16	1.29
4	0.79	1.07	1.11	1.15	1.30
High β	0.34	0.64	0.72	0.86	1.06
Panel B. Average excess returns (percent)					
	Low Z*	2	3	4	High Z*
Low β	0.12	0.48	0.45	0.52	0.63
2	0.60	0.75	0.71	0.70	0.78
3	0.51	0.78	0.78	0.77	0.90
4	0.41	0.68	0.73	0.76	0.91
High β	−0.05	0.25	0.33	0.48	0.68
Panel C. Standard deviation (percent)					
	Low Z*	2	3	4	High Z*
Low β	6.13	3.69	3.19	3.21	4.41
2	6.20	4.38	3.93	3.86	4.25
3	6.89	5.32	4.90	4.77	4.99
4	8.25	6.47	5.98	5.65	5.99
High β	10.67	8.59	7.89	7.61	7.91

This table reports the average equal-weighted monthly returns (in percent) for 25 portfolios sorted on estimated beta and zeta coefficients in the ZCAPM. These coefficients are estimated in the prior 6-month period using daily returns. Out-of-sample returns are computed for each portfolio in the one-month-period ahead of the 6-month estimation period. The estimation period is rolled forward one month at a time and a monthly time series of returns for each portfolio is generated in the analysis period 1965 to 2018. Averages of these monthly times-series returns are computed (Panel A), in addition to their excess returns over the average one-month Treasury bill rate (Panel B), and the time-series standard deviation of monthly returns (Panel C)

Focusing on the columns in Panel A of Table 5.2, it is obvious that no relation exists between beta risk (β) and average value-weighted returns. Indeed, in the first three columns, low β portfolios have average returns greater than the high β portfolios, which disagrees with the hypothesized positive beta relation in the CAPM. In Panel B average excess returns follow similar patterns. Likewise, in Table 5.3 using equal-weighted returns, no positive relation between beta risk and average returns emerges.

Lastly, we gathered additional test asset portfolios for the purpose of robustness checks to further corroborate our cross-sectional test findings for the ZCAPM. In Chapter 7 we utilize test assets formed on different size

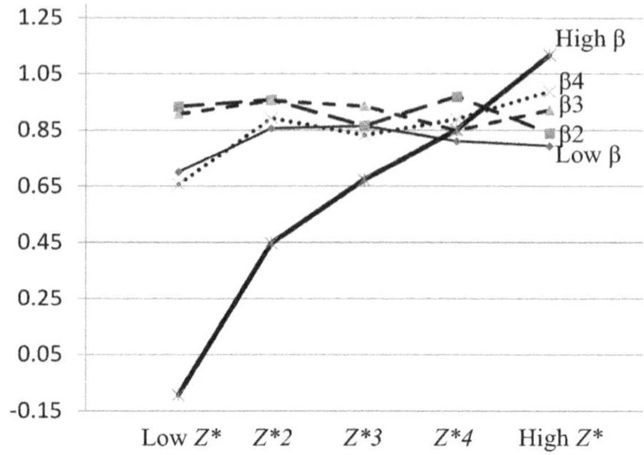

Fig. 5.1 Average out-of-sample, value-weighted monthly returns are shown for 25 beta-zeta portfolios. Zeta risk portfolios are sorted into quintiles from low to high within each beta risk quintile portfolio. The analysis period is January 1965 to December 2018

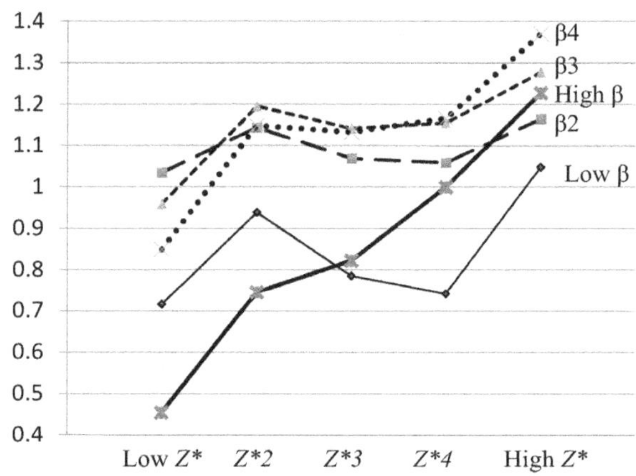

Fig. 5.2 Average out-of-sample, equal-weighted monthly returns are shown for 25 beta-zeta risk portfolios. Zeta risk portfolios are sorted into quintiles from low to high within each beta risk quintile portfolio. The analysis period is January 1965 to December 2018

groups (i.e., microcap stocks in the bottom quintile of market capitalization versus larger stocks), profit and investment firm characteristics in recent work by Fama and French (2015, 2018), and individual common stocks that are among the largest 500 stocks by market capitalization.

5.3 Cross-Sectional Tests

To conduct formal cross-sectional tests of the empirical ZCAPM compared to other asset pricing models, we employ the renowned Fama and MacBeth (1973) test procedure. This cross-sectional test has been implemented to evaluate the validity of virtually every asset pricing model in the literature. As ascertained by Fama and French (2020, p. 1891), factors in time-series models are normally selected based on their success in cross-sectional tests. We implement the standard monthly rolling Fama and MacBeth approach with month-by-month estimates of the market prices of risk based on factor loadings and excess returns in each month of the analysis period. Out-of-sample cross-sectional tests are conducted using one-month-ahead portfolio returns. As discussed earlier, the practical utility of asset pricing models is best judged in out-of-sample (rather than in-sample) tests wherein model parameters are estimated with data before one-month-ahead returns.

According to the Fama and MacBeth procedure, in the first step we estimate the following time-series regression for each asset pricing model:

$$R_{it} - R_{ft} = \alpha_i + \beta_{i,1} F_{1t} + \beta_{i,2} F_{2t} + \cdots + \beta_{i,K} F_{Kt} + e_{it}, \tag{5.1}$$

where R_{it} is the realized return on the ith stock portfolio (or stock) at time t, R_{ft} is the riskless rate (e.g., Treasury bill rate), α_i is the intercept term, $F_{1t}, F_{2t}, \ldots, F_{Kt}$ are $k = 1, \ldots, K$ asset pricing factors, $\beta_{i,1}, \beta_{i,2}, \ldots, \beta_{i,K}$ are corresponding $k = 1, \ldots, K$ beta risk loadings for the ith stock portfolios (or stocks), $e_{it} \sim$ iid $\mathrm{N}(0, \sigma_i^2)$, $t = 1, \ldots, T$ is the estimation period, and $i = 1, \ldots, N$ is the number of stock portfolios (or stocks) used as test assets. Factors F_{kt} are most commonly zero-investment portfolios comprised of long-minus-short holdings in stocks with various firm and other characteristics, which are defined below for popular asset pricing models.

In the second step of the Fama and MacBeth procedure, using estimates of betas from time-series regression (5.1), we estimate the following out-of-sample cross-sectional relation:

$$R_{iT+1} - R_{fT+1} = \lambda_0 + \lambda_1 \hat{\beta}_{i,1} + \lambda_2 \hat{\beta}_{i,2} + \cdots + \lambda_K \hat{\beta}_{i,K} + u_{iT+1}, \quad i = 1, \ldots, N, \tag{5.2}$$

where R_{iT+1} is the realized return on the ith stock portfolio (or stock) in out-of-sample time period $T+1$ (e.g., one-month-ahead), R_{fT+1} is the riskless rate, $\hat{\beta}_{i,1}, \hat{\beta}_{i,2}, \ldots, \hat{\beta}_{i,K}$ are $k = 1, \ldots, K$ beta risk loadings estimated using Eq. (5.1) for $i = 1, \ldots, N$ stock portfolios (or stocks) in the prior estimation period $t = 1, \ldots, T$, λ_0 is the intercept term,[5] $\lambda_1, \lambda_2, \ldots, \lambda_K$ are correponding estimated $k = 1, \ldots, K$ market prices of beta risk loadings, and $u_{iT+1} \sim$ iid $N(0, \sigma_i^2)$. The null hypotheses are: $E(\lambda_0) = 0$ (i.e., no mispricing or omitted risk factors), and $E(\lambda_1), E(\lambda_2), \ldots, E(\lambda_K)$ correspond to expected risk premiums associated with each factor.

As recognized by Ferson (2019, p. 223), cross-sectional regressions automatically construct a mimicking portfolio for each λ_k that is long the high-risk-loading assets minus short the low-risk loading assets. Hence, for the kth factor, regardless of whether it is traded (e.g., zero-investment factors) or nontraded,[6] its estimated risk premium λ_k approximates the return on the factor mimicking portfolio. In this regard, Koijen et al. (2017) have empirically demonstrated that cross-sectional risk premiums are linked to systematic time-series regression factors. Citing their work, Lettau and Pelger (2020, p. 2275) argued that a close connection exists between systematic factors in Eq. (5.1) and risk premiums in Eq. (5.2).

Similar to Bali et al. (2017), time-series model (5.1) is estimated using one-year of daily returns. In the first step, starting with daily returns in the year 1964, we estimate model (5.1). In the second step, we estimate cross-sectional relation (5.2) in January 1965. The estimation period for the time-series model is rolled forward one month, and the cross-sectional test is repeated in February 1965. This procedure is rolled forward one month at a time until December 2018. We retain monthly time series of 648 estimated out-of-sample factor prices of risk $\hat{\lambda}_k$ for the kth factor from January 1965 to December 2018. These series are used to compute the average values of $\hat{\lambda}_k$

[5] Fama and French (2020, p. 1892) have defined λ_0 as the common return in month $T+1$ among the test asset porfolios not explained by the independent variables in the regression equation.

[6] According to Ferson (2019), if a nontraded firm characteristic such as the book-to-market equity ratio were used in place of its beta on the right-hand-side of a cross-sectional regression, the estimated λ_k would be a long/short mimicking portfolio return (i.e., long high ratio stocks and short low ratio stocks). In a recent paper, Fama and French (2020) used this approach to cross-sectionally estimate mimicking portfolio returns for any given month for characteristic values of size, value, profit, and capital investment, in addition to tradeable momentum returns. They then inserted the time-series of mimicking portfolio returns as factors (i.e., X variables) in the time-series regression model.

in percent per month and associated t-statistics. Cochrane (2005, pp. 250–251) has commented that t-statistics associated with $\hat{\lambda}_k$s are corrected for cross-sectional correlation of residual errors in the monthly rolling Fama–MacBeth approach, which are equivalent to Shanken (1992) corrected OLS standard errors.

Lastly, consistent with Jagannathan and Wang (1996) and Lettau and Ludvigson (2001, footnote 17, p. 1254), we evaluate the goodness-of-fit of the cross-sectional regressions using the R^2 statistic from the single regression approach. Regarding the latter approach, average monthly returns for all test asset stock portfolios (or stocks) in the sample period are regressed on their average monthly estimates of $\hat{\lambda}_K$ (i.e., 648 monthly estimates in which we compute average returns for each test asset as well as their average market prices of K risk factors). This approach is consistent with Cochrane (1996), who proposed that goodness-of-fit can be assessed for a model by plotting a simple graph of average realized returns (Y-axis) and average predicted returns (X-axis).[7]

5.4 Benchmark Time-Series Multifactor Models

To evaluate the performance of the ZCAPM, we benchmark our results against five popular models[8]:

- CAPM market model with excess market returns defined as proxy market returns R_{mt} (value-weighted CRSP index returns) minus riskless rates R_{ft} (Treasury bill rates);
- Fama and French's (1992, 1993, 1995) three-factor model based on augmenting the CAPM market model with a size factor (viz., small minus large firms' stock returns, or *SMB*) and value factor (viz., high B/M minus low B/M firms' stock returns, or *HML*);
- Carhart's (1997) four-factor model based on augmenting the three-factor model with a momentum factor (viz., firms with high past return stock returns minus low past stock returns, or *MOM*);

[7] Ferson (2019, p. 227) has noted that the average of the cross-sectional regression R^2 values for all sample period months is reported by many researchers but is unreliable as a measure of goodness-of-fit.

[8] In forthcoming robustness checks in Chapter 7, we also test recently proposed four-factor models by Hou et al. (2015) and Stambaugh and Yuan (2017).

- Fama and French's (2015) five-factor model based on augmenting their three-factor model with a profit factor (viz., robust operating profitability minus weak operating profitability returns, or *RMW*) and capital investment factor (viz., conservative investment minus aggressive investment returns, or *CMA*); and
- Fama and French's (2018) six-factor model based on augmenting their five-factor model with a momentum factor.

It is worth noting that none of the zero-investment factors in the Fama and French and Carhart models, including *SMB*, *HML*, *MOM*, *RMW*, and *CMA*, can be implemented in the real world. The main problem is that large short positions are required which would be difficult to create or manage by an investor on a daily or monthly basis over time. Hence, so-called *multifactors* are best viewed as theoretical portfolios rather than investable portfolios. Even so, these multifactors are the most widely accepted factors among academics and practitioners around the world. Using the above Fama and French as well as Carhart models as benchmarks against which to evaluate our ZCAPM in forthcoming comparative tests in Chapters 6 and 7 is a high bar to clear. If the ZCAPM outperforms these state-of-the-art models, it most certainly deserves recognition.

It may be possible to construct proxies for multifactors by forming long and short positions in exchange traded funds (ETFs). Nowadays there are many ETFs that span different investment styles as well as bull and bear funds that correspond to long and short portfolios, respectively. To the authors' knowledge, no research has been published on this possibility to determine if proxy ETF factors can price stocks as well as theoretical zero-investment factors.

Unlike multifactor models, the CAPM market model is based on an investable zero-investment portfolio—namely, long CRSP value-weighted index and short Treasury bills. Our empirical ZCAPM utilizes this investable long-CRSP-index/short-Treasury-bill portfolio as one key factor that proxies average excess market returns (rather than market portfolio *M*'s excess return in the context of the CAPM). The ZCAPM's other key factor is the cross-sectional standard deviation of individual stocks' returns in the CRSP index (return dispersion or *RD*). The latter factor is not investable but is a macro state variable that investors can readily compute on a daily basis.

5.5 Time-Series and Cross-Sectional Regressions for the ZCAPM

In Chapter 3 we mathematically derived the *theoretical ZCAPM* as a special case of Black's (1972) zero-beta CAPM.[9] As specified there in Eq. (3.33), the expected return on the ith asset is:

$$E(R_{it}) - R_{ft} = \beta_{i,a}[E(R_{at}) - R_{ft}] + Z^{*}_{i,a}\sigma_{at}, \tag{5.3}$$

where $E(R_{at})$ is the expected market return based on the average return of all assets at time t (rather than a proxy m for the theoretical market portfolio M), R_{ft} is the riskless rate, $\beta_{i,a}$ is the beta risk coefficient measuring sensitivity to expected excess market returns, σ_{at} is the cross-sectional standard deviation of all asset returns (or return dispersion denoted RD) at time t, and $Z^{*}_{i,a}$ is the zeta risk coefficient measuring dichotomous positive or negative sensitivity to return dispersion.[10] The asterisk on $Z^{*}_{i,a}$ denotes its relation to orthogonal portfolios I^{*} and ZI^{*} on the mean-variance investment parabola. Zero-beta portfolio ZI^{*} and efficient portfolio I^{*} are unique due to their equal return variances.

To model the dual opposing effects of RD on asset returns, we allowed the sign of the zeta risk coefficient in ZCAPM relation (5.3) to change over time. The following *empirical ZCAPM* was specified as a time-series regression model[11]:

$$R_{it} - R_{ft} = \beta_{i,a}(R_{at} - R_{ft}) + Z_{i,a}D_{it}\sigma_{at} + u_{it}, \quad t = 1, \ldots, T \tag{5.4}$$

where $R_{it} - R_{ft}$ is the excess return for the ith stock portfolio (or stock) over the riskless rate at time t, $\beta_{i,a}$ measures sensitivity to excess average market returns equal to $R_{at} - R_{ft}$, $Z_{i,a}$ measures sensitivity to return dispersion σ_{at} (or RD), D_{it} is a signal variable with values $+1$ and -1 representing positive and negative RD effects on stock returns, respectively, and $u_{it} \sim$ iid $N(0, \sigma_i^2)$. As discussed in Chapter 4, among other reasons, no mispricing error is included (i.e., $\alpha_i = 0$) in Eq. (5.4) due to our emphasis on out-of-sample cross-sectional results, rather than in-sample time-series regression analyses.

[9] See earlier work in Liu et al. (2012) and Liu (2013).

[10] Since RD is a nontraded factor, we designate its factor loading as Z rather than β to distinguish it from commonly used tradable zero-investment factors.

[11] See also Liu et al. (2020).

Since we do not know a priori the value of signal variable D_{it}, it is a latent or hidden variable. However, we can define D_{it} as an independent random variable with the following two-point distribution:

$$D_{it} = \begin{cases} +1 & \text{with probability } p_i \\ -1 & \text{with probability } 1 - p_i, \end{cases} \tag{5.5}$$

where p_i (or $1 - p_i$) is the probability of a positive (or negative) return dispersion effect, and D_{it} are independent of u_{it}. To estimate parameters $\theta_i = (\beta_{i,a}, Z_{i,a}, p_i)$, we utilize an expectation–maximization (EM) algorithm (see Dempster et al. 1977).[12]

As specified in Eq. (4.12) of Chapter 4, given that $E(D_{it}) = 2p_i - 1$, the marginal form of the empirical ZCAPM is:

$$R_{it} - R_{ft} = \beta_{i,a}(R_{at} - R_{ft}) + Z^*_{i,a}\sigma_{at} + u^*_{it}, \quad t = 1, \ldots, T, \tag{5.6}$$

where $\beta_{i,a}$ is the beta risk coefficient, $Z^*_{i,a} = Z_{i,a}(2p_i - 1)$ is the zeta risk coefficient, u^*_{it} is the error term with variance dependent on return dispersion as shown in Eq. (4.13), and other notation is as before.

Using estimates of beta and zeta risk coefficients from time-series regression (5.6) above, we estimate the following cross-sectional OLS regression:

$$R_{i,T+1} - R_{fT+1} = \lambda_0 + \lambda_a\hat{\beta}_{i,a} + \lambda_{RD}\hat{Z}^*_{i,a} + u_{it}, i = 1, \ldots, N, \tag{5.7}$$

where the coefficients denoted λ_a and λ_{RD} provide estimates of the market prices of the beta and zeta risk factors in percent terms, respectively, and other notation is as before. Referring to our earlier discussion of Eq. (5.2), the estimated risk premium λ_a (λ_{RD}) approximates a mimicking portfolio return that is long stocks with higher betas (zetas) and short stocks with lower betas (zetas).

Beta loadings are benchmarked to one on average for the average market index but not zeta loadings. For this reason, it is important to interpret $\hat{\lambda}_{RD}$ associated with RD as the risk premium per unit zeta risk. Also, beta loadings are time invariant for the most part as similar estimated values are obtained using daily versus monthly returns. By comparison, zeta

[12] See Chapter 4 for detailed discussion of the EM algorithm and further citations to literature.

loadings are affected by the holding period used in the time-series regression model.[13] Because zeta loadings are estimated in a time-series regression (5.6) with daily returns, and one-month-ahead excess returns are used as the dependent variable in cross-sectional regression Eq. (5.7), we rescale $\hat{Z}^*_{i,a}$ from a daily to monthly basis as follows:

$$R_{i,T+1} - R_{fT+1} = \lambda_0 + \lambda_a \hat{\beta}_{i,a,} + \lambda_{RD} \hat{Z}^*_{i,a} N_{T+1} + +u_{it}, i = 1, \ldots, N, \quad (5.8)$$

where N_{T+1} is the number of trading days in month $T + 1$ (i.e., 21 days), $\hat{Z}^*_{i,a} N_{T+1}$ is the monthly estimated zeta risk, and λ_{RD} is the monthly risk premium associated with zeta risk. The risk premium $\hat{\lambda}_{RD}$ per unit zeta risk is unchanged by this rescaling. However, without rescaling $\hat{Z}^*_{i,a}$ up to a monthly basis, much larger λ_{RD} estimates would not be comparable to λ_a estimates associated with beta loadings.

Matlab programs for estimating the empirical ZCAPM and conducting cross-sectional regression tests are available at the end of the book in the Compendium. Additionally, R programs for these analyses can be downloaded from GitHub (https://github.com/zcapm). R is a free software environment available on the internet. Our R programs run faster in terms of estimating the empirical ZCAPM than the Matlab programs.

5.6 Summary

A long sample period covering over 50 years was used to gather data for all U.S. common stock returns from the CRSP database. Descriptive statistics for market index returns, riskless rates, and several popular zero-investment factors in our analysis period January 1965 to December 2018 were documented. Also, we constructed beta-zeta risk sorted portfolios using the empirical ZCAPM. One-month-ahead (out-of-sample) value- and equal-weighted returns for these portfolios were computed in the sample period. Our results showed that equal-weighted returns are less confounded with size effects inherent in value-weighted returns. For equal-weighted returns, a strong relation between average returns and zeta risk is apparent, but no such relation is found for beta risk. This preliminary evidence supports the ZCAPM's proposition that returns are increasing in zeta risk.

[13] The invariance of beta to holding period returns can be attributed to the linearity property of returns, i.e., the monthly return is roughly approximated by the sum of 21 daily returns in the month. This linearity does not hold for return dispersion (*RD*).

To test our empirical ZCAPM in forthcoming chapters, we follow standard practices in the asset pricing literature. In this regard, we described widely applied Fama and MacBeth (1973) cross-sectional test methods. These out-of-sample tests estimate the risk parameters of models in an estimation period, and then relate risk parameters to stock returns in the next month. Using this well-known two-step approach, there is no possibility of cheating in tests of different models. As reviewed in this chapter, our ZCAPM results are benchmarked against a number of asset pricing models, including the CAPM market model in addition to popular asset pricing models by Fama and French and other researchers. Both time-series and cross-sectional regression models for the empirical ZCAPM were specified for these purposes.

As we will see in forthcoming Chapters 6 and 7, the ZCAPM consistently outperforms other models across a wide variety of test assets in different sample periods. When industry portfolios are included in the test assets, which are entirely exogenous to asset pricing models due to not containing an industry factor, our ZCAPM does particularly well compared to other models. Also, the ZCAPM outperforms other models using individual stocks as test assets. Our empirical results suggest that the ZCAPM—itself another form of the CAPM in general and zero-beta CAPM in particular—dominates popular multifactor asset pricing models.

Bibliography

Bali, T., & G., R. F. Engle, and Y. Tang,. (2017). Dynamic conditional beta is alive and well in the cross section of daily stock returns. *Management Science, 63*, 3760–3779.

Black, F. (1972). Capital market equilibrium with restricted borrowing. *Journal of Business, 45*, 444–454.

Black, F., Jensen, M. C., & Scholes, M. (1972). The capital asset pricing model: Some empirical tests. In M. C. Jensen (Ed.), *Studies in the Theory of Capital Markets*. New York, NY: Praeger.

Carhart, M. M. (1997). On persistence in mutual fund performance. *Journal of Finance, 52*, 57–82.

Cochrane, J. H. (1996). A cross-sectional test of an investment-based asset pricing model. *Journal of Political Economy, 104*, 572–621.

Cochrane, J. H. (2005). *Asset Pricing* (Revised ed.). Princeton, NJ: Princeton University Press.

Daniel, K., & Titman, S. (2012). Testing factor-model explanations of market anomalies. *Critical Finance Review, 1*, 103–139.

Dempster, A. P., Laird, N. M., & Rubin, D. B. (1977). Maximum likelihood from incomplete data via the EM algorithm. *Journal of the Royal Statistical Society, 39*, 1–38.

Fama, E. F., & French, K. R. (1992). The cross-section of expected stock returns. *Journal of Finance, 47*, 427–465.

Fama, E. F., & French, K. R. (1993). The cross-section of expected returns. *Journal of Financial Economics, 33*, 3–56.

Fama, E. F., & French, K. R. (1995). Size and book-to-market factors in earnings and returns. *Journal of Finance, 50*, 131–156.

Fama, E. F., & French, K. R. (2015). A five-factor asset pricing model. *Journal of Financial Economics, 116*, 1–22.

Fama, E. F., & French, K. R. (2018). Choosing factors. *Journal of Financial Economics, 128*, 234–252.

Fama, E. F., & French, K. R. (2020). Comparing cross-section and time-series factor models. *Review of Financial Studies, 33*, 1892–1926.

Fama, E. F., & MacBeth, J. D. (1973). Risk, return, and equilibrium: Empirical tests. *Journal of Political Economy, 81*, 607–636.

Ferson, W. E. (2019). *Empirical Asset Pricing: Models and Methods.* Cambridge, MA: The MIT Press.

Ferson, W. E., Nallareddy, S. K., & Xie, B. (2013). The "out-of-sample" performance of long-run risk models. *Journal of Financial Economics, 107*, 537–556.

Ferson, W. E., Sarkissian, S., Simin, T., & T.,. (1999). The alpha factor asset pricing model: A parable. *Journal of Financial Markets, 2*, 49–68.

Hou, K., Xue, C., & Zhang, L. (2015). Digesting anomalies: An investment approach. *Review of Financial Studies, 28*, 650–705.

Jagannathan, R., & Wang, Z. (1996). The conditional CAPM and the cross-section of asset returns. *Journal of Finance, 51*, 3–53.

Koijen, R. S., Lustig, H., & Van Nieuwerburgh, S. (2017). The cross-section and time series of stock and bond returns. *Journal of Monetary Economics, 88*, 50–69.

Lettau, M., & Ludvigson, S. (2001). Consumption, aggregate wealth, and expected stock returns. *Journal of Finance, 56*, 815–849.

Lettau, M., & Pelger, M. (2020). Factors that fit the time series and cross-section of stock returns. *Review of Financial Studies, 33*, 2274–2325.

Lewellen, J., Nagel, S., & Shanken, J. A. (2010). A skeptical appraisal of asset pricing tests. *Journal of Financial Economics, 96*, 175–194.

Liu, W., 2013, *A New Asset Pricing Model Based on the Zero-Beta CAPM: Theory and Evidence*, Doctoral dissertation, Texas A&M University.

Liu, W., Kolari, J. W., & Huang, J. Z. (2012). *A new asset pricing model based on the zero-beta CAPM.* Atlanta, GA (October): Presentation at the annual meetings of the Financial Management Association.

Liu, W., Kolari, J. W., & Huang, J. Z. (2020). *Return dispersion and the cross-section of stock returns.* Palm Springs, CA (October): Presentation at the annual meetings of the Southern Finance Association.

Lo, A. W., & MacKinlay, A. C. (1990). Data snooping in tests of financial asset pricing models. *Review of Financial Studies, 3*, 431–467.

MacKinlay, A. C. (1995). Multifactor models do not explain deviations from the CAPM. *Journal of Financial Economics, 38*, 3–28.

Shanken, J. (1992). On the estimation of beta pricing models. *Review of Financial Studies, 5*, 1–34.

Sharpe, W. F. (1964). Capital asset prices: A theory of market equilibrium under conditions of risk. *Journal of Finance, 19*, 425–442.

Simin, T. (2008). The poor performance of asset pricing models. *Journal of Financial and Quantitative Analysis, 43*, 335–380.

Stambaugh, R. F., & Yuan, Y. (2017). Mispricing factors. *Review of Financial Studies, 30*, 1270–1315.

CHAPTER 6

Empirical Tests of the ZCAPM

Abstract This chapter presents evidence in support of the empirical ZCAPM. Based on U.S. common stock returns in the period January 1965 to December 2018, across a variety of test asset portfolios, out-of-sample cross-sectional tests of the traditional approach to specifying return dispersion (*RD*) in an asset pricing model yield insignificant or marginally significant estimated prices of risk in most cases. The failure of this traditional model justifies using the ZCAPM to take into account the symmetric effects of *RD* on stock returns. Graphical analyses of the empirical ZCAPM estimated via the EM algorithm show a close relation between zeta risk and one-month-ahead (out-of-sample) cross-sectional excess returns for a variety of test asset portfolios. Interestingly, zeta risk exhibits strong goodness-of-fit with the one-month-ahead returns of widely used size and book-to-market equity portfolios by Fama and French (1992, 1993). Further graphical results show that the empirical ZCAPM outperforms popular Fama and French (1992, 1993, 1995, 1996, 2015, 2018) three-, five-, and six-factor models in terms of predicting one-month-ahead stock returns, especially among industry portfolios. The latter poor cross-sectional performances of these popular models across different industry portfolios is a major shortfall that appears to be attributable to their inability to add much explanatory power in time-series regressions to the CAPM market model. In sum, graphical evidence based on out-of-sample returns lends strong support for the ZCAPM.

J. W. Kolari et al., *A New Model of Capital Asset Prices*,
https://doi.org/10.1007/978-3-030-65197-8_6

Keywords Asset pricing · Beta risk · CAPM · Cross-sectional tests · Empirical ZCAPM · Expectation–Maximization (EM) algorithm · Fitted returns · Fama and French · Industry portfolios · Multifactor models · Out-of-sample returns · Predicted returns · Return dispersion · Securities investment · Signal variable · Stock market · ZCAPM · Zero-beta CAPM · Zeta risk

6.1 Traditional Model Results

Chapter 4 reviewed previous studies by Jiang (2010), Demirer and Jategaonkar (2013), Garcia et al. (2014), Chichernea et al. (2015), and Verousis and Voukelators (2015) that conducted empirical tests of cross-sectional return dispersion (RD) as an asset pricing factor. In these studies, a straightforward approach is used that augments the market factor with RD. More specifically, as specified earlier in Eq. (4.6) in Chapter 4, the following time-series OLS regression model is estimated in period $t = 1, \cdots, T$:

$$R_{it} - R_{ft} = \alpha_i + \beta_{i,m}(R_{mt} - R_{ft}) + Z_{i,m}\sigma_{mt} + u_{it}, \tag{6.1}$$

where $R_{it} - R_{ft}$ is the excess return of the ith stock portfolio (or stock) over the riskless rate, α_i is the mispricing term, $R_{mt} - R_{ft}$ is the excess market return based on market proxy m, $\beta_{i,m}$ captures beta risk associated with sensitivity to market proxy excess returns, σ_{mt} is RD at time t, $Z_{i,m}$ measures sensitivity to RD, and $u_{it} \sim$ iid $\mathrm{N}(0, \sigma_i^2)$. Because RD is a nontraded factor, we designate its factor loading as Z rather than β to distinguish it from commonly used tradable zero-investment factors. According to relation Eq. (6.1), stock returns depend on two risk premia—namely, a market risk premium associated with beta risk loading $\beta_{i,m}$ as in the static CAPM (Treynor 1961, 1962; Sharpe 1964; Lintner 1965; 1966; 1972) and an RD risk premium associated with the zeta risk loading $Z_{i,m}$. As discussed in Chapters 3 and 4, studies link RD to macroeconomic variables, business cycles, aggregate market volatility, and aggregate idiosyncratic volatility.[1]

Applying the rolling Fama and MacBeth (1973) cross-sectional test procedure described in Eqs. (5.1) and (5.2) in Chapter 5, empirical results for the traditional model are produced. Reviewing this procedure, for each

[1] See Loungani et al. (1990), Adrian and Rosenberg (1994), Chichernea et al. (2001), Choudhry et al. (2003), Christie and Huang (2003), Connolly and Stivers (2006), Demirer et al. (2008), Duffee (2015), Gomes et al. (2016), Zhang (2019), and others.

stock portfolio, the traditional time-series regression model is estimated using 12-months of daily returns beginning in 1964, and then one-month-ahead returns in January 1965 for portfolios are cross-sectionally regressed on the previously estimated factor loadings. The cross-sectional regression is:

$$R_{iT+1} - R_{fT+1} = \lambda_0 + \lambda_m \hat{\beta}_{i,m} + \lambda_{RD} \hat{Z}_{i,m} + u_{iT+1}, \quad i = 1, ..., N, \quad (6.2)$$

where R_{iT+1} is the realized return on the ith stock portfolio (or stock) in out-of-sample time period $T + 1$ (e.g., one-month-ahead), R_{fT+1} is the riskless rate, $\hat{\beta}_{i,m}$ and $\hat{Z}_{i,m}$ are the risk loadings estimated using Eq. (6.1) for $i = 1, ..., N$ stock portfolios in the prior estimation period $t = 1, ..., T$, λ_0 is the intercept term, λ_m and λ_{RD} are corresponding estimated market prices of the risk loadings, and $u_{iT+1} \sim \text{iid N}(0, \sigma_i^2)$. This two-step process is rolled forward month-by-month until December 2018 to produce a time series of 648 monthly estimates of λ_m and λ_{RD}. Daily returns for a variety of stock portfolios are downloaded from Kenneth French's data library website.[2]

Table 6.1 presents our cross-sectional test results. For the eight different stock portfolios (i.e., test assets) shown there, estimates of $\hat{\lambda}_{RD}$ associated with factor loadings $\hat{Z}_{i,m}$ are not generally significant. However, in three test asset portfolios containing 47 industry portfolios, 25 B/M-profit, and 25 B/M-investment portfolios, $\hat{Z}_{i,m}$ is negatively priced at significant levels with $t = -1.97$, $t = -2.19$, and $t = -1.88$, respectively. Verousis and Voukelators (2015) found $\hat{Z}_{i,m}$ to be negatively priced also. By contrast, Demirer and Jategaonkar (2010), Garcia et al. (2013), Jiang (2014), and Chichernea (2015) reported positive and significant prices of risk related to *RD*. We should mention that our results may diverge from those of previous studies due to conducting out-of-sample rather than in-sample cross-sectional tests in addition to using daily instead of monthly returns.

We infer from the results in Table 6.1 that return dispersion loadings in the traditional model are insignificant or marginally priced in most test assets. Given that the traditional approach to incorporating return dispersion in asset pricing models does not work on the whole, justification for our ZAPM approach is garnered.

[2] See https://mba.tuck.dartmouth.edu/pages/faculty/ken.french/data_library.

Table 6.1 Out-of-sample Fama-MacBeth cross-sectional tests of the traditional model based on market and return dispersion (*RD*) factors in the period January 1965 to December 2018: 12-month rolling windows

Test asset portfolios	Cross-sectional regression results			
	$\hat{\alpha}$	$\hat{\lambda}_m$	$\hat{\lambda}_{RD}$	R^2
25 size-B/M	0.886	−0.28	−0.32	0.45
	(3.90)	(−1.19)	(−0.62)	
47 industry	0.48	0.08	−0.64	0.01
	(2.49)	(0.37)	(−1.97)	
25 size-B/M + 47 industry	0.64	−0.05	−0.65	0.02
	(3.50)	(−0.05)	(−0.65)	
20 smallest (microcap)	1.26	−0.74	0.13	0.78
	(6.19)	(−2.85)	(0.29)	
76 largest size	0.55	0.06	−0.29	0.25
	(2.81)	(0.25)	(−1.01)	
25 B/M-profit	0.85	−0.33	−0.86	0.70
	(3.47)	(−1.20)	(−2.19)	
25 B/M-investment	0.48	0.08	−0.81	0.36
	(2.02)	(0.31)	(−1.88)	
25 profit-investment	0.71	−0.16	−0.11	0.31
	(3.20)	(−0.62)	(−0.34)	

Based on value-weighted returns, this table reports out-of-sample cross-sectional tests using the monthly rolling approach for the traditional model previously employed in the literature. The traditional two-factor model is:

$$\widetilde{R}_{it} - R_{ft} = \alpha_i + \beta_{i,m}(\widetilde{R}_{mt} - R_{ft}) + Z_{i,m}\widetilde{\sigma}_{mt} + \widetilde{u}_{it}, \quad t = 1, \cdots, T,$$

where $\widetilde{R}_{it}$ is the daily rate of return for the ith test asset portfolio, R_{ft} is the riskless Treasury bill rate at time t, $\widetilde{R}_{mt}$ is the value-weighted CRSP market index return as a proxy m for the theoretical market portfolio M of Sharpe (1964), beta risk coefficient $\beta_{i,m}$ measures sensitivity to excess market returns, $\widetilde{\sigma}_{mt}$ is the cross-sectional standard deviation of value-weighted CRSP index returns (or *RD*) at time t, zeta risk coefficient $Z_{i,m}$ measures sensitivity to *RD*, and $\widetilde{u}_{it}$ is the error term. The following two-step Fama and MacBeth (1973) procedure is used: (1) time-series regressions of the respective factor model are fitted using daily returns in a 12-month period to estimate factor loadings; and (2) in the subsequent out-of-sample month, a cross-sectional regression is run to estimate the out-of-sample factor prices of risk denoted λ_k for the kth factor in monthly percent return terms. The analyses are rolled forward one month at a time to enable cross-sectional regressions in each month from January 1965 to December 2018. The time-series average of $t = 1, \cdots, 648$ estimated factor prices for the kth factor is denoted $\hat{\lambda}_k$ (t-statistics in parentheses). Results are shown for different sets of stock portfolios as test assets

6.2 Graphical Evidence for the ZCAPM

6.2.1 Excess Returns and Factor Loadings

Commenting on asset pricing models, Fama and MacBeth (1973, p. 613) observed: "As a normative theory the model only has content if there is some relation between future returns and estimates of risk that can be made on the basis of current information." Given this criterion, we examine the relationship between one-month-ahead stock returns and prior estimated beta and zeta risks in our empirical ZCAPM.

Recap of the ZCAPM. Briefly reviewing Chapters 3 and 4, our ZCAPM was mathematically derived as a special case of Black's (1972) zero-beta CAPM.[3] According to the *theoretical ZCAPM*, the return generating process for the ith asset is as follows:

$$E(R_{it}) - R_{ft} = \beta_{i,a}[E(R_{at}) - R_{ft}] + Z^{*}_{i,a}\sigma_{at}, \tag{6.3}$$

where $E(R_{at})$ is the expected market return based on the average return of all assets at time t, R_{ft} is the riskless rate, $\beta_{i,a}$ is the beta risk coefficient measuring sensitivity to expected excess market returns, σ_{at} is the cross-sectional standard deviation of all asset returns (or return dispersion denoted RD) at time t, and $Z^{*}_{i,a}$ is the zeta risk coefficient measuring dichotomous positive or negative sensitivity to return dispersion.[4]

To estimate the ZCAPM, we proposed the following time-series regression model dubbed the *empirical ZCAPM*[5]:

$$R_{it} - R_{ft} = \beta_{i,a}(R_{at} - R_{ft}) + Z_{i,a}D_{it}\sigma_{at} + u_{it}, \quad t = 1, \cdots, T, \tag{6.4}$$

where $R_{it} - R_{ft}$ is the daily excess return of the ith stock portfolio (or stock) over the Treasury bill rate in a one-year period with $t = 1, \cdots, T$, $R_{at} - R_{ft}$ is the excess average market return of the value-weighted CRSP index associated with beta risk coefficient $\beta_{i,a}$, σ_{at} is the cross-sectional standard deviation of value-weighted returns in the CRSP index (return dispersion or

[3] See earlier work in Liu et al. (2012) and Liu (2013).

[4] Since RD is a nontraded factor, we designate its factor loading as Z rather than β to distinguish it from commonly-used tradable zero-investment factors. Also, an asterisk superscript is added to denote its relation to orthogonal portfolios I^* and ZI^* on the mean-variance investment parabola. Portfolio ZI^* is the zero-beta counterpart of efficient portfolio I^*, which are a unique pair of portfolios with equal return variance.

[5] See also Liu et al. (2020).

RD) related to zeta risk coefficient $Z_{i,a}$, signal variable $D_{it} = +1$ or -1, and $u_{it} \sim$ iid $N(0, \sigma_i^2)$. Our empirical ZCAPM differs from the traditional model in the previous section in three ways: (1) no intercept (i.e., α_i) term is included; (2) the CRSP index return is associated with the average market return located on the axis of symmetry of the mean-variance parabola, as opposed to the return on proxy portfolio m representing tangent market portfolio M in Sharpe's (1964) CAPM; and (3) signal variable D_{it} captures positive and negative sensitivity of stock returns to return dispersion movements on day t. Regarding these differences, the assumption that $\alpha_i = 0$ has little or no effect on the out-of-sample cross-sectional regression results in this chapter.[6] Also, we assume that signal variable D_{it} is latent or unobserved. It can be defined as an independent random variable with the following two-point distribution:

$$D_{it} = \begin{cases} +1 & \text{with probability } p_i \\ -1 & \text{with probability } 1 - p_i, \end{cases} \tag{6.5}$$

where p_i (or $1 - p_i$) is the probability of a positive (or negative) return dispersion effect, and D_{it} are independent of u_{it}.

To estimate the aforementioned probabilities and other parameters in the empirical ZCAPM, we employ the expectation–maximization (EM) algorithm (see Dempster et al. (1977)).[7] Since $E(D_{it}) = 2p_i - 1$, ZCAPM relation Eq. (6.4) can be rewritten in marginal form as:

$$R_{it} - R_{ft} = \beta_{i,a}(R_{at} - R_{ft}) + Z^*_{i,a}\sigma_{at} + u^*_{it}, \quad t = 1, \cdots, T, \tag{6.6}$$

where $\beta_{i,a}$ is the beta risk loading, $\hat{Z}^*_{i,a} = \hat{Z}_{i,a}(2\hat{p}_i - 1)$ is the zeta risk loading, u^*_{it} is the error term with variance dependent on return dispersion (see Eq. [4.13] of Chapter 4), and other notation is as before. Using daily returns for different stock portfolios, a 12-month estimation period is used to estimate the empirical ZCAPM specified in relation to Eq. (6.6). For each stock portfolio, we begin by estimating $\beta_{i,a}$ and $Z^*_{i,a}$ in 1964 and record its out-of-sample (one-month-ahead) excess return in January 1965. Rolling forward one month at a time until November 2018, time series of $\beta_{i,a}$ and $Z^*_{i,a}$ coefficients and related one-month-ahead excess returns are con-

[6] See Chapter 4 for further discussion and rationale for dropping this mispricing error term.

[7] See Chapter 4 for detailed discussion of the EM algorithm and further citations to literature.

structed for all stock portfolios. These series afford the computation of average one-month-ahead returns and lagged average beta and zeta risk coefficients (estimated in the prior year) for all portfolios over 648 months from January 1965 to December 2018.

Matlab programs for estimating the empirical ZCAPM are available at the end of the book in the Compendium. Additionally, R programs for these analyses can be downloaded from GitHub (https://github.com/zcapm). R is a free software environment available on the internet. Our R programs run faster in terms of estimating the empirical ZCAPM than the Matlab programs.

Graphical Results. Figure 6.1 shows the relation between average one-month-ahead excess returns in percent (Y-axis) and time-series average zeta risk $\hat{Z}^*_{i,a}$ (X-axis) in the previous 12-month estimation period for sample portfolios. A sample of 97 combined stock portfolios is used, which is comprised of 25 size-B/M sorted plus 47 industry plus 25 beta-zeta sorted portfolios. Portfolios are sorted into beta risk $\hat{\beta}_{i,a}$ quintiles and then zeta risk $\hat{Z}^*_{i,a}$ quintiles within each $\hat{\beta}_{i,a}$ quintile. Casual inspection of Fig. 6.1 suggests that a definite positive relation exists between out-of-sample average excess returns and average zeta risk in our analysis period from January 1965 to December 2018.

Repeating the above steps to show the relation between average one-month-ahead excess returns and average beta risk (i.e., portfolios are now sorted into $\hat{Z}^*_{i,a}$ quintiles and then $\hat{\beta}_{i,a}$ quintiles), Fig. 6.2 confirms the familiar lack of a positive association between average one-month-ahead excess returns and average beta risk.

Similar graphical analyses are produced using the often-studied 25 size-B/M portfolios in the Fama and French studies (1992, 1993, 1995, 2015, 2018). Figure 6.3 illustrates a very close relation between zeta risk and one-month-ahead cross-sectional excess returns for these portfolios. Also, there appears to be an inverse relation between beta risk and zeta risk—that is, small $\hat{\beta}$ quintile stocks have the highest positive $\hat{Z}^*$ values, and the big $\hat{\beta}$ quintile stocks have the lowest negative $\hat{Z}^*_i$ values.

Comparing Fig. 6.3 and previous Fig. 6.1, the range of average estimated zeta risk coefficients for the 25 size-B/M portfolios is similar to the broader set of 97 portfolios. We infer that the size-B/M sorted portfolios do a good job of spanning zeta risk in the population of U.S. stocks. Also, as shown in Fig. 6.3, $\hat{Z}^*$ values range from about −0.2 to 0.4 and average one-month-ahead excess returns from about 0.2 to 1.0%, which implies a slope

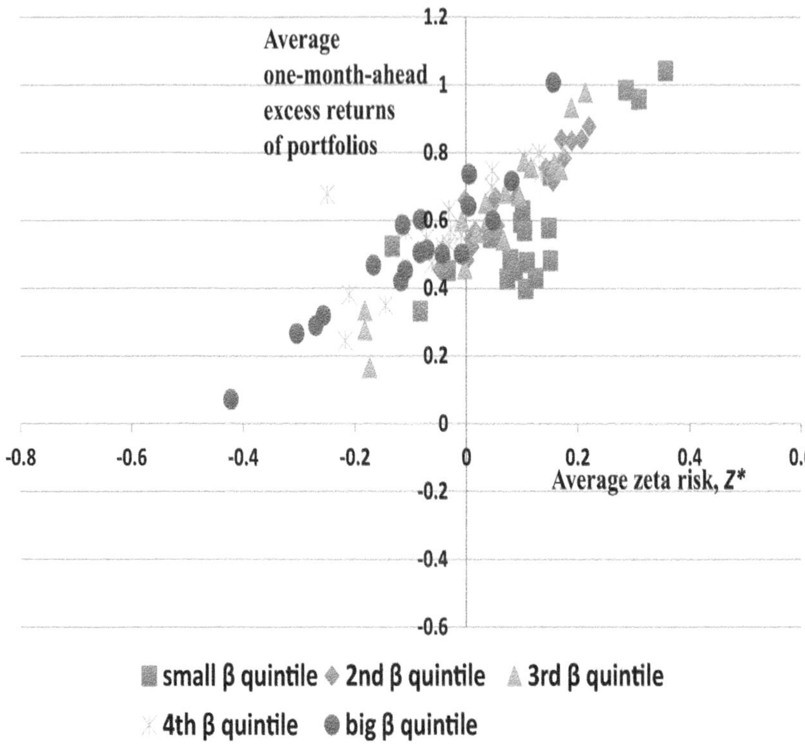

Fig. 6.1 Out-of-sample cross-sectional ZCAPM relationship between average one-month-ahead realized excess returns in percent (Y-axis) and average zeta risk $\hat{Z}^*_{i,a}$ in the previous 12-month estimation period (X-axis). Results are shown for 97 portfolios consisting of 25 size-B/M sorted plus 47 industry plus 25 beta-zeta sorted portfolios. These portfolios are sorted into beta risk $\hat{\beta}_{i,a}$ quintiles and then zeta risk $\hat{Z}^*_{i,a}$ quintiles within each $\hat{\beta}_{i,a}$ quintile. The analysis period is January 1965 to December 2018

of approximately 1.3% monthly risk premium per unit zeta risk (i.e., about 1.1% in Fig. 6.1). Hence, the *RD* risk premium is economically meaningful.

By contrast, for the 25 size-B/M portfolios, Fig. 6.4 shows that beta risk and average one-month-ahead excess returns are less closely and inversely related to one another. Comparing Fig. 6.4 to previous Fig. 6.2, we see that the 25 size-B/M portfolios have beta estimates that are closer to 1.0

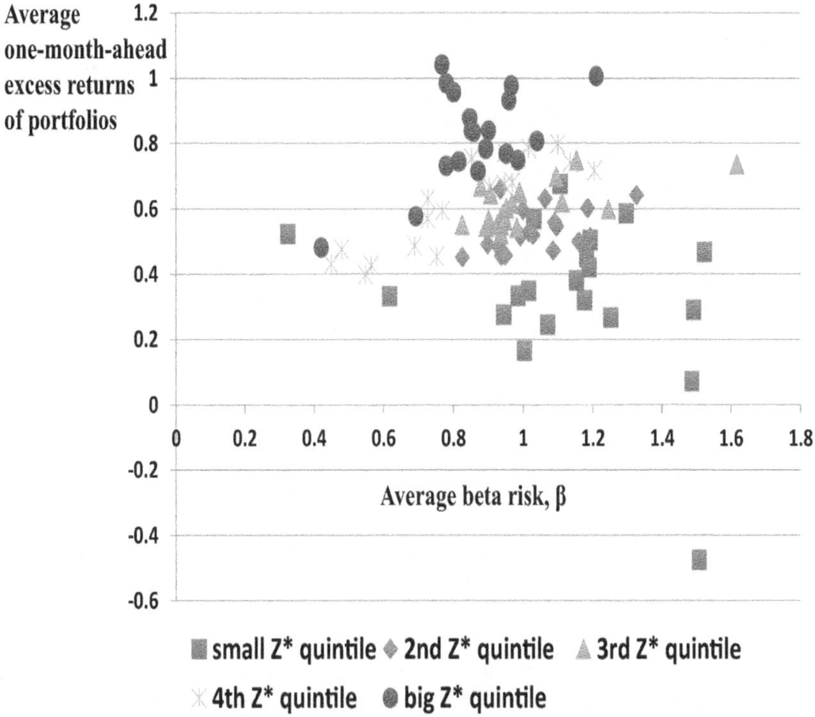

Fig. 6.2 Out-of-sample cross-sectional ZCAPM relationship between average one-month-ahead realized excess returns in percent (Y-axis) and average beta risk $\hat{\beta}_{i,a}$ in the previous 12-month estimation period (X-axis). Results are shown for 97 portfolios consisting of 25 size-B/M sorted plus 47 industry plus 25 beta-zeta sorted portfolios. These portfolios are sorted into zeta risk $\hat{Z}^{*}_{i,a}$ quintiles and then beta risk $\hat{\beta}_{i,a}$ quintiles within each $\hat{Z}^{*}_{i,a}$ quintile. The analysis period is January 1965 to December 2018

than the broader set of 97 portfolios. Hence, sorting stocks by size and B/M ratios forms portfolios with divergent zeta risk but similar beta risk.

Finally, Figs. 6.5 and 6.6 sort the 25 size-B/M stock portfolios into size and B/M quintiles to better reveal size and value effects, respectively. In both cases, a strong linear relation is evident between average one-month-ahead excess returns and average zeta risk in our analysis period. In Fig. 6.5

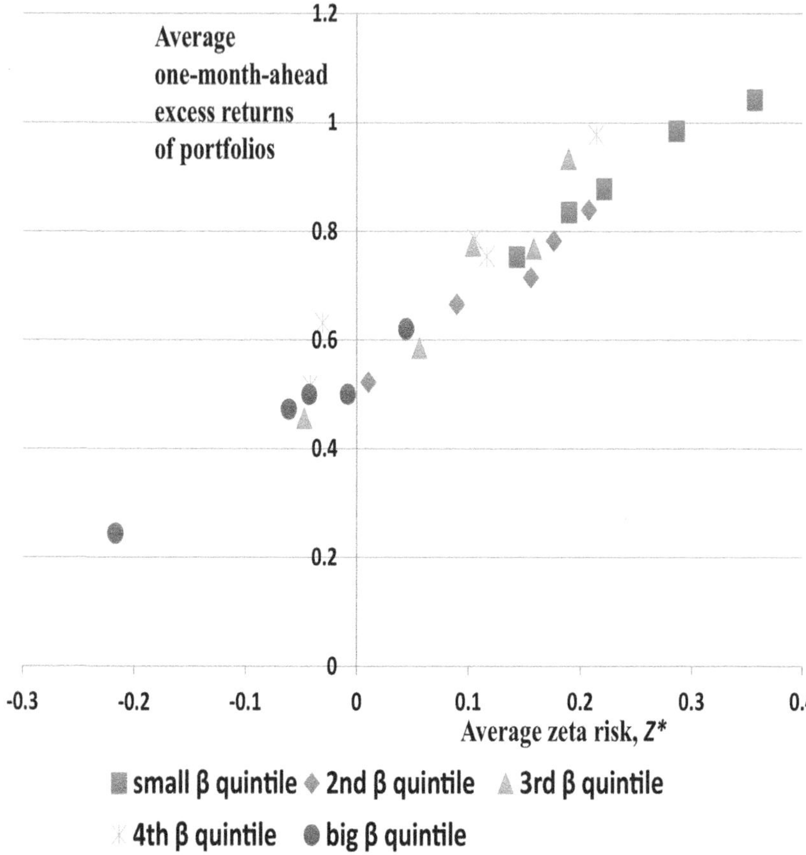

Fig. 6.3 Out-of-sample cross-sectional ZCAPM relationship between average one-month-ahead realized excess returns in percent (Y-axis) and average zeta risk $\hat{Z}^*_{i,a}$ in the previous 12-month estimation period (X-axis). Results are shown for 25 size-B/M portfolios often-used in the Fama and French (1992, 1993, 1995, 2015, 2018) studies. These portfolios are sorted into beta risk $\hat{\beta}_{i,a}$ quintiles and then zeta risk $\hat{Z}^*_{i,a}$ quintiles within each $\hat{\beta}_{i,a}$ quintile. The analysis period is January 1965 to December 2018

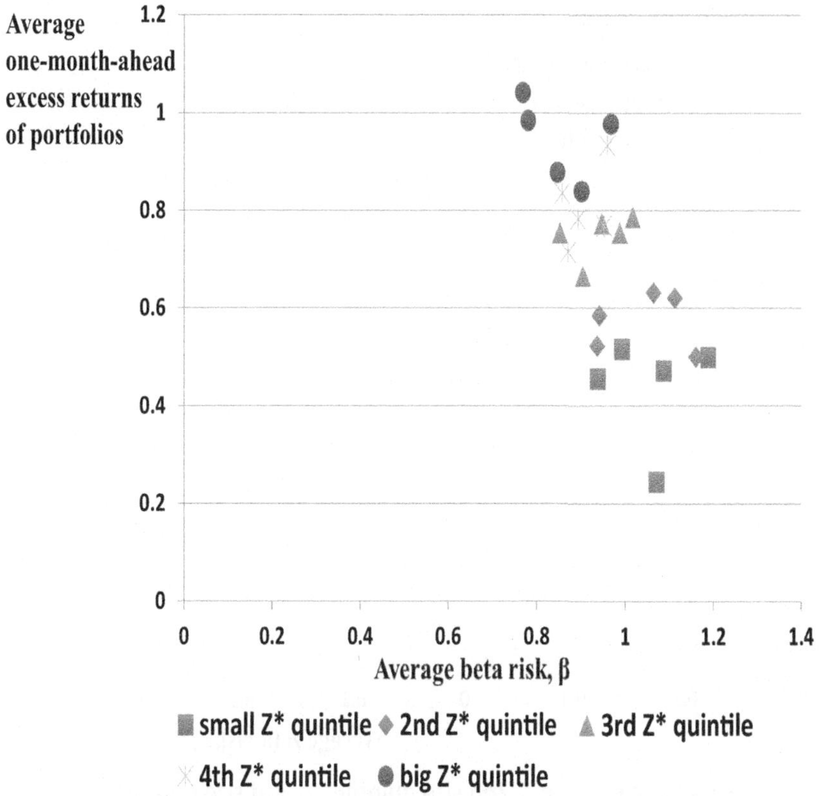

Fig. 6.4 Out-of-sample cross-sectional ZCAPM relationship between average one-month-ahead realized excess returns in percent (Y-axis) and average beta risk $\hat{\beta}_{i,a}$ in the previous 12-month estimation period (X-axis). Results are shown for 25 size-B/M portfolios often-used in the Fama and French (1992, 1993, 1995, 2015, 2018) studies. These portfolios are sorted into zeta risk $\hat{Z}^*_{i,a}$ quintiles and then beta risk $\hat{\beta}_{i,a}$ quintiles within each $\hat{Z}^*_{i,a}$ quintile. The analysis period is January 1965 to December 2018

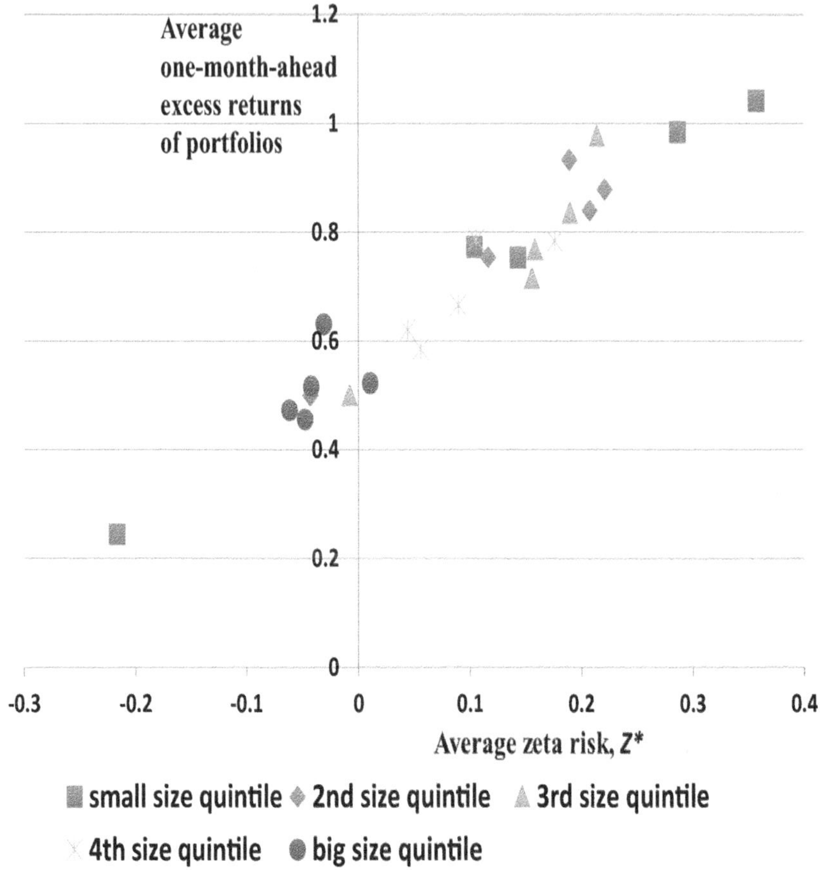

Fig. 6.5 Out-of-sample cross-sectional ZCAPM relationship between average one-month-ahead realized excess returns in percent (Y-axis) and average zeta risk $\hat{Z}^*_{i,a}$ in the previous 12-month estimation period (X-axis). A total of 25 size-B/M portfolios are sorted into size quintiles and then zeta risk $\hat{Z}^*_{i,a}$ quintiles within each size quintile. The analysis period is January 1965 to December 2018

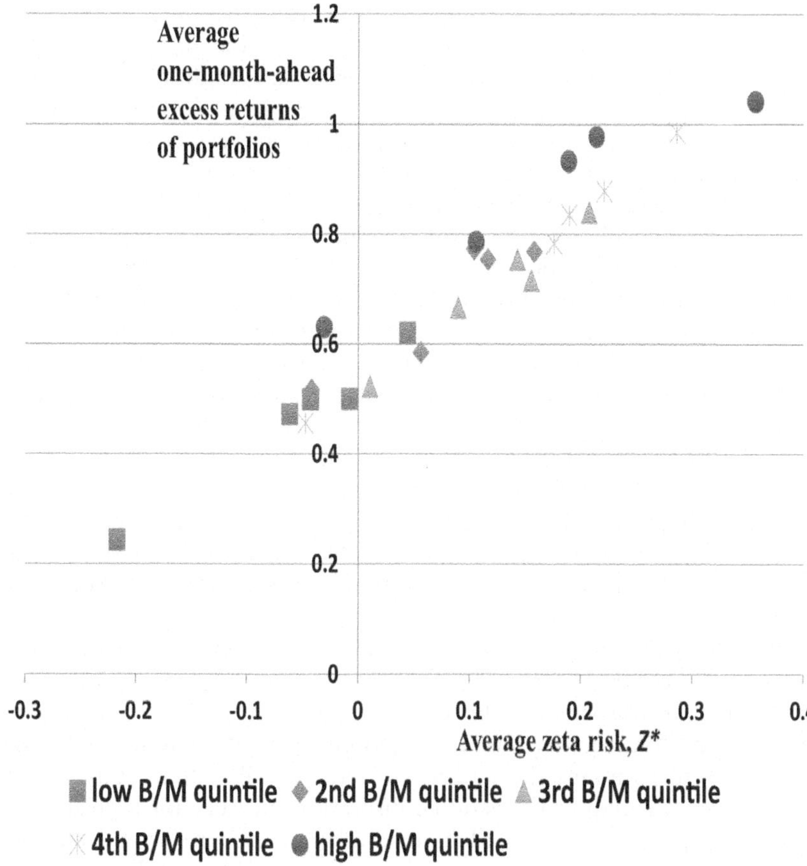

Fig. 6.6 Out-of-sample cross-sectional ZCAPM relationship between average one-month-ahead realized excess returns in percent (Y-axis) and average zeta risk $\hat{Z}^*_{i,a}$ in the previous 12-month estimation period (X-axis). A total of 25 size-B/M portfolios are sorted into B/M quintiles and then zeta risk $\hat{Z}^*_{i,a}$ quintiles within each B/M quintile. The analysis period is January 1965 to December 2018

small size quintile portfolios completely span the range of zeta risk, with the smallest-size/lowest-B/M (growth) stocks on the far left having the lowest average excess returns, and the smallest-size/highest-B/M (value) stocks on the far right having the highest average excess returns. Some relation between zeta risk and market capitalization is evident, with smaller stocks generally having higher zeta risk than larger stocks. Also, Fig. 6.6 shows that zeta risk is positively related to B/M ratios.

An interesting observation from Figs. 6.5 and 6.6 that display the 25 size-B/M sorted portfolios for different size and B/M ratio quintiles, respectively, is that, given a particular level of zeta risk as measured by $\hat{Z}^*$, there is very little variation around the line fitting average one-month-ahead excess returns and zeta risk estimated in the previous year. We interpret this close goodness-of-fit to mean that, after taking into account zeta risk, incremental contributions to returns from size and B/M ratios are negligent. Instead, these potential sources of return variation in stock returns are captured by zeta risk for the most part. Defining patterns of average stock returns not explained by the CAPM as anomalies (see Fama and French 1996, p. 55), our findings indicate that the empirical ZCAPM helps to explain the anomalous effects of firm size and value characteristics on stock returns.

We infer from these findings that the zero-investment portfolio size and value factors proxy (to some extent) market risk associated with cross-sectional return dispersion. This inference is not surprising to the extent that these multifactors are based on zero-investment portfolios with long portfolio returns minus short portfolio returns. The latter return difference is itself a rough cross-sectional dispersion measure for a given time period (e.g., day or month). Many researchers consider size and value to be anomalous factors not explained by general market risk. While movements in average market returns over time (i.e., beta risk) do not explain the size and value factors, zeta risk associated with return dispersion does a very good job of explaining them. Because the well-known size and value factors are explained by general market risk manifested in return dispersion, these firm characteristics are not associated with anomalous returns as previously believed.

6.2.2 *Predicted and Realized Excess Returns*

We next provide graphs of realized excess returns (Y-axis) and predicted excess returns (X-axis) for different stock portfolios based on different asset pricing models. Both Cochrane (1996) and Lettau and Ludvigson (2001) have recommended such graphs as a tool in evaluating the goodness-of-fit of asset pricing models.

Comparative Analyses. To gauge empirical ZCAPM results, we graphically compare them to those produced by the three-, five-, and six-factor models of Fama and French (1992, 1993, 1995, 2015, 2018). Our results are based on the time-series averages of one-month-ahead realized and predicted (or fitted) excess returns for portfolios in each out-of-sample month. To obtain these time series, the risk parameters for each model are estimated using daily returns of stock portfolios in the 12-months prior to one-month-ahead realized returns. In the one-month-ahead period, we compute predicted returns using the previously estimated risk parameters of each model multiplied by the coincident factors in that month. The estimation period is rolled forward one month at a time to obtain out-of-sample time series of these monthly returns from January 1965 to December 2018. Averages of these one-month-ahead realized and predicted return series are computed for each stock portfolio.

Graphical Results. Based on the 25 size and B/M stock portfolios typically used in many studies, as shown in Fig. 6.7, both Fama and French's three-factor model and our empirical ZCAPM generate predicted excess returns that fit average realized excess returns fairly well. One exception is the stock portfolio in the three-factor model results (Panel A) that corresponds to the smallest-size/lowest-B/M (growth) portfolio with the lowest average realized excess return. It is well known that the three-factor model has difficulty explaining this anomalous small, growth portfolio (e.g., see Fama and French 1996).[8] By contrast, the empirical ZCAPM appears to explain this anomalous small stock portfolio, for it lies reasonably close to the 45-degree line of realized/predicted excess returns.

More generally, the ZCAPM provides a closer realized/predicted excess return relation than the three-factor model. This closer fit is obvious in terms of the lower dispersion of the 25 size-B/M portfolios around the 45-degree line in Panel B for the empirical ZCAPM compared to the three-factor model in Panel A. This goodness-of-fit is consistent with forthcoming cross-sectional tests in Chapter 7. There we find that, for the 25 size-B/M

[8] Some authors (e.g., see Lettau and Ludvigson 2001; Petkova2006) have observed similar problems in the three-factor model with respect to selected stock portfolios in the 25 size-B/M sorted test assets.

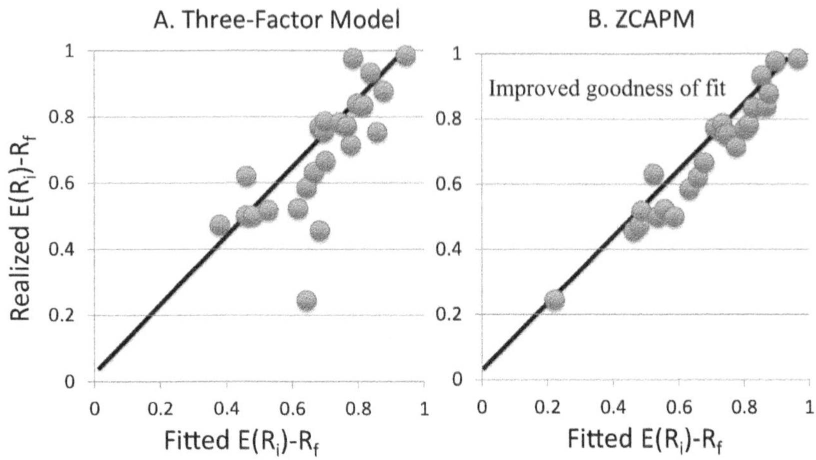

Fig. 6.7 Out-of-sample cross-sectional relationship between average one-month-ahead realized excess returns in percent (Y-axis) and average one-month-ahead predicted (fitted) excess returns in percent (X-axis) for 25 size-B/M sorted portfolios: Fama and French three-factor model in Panel A and empirical ZCAPM in Panel B. The analysis period is January 1965 to December 2018

portfolios, the empirical ZCAPM has an estimated R^2 value of 94 percent versus 63% for the three-factor model (see Table 7.1).

We infer from this evidence that the empirical ZCAPM outperforms the Fama and French three-factor model in terms of its ability to predict one-month-ahead realized returns. These results are remarkable in the sense that the 25 size and B/M stock portfolios are related to Fama and French's size and B/M (value) factors but entirely exogenous to the ZCAPM's average market return and *RD* factors. Fama and French rely heavily on these portfolios to support their three-factor model. Strikingly, our results suggest that no more factors are needed beyond the ZCAPM to price the size and B/M test assets.

Comparing one-month-ahead predicted versus realized excess returns for 72 combined stock portfolios composed of 25 size-B/M sorted plus 47 industry portfolios, the results are compelling. Following the same procedures used to create Fig. 6.7, Fig. 6.8 shows that the three-factor model in Panel A does a poor job of predicting average one-month-ahead realized excess returns compared to the empirical ZCAPM in Panel B. In Panel A,

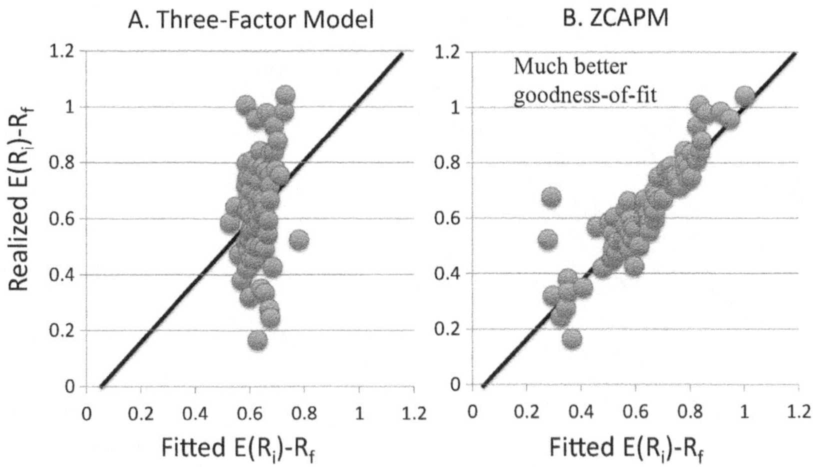

Fig. 6.8 Out-of-sample cross-sectional relationship between average one-month-ahead realized excess returns in percent (Y-axis) and average one-month-ahead predicted (fitted) excess returns in percent (X-axis) for 25 size-B/M sorted plus 47 industry portfolios: Fama and French Fama and French three-factor model in Panel A and empirical ZCAPM in Panel B. The analysis period is January 1965 to December 2018

the average fitted excess returns from the three-factor model bunch up into a much smaller range of values than those for average realized excess returns. By contrast, with only a few exceptions,[9] average fitted excess returns for the ZCAPM are spread out and fall fairly close to the 45-degree line from the origin with respect to average realized excess returns. Again, in forthcoming cross-sectional tests reported in Chapter 7 using these stock portfolios as test assets, the cross-sectional R^2 for the ZCAPM is 79% versus only 6% for the three-factor model (see Table 7.1). In terms of explaining expected returns, defined as average predicted returns in the month ahead,

[9] There are two undiversified industry portfolios that lie well above the 45-degree line corresponding to gold and coal producing companies.

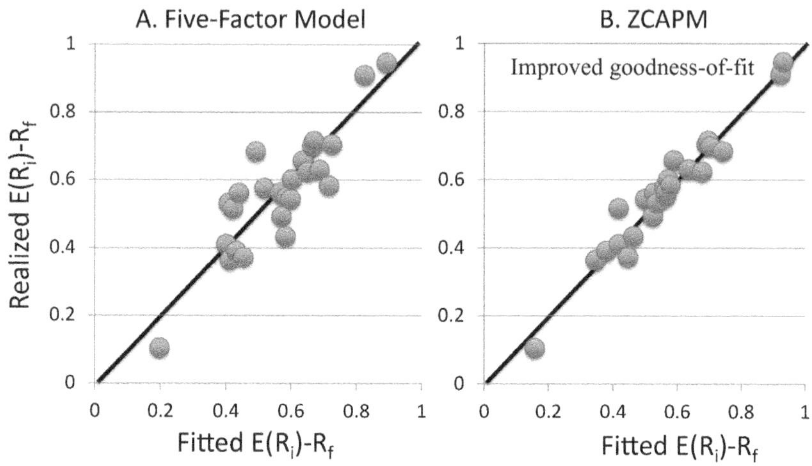

Fig. 6.9 Out-of-sample cross-sectional relationship between average one-month-ahead realized excess returns in percent (Y-axis) and average one-month-ahead predicted (fitted) excess returns in percent (X-axis) for 25 profit-investment sorted portfolios: Fama and French five-factor model in Panel A and empirical ZCAPM in Panel B. The analysis period is January 1965 to December 2018

the empirical ZCAPM dramatically improves upon the Fama and French three-factor model.[10]

A major problem with the three-factor model can be observed by comparing Panel A in Figs. 6.7 and 6.8. It is apparent from these two graphs that the three-factor model is almost useless in terms of predicting exogenous industry portfolio returns. This problem occurs in other well-known asset pricing models also. For example, Daniel and Titman (2012) have shown that, based on the consumption CAPM (CCAPM) of Lettau and Ludvigson (2001), there is no relation between realized and fitted returns for 38 industry portfolios.[11] Conversely, comparing Panel B in Figs. 6.7 and 6.8,

[10] In unreported results, we repeated Figs. 6.7 and 6.8 using the Carhart (1997) four-factor model that augments the Fama and French three-factor model with a momentum factor but obtained similar results to those for the three-factor model.

[11] Daniel and Titman (2012) have argued that cross-sectional tests have low power when based on test assets that have loadings on proposed factors that are highly correlated with test asset characteristics (e.g., size and B/M ratios).

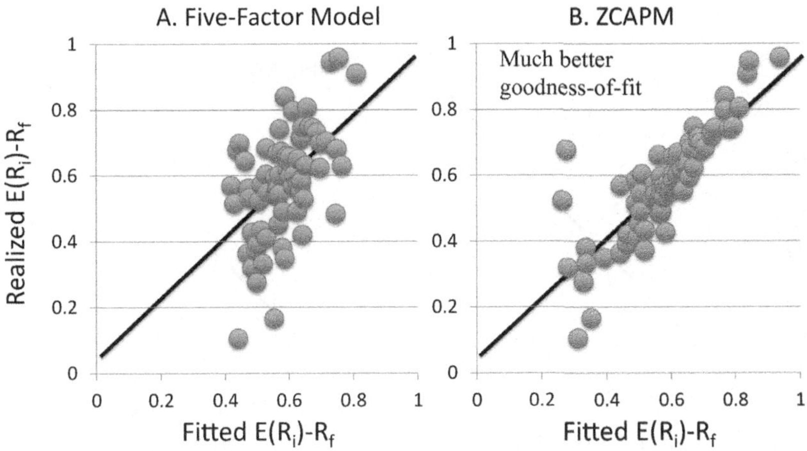

Fig. 6.10 Out-of-sample cross-sectional relationship between average one-month-ahead realized excess returns in percent (Y-axis) and average one-month-ahead predicted (fitted) excess returns in percent (X-axis) for 25 profit-investment sorted plus 47 industry portfolios: Fama and French Fama and French five-factor model in Panel A and empirical ZCAPM in Panel B. The analysis period is January 1965 to December 2018

the ZCAPM continues to do a good job of predicting one-month-ahead returns for industry stock portfolios.

In unreported results, we repeated the comparative results in Panel A of Figs. 6.7 and 6.8 using the Stambaugh and Yuan (2017) four-factor model with novel mispricing factors. We discuss this model in further detail in Chapter 7. Our results suggest that this model performs almost as well as the Fama and French three-factor model for the 25 size and B/M stock portfolios. However, for the combined 25 size-B/M plus 47 industry portfolios, like the Fama and French model in Panel A of Fig. 6.8, the Stambaugh and Yuan four-factor model does not predict their out-of-sample returns. In both cases, especially for test assets containing industry portfolios, the empirical ZCAPM outperforms their four-factor model.

Following the same procedures, we compare the Fama and French five-factor model and empirical ZCAPM by replicating Figs. 6.7 and 6.8 using 25 profit-investment sorted portfolios downloaded from Kenneth French's website. Using these 25 portfolios, Fig. 6.9 shows that the ZCAPM out-

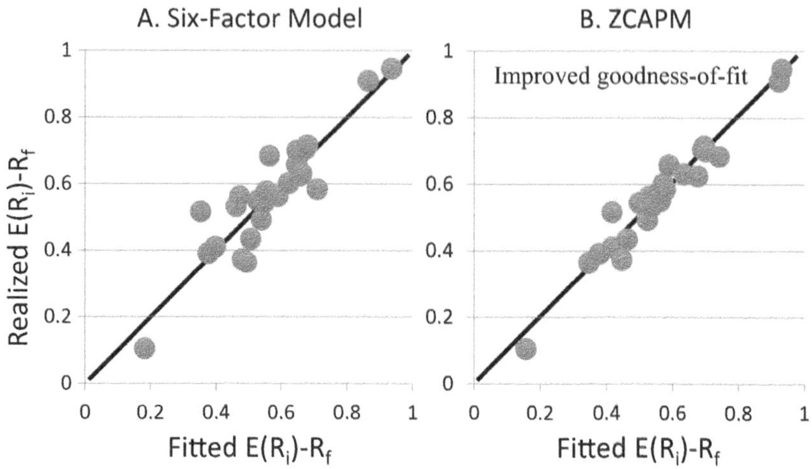

Fig. 6.11 Out-of-sample cross-sectional relationship between average one-month-ahead realized excess returns in percent (Y-axis) and average one-month-ahead predicted (fitted) excess returns in percent (X-axis) for 25 profit-investment sorted portfolios: Fama and French six-factor model in Panel A and empirical ZCAPM in Panel B. The analysis period is January 1965 to December 2018

performs the five-factor model. Figure 6.10 shows the comparative results for the combined 72 portfolios containing 25 profit-investment plus 47 exogenous industry portfolios. Similar to the three-factor model results in Fig. 6.8, the five-factor model does not predict their returns very well (albeit somewhat better than the three-factor model). By contrast, the ZCAPM does a good job of predicting these combined portfolio returns.

Lastly, we compare the Fama and French six-factor model to the empirical ZCAPM in Figs. 6.11 and 6.12. As before, the ZCAPM outperforms the six-factor model for the 25 profit-investment sorted portfolios and especially so for the combined 72 portfolios incorporating industry portfolios. Also, comparing the Fama and French five- and six-factor models in Panel A of Figs. 6.10 and 6.12, which are based on the combined 72 portfolios with 25 profit-investment and 47 industry portfolios, the momentum factor appears to have improved the fit between realized and predicted returns to some degree.

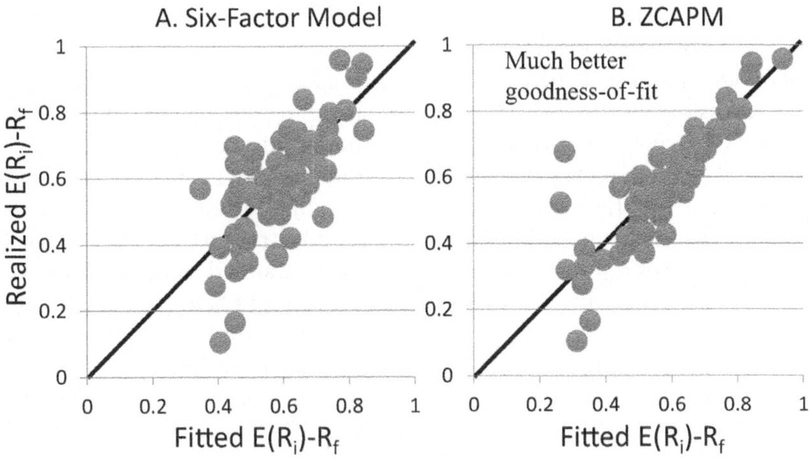

Fig. 6.12 Out-of-sample cross-sectional relationship between average one-month-ahead realized excess returns in percent (Y-axis) and average one-month-ahead predicted (fitted) excess returns in percent (X-axis) for 25 profit-investment sorted plus 47 industry portfolios: Fama and French Fama and French six-factor model in Panel A and empirical ZCAPM in Panel B. The analysis period is January 1965 to December 2018

In sum, our evidence suggests that the Fama and French three-, five-, and six-factor models, which are exemplary of the step-by-step evolution of multifactor models and state-of-the-art in asset pricing models over time, are outperformed by the ZCAPM in terms of explaining the out-of-sample cross section of average stock returns. For industry portfolios, excluding the momentum factor, the three- and five-factor models perform so poorly that they are almost useless. With the inclusion of the momentum factor to form a six-factor model, there appears to be some relationship between realized and predicted stock returns, but the empirical ZCAPM clearly outperforms the six-factor model.

6.2.3 *Why Do Multifactor Models Do Poorly with Industries?*

Based on the analyses and findings in the previous subsection, a natural question arises: Why is the cross-sectional performance of multifactor models so poor in the case of industry portfolios? To answer this question, we ran time-series regressions for the multifactor models using daily returns for the 47 industry portfolios from January 1965 to December 2018. The dependent variable is the excess return for each industry portfolio.

Regression results for different industries are shown in Table 6.2. To conserve space, we report results for selected industries: agriculture (Panel A), oil (Panel B), steel (Panel C), telecommunications (Panel D), and transportation (Panel E). Other industries yield similar results. Comparing the R^2 values for different models across these industries, we see that explanatory power does not increase much as factors are added to the CAPM market model. At most the R^2 values increase by about 6% for the oil industry (i.e., from 50% for the CAPM to 56% for the five- and six-factor models), and the smallest increase in R^2 values is only 2% for the agriculture industry (i.e., from 29% for the CAPM to 31% for the five- and six-factor models).

By contrast, in unreported results, for the 25 size-B/M portfolios, R^2 values typically increase substantially to around 90 percent for the three-factor model. As more factors are added to the three-factor model up the six-factor model, only marginal improvement of a few percent in R^2 values is achieved.

We infer that, with respect to industry portfolios, the multifactor models under study have poor incremental goodness-of-fit compared to the CAPM market model. This lack of time-series regression explanatory power helps to explain the relatively poor performance of these models in terms of out-of-sample cross-sectional realized versus predicted returns.

6.3 Summary

Previous studies have investigated return dispersion (*RD*) as an asset pricing factor by specifying a two-factor model with market and *RD* factors. Based on our empirical tests using U.S. stock returns in the period January 1965 to December 2018, this traditional model is not supported. Modifying the traditional model, our empirical ZCAPM adds a dummy signal variable to capture positive and negative sensitivity to *RD* at any given time *t* (e.g., daily). Assets with positive (negative) *RD* sensitivity are conjectured to experience increasing (decreasing) returns as cross-sectional market dispersion increases, and vice versa as dispersion decreases. According to our empirical ZCAPM, asset returns consist of an excess market return factor associated with beta risk and an *RD* factor related to zeta risk that captures asymmetric positive and negative sensitivity to *RD*. To estimate beta

Table 6.2 Time-series regression results for the CAPM and multifactor models in the period January 1965 to December 2018

Panel A: Agriculture

Model	$\hat{\alpha}$	$\hat{\beta}_{i,m}$	$\hat{\beta}_{i,S}$	$\hat{\beta}_{i,V}$	$\hat{\beta}_{i,MOM}$	$\hat{\beta}_{i,R}$	xs$\hat{\beta}_{i,C}$	R^2
CAPM	0.01	0.75						0.29
	(1.01)	(73.99)						
Three-factor	0.01	0.78	0.26	0.15				0.30
	(0.67)	(74.19)	(13.87)	(7.05)				
Four-factor	0.00	0.78	0.26	0.17	0.05			0.30
	(0.46)	(73.54)	(13.83)	(7.72)	(3.44)			
Five-factor	0.00	0.82	0.37	0.02		0.31	0.14	0.31
	(0.05)	(72.69)	(18.51)	(0.89)		(10.47)	(3.97)	
Six-factor	0.00	0.82	0.37	0.03	0.01	0.30	0.13	0.31
	(0.0)	(72.46)	(18.4)	(1.16)	(0.98)	(10.34)	(3.75)	

Panel B: Oil

Model	$\hat{\alpha}$	$\hat{\beta}_{i,m}$	$\hat{\beta}_{i,S}$	$\hat{\beta}_{i,V}$	$\hat{\beta}_{i,MOM}$	$\hat{\beta}_{i,R}$	$\hat{\beta}_{i,C}$	R^2
CAPM	0.01	0.94						0.50
	(0.67)	(117.67)						
Three-factor	0.00	1.00	−0.21	0.48				0.55
	(−0.22)	(124.64)	(−14.25)	(30.3)				
Four-factor	0.00	1.01	−0.21	0.51	0.08			0.55
	(−0.64)	(123.93)	(−14.36)	(31.1)	(6.94)			
Five-factor	−0.01	1.07	−0.05	0.17		0.43	0.60	0.56
	(−1.84)	(126.28)	(−3.26)	(9.27)		(19.5)	(22.87)	
Six-factor	−0.01	1.07	−0.05	0.16	−0.01	0.43	0.60	0.56
	(−1.81)	(125.67)	(−3.21)	(8.54)	(−0.65)	(19.48)	(22.66)	

Panel C: Steel

Model	$\hat{\alpha}$	$\hat{\beta}_{i,m}$	$\hat{\beta}_{i,S}$	$\hat{\beta}_{i,V}$	$\hat{\beta}_{i,MOM}$	$\hat{\beta}_{i,R}$	$\hat{\beta}_{i,C}$	R^2
CAPM	−0.02	1.25						0.62
	(−1.85)	(148.35)						
Three-factor	−0.03	1.34	0.47	0.53				0.67
	(−3.74)	(163.21)	(31.31)	(32.8)				
Four-factor	−0.02	1.33	0.47	0.49	−0.11			0.67
	(−3.18)	(159.03)	(31.53)	(29.12)	(−9.47)			
Five-factor	−0.02	1.31	0.42	0.35		−0.24	0.10	0.66
	(−3.05)	(147.17)	(26.05)	(18.33)		(−10.21)	(3.53)	
Six-factor	−0.02	1.3	0.43	0.28	−0.12	−0.22	0.14	0.67
	(−2.55)	(146.12)	(26.75)	(14.06)	(−10.02)	(−9.31)	(5.17)	

(continued)

Table 6.2 (continued)

Panel D: Telecommunications

Model	$\hat{\alpha}$	$\hat{\beta}_{i,m}$	$\hat{\beta}_{i,S}$	$\hat{\beta}_{i,V}$	$\hat{\beta}_{i,MOM}$	$\hat{\beta}_{i,R}$	$\hat{\beta}_{i,C}$	R^2
CAPM	0.00	0.88						0.64
	(0.24)	(155.42)						
Three-factor	0.00	0.90	−0.20	0.19				0.66
	(−0.07)	(156.13)	(−19.29)	(16.7)				
Four-factor	0.00	0.89	−0.20	0.16	−0.06			0.66
	(0.41)	(152.19)	(−19.23)	(13.95)	(−8.02)			
Five-factor	0.00	0.89	−0.25	0.11		−0.22	0.23	0.67
	(0.25)	(145.77)	(−22.45)	(8.71)		(−14.13)	(12.11)	
Six-factor	0.00	0.88	−0.24	0.07	−0.07	−0.21	0.25	0.67
	(0.68)	(144.72)	(−21.91)	(5.44)	(−8.47)	(−13.34)	(13.39)	

Panel E: Transportation

Model	$\hat{\alpha}$	$\hat{\beta}_{i,m}$	$\hat{\beta}_{i,S}$	$\hat{\beta}_{i,V}$	$\hat{\beta}_{i,MOM}$	$\hat{\beta}_{i,R}$	$\hat{\beta}_{i,C}$	R^2
CAPM	0.00	1.02						0.68
	−0.15	(171.17)						
Three-factor	−0.01	1.06	0.22	0.26				0.70
	(−1.04)	(176.26)	(20.28)	(22.11)				
Four-factor	−0.01	1.06	0.22	0.26	−0.01			0.70
	(−1.00)	(172.99)	(20.29)	(21.12)	(−0.64)			
Five-factor	−0.01	1.10	0.34	0.17		0.32	0.11	0.71
	(−2.21)	(172.06)	(29.24)	(12.34)		(19.58)	(5.8)	
Six-factor	−0.01	1.09	0.34	0.15	−0.04	0.33	0.13	0.71
	(−1.99)	(171.01)	(29.49)	(10.22)	(−4.37)	(19.91)	(6.45)	

This table is based on daily returns from January 1965 to December 2018. We report time-series regression results for the CAPM and different multifactor models, where the dependent variable is the daily excess returns for each industry. As discussed in Chapters 2 and 5, the following models are tested: CAPM market model, Fama and French (1992, 1993, 1995) three-factor model, Carhart (1997) four-factor model, Fama and French (2015) five-factor model, and Fama and French (2018) six-factor model. Estimated factor loadings (and associated factors) are denoted as follows: $\hat{\beta}_{i,m}$ (CRSP index excess return factor as proxy for the market portfolio), $\hat{\beta}_{i,S}$ (size factor *SMB*), $\hat{\beta}_{i,V}$ (value factor *HML*), $\hat{\beta}_{i,MOM}$ (momentum factor *MOM*), $\hat{\beta}_{i,R}$ (profit factor *RMW*), and $\hat{\beta}_{i,C}$ (capital investment factor *CMA*). Daily CRSP index returns, one-month Treasury bill rates, and industry portfolio returns are downloaded Kenneth French's website. For all models, *t*-statistics (in parentheses) and R^2 values are reported. Results are shown for different industry stock portfolios as test assets and zeta risk loadings, we employed the expectation–maximization (EM) algorithm.

Graphical analyses demonstrated that a close relation exists between zeta risk (associated with *RD*) and one-month-ahead returns for different stock portfolios. However, confirming prior studies, CAPM beta estimated using the market model was not related to one-month-ahead returns. Concerning the often-studied Fama and French size and B/M sorted portfolios, zeta risk was closely related to their one-month-ahead returns. As such, our results show that previous anomalous returns among stocks based on size and value firm characteristics are explained by zeta risk in the empirical ZCAPM.

Further graphical analyses of stock portfolios showed that the empirical ZCAPM does a good job of predicting one-month-ahead returns compared to the widely used Fama and French three-, five-, and six-factor models. Our ZCAPM demonstrated a closer relationship between one-month-ahead realized and predicted excess returns than the Fama and French (1992, 1993, 1995) three-factor model even for the small, growth portfolio that is known to be problematic for this model. Combining size and B/M sorted portfolios with industry portfolios and beta-zeta sorted portfolios, the empirical ZCAPM again provided a close relation between one-month-ahead realized and predicted stock returns, but the three-factor model exhibited little or no relation. Additional out-of-sample tests using profit and investment sorted portfolios that compared Fama and French's (2015, 2018) five- and six-factor models to the empirical ZCAPM confirmed the relatively higher predictive ability of the ZCAPM.

Whenever industry portfolios were included in the test asset portfolios, the performance of the Fama and French three-, five- and six-factor models broke down in terms of the goodness-of-fit between out-of-sample predicted and realized excess returns. By contrast, the empirical ZCAPM continued to provide strong goodness-of-fit with respect to industry portfolios. Interestingly, the ZCAPM provided a remarkably close fit between realized and predicted returns among Fama and French's frequently used 25 size-B/M sorted portfolios that improved upon their three-factor model. Since these portfolios are entirely exogenous to the ZCAPM, this evidence corroborates our earlier inference that anomalous return patterns in size and B/M firm characteristics are almost completely explained by the ZCAPM. Moreover, the profit-investment sorted portfolios are better explained by the ZCAPM than the five- and six-factor models of Fama and French even though these test assets are exogenous to the ZCAPM but endogenous to the Fama and French models. Like the size and value firm characteristics, anomalous returns associated with profit and investment characteristics of firms are largely explained by the empirical ZCAPM.

In sum, our graphical ZCAPM results are striking. The Fama and French models have been developed over the past 30 years in numerous papers published in top tier finance journals. Their widespread usage among academics and practitioners around the world attests to the fact that they represent the state-of-the-art in asset pricing. In this context, it is extraordinary that, in out-of-sample cross-sectional graphical analyses, the empirical ZCAPM outperforms these popular models using stock portfolios that are endogenous to these models but exogenous to the ZCAPM. Moreover, the impressive performance of the ZCAPM using exogenous industry portfolios compared to the poor performance of the Fama and French three-, five-, and six-factor models is remarkable. As an explanation for this poor cross-sectional performance of multifactor models, we presented evidence that they do not contribute much to the time-series regression explanatory power of industry portfolio returns compared to the CAPM market model.

Consistent with our earlier quotation of Fama and MacBeth (1973), because estimates of beta and zeta risks made from existing information are closely related to future returns, our empirical ZCAPM is a valid asset pricing model. In this regard, it is not the returns themselves that are predicted but the order of returns. Low (high) risk assets should have lower (higher) future returns. In a random walk market, nobody can predict the future level of returns. However, the order of future returns should be related to the previous order of their risk as measured by an asset pricing model. Not only does our empirical ZCAPM do a very good job in this respect, it clearly dominates extant asset pricing models.

Bibliography

Adrian, T., & Rosenberg, J. (2008). Stock returns and volatility: Pricing the short-run and long-run components of market risk. *Journal of Finance*, *63*, 2997–3030.

Black, F. (1972). Capital market equilibrium with restricted borrowing. *Journal of Business*, *45*, 444–454.

Carhart, M. M. (1997). On persistence in mutual fund performance. *Journal of Finance*, *52*, 57–82.

Chichernea, D. C., Holder, A. D., & Petkevich, A. (2015). Does return dispersion explain the accrual and investment anomalies? *Journal of Accounting and Economics, 60*, 133–148.

Choudhry, T., Papadimitriou, F. I., & Shabi, S. (2016). Stock market volatility and business cycle: Evidence from linear and nonlinear causality tests. *Journal of Banking and Finance, 66*, 89–101.

Christie, W., & Huang, R. (1994). The changing functional relation between stock returns and dividend yields. *Journal of Empirical Finance, 1*, 161–191.

Cochrane, J. H. (1996). A cross-sectional test of an investment-based asset pricing model. *Journal of Political Economy, 104*, 572–621.

Connolly, R., & Stivers, C. (2003). Momentum and reversals in equity index returns during periods of abnormal turnover and return dispersion. *Journal of Finance, 58*, 1521–1556.

Daniel, K., & Titman, S. (2012). Testing factor-model explanations of market anomalies. *Critical Finance Review, 1*, 103–139.

Demirer, R., Gupta, R., Zhihu, L., & Wing-Keung, W. (2019). Equity return dispersion and stock market volatility: Evidence from multivariate linear and nonlinear causality tests. *Sustainability, 11*, 1–15.

Demirer, R., & Jategaonkar, S. P. (2013). The conditional relation between dispersion and return. *Review of Financial Economics, 22*, 125–134.

Dempster, A. P., Laird, N. M., & Rubin, D. B. (1977). Maximum likelihood from incomplete data via the EM algorithm. *Journal of the Royal Statistical Society, 39*, 1–38.

Duffee, G. R. (2001). Asymmetric cross-sectional dispersion in stock returns: Evidence and implications (Working paper). University of California, Berkeley, CA.

Fama, E. F., & French, K. R. (1992). The cross-section of expected stock returns. *Journal of Finance, 47*, 427–465.

Fama, E. F., & French, K. R. (1993). The cross-section of expected returns. *Journal of Financial Economics, 33*, 3–56.

Fama, E. F., & French, K. R. (1995). Size and book-to-market factors in earnings and returns. *Journal of Finance, 50*, 131–156.

Fama, E. F., & French, K. R. (1996). Multifactor explanations of asset pricing anomalies. *Journal of Finance, 51*, 55–84.

Fama, E. F., & French, K. R. (1996). The CAPM is wanted, dead or alive. *Journal of Finance, 51*, 1947–1958.

Fama, E. F., & French, K. R. (2015). A five-factor asset pricing model. *Journal of Financial Economics, 116*, 1–22.

Fama, E. F., & French, K. R. (2018). Choosing factors. *Journal of Financial Economics, 128*, 234–252.

Fama, E. F., & MacBeth, J. D. (1973). Risk, return, and equilibrium: Empirical tests. *Journal of Political Economy, 81*, 607–636.

Garcia, R., Mantilla-Garcia, D., & Martellini, L. (2014). A model-free measure of aggregate idiosyncratic volatility and the prediction of market returns. *Journal of Financial and Quantitative Analysis, 49*, 1133–1165.
Gomes, J., Kogan, L., & Zhang, L. (2003). Equilibrium cross section of returns. *Journal of Political Economy, 111*, 693–732.
Jiang, X. (2010). Return dispersion and expected returns. *Financial Markets and Portfolio Management, 24*, 107–135.
Lettau, M., & Ludvigson, S. (2001). Consumption, aggregate wealth, and expected stock returns. *Journal of Finance, 56*, 815–849.
Lintner, J. (1965). The valuation of risk assets and the selection of risky investments in stock portfolios and capital budgets. *Review of Economics and Statistics, 47*, 13–37.
Liu, W. (2013). *A new asset pricing model based on the zero-beta CAPM: Theory and evidence*. Doctoral dissertation, Texas A&M University.
Liu, W., Kolari, J. W., & Huang, J. Z. (2012, October). *A new asset pricing model based on the zero-beta CAPM*. Atlanta, GA: Presentation at the Annual Meetings of the Financial Management Association.
Liu, W., Kolari, J. W., & Huang, J. Z. (2020, October). *Return dispersion and the cross-section of stock returns*. Palm Springs, CA: Presentation at the Annual Meetings of the Southern Finance Association.
Loungani, P., Rush, M., & Tave, W. (1990). Stock market dispersion and unemployment. *Journal of Monetary Economics, 25*, 367–388.
Mossin, J. (1966). Equilibrium in a capital asset market. *Econometrica, 34*, 768–783.
Petkova, R. (2006). Do the Fama-French factors proxy for innovations in predictive variables? *Journal of Finance, 61*, 581–612.
Sharpe, W. F. (1964). Capital asset prices: A theory of market equilibrium under conditions of risk. *Journal of Finance, 19*, 425–442.
Stambaugh, R. F., & Yuan, Y. (2017). Mispricing factors. *Review of Financial Studies, 30*, 1270–1315.
Treynor, J. L. (1961). *Market value, time, and risk* (Unpublished manuscript).
Treynor, J. L. (1962). *Toward a theory of market value of risky assets* (Unpublished manuscript).
Verousis, T., & Voukelators, N. (2015). *Cross-sectional dispersion an expected returns*. 5th Annual Conference of the Financial Engineering and Banking Society. France: Nantes.
Zhang, X. F. (2006). Information uncertainty and stock returns. *Journal of Finance, 61*, 105–136.

CHAPTER 7

Cross-Sectional Tests of the ZCAPM

Abstract This chapter reports formal cross-sectional tests of the empirical ZCAPM compared to popular asset pricing models. As in the previous chapter, our tests utilize all U.S. common stock returns from January 1965 to December 2018. We report extensive out-of-sample Fama and MacBeth (1973) cross-sectional tests of the ZCAPM compared to other asset pricing models. Our goal is to demonstrate using a weight of stock return evidence that the ZCAPM is the dominant asset pricing model relative to existing prominent models. In brief, the results of our tests strongly favor the empirical ZCAPM over other models. In test-after-test, zeta risk loadings in the ZCAPM have the highest t-values in cross-sectional regression analyses in the range of 3–6 that well exceed all multifactors in popular models. Not only are the t-values exceptionally high by any recommended threshold in the asset pricing literature, but zeta risk loadings are consistently positive and significant in terms of pricing return dispersion sensitivity in virtually all test assets investigated here. Additionally, across a variety of test assets, goodness-of-fit as measured by R^2 values is exceptionally high in our cross-sectional tests ranging from a low of approximately 70% to a high of 98%. In several commonly used test assets, little or no residual error remains to be explained by other potential factors. By contrast, popular multifactors' loadings rarely achieve a cross-sectional t-value exceeding 3, are much less consistently priced across different test assets, and have markedly lower R^2

J. W. Kolari et al., *A New Model of Capital Asset Prices*,
https://doi.org/10.1007/978-3-030-65197-8_7

values in most test assets. Based on these extensive tests, we conclude that the ZCAPM represents a pathbreaking innovation in asset pricing for academic research and investment practice.

Keywords Asset pricing · Beta risk · CAPM · Cross-sectional regression tests · Empirical ZCAPM · Expectation-maximization (EM) algorithm · Fama and MacBeth · Fama and French · Industry portfolios · Microcap stocks · Multifactor models · Out-of-sample returns · Return dispersion · Securities investment · Signal variable · Stock market · Test assets · ZCAPM · Zero-beta CAPM · Zeta risk

7.1 Preview of Empirical Evidence

Fama and MacBeth (1973) cross-sectional tests are the most widely accepted means by which to evaluate the validity of different contender asset pricing models. In this chapter we show that zeta risk loadings in the empirical ZCAPM estimated via the expectation-maximization (EM) algorithm are consistently significant for out-of-sample (one-month-ahead) stock returns. Indeed, the price of zeta risk loadings is significant at a higher level than any factor in prior literature documenting out-of-sample cross-sectional tests to the authors' knowledge. By comparison, the familiar general market index, size, value, momentum, profit, and capital investment factors in the Fama and French (1992, 1993, 1995, 1996) three-factor model, Carhart (1997) four-factor model, and Fama and French (2015, 2018) five- and six-factor models are less significant and priced in some but not all test assets. For a variety of different test assets, including portfolios sorted on size, book-to-market (value), profit, capital investment, beta and zeta risk coefficients, and industries, out-of-sample cross-sectional tests with one-month-ahead stock returns show that the market price of zeta risk associated with return dispersion (denoted *RD*) has t-values in the range of approximately 3–6 using the standard Fama-MacBeth monthly rolling approach. These out-of-sample zeta risk t-statistic results surpass the 3.0 and 3.4 hurdle rates recently established by Harvey et al. (2015) and Chordia et al. (2020), respectively, for the significance of asset pricing factors. By contrast, with only rare exceptions, cross-sectional t-values associated with size, value, momentum, profit, and capital investment risk loadings in the three-, four-, five-, and six-factor models do not pass the 3.0 hurdle rate in different test asset portfolios.

In addition to high statistical significance, risk premium estimates associated with zeta risk are economically substantial in the range of approximately 0.30% to 0.50% per month per unit estimated zeta coefficient across different test assets. Also, cross-sectional R^2 values for the ZCAPM are relatively high compared to other models ranging typically from approximately 70% to as high as 98%. Strikingly, the ZCAPM achieves a 94% R^2 value using Fama and French's often-studied 25 size and book-to-market (B/M) test assets, which are exogenous to the ZCAPM. In these test assets, no more factors than the empirical ZCAPM's average market return and *RD* factors are needed to price stock return risks. By comparison, even with the benefit of using size and value (B/M) test assets that are endogenous to their model, Fama and French's three-factor model achieves a substantially lower R^2 value of 63%. The Fama and French six-factor model boosts the cross-sectional R^2 value to 80%, but this multifactor model maximum is still well below the ZCAPM at 94%. Another important finding is that the R^2 values of multifactor models dramatically drop when industry portfolios are included in the test assets. For example, combining the 25 size and B/M portfolios with 47% industry portfolios, the three- and six-factor models' R^2 values drop to 6 and 36%, respectively, in the cross section of average stock returns. For these test assets, the ZCAPM's R^2 value is substantially higher at 79%. We infer that, unlike other popular models, the empirical ZCAPM generally explains most of the cross section of average stock returns in different test assets and almost all cross-sectional returns in some test assets.

An important implication of our findings is that the numerous factors proposed by many researchers over the past 30 years are no longer necessary. The empirical ZCAPM essentially sweeps these factors off the table as superfluous explanatory variables. This conclusion should not be surprising for two reasons. First, most factors—defined as zero-investment portfolios based on long minus short positions—are themselves rough measures of return dispersion. These long/short factors measure different slices of the total return dispersion of stock returns in the market and therefore capture different pieces of the total return dispersion. Collectively, these zero-investment factors are subsumed within total return dispersion in the ZCAPM.

Second, Sharpe's (1964) CAPM theory says that only systematic market risk associated with market portfolio *M* is priced by investors. Unsystematic risks specific to firms are diversifiable and therefore not priced. The problem with the CAPM is that, as the Roll (1977) critique argues, *M* is not observable so it cannot be tested. As shown in Chapter 3, our theoretical ZCAPM is an alternative form of the CAPM. We proxy market portfolio *M* differently than in the past. Rather than proxy *M* using market index returns (i.e., CRSP index, S&P 500 index, etc.), we use both average market index returns and their cross-sectional return dispersion. According to ZCAPM geometry, we move horizontally along the axis of symmetry of the mean-variance investment parabola (i.e., average market index returns) and then vertically up or down by means of the cross-sectional standard deviation of all stocks' returns (i.e., return dispersion) toward portfolios on the efficient frontier or inefficient lower boundary of the parabola, respectively. Since any two orthogonal portfolios on the upper and lower boundaries of the parabola can be used to proximate *M* in line with Black's (1972) zero-beta CAPM, our ZCAPM enables estimation of the CAPM in another form. Hence, our cross-sectional test results summarized above not only support the theoretical ZCAPM but Sharpe's CAPM and Black's zero-beta CAPM. All three CAPM theories posit that no other market risks are needed to price assets in equilibrium.

We perform a variety of robustness checks with split subsample periods and different test assets based on microcap and larger market capitalization portfolios, profit and capital investment portfolios, and the largest 500 individual stocks by market capitalization. Also, out-of-sample periods greater than one month are tested. Overall, we find that *RD* loadings (i.e., zeta risk) are the only factor risk loadings consistently priced in these robustness checks with *t*-values that exceed the hurdle rate of 3.0 in most cases. Lastly, we test recently proposed four-factor models by Hou et al. (2015) and Stambaugh and Yuan (2017) and find that their new factors are generally significant across different test assets but have *t*-values less than the 3.00 threshold. Similar to the consistent outperformance of the empirical ZCAPM relative to the Fama and French models, the ZCAPM clearly outperforms these four-factor models across a variety of test asset portfolios, especially when industry portfolios are included in the test assets.

These and other empirical results suggest that: (1) zeta risk associated with cross-sectional return dispersion is a salient asset pricing factor, and (2) the empirical ZCAPM explains most of the cross-sectional variation in stock returns. Based on our empirical results, we conclude that the ZCAPM represents a pathbreaking innovation in asset pricing for academic research and investment practice.

7.2 Out-of-Sample Cross-Sectional Tests

Our cross-sectional tests are out-of-sample in the sense that the risk parameters of a model are estimated in step one time-series regressions and, subsequently, *one-month-ahead* excess returns are cross-sectionally regressed in step two on the estimated risk parameters. We benchmark our empirical ZCAPM results against those for the CAPM as well as popular three-, four-, five-, and six-factor models defined in Chapter 5.

7.2.1 Overview of the ZCAPM and Cross-Sectional Regression Procedure

Before reporting test results, we review the theoretical and empirical ZCAPM from Chapters 3 and 4 as well as cross-sectional test procedure from Chapter 5. Mathematically derived as a special case of Black's (1972) zero-beta CAPM,[1] the *theoretical ZCAPM* is:

$$E(R_{it}) - R_{ft} = \beta_{i,a}[E(R_{at}) - R_{ft}] + Z^*_{i,a}\sigma_{at}, \tag{7.1}$$

where $E(R_{it})$ is the expected return on the ith asset at time t, $E(R_{at})$ is the expected market return based on the average return of all assets (rather than a proxy market index m for the theoretical market portfolio M), R_{ft} is the riskless rate, $\beta_{i,a}$ is the beta risk coefficient measuring sensitivity to expected excess market returns, σ_{at} is the cross-sectional standard deviation of all asset returns (or return dispersion denoted RD) at time t, and $Z^*_{i,a}$ is the zeta risk coefficient measuring dichotomous positive or negative sensitivity to return dispersion.[2]

To take into account both positive and negative signs on zeta risk coefficient $Z^*_{i,a}$, we proposed the following *empirical ZCAPM*[3]:

$$R_{it} - R_{ft} = \beta_{i,a}(R_{at} - R_{ft}) + Z_{i,a}D_{it}\sigma_{at} + u_{it}, \quad t = 1, \cdots, T, \tag{7.2}$$

[1] See earlier work in Liu et al. (2012) and Liu (2013).

[2] Because RD is a nontraded factor, we denote its factor loading as Z to distinguish it from tradeable zero-investment factor β loadings. Also, the asterisk denotes its relation to efficient portfolio I^* and its zero-beta portfolio ZI^* on the mean-variance investment parabola. These two orthogonal portfolios are unique due to having equal return variances.

[3] See Liu et al. (2020).

where $R_{it} - R_{ft}$ is the daily excess return over the Treasury bill rate for the ith stock portfolio (or stock) in a one-year period with $t = 1, \cdots, T$, $R_{at} - R_{ft}$ is the excess average market return of the value-weighted CRSP index associated with beta risk coefficient $\beta_{i,a}$, σ_{at} is the cross-sectional standard deviation of value-weighted returns in the CRSP index (return dispersion or RD) related to zeta risk coefficient $Z_{i,a}$, signal variable $D_{it} = +1$ or -1, and $u_{it} \sim$ iid $N(0, \sigma_i^2)$.[4] Signal variable D_{it} is a latent (unobserved) independent random variable with the following two-point distribution:

$$D_{it} = \begin{cases} +1 & \text{with probability } p_i \\ -1 & \text{with probability } 1 - p_i, \end{cases} \tag{7.3}$$

where p_i (or $1 - p_i$) is the probability of a positive (or negative) return dispersion effect, and D_{it} is independent of u_{it}.

Subsequently, we can rewrite ZCAPM relation (7.2) in its marginal form as:

$$R_{it} - R_{ft} = \beta_{i,a}(R_{at} - R_{ft}) + Z^*_{i,a}\sigma_{at} + u^*_{it}, \quad t = 1, \cdots, T, \tag{7.4}$$

where $\hat{\beta}_{i,a}$ is the beta risk coefficient, $\hat{Z}^*_{i,a} = \hat{Z}_{i,a}(2\hat{p}_i - 1)$ is the zeta risk coefficient, u^*_{it} is the error term with variance dependent on return dispersion (see Eq. 4.13 in Chapter 4), and other notation is as before. Using 12 months of daily returns, the empirical ZCAPM in Eq. (7.4) is estimated via the expectation-maximization (EM) algorithm (see Dempster et al. 1977).[5]

Next we cross-sectionally regress one-month-ahead (out-of-sample) returns for stock portfolios on $\hat{\beta}_{i,a}$ and $\hat{Z}^*_{i,a}$ loadings:

$$R_{iT+1} - R_{fT+1} = \lambda_0 + \lambda_a\hat{\beta}_{i,a} + \lambda_{RD}\hat{Z}^*_{i,a} + u_{it}, i = 1, ..., N, \tag{7.5}$$

where λ_0 is the intercept term, λ_a and λ_{RD} are coefficient estimates of the market prices of the beta and zeta risk loadings in percent terms, respectively, and other notation is as before. Because one-month-ahead excess

[4] As discussed in Chapter 4, several theoretical and empirical reasons justify dropping an intercept mispricing error term in Eq. (7.2). In the present context, because our interest is in forthcoming out-of-sample cross-sectional regression tests, rather than in-sample time-series regression tests, we set $\alpha_i = 0$.

[5] See Chapter 4 for detailed discussion of the EM algorithm and further citations to literature.

returns are used as the dependent variable in cross-sectional regression Eq. (7.5), and zeta loadings are estimated in time-series regression (7.2) with daily returns, $\hat{Z}^*_{i,a}$ must be rescaled from a daily to monthly basis as follows:

$$R_{i,T+1} - R_{fT+1} = \lambda_0 + \lambda_M \hat{\beta}_{i,a,} + \lambda_{RD} \hat{Z}^*_{i,a} N_{T+1} + +u_{it}, i = 1, ..., N, \quad (7.6)$$

where N_{T+1} is the number of trading days in a month $T + 1$ (i.e., 21 days), $Z^*_{i,T} N_{T+1}$ is the monthly estimated zeta risk, and λ_{RD} is the monthly risk premium associated with zeta risk. This rescaling does not change the risk premium $\hat{\lambda}_{RD}$ per unit zeta risk; however, rescaling $Z^*_{i,T}$ to a monthly basis makes λ_{RD} estimates comparable to λ_a estimates associated with beta loadings.

The rolling Fama and MacBeth cross-sectional test procedure is utilized. This two-step procedure begins as follows:

(1) in 1964 the empirical ZCAPM in Eq. (7.4) is estimated using daily returns for each stock portfolio (or stock); and
(2) one-month-ahead returns in January 1965 for all test asset stock portfolios (or stocks) are cross-sectionally regressed on beta and zeta risk loadings using Eq. (7.6).

Rolling forward one month at a time, a time series of 648 estimates of market prices λ_{RD} and λ_a are generated for the analysis period from January 1965 to December 2018. Averages of these estimated market prices and associated t-statistics are computed.

Matlab programs for estimating the empirical ZCAPM and conducting cross-sectional regression tests are available at the end of the book in the Compendium. Additionally, R programs for these analyses can be downloaded from GitHub (https://github.com/zcapm). R is a free software environment available on the internet. Our R programs run faster in terms of estimating the empirical ZCAPM than the Matlab programs.

7.2.2 *Empirical Results*

Turning to results, across different test assets, Table 7.1 shows that return dispersion (RD) loadings are highly significant in terms of pricing their risk. For example, in Panel A based on Fama and French's often-used 25 size-B/M sorted portfolios, the market price of RD zeta risk is $\hat{\lambda}_{RD} = 0.46\%$ per

Table 7.1 Out-of-sample Fama-MacBeth cross-sectional tests for ZCAPM regression factor loadings compared to other asset pricing models in the period January 1965 to December 2018: 12-month rolling windows

Panel A: 25 size-B/M sorted portfolios

Model	$\hat{\alpha}$	$\hat{\lambda}_m$	$\hat{\lambda}_{RD}$	$\hat{\lambda}_{SMB}$	$\hat{\lambda}_{HML}$	$\hat{\lambda}_{MOM}$	$\hat{\lambda}_{RMW}$	$\hat{\lambda}_{CMA}$	R^2
CAPM	0.98	−0.35							0.48
	(4.03)	(−0.35)							
ZCAPM	0.78	−0.19	0.46						0.94
	(3.26)	(−0.77)	(4.22)						
Three-factor	0.93	−0.41		0.17	0.31				0.63
	(4.98)	(−1.96)		(1.27)	(2.64)				
Four-factor	1.12	−0.60		0.16	0.29	0.08			0.69
	(5.84)	(−2.83)		(1.29)	(2.57)	(0.35)			
Five-factor	0.98	−0.45		0.21	0.28		0.13	0.11	0.75
	(4.94)	(−2.06)		(1.73)	(2.49)		(1.10)	(0.84)	
Six-factor	1.07	−0.55		0.22	0.30	0.16	0.12	0.06	0.80
	(5.39)	(−2.52)		(1.80)	(2.69)	(0.68)	(1.03)	(0.45)	

Panel B: 47 industry portfolios

Model	$\hat{\alpha}$	$\hat{\lambda}_m$	$\hat{\lambda}_{RD}$	$\hat{\lambda}_{SMB}$	$\hat{\lambda}_{HML}$	$\hat{\lambda}_{MOM}$	$\hat{\lambda}_{RMW}$	$\hat{\lambda}_{CMA}$	R^2
CAPM	0.57	0.03							0.00
	(2.95)	(0.15)							
ZCAPM	0.49	0.11	0.32						0.70
	(2.71)	(0.53)	(4.07)						
Three-factor	0.43	0.11		0.02	0.14				0.15
	(2.21)	(0.48)		(0.14)	(1.17)				
Four-factor	0.46	0.08		0.04	0.08	0.43			0.39
	(2.31)	(0.37)		(0.31)	(0.73)	(2.09)			
Five-factor	0.36	0.19		0.07	0.09		0.20	0.24	0.18
	(1.78)	(0.83)		(0.51)	(0.76)		(2.03)	(2.48)	
Six-factor	0.51	0.04		0.04	0.06	0.39	0.20	0.17	0.50
	(2.53)	(0.16)		(0.32)	(0.52)	(1.92)	(2.05)	(1.78)	

Panel C: 25 beta-zeta sorted portfolios

Model	$\hat{\alpha}$	$\hat{\lambda}_m$	$\hat{\lambda}_{RD}$	$\hat{\lambda}_{SMB}$	$\hat{\lambda}_{HML}$	$\hat{\lambda}_{MOM}$	$\hat{\lambda}_{RMW}$	$\hat{\lambda}_{CMA}$	R^2
CAPM	0.49	−0.06							0.11
	(3.23)	(−0.26)							
ZCAPM	0.29	0.17	0.35						0.96
	(1.91)	(0.83)	(4.03)						
Three-factor	0.66	−0.05		−0.28	0.14				0.65
	(3.34)	(−0.24)		(−1.49)	(1.00)				
Four-factor	0.54	−0.03		−0.25	0.25	0.28			0.70
	(3.50)	(−0.15)		(−1.51)	(1.76)	(1.61)			
Five-factor	0.52	−0.03		−0.19	0.25		0.17	0.09	0.67
	(3.06)	(−0.13)		(−1.11)	(1.56)		(1.18)	(0.77)	
Six-factor	0.62	−0.11		−0.14	0.30	0.26	0.17	0.02	0.76
	(3.86)	(−0.54)		(−0.88)	(1.90)	(1.50)	(1.30)	(0.14)	

(continued)

Table 7.1 (continued)

Panel D: 25 size-B/M sorted plus 47 industry portfolios

Model	$\hat{\alpha}$	$\hat{\lambda}_m$	$\hat{\lambda}_{RD}$	$\hat{\lambda}_{SMB}$	$\hat{\lambda}_{HML}$	$\hat{\lambda}_{MOM}$	$\hat{\lambda}_{RMW}$	$\hat{\lambda}_{CMA}$	R^2
CAPM	0.72	−0.09							0.03
	(3.82)	(−0.41)							
ZCAPM	0.59	0.03	0.37						0.79
	(3.38)	(0.14)	(4.99)						
Three-factor	0.54	0.01		0.11	0.16				0.06
	(3.08)	(−0.03)		(0.86)	(1.41)				
Four-factor	0.58	−0.04		0.12	0.15	0.43			0.24
	(3.33)	(−0.18)		(0.96)	(1.44)	(2.16)			
Five-factor	0.48	0.06		0.16	0.13		0.19	0.22	0.11
	(2.83)	(0.30)		(1.38)	(1.22)		(1.92)	(2.42)	
Six-factor	0.64	−0.09		0.16	0.16	0.40	0.18	0.18	0.36
	(3.70)	(−0.47)		(1.35)	(1.50)	(2.07)	(1.87)	(2.00)	

Panel E: 97 combined portfolios

Model	$\hat{\alpha}$	$\hat{\lambda}_m$	$\hat{\lambda}_{RD}$	$\hat{\lambda}_{SMB}$	$\hat{\lambda}_{HML}$	$\hat{\lambda}_{MOM}$	$\hat{\lambda}_{RMW}$	$\hat{\lambda}_{CMA}$	R^2
CAPM	0.64	−0.06							0.05
	(3.93)	(−0.31)							
ZCAPM	0.48	0.09	0.38						0.83
	(3.24)	(0.47)	(5.42)						
Three-factor	0.52	0.002		0.06	0.18				0.06
	(3.55)	(0.01)		(0.49)	(1.64)				
Four-factor	0.53	−0.01		0.09	0.17	0.43			0.28
	(3.75)	(−0.06)		(0.75)	(1.64)	(2.54)			
Five-factor	0.44	0.09		0.12	0.14		0.21	0.21	0.22
	(2.97)	(0.45)		(1.02)	(1.35)		(1.99)	(2.36)	
Six-factor	0.57	−0.04		0.14	0.17	0.40	0.19	0.16	0.35
	(4.02)	(−0.24)		(1.20)	(1.68)	(2.40)	(1.94)	(1.84)	

Using value-weighted returns, this table contains results for the analysis period January 1965 to December 2018. We report out-of-sample (one-month-ahead) estimated prices of risk based on standard two-step Fama-MacBeth cross-sectional tests. Estimated prices of risk are denoted $\hat{\lambda}_k$ for the kth factor in monthly percent return terms (t-statistics in parentheses). Factors are denoted as m (CRSP index, see footnote 1), *RD* (return dispersion), *SMB* (size), *HML* (value), *MOM* (momentum), *RMW* (profit), and *CMA* (capital investment). Results are shown for different sets of test asset portfolios

[1] In the ZCAPM, the price of beta risk associated with CRSP index excess returns is denoted $\hat{\lambda}_a$ rather than $\hat{\lambda}_m$ in the other models

month per unit estimated zeta coefficient (t = 4.22). In Panel B using 47 industry portfolios, we again obtain highly statistically significant market prices of *RD* risk equal to $\hat{\lambda}_{RD}$ = 0.32% per month (t = 4.07). These results strongly support the ZCAPM.

However, the results for factors in popular asset pricing models are not nearly as strong as the ZCAPM. Section 5.4 in Chapter 5 reviewed the Fama and French and Carhart models containing zero-investment (long/short) factors, including size, value, momentum, profit, and capital investment. As shown in Table 7.1, none of these factors is consistently priced in the 25 size-B/M portfolios and industry portfolios in Panels A and B, respectively. We summarize the results below.

- The *SMB* (size) factor is not priced in Panel A for the three- and four-factor models but is nominally significant at the ten percent level in the five- and six-factor models with $\hat{\lambda}_{SMB}$ = 0.21% per month (t = 1.73) and $\hat{\lambda}_{SMB}$ = 0.22% per month (t = 1.80), respectively. In Panel B for industry portfolios, *SMB* is not priced in any of the models.
- The *HML* (value) factor is significantly priced at the one percent level in Panel A for the three-, four-, five-, and six-factor models with $\hat{\lambda}_{HML}$ = 0.31% per month (t = 2.64), $\hat{\lambda}_{HML}$ = 0.29%(t = 2.57), $\hat{\lambda}_{HML}$ = 0.28% (t = 2.49), and $\hat{\lambda}_{HML}$ = 0.30% (t = 2.69), respectively. In Panel B for industry portfolios, *HML* is not priced in any of the models.
- The *MOM* (momentum) factor in the four-factor model is significantly priced in Panel B for industry portfolios at the five percent level with $\hat{\lambda}_{MOM}$ = 0.43% per month (t = 2.09) and at the ten percent level for the six-factor model with $\hat{\lambda}_{MOM}$ = 0.39% per month (t = 1.92). In Panel A for the 25 size-B/M sorted portfolios, *MOM* is not priced in the four- and six-factor models.
- The *RMW* (profit) factor is significantly priced in the five- and six-factor models in Panel B for industry portfolios at the five percent level with $\hat{\lambda}_{RMW}$ = 0.20% per month (t = 2.03) and $\hat{\lambda}_{RMW}$ = 0.20% (t = 2.05), respectively. In Panel A for 25 size-B/M portfolios, *RMW* is not priced in the five- and six-factor models.
- The *CMA* (capital investment) factor is significantly priced in the five-factor model in Panel B for industry portfolios at the five percent level with $\hat{\lambda}_{CMA}$ = 0.24% per month (t = 2.48) and in the six-factor model at the marginal 10% level with $\hat{\lambda}_{CMA}$ = 0.17% (t = 1.78). In Panel A for 25 size-B/M portfolios, *CMA* is not priced in the five- and six-factor models.

Importantly, only the *RD* (return dispersion) factor is associated with estimated risk premiums with t-statistics consistently greater than 3. In the 97 combined portfolios in Panel E, the t-value associated with *RD* factor loadings reaches a maximum of 5.42, which is very high compared to other popular factors. As mentioned earlier, Harvey et al. (2015) and Chordia et al. (2020) have recommended that proposed factors should have a t-statistic of more than 3.0 to avoid data-snooping biases inherent in testing for valid asset pricing factors. The Fama and French factors fail to clear these hurdles.

Previous asset pricing studies normally test the CAPM market model and multifactor models using five years of monthly returns. Consequently, we repeated the analyses for these models using a five-year period to estimate time-series regression loadings. In general, our unreported results are similar to those using daily returns in a one-year estimation period in Table 7.1, with the exception that *HML* is more significantly priced across different test asset portfolios. In these tests, *RMW* loadings generate a t-value greater than 3 for the 25 size-B/M sorted portfolios.

Due to the exclusion of an intercept in the first step time-series regression estimates of the empirical ZCAPM, we compared the monthly rolling approach results in Table 7.1 with and without estimated intercepts ($\hat{\alpha}$s) for the CAPM and three-, four-, five-, and six-factor models. In unreported results, we find little or no change in the factor prices $\hat{\lambda}_k$ for these models with or without estimated intercepts in time-series regressions.[6] We infer that cross-sectional tests of factor prices are unaffected by time-series regressions that set the intercept to zero. In this regard, an anonymous reviewer of our book was concerned that the absence of an intercept term in the empirical ZCAPM impacted the beta risk and zeta risk factor loadings and, in turn, our cross-sectional test results. However, our tests of other CAPM and multifactor models with and without intercepts indicate that the zero intercept in the empirical ZCAPM likely has little or no effect on our test results.

Confirming previous tests of CAPM beta, the average price of risk $\hat{\lambda}_m$ associated with beta is not generally significant across models and test assets in Table 7.1, with the exception that it is significantly but negatively priced in the three-, four-, five-, and six-factor models in Panel A for 25 size-B/M sorted portfolios. These results are not consistent with the positive relation

[6] Results are available upon request from the authors.

between market beta and returns in CAPM theory. However, they agree with the poor cross-sectional relation between excess returns and beta risk in Figure 6.2 in Chapter 6, as well as their apparent inverse relation in Figure 6.4. Also, they agree with Fama and French (1992, 1995, 1996) and many others that generally find that market beta is not priced in the cross section.[7]

As discussed in Chapters 4–6, market model specifications of the CAPM typically use the CRSP index to proxy the true market portfolio *M* in Sharpe's (1964) CAPM. However, the ZCAPM does not view the CRSP index as a proxy for the true market portfolio *M* but rather the average return on all stocks in the market. According to ZCAPM theory, average market returns lie approximately on the axis of symmetry of the mean-variance investment parabola, not on the efficient frontier at the tangent point between the Capital Market Line (CML) connecting the frontier and the riskless rate of interest. For this reason, the ZCAPM denotes $\hat{\lambda}_m$ as $\hat{\lambda}_a$ in recognition of this very different perspective on market beta associated with CRSP index excess returns.

Referring to results based on beta-zeta sorted portfolios in Panel C of Table 7.1, we see that the only significantly priced factor at the one percent level or lower across different models is *RD*. *HML* is marginally priced (at the 10% level) in the four- and six-factor models. For portfolios containing industries in Panels D and E, *SMB* in the three-, four-, five-, and six-factor models is not priced. *HML* is marginally priced in Panel E in the six-factor model. And, *MOM*, *RMW*, and *CMA* are significantly priced at the 5% level or lower. Again, *RD* has a fairly large economic magnitude and is more significantly priced in Panels D and E than other tested factors with $\hat{\lambda}_V = 0.37\%$ per month ($t = 4.99$) and $\hat{\lambda}_V = 0.38\%$ ($t = 5.42$), respectively. Notice that the latter *t*-statistics are exceptionally high at 5 or more.

In sum, we infer from the results in Table 7.1 that *RD* is more consistently and significantly priced in the cross section of average stock returns than other factors in popular asset pricing models. More generally, *t*-values associated with the market price of *RD* loadings are relatively high compared to those of other studies in the asset pricing literature.[8]

[7] See the excellent survey article by Fama and French (2004).

[8] It is worth mentioning that Adrian et al. (2014) proposed a new security broker-dealer leverage factor. Using quarterly data series in the sample period 1968 to 2009, cross-sectional tests for a combination of 25 size-B/M, 10 momentum, and 6 Treasury bond portfolios were conducted. For each portfolio they estimated the beta factor loading for the broker-dealer

With respect to goodness-of-fit, for the 25 size-B/M sorted and 25 beta-zeta sorted portfolios in Panels A and C of Table 7.1, respectively, estimated R^2 values are typically higher than for other test assets in Panels B, D, and E that contain industry portfolios. For example, in Panel A using the 25 size-B/M portfolios, R^2 values are 0.48, 0.94, 0.63, 0.69, 0.75, and 0.80 for the CAPM, ZCAPM, three-, four-, five-, and six-factor models, respectively, compared to 0.00, 0.70, 0.15, 0.39, 0.18, and 0.50 in Panel B using 47 industry portfolios. In Panels A and C, the very high R^2 values of 0.94 and 0.96, respectively, for our ZCAPM using 25 size-B/M sorted and 25 beta-zeta sorted portfolios are outstanding but should be interpreted with some caution due to the exclusion of industry portfolios. Nonetheless, based on the consistency of the results across different test assets, we infer from the R^2 results that the ZCAPM has stronger goodness-of-fit than the other models in terms of explaining cross-sectional variation of average returns. With R^2 values in the range of 70%–96%, it is apparent that the ZCAPM does an excellent job of explaining cross-sectional stock returns. Little residual error remains for other potential risk factors to explain, especially in size-B/M sorted and 25 beta-zeta sorted portfolios.

The relatively high R^2 values and t-values associated with the ZCAPM in cross-sectional tests help to explain the relatively high magnitudes of estimated market prices of zeta risk loadings. According to the descriptive statistics in Table 5.1 in Chapter 5, the average market risk premium (i.e., $R_a - R_f$) is approximately 0.50% per month in the sample period January 1965 to December 2018. In Table 7.1 the estimated values of the market premium for zeta risk loadings, or $\hat{\lambda}_{RD}$, in the ZCAPM for different test assets range from 0.32% to 0.46% per month. Note that these estimates have some relation to the R^2 values. For example, in Panel B the R^2 value is 70% for the ZCAPM and $\hat{\lambda}_{RD}$ = 0.32%, whereas in Panel A the R^2 value is 94% for the ZCAPM and $\hat{\lambda}_{RD}$ = 0.46%. The latter estimate accounts for 92% of the average market premium in the sample period which is

leverage factor using one time-series regression for the full sample period. The average quarterly excess returns over the full sample period were then regressed on the full-sample beta factor loadings in a single cross-sectional regression. This in-sample cross-sectional test procedure yielded one estimate of the market price of broker-dealer leverage risk. They obtained relatively high t-values in the range from 3.1 to 3.7 for their leverage factor. However, they do not report out-of-sample test results, which are less prone to evaluation problems mentioned earlier. It is reasonable to believe that their t-values would be reduced in out-of-sample tests. In our analyses, we only report out-of-sample test results. Also, they do not include industry portfolios in their test assets, which would present a more difficult challenge in tests.

made possible by the almost perfect relationship between average monthly realized returns and average monthly fitted returns in the 25 size-B/M test asset portfolios. Of course, high $\hat{\lambda}_{RD}$ estimates are associated with high t-values (i.e., ranging from 4.03 to 5.42).

The only other factor to yield an estimate of $\hat{\lambda}$ that compares with $\hat{\lambda}_{RD}$ is momentum. In Panels B, D, and E of Table 7.1 containing results with industry portfolios, $\hat{\lambda}_{MOM}$ ranges from 0.28% to 0.43% per month. In these instances, the associated t-values are relatively high compared to other popular multifactors including size, value, profit, and investment, and R^2 values range from 24% to 80% for models containing momentum. In Table 7.1 the other four multifactors have $\hat{\lambda}$s in the range of −0.28% to 0.31%, and the market factor has estimates from −0.60% to 0.19%, both of which are less than those for zeta risk and momentum loadings.

Across different test assets in Table 7.1, $\hat{\alpha}$s (intercepts) are typically positive, similar in magnitude, and significant in different asset pricing models. Estimated $\hat{\alpha}$s range from 0.36% to 1.12% per month, with noticeably higher values in the 25 size-B/M sorted assets. These intercepts represent average stock returns when all factor loadings (i.e., independent variables) are set to zero.

7.3 Robustness Checks

As robustness checks, we repeat the out-of-sample cross-sectional tests in Table 7.1 using split subsample periods as well as different test asset portfolios (based on size groups in addition to profit and capital investment firm characteristics) and individual stocks.[9] Also, we generate tests using longer out-of-sample periods than one month. Finally, we provide comparative results for recent four-factor models by Hou et al. (2015) and Stambaugh and Yuan (2017).

[9] Ang et al. (2020) have reported evidence that the efficiency of cross-sectional tests is improved by using individual stocks rather than portfolios as test assets. Other researchers have advocated for using individual stocks over stock portfolios in cross-sectional tests also (e.g., see Kim 1995; Gagliardini et al. 2016). Of course, individual stocks enable wider ranging risk parameter (i.e., regression coefficient) estimates than portfolios to better observe the total spread of risk and return among test assets but introduce error-in-the-variables problems. See Subsection 2.1.2 in Chapter 2 for discussion per Black et al. (1972) in this regard.

7.3.1 Split Subsample Period Results

Tables 7.2 and 7.3 report cross-sectional test results for the two subperiods January 1965 to December 1989 and January 1990 to December 2018, respectively. The results for the first subperiod in Table 7.2 are very similar to the full sample results in Table 7.1. Again *RD* loadings are the most consistently and significantly priced with *t*-values in the range of 3.31 to 5.52 in different test asset portfolios. As before, some multifactors are significant but not consistently priced in different models and test assets. For example, across different test asset portfolios, the ranges of *t*-values for different multifactors are as follows: *SMB* from −1.54 to 1.91, *HML* from 0.66 to 3.18, *MOM* from −0.36 to 2.07, *RMW* from −0.52 to 0.79, and *CMA* from −0.06 to 3.81.

The results for the second subperiod in Table 7.3 are quite different from Table 7.1. Not only is the market factor normally not priced, but now the multifactors are generally not significantly priced also. An exception is that *RMW* is significantly priced at the five percent level in the five- and six-factor models for industry portfolios in Panel B, size-B/M sorted plus industry portfolios in Panel D, and 97 combined portfolios in Panel E. By contrast, our *RD* risk factor is significantly priced in all five different test assets in Table 7.3, albeit at a marginal 10% level for industry portfolios in Panel B. In this sample period from January 1990 to December 2018, it is possible that market turmoil in the 2000 technology bubble and later 2008–2009 financial crisis reduced the asset pricing ability of *RD* to some degree and the multifactors to a larger extent. Alternatively, the significance of multifactors may not be persistent over time due to increased informational efficiency arising from publication of their anomalous return behavior (e.g., see Schwert 2003; Chordia et al. 2014; Hou et al. 2015; McLean and Ponti 2016; Green et al. 2016; Harvey 2017; Linnainmaa and Roberts 2018, and others). A problem in the latter argument is that the profit and capital investment factors were not featured prominently in the asset pricing literature until after 2010. Hence, we believe that severe market volatility is responsible for the diminished performance of different asset pricing models in the January 1990 to December 2018 period. Even so, the empirical ZCAPM holds up and is able to explain from 67% to 93% of the cross section of average returns in Table 7.3.

Table 7.2 Split subsample period results for out-of-sample Fama-MacBeth cross-sectional tests from January 1965 to December 1989: 12-month rolling windows

Model	$\hat{\alpha}$	$\hat{\lambda}_m$	$\hat{\lambda}_{RD}$	$\hat{\lambda}_{SMB}$	$\hat{\lambda}_{HML}$	$\hat{\lambda}_{MOM}$	$\hat{\lambda}_{RMW}$	$\hat{\lambda}_{CMA}$	R^2
Panel A: 25 size-B/M sorted portfolios									
CAPM	0.86	−0.32							0.50
	(2.35)	(−0.91)							
ZCAPM	0.90	−0.42	0.45						0.91
	(2.46)	(−1.22)	(3.31)						
Three-factor	0.75	−0.39		0.28	0.49				0.74
	(2.87)	(−1.44)		(1.60)	(3.00)				
Four-factor	0.98	−0.62		0.29	0.49	0.04			0.75
	(3.67)	(−2.30)		(1.60)	(3.00)	(0.14)			
Five-factor	0.78	−0.41		0.34	0.47		−0.04	0.15	0.78
	(2.69)	(−1.41)		(1.87)	(2.90)		(−0.28)	(0.87)	
Six-factor	0.82	−0.547		0.35	0.50	0.21	0.04	0.05	0.79
	(2.97)	(−1.64)		(1.91)	(3.09)	(0.67)	(0.25)	(0.26)	
Panel B: 47 industry portfolios									
CAPM	0.84	−0.33							0.00
	(3.06)	(−1.20)							
ZCAPM	0.78	−0.27	0.43						0.79
	(2.92)	(−1.03)	(4.25)						
Three-factor	0.68	−0.25		0.13	0.44				0.12
	(2.42)	(−0.78)		(0.81)	(2.76)				
Four-factor	0.59	−0.15		0.16	0.25	0.53			0.22
	(2.23)	(−0.50)		(0.94)	(1.55)	(1.94)			
Five-factor	0.55	−0.12		0.25	0.24		0.03	0.51	0.17
	(2.12)	(−0.38)		(1.47)	(1.52)		(0.23)	(3.75)	
Six-factor	0.64	−0.23		0.20	0.19	0.53	0.01	0.32	0.37
	(2.45)	(−0.75)		(1.20)	(1.14)	(2.01)	(0.05)	(2.28)	
Panel C: 25 beta-zeta sorted portfolios									
CAPM	0.63	−0.28							0.17
	(2.58)	(−1.03)							
ZCAPM	0.43	−0.04	0.46						0.97
	(1.62)	(−0.13)	(4.45)						
Three-factor	0.79	−0.36		−0.19	0.13				0.48
	(3.31)	(−1.28)		(−0.91)	(0.66)				
Four-factor	0.77	−0.34		−0.20	0.29	0.17			0.56
	(2.91)	(−1.18)		(−1.00)	(1.41)	(0.68)			
Five-factor	0.68	−0.24		−0.24	0.17		0.14	−0.01	0.59
	(2.69)	(−0.88)		(−1.17)	(0.89)		(0.79)	(−0.06)	
Six-factor	0.78	−0.36		−0.30	0.24	−0.09	0.09	0.11	0.63
	(2.67)	(−1.16)		(−1.54)	(1.13)	(−0.36)	(−0.52)	(0.60)	

(continued)

Table 7.2 (continued)

Panel D: 25 size-B/M sorted plus 47 industry portfolios

Model	$\hat{\alpha}$	$\hat{\lambda}_m$	$\hat{\lambda}_{RD}$	$\hat{\lambda}_{SMB}$	$\hat{\lambda}_{HML}$	$\hat{\lambda}_{MOM}$	$\hat{\lambda}_{RMW}$	$\hat{\lambda}_{CMA}$	R^2
CAPM	0.94	−0.40							0.09
	(3.39)	(−1.50)							
ZCAPM	0.84	−0.33	0.48						0.83
	(3.18)	(−1.30)	(4.95)						
Three-factor	0.69	−0.27		0.20	0.44				0.21
	(2.73)	(−0.92)		(1.25)	(3.00)				
Four-factor	0.68	−0.24		0.21	0.34	0.48			0.26
	(2.83)	(−0.89)		(1.27)	(2.25)	(1.84)			
Five-factor	0.58	−0.15		0.28	0.32		0.01	0.49	0.20
	(2.45)	(−0.52)		(1.68)	(2.17)		(0.09)	(3.81)	
Six-factor	0.70	−0.29		0.26	0.31	0.52	−0.02	0.36	0.32
	(2.96)	(−1.05)		(1.57)	(2.07)	(2.05)	(−0.18)	(2.71)	

Panel E: 97 combined portfolios

Model	$\hat{\alpha}$	$\hat{\lambda}_m$	$\hat{\lambda}_{RD}$	$\hat{\lambda}_{SMB}$	$\hat{\lambda}_{HML}$	$\hat{\lambda}_{MOM}$	$\hat{\lambda}_{RMW}$	$\hat{\lambda}_{CMA}$	R^2
CAPM	0.87	−0.38							0.11
	(3.58)	(−1.55)							
ZCAPM	0.76	−0.28	0.48						0.86
	(3.24)	(−1.19)	(5.52)						
Three-factor	0.74	−0.34		0.14	0.45				0.17
	(3.54)	(−1.30)		(0.87)	(3.18)				
Four-factor	0.66	−0.24		0.16	0.35	(0.45)			0.26
	(3.11)	(−0.94)		(0.97)	(2.41)	(2.00)			
Five-factor	0.62	−0.20		0.22	0.32		0.08	0.44	0.22
	(3.03)	(−0.80)		(1.38)	(2.24)		(0.73)	(3.52)	
Six-factor	0.63	−0.23		0.20	0.31	0.44	0.04	0.35	0.29
	(2.93)	(−0.89)		(1.26)	(2.12)	(2.07)	(0.33)	(2.78)	

Using value-weighted returns, this table repeats results in Table 7.1 for the subsample period January 1965 to December 1989. We report out-of-sample (one-month-ahead) estimated prices of risk based on standard two-step Fama-MacBeth cross-sectional tests. Estimated prices of risk are denoted $\hat{\lambda}_k$ for the kth factor in monthly percent return terms (t-statistics in parentheses). Factors are denoted as m (CRSP index, see footnote 1), *RD* (return dispersion), *SMB* (size), *HML* (value), *MOM* (momentum), *RMW* (profit), and *CMA* (capital investment). Results are shown for different sets of test asset portfolios

[1] In the ZCAPM, the price of beta risk associated with CRSP index excess returns is denoted $\hat{\lambda}_a$ rather than $\hat{\lambda}_m$ in the other models

Table 7.3 Split subsample period results for out-of-sample Fama-MacBeth cross-sectional tests from January 1990 to December 2018: 12-month rolling windows

Panel A: 25 size-B/M sorted portfolios

Model	$\hat{\alpha}$	$\hat{\lambda}_m$	$\hat{\lambda}_{RD}$	$\hat{\lambda}_{SMB}$	$\hat{\lambda}_{HML}$	$\hat{\lambda}_{MOM}$	$\hat{\lambda}_{RMW}$	$\hat{\lambda}_{CMA}$	R^2
CAPM	1.10	−0.39							0.25
	(3.39)	(−1.09)							
ZCAPM	0.66	0.03	0.47						0.79
	(2.11)	(0.08)	(2.83)						
Three-factor	1.10	−0.43		0.06	0.15				0.30
	(4.09)	(−1.32)		(0.28)	(0.86)				
Four-factor	1.23	−0.56		0.06	0.13	0.11			0.40
	(4.51)	(−1.79)		(0.31)	(0.80)	(0.29)			
Five-factor	1.13	−0.48		0.11	0.14		0.27	0.11	0.51
	(3.98)	(−1.41)		(0.65)	(0.87)		(1.36)	(0.55)	
Six-factor	1.23	−0.58		0.10	0.13	0.25	0.24	0.07	0.58
	(4.57)	(−1.82)		(0.64)	(0.84)	(0.66)	(1.28)	(0.38)	

Panel B: 47 industry portfolios

Model	$\hat{\alpha}$	$\hat{\lambda}_m$	$\hat{\lambda}_{RD}$	$\hat{\lambda}_{SMB}$	$\hat{\lambda}_{HML}$	$\hat{\lambda}_{MOM}$	$\hat{\lambda}_{RMW}$	$\hat{\lambda}_{CMA}$	R^2
CAPM	0.31	0.39							0.05
	(1.14)	(1.14)							
ZCAPM	0.25	0.44	0.22						0.67
	(0.99)	(1.40)	(1.87)						
Three-factor	0.20	0.47		−0.09	−0.14				0.33
	(0.72)	(1.35)		(−0.39)	(−0.81)				
Four-factor	0.34	0.29		−0.06	−0.06	0.34			0.53
	(1.18)	(0.84)		(−0.27)	(−0.39)	(1.13)			
Five-factor	0.18	0.46		−0.08	−0.05		0.35	0.01	0.30
	(0.62)	(1.34)		(−0.39)	(−0.34)		(2.39)	(0.11)	
Six-factor	0.45	0.18		−0.10	−0.04	0.23	0.41	0.01	0.64
	(1.49)	(0.54)		(−0.49)	(−0.24)	(0.76)	(2.55)	(0.18)	

Panel C: 25 beta-zeta sorted portfolios

Model	$\hat{\alpha}$	$\hat{\lambda}_m$	$\hat{\lambda}_{RD}$	$\hat{\lambda}_{SMB}$	$\hat{\lambda}_{HML}$	$\hat{\lambda}_{MOM}$	$\hat{\lambda}_{RMW}$	$\hat{\lambda}_{CMA}$	R^2
CAPM	0.52	0.03							0.10
	(2.52)	(0.07)							
ZCAPM	0.37	0.20	0.28						0.93
	(1.94)	(0.40)	(2.10)						
Three-factor	0.49	0.13		−0.40	0.19				0.76
	(2.01)	(0.40)		(−1.26)	(0.87)				
Four-factor	0.44	0.17		−0.46	0.28	0.25			0.81
	(2.03)	(0.59)		(−1.78)	(0.29)	(0.25)			
Five-factor	0.52	−0.03		−0.19	0.25		0.17	0.09	0.67
	(3.06)	(−0.13)		(−1.11)	(0.25)		(0.17)	(0.09)	
Six-factor	0.69	−0.09		−0.28	0.39	0.22	0.11	0.03	0.84
	(3.05)	(−0.29)		(−1.13)	(1.63)	(0.90)	(0.52)	(0.19)	

(continued)

Table 7.3 (continued)

Panel D: 25 size-B/M sorted plus 47 industry portfolios

Model	$\hat{\alpha}$	$\hat{\lambda}_m$	$\hat{\lambda}_{RD}$	$\hat{\lambda}_{SMB}$	$\hat{\lambda}_{HML}$	$\hat{\lambda}_{MOM}$	$\hat{\lambda}_{RMW}$	$\hat{\lambda}_{CMA}$	R^2
CAPM	0.51	0.21							0.01
	(1.99)	(0.67)							
ZCAPM	0.37	0.34	0.28						0.67
	(1.61)	(1.13)	(2.53)						
Three-factor	0.39	0.27		0.02	−0.11				0.03
	(1.62)	(0.84)		(0.09)	(−0.65)				
Four-factor	0.50	0.48		0.03	−0.01	0.38			0.31
	(1.98)	(0.46)		(0.20)	(−0.06)	(1.30)			
Five-factor	0.39	0.25		0.06	−0.04		0.35	−0.01	0.07
	(1.62)	(0.81)		(0.37)	(−0.27)		(2.28)	(−0.07)	
Six-factor	0.62	0.01		0.07	0.04	0.29	0.39	0.01	0.48
	(2.47)	(0.04)		(0.41)	(0.28)	(0.98)	(2.48)	(0.06)	

Panel E: 97 combined portfolios

Model	$\hat{\alpha}$	$\hat{\lambda}_m$	$\hat{\lambda}_{RD}$	$\hat{\lambda}_{SMB}$	$\hat{\lambda}_{HML}$	$\hat{\lambda}_{MOM}$	$\hat{\lambda}_{RMW}$	$\hat{\lambda}_{CMA}$	R^2
CAPM	0.50	0.18							0.01
	(2.26)	(0.56)							
ZCAPM	0.33	0.33	0.30						0.75
	(1.71)	(1.16)	(2.84)						
Three-factor	0.39	0.25		−0.03	−0.05				0.02
	(1.95)	(0.84)		(−0.14)	(−0.28)				
Four-factor	0.47	0.15		0.01	0.02	0.34			0.26
	(2.40)	(0.55)		(0.07)	(0.16)	(1.40)			
Five-factor	0.37	0.26		0.02	0.01		0.31	−0.003	0.18
	(1.93)	(0.95)		(0.15)	(0.06)		(1.95)	(−0.02)	
Six-factor	0.56	0.06		0.05	0.07	0.25	0.34	0.02	0.34
	(2.91)	(0.21)		(0.32)	(0.47)	(1.01)	(2.25)	(0.14)	

Using value-weighted returns, this table repeats results in Table 7.1 for the subsample period January 1990 to December 2018. We report out-of-sample (one-month-ahead) estimated prices of risk based on standard two-step Fama-MacBeth cross-sectional tests. Estimated prices of risk are denoted $\hat{\lambda}_k$ for the kth factor in monthly percent return terms (t-statistics in parentheses). Factors are denoted as m (CRSP index, see footnote 1), *RD* (return dispersion), *SMB* (size), *HML* (value), *MOM* (momentum), *RMW* (profit), and *CMA* (capital investment). Results are shown for different sets of test asset portfolios

[1] In the ZCAPM, the price of beta risk associated with CRSP index excess returns is denoted $\hat{\lambda}_a$ rather than $\hat{\lambda}_m$ in the other models

7.3.2 *Size Group Results*

Table 7.4 gives results for different size groups. For this purpose we employ 100 size-B/M sorted portfolios downloaded from Kenneth French's website. Four of these portfolios are dropped due to incomplete daily return series in our sample period. The results for 96 size-B/M portfolios in Panel A show that: *RD* is highly significant with $\hat{\lambda}_{RD} = 0.29\%$ (t-value = 3.67), and *HML* is significant at the five percent level or lower in the three-, four-,

Table 7.4 Size group results for different asset pricing models using out-of-sample Fama-MacBeth cross-sectional regressions in the period January 1965 to December 2018: 12-month rolling windows

Panel A: 96 size-B/M sorted portfolios

Model	$\hat{\alpha}$	$\hat{\lambda}_m$	$\hat{\lambda}_{RD}$	$\hat{\lambda}_{SMB}$	$\hat{\lambda}_{HML}$	$\hat{\lambda}_{MOM}$	$\hat{\lambda}_{RMW}$	$\hat{\lambda}_{CMA}$	R^2
CAPM	0.89	−0.23							0.33
	(4.33)	(−1.10)							
ZCAPM	0.76	−0.11	0.29						0.91
	(3.96)	(−0.57)	(3.67)						
Three-factor	0.81	−0.25		0.11	0.31				0.49
	(5.05)	(−1.51)		(0.85)	(2.63)				
Four-factor	0.82	−0.27		0.12	0.29	−0.01			0.51
	(5.27)	(−1.68)		(0.93)	(2.57)	(−0.03)			
Five-factor	0.79	−0.22		0.17	0.25		0.19	0.08	0.56
	(5.05)	(−1.36)		(1.37)	(2.19)		(1.85)	(0.99)	
Six-factor	0.85	−0.29		0.18	0.26	−0.01	0.17	0.11	0.60
	(5.51)	(−1.84)		(1.50)	(2.32)	(−0.04)	(1.73)	(1.27)	

Panel B: 20 smallest (microcap) size sorted portfolios

Model	$\hat{\alpha}$	$\hat{\lambda}_m$	$\hat{\lambda}_{RD}$	$\hat{\lambda}_{SMB}$	$\hat{\lambda}_{HML}$	$\hat{\lambda}_{MOM}$	$\hat{\lambda}_{RMW}$	$\hat{\lambda}_{CMA}$	R^2
CAPM	1.45	−0.98							0.45
	(6.91)	(−3.44)							
ZCAPM	0.98	−0.33	0.39						0.98
	(4.49)	(−1.37)	(4.24)						
Three-factor	1.29	0.35		−1.04	0.68				0.75
	(5.70)	(0.93)		(−2.77)	(3.37)				
Four-factor	1.15	0.22		−0.79	0.68	−0.17			0.75
	(5.21)	(0.64)		(−2.26)	(3.63)	(−0.48)			
Five-factor	1.19	0.27		−0.73	0.49		0.52	0.25	0.78
	(5.37)	(0.77)		(−2.14)	(2.38)		(2.44)	(1.16)	
Six-factor	1.10	0.19		−0.59	0.60	−0.25	0.50	0.29	0.80
	(4.90)	(0.56)		(−1.77)	(2.84)	(−0.68)	(2.37)	(1.29)	

(continued)

Table 7.4 (continued)

Panel C: 76 largest size sorted portfolios

Model	$\hat{\alpha}$	$\hat{\lambda}_m$	$\hat{\lambda}_{RD}$	$\hat{\lambda}_{SMB}$	$\hat{\lambda}_{HML}$	$\hat{\lambda}_{MOM}$	$\hat{\lambda}_{RMW}$	$\hat{\lambda}_{CMA}$	R^2
CAPM	0.70	−0.02							0.26
	(3.32)	(−0.11)							
ZCAPM	0.64	0.01	0.22						0.89
	(3.20)	(0.04)	(3.08)						
Three-factor	0.62	−0.09		0.18	0.270				0.56
	(3.35)	(−0.42)		(1.52)	(2.32)				
Four-factor	0.771	−0.18		0.19	0.26	−0.03			0.58
	(4.04)	(−0.95)		(1.67)	(2.30)	(−0.15)			
Five-factor	0.70	−0.15		0.23	0.22		0.07	0.12	0.56
	(3.71)	(−0.74)		(2.05)	(1.98)		(0.72)	(1.39)	
Six-factor	0.78	−0.25		0.23	0.24	−0.01	0.08	0.13	0.63
	(4.41)	(−1.27)		(2.10)	(2.15)	(−0.06)	(0.89)	(1.50)	

Using value-weighted returns, this table repeats results in Table 7.1 for different size groups in the analysis period January 1965 to December 2018. We report out-of-sample (one-month-ahead) estimated prices of risk based on standard two-step Fama-MacBeth cross-sectional tests. Estimated prices of risk are denoted $\hat{\lambda}_k$ for the *k*th factor in monthly percent return terms (*t*-statistics in parentheses). Factors are denoted as *m* (CRSP index, see footnote 1), *RD* (return dispersion), *SMB* (size), *HML* (value), *MOM* (momentum), *RMW* (profit), and *CMA* (capital investment). Results are shown for different sets of test asset portfolios

[1] In the ZCAPM, the price of beta risk associated with CRSP index excess returns is denoted $\hat{\lambda}_a$ rather than $\hat{\lambda}_m$ in the other models

five-, and six-factor models (*t*-values in the range of 2.19 to 2.63). Panels B and C break down these results into size groups by separately testing the 20 smallest (microcap) portfolios and 76 larger market capitalization portfolios.

For microcaps in Panel B, the most significant factor is *RD* (*t*-value = 4.24), and multifactors *SMB*, *HML*, and *RMW* are significant at the five percent level or lower. *HML* achieves relatively high multifactor *t*-values ranging from 2.38 to 3.63 in the three-, four-, five- and six-factor models. In the three- and four-factor models, the *t*-values for the price of *HML* are 3.37 and 3.63, respectively, which exceed the 3.0 hurdle. The size factor is negative and significantly priced in the three-, four-, and five-factor models with *t*-values in the range −2.77 to −1.77, which is difficult to explain given its positive significance in Panel A of Table 7.1 using 25 size-B/M sorted portfolios. Note that the R^2 values for the microcap portfolios across all models are somewhat higher than for the total sample of 96 portfolios.

For the microcap portfolios the ZCAPM reaches a maximum R^2 value of 98%, which is outstanding.

For the 76 largest stock portfolios in Panel C, the results are similar to those for the total 96 portfolios in Panel A. The *RD* factor is again positive and significantly priced with a *t*-value equal to 3.08. Compared to the microcaps, the market price of *SMB* risk flips to become positive and significant at the one percent level in the four-factor model and the five percent level in the five- and six-factor models. Also, *HML* is significantly priced with *t*-values in the range 1.98 to 2.32 in the three-, four-, five-, and six-factor models. Across all models, the R^2 values are similar to the total 96 portfolios in Panel A but lower than the 20 microcap portfolios in Panel B. Nonetheless, among larger stocks, the R^2 value for the ZCAPM at 89% well exceeds that of the best multifactor performance by the six-factor model at 63%.

7.3.3 *Profit and Capital Investment Results*

In view of Fama and French's five- and six-factor models, we tested portfolios sorted on profit and capital investment firm characteristics. Table 7.5 gives the results. For 25 B/M-profit sorted portfolios in Panel A, *RD* is most significantly priced with $\hat{\lambda}_{RD} = 0.36\%$ (*t*-value = 4.15). Multifactor *HML* is significantly priced at the five percent level in the three-, four-, five- and six-factor models (*t*-values ranging from 1.74 to 2.52), and *SMB* is significantly priced at the five percent level in the six-factor model ($t = 2.07$). Notably, the R^2 value for the six-factor model is 93% for these test assets, which is higher than the ZCAPM at 81%. This is the only test in which the ZCAPM did not have the highest R^2 value. For the 25 B/M-investment and 25 profit-investment sorted portfolios in Panels B and C, respectively, *RD* remains highly significant (*t*-values exceeding 4.5). By contrast, the multifactors exhibit changing patterns of significance across different models and test assets with a maximum *t*-value of 3.11 for *RMW* in the six-factor model. Also, for test assets in Panels B and C, the ZCAPM once again has the highest R^2 values of 83% and 95%, respectively, compared to the other models.

7.3.4 *Individual Stock Results*

Here we repeat the cross-sectional tests of different models using the largest 500 market capitalization stocks. For the initial one-year window to estimate model parameters from January 1964 to December 1964, we select all common stocks with daily stock returns available from January 1964 to January 1965. Market capitalization is measured in December 1964 for all stocks, and the top 500 stocks by market capitalization are selected to gather daily returns from January 1964 to January 1965. This process is rolled forward one month at a time to create daily return time series for individual stocks from January 1964 to December 2018.

Table 7.5 Profit and capital investment sorted results for different asset pricing models using out-of-sample Fama-MacBeth cross-sectional regressions in the period January 1965 to December 2018: 12-month rolling windows

Panel A: 25 B/M-profit sorted portfolios									
Model	$\hat{\alpha}$	$\hat{\lambda}_m$	$\hat{\lambda}_{RD}$	$\hat{\lambda}_{SMB}$	$\hat{\lambda}_{HML}$	$\hat{\lambda}_{MOM}$	$\hat{\lambda}_{RMW}$	$\hat{\lambda}_{CMA}$	R^2
CAPM	1.07	−0.51							0.23
	(4.48)	(−1.94)							
ZCAPM	0.80	−0.26	0.36						0.81
	(3.49)	(−1.06)	(4.15)						
Three-factor	0.76	−0.29		0.04	0.30				0.89
	(3.07)	(−1.04)		(0.30)	(2.52)				
Four-factor		0.66	−0.19		0.05	0.27	−0.09		0.87
	(2.62)	(−0.70)		(0.37)	(2.38)	(−0.42)			
Five-factor	0.89	−0.38		0.20	0.19		0.16	0.11	0.90
	(4.50)	(−1.39)		(1.33)	(1.74)		(1.49)	(1.03)	
Six-factor	0.94	−0.45		0.31	0.20	−0.20	0.16	0.10	0.93
	(3.68)	(−1.65)		(2.07)	(1.82)	(−0.90)	(1.87)	(0.87)	
Panel B: 25 B/M-investment sorted portfolios									
Model	$\hat{\alpha}$	$\hat{\lambda}_m$	$\hat{\lambda}_{RD}$	$\hat{\lambda}_{SMB}$	$\hat{\lambda}_{HML}$	$\hat{\lambda}_{MOM}$	$\hat{\lambda}_{RMW}$	$\hat{\lambda}_{CMA}$	R^2
CAPM	0.59	0.01							0.09
	(2.45)	(0.04)							
ZCAPM	0.49	0.09	0.38						0.83
	(3.24)	(0.47)	(5.42)						
Three-factor	0.27	0.24		0.21	0.19				0.52
	(1.09)	(0.91)		(1.45)	(1.69)				
Four-factor		0.11	0.40		0.13	0.15	0.10		0.62
	(0.47)	(1.58)		(0.87)	(1.36)	(0.49)			
Five-factor	0.17	0.35		0.20	0.14		(0.06)	(0.11)	0.58
	(0.66)	(1.38)		(1.31)	(1.25)		0.60	1.66	
Six-factor	0.04	0.47		0.18	0.12	0.07	0.06	0.14	0.68
	(0.16)	(1.85)		(1.12)	(1.10)	(0.34)	(0.54)	(1.73)	

(continued)

Table 7.5 (continued)

Panel C: 25 profit-investment sorted portfolios

Model	$\hat{\alpha}$	$\hat{\lambda}_m$	$\hat{\lambda}_{RD}$	$\hat{\lambda}_{SMB}$	$\hat{\lambda}_{HML}$	$\hat{\lambda}_{MOM}$	$\hat{\lambda}_{RMW}$	$\hat{\lambda}_{CMA}$	R^2
CAPM	0.63	−0.08							0.24
	(2.94)	(−0.33)							
ZCAPM	0.66	−0.11	0.34						0.95
	(3.03)	(−0.44)	(4.51)						
Three-factor	0.34	0.17		0.11	0.18				0.24
	(1.51)	(0.68)		(0.81)	(1.47)				
Four-factor		0.57	−0.05		0.09	0.14	0.35		0.44
	(2.41)	(−0.19)		(0.66)	(1.19)	(1.91)			
Five-factor	0.43	0.10		0.30	0.09		0.23	0.15	0.78
	(1.80)	(0.39)		(2.03)	(0.76)		(2.92)	(1.79)	
Six-factor	0.60	−0.08		0.30	0.09	0.20	0.25	0.15	0.83
	(2.45)	(−0.30)		(1.92)	(0.79)	(0.97)	(3.11)	(1.81)	

Using value-weighted returns, this table repeats results in Table 7.1 for test asset portfolios sorted on profit and capital investment firm characteristics in the analysis period from January 1965 to December 2018. We report out-of-sample (one-month-ahead) estimated prices of risk based on standard two-step Fama-MacBeth cross-sectional tests. Estimated prices of risk are denoted $\hat{\lambda}_k$ for the kth factor in monthly percent return terms (t-statistics in parentheses). Factors are denoted as m (CRSP index, see footnote 1), *RD* (return dispersion), *SMB* (size), *HML* (value), *MOM* (momentum), *RMW* (profit), and *CMA* (capital investment). Results are shown for different sets of test asset portfolios

[1] In the ZCAPM, the price of beta risk associated with CRSP index excess returns is denoted $\hat{\lambda}_a$ rather than $\hat{\lambda}_m$ in the other models

In cross-sectional test results shown in Table 7.6, only *RD* and *RMW* are significant with t-values equal to 2.81 for *RD* and 2.43 for *RMW* in both five- and six-factor models. Because it is well known that it is difficult to obtain significant results using individual stocks, these unaggregated stock results lend further support for *RD* as a significant asset pricing factor.[10]

7.3.5 Out-of-Sample Periods Greater Than One Month

As another robustness check, we conduct Fama-MacBeth cross-sectional tests using the monthly rolling approach based on out-of-sample periods greater than one month. Following the methodology in Table 7.1 with 72 combined portfolios (viz., 25 size-B/M sorted and 47 industry portfo-

[10] As in Table 7.1, we do not report R^2 values due to changing samples of individual stocks over time.

Table 7.6 Largest 500 common stocks' results by market capitalization for different asset pricing models using out-of-sample Fama-MacBeth cross-sectional regressions in the period January 1965 to December 2018: 12-month rolling windows

Model	$\hat{\alpha}$	$\hat{\lambda}_m$	$\hat{\lambda}_{RD}$	$\hat{\lambda}_{SMB}$	$\hat{\lambda}_{HML}$	$\hat{\lambda}_{MOM}$	$\hat{\lambda}_{RMW}$	$\hat{\lambda}_{CMA}$
CAPM	0.51	0.04						
	(3.49)	(0.25)						
ZCAPM	0.42	0.04	0.14					
	(3.32)	(0.25)	(2.81)					
Three-factor	0.42	0.11		0.01	0.12			
	(3.22)	(0.66)		(0.07)	(1.34)			
Four-factor		0.42	0.22		−0.02	−0.06	0.16	
	(2.52)	(0.90)		(−0.14)	(−0.40)	(0.67)		
Five-factor	0.32	0.33		0.02	−0.10		0.29	−0.06
	(2.12)	(1.52)		(0.14)	(−0.75)		(2.43)	(−0.53)
Six-factor	0.43	0.12		0.10	0.06	0.17	0.17	0.05
	(3.54)	(0.78)		(1.11)	(0.66)	(1.21)	(2.43)	(0.67)

This table repeats results in Table 7.1 for individual stocks in the analysis period from January 1965 to December 2018. We report out-of-sample (one-month-ahead) estimated prices of risk based on standard two-step Fama-MacBeth cross-sectional tests. Estimated prices of risk are denoted $\hat{\lambda}_k$ for the kth factor in monthly percent return terms (t-statistics in parentheses). Factors are denoted as m (CRSP index, see footnote 1), *RD* (return dispersion), *SMB* (size), *HML* (value), *MOM* (momentum), *RMW* (profit), and *CMA* (capital investment)

[1] In the ZCAPM, the price of beta risk associated with CRSP index excess returns is denoted $\hat{\lambda}_a$ rather than $\hat{\lambda}_m$ in the other models

lios) and a 12-month estimation window for time-series regression models, Table 7.7 shows the cross-sectional regression results for 3-, 6-, 12-, and 24-month out-of-sample periods. The *RD* factor again is significantly priced in 3-, 6-, and 12-month out-of-sample periods but not 24-months. The multifactors are normally not significantly priced in these tests, with the exceptions of *RMW* in the 3-month out-of-sample period for the five- and six-factor models (i.e., 5% level).

We observe that the cross-sectional R^2 values for the ZCAPM remain at relatively high levels compared to other models—namely, 0.78, 0.72, 0.74, and 0.36 for 3-, 6-, 12-, and 24-months, respectively, for the ZCAPM versus at most 0.39, 0.36, 0.32, and 0.31, respectively, for other models in these longer out-of-sample tests. Even in 12-month out-of-sample tests, the goodness-of-fit for the ZCAPM is relatively high, which thereafter declines in the 24-month tests. This evidence suggests that zeta risk in the ZCAPM is a persistent common factor in stock returns not captured in the CAPM

Table 7.7 Comparisons of different asset pricing models based on out-of-sample Fama-MacBeth cross-sectional regressions in the period January 1965 to December 2018: Robustness tests using out-of-sample rolling windows greater than one month

Panel A: 3-month out-of-sample period

Model	$\hat{\alpha}$	$\hat{\lambda}_m$	$\hat{\lambda}_{RD}$	$\hat{\lambda}_{SMB}$	$\hat{\lambda}_{HML}$	$\hat{\lambda}_{MOM}$	$\hat{\lambda}_{RMW}$	$\hat{\lambda}_{CMA}$	R^2
CAPM	0.67	−0.0002							0.01
	(3.32)	(−0.001)							
ZCAPM	0.55	0.11	0.29						0.78
	(2.86)	(0.52)	(3.73)						
Three-factor	0.53	0.04		0.14	0.12				0.07
	(2.68)	(0.17)		(1.16)	(1.00)				
Four-factor		0.61	−0.03		0.14	0.10	0.27		0.26
	(3.05)	(−0.15)		(1.18)	(0.92)	(1.33)		4	
Five-factor	0.53	0.03		0.20	0.13		0.21	0.14	0.14
	(2.83)	(0.14)		(1.57)	(1.12)		(2.19)	(1.39)	
Six-factor	0.74	−0.18		0.19	0.13	0.25	0.20	0.11	0.39
	(3.91)	(−0.87)		(1.57)	(1.19)	(1.26)	(2.11)	(1.06)	

Panel B: 6-month out-of-sample period

Model	$\hat{\alpha}$	$\hat{\lambda}_m$	$\hat{\lambda}_{RD}$	$\hat{\lambda}_{SMB}$	$\hat{\lambda}_{HML}$	$\hat{\lambda}_{MOM}$	$\hat{\lambda}_{RMW}$	$\hat{\lambda}_{CMA}$	R^2
CAPM	0.72	−0.05							0.01
	(3.25)	(−0.23)							
ZCAPM	0.68	−0.02	0.20						0.72
	(3.13)	(−0.08)	(2.51)						
Three-factor	0.60	−0.02		0.14	0.12				0.07
	(2.77)	(−0.10)		(1.20)	(1.09)				
Four-factor		0.65	−0.09		0.14	0.12	0.18		0.24
	(3.37)	(−0.41)		(1.14)	(1.06)	(1.23)			
Five-factor	0.53	0.03		0.18	0.13		0.15	0.14	0.13
	(2.86)	(0.15)		(1.39)	(1.06)		(1.53)	(1.41)	
Six-factor	0.70	−0.15		0.17	0.14	0.16	0.13	0.12	0.36
	(3.62)	(−0.65)		(1.35)	(1.11)	(0.81)	(1.42)	(1.22)	

Panel C: 12-month out-of-sample period

Model	$\hat{\alpha}$	$\hat{\lambda}_m$	$\hat{\lambda}_{RD}$	$\hat{\lambda}_{SMB}$	$\hat{\lambda}_{HML}$	$\hat{\lambda}_{MOM}$	$\hat{\lambda}_{RMW}$	$\hat{\lambda}_{CMA}$	R^2
CAPM	0.84	−0.14							0.003
	(3.72)	(−0.55)							
ZCAPM	0.78	−0.10	0.17						0.74
	(3.34)	(−0.42)	(2.25)						
Three-factor	0.75	−0.17		0.17	0.15				0.06
	(3.93)	(−0.77)		(1.21)	(1.04)				
Four-factor		0.77	−0.19		0.15	0.11	0.03		0.13
	(3.89)	(−0.85)		(1.06)	(0.81)	(0.18)			
Five-factor	0.69	−0.11		0.21	0.14		0.10	0.19	0.13
	(3.59)	(−0.50)		(1.45)	(1.01)		(0.98)	(1.60)	
Six-factor	0.82	−0.25		0.19	0.13	−0.03	0.12	0.13	0.32
	(4.17)	(−1.17)		(1.30)	(0.94)	(−0.14)	(1.23)	(1.07)	

(continued)

Table 7.7 (continued)

Panel D: 24-month out-of-sample period

Model	$\hat{\alpha}$	$\hat{\lambda}_m$	$\hat{\lambda}_{RD}$	$\hat{\lambda}_{SMB}$	$\hat{\lambda}_{HML}$	$\hat{\lambda}_{MOM}$	$\hat{\lambda}_{RMW}$	$\hat{\lambda}_{CMA}$	R^2
CAPM	0.96	−0.18							0.003
	(3.12)	(−0.71)							
ZCAPM	0.89	−0.12	0.06						0.36
	(2.83)	(−0.45)	(0.65)						
Three-factor	0.83	−019		0.23	0.13				0.10
	(2.90)	(−0.67)		(1.18)	(1.15)				
Four-factor		0.78	−0.14		0.23	0.12	−0.07		0.19
	(3.29)	(−0.59)		(1.12)	(0.91)	(−0.31)			
Five-factor	0.86	−0.23		0.27	0.16		0.03	0.12	0.12
	(3.36)	(−0.87)		(1.27)	(1.39)		(0.26)	(1.15)	
Six-factor	1.00	−0.37		0.25	0.15	−0.13	0.04	0.09	0.31
	(4.46)	(−1.87)		(1.19)	(1.14)	(−0.55)	(0.49)	(0.81)	

This table repeats the results in Table 7.1 for out-of-sample periods longer than one month. We report out-of-sample (one-month-ahead) estimated prices of risk based on standard two-step Fama-MacBeth cross-sectional tests. Estimated prices of risk are denoted $\hat{\lambda}_k$ for the kth factor in monthly percent return terms (t-statistics in parentheses). Factors are denoted as m (CRSP index, see footnote 1), *RD* (return dispersion), *SMB* (size), *HML* (value), *MOM* (momentum), *RMW* (profit), and *CMA* (capital investment). Results are shown in the following panels: (A) 3-months, (B), 6-months, (C) 12-months, and (D) 24-months. As in previous analyses, time-series regressions of the respective model are fitted using daily returns in a 12-month period to estimate factor loadings for test asset portfolios. However, unlike our previous analyses using one-month-ahead returns, cross-sectional regressions are run using 3-, 6-, 12-ahead portfolio , and 24-months ahead returns. The results are shown for 72 tests assets comprised of 25 size-B/M sorted plus 47 industry portfolios

[1]In the ZCAPM, the price of beta risk associated with CRSP index excess returns is denoted $\hat{\lambda}_a$ rather than $\hat{\lambda}_m$ in the other models

market model as well as three-, four-, five-, and six-factor models.[11] Related to these findings, Ferson et al. (2013) have found little predictive power among alternative long-run asset pricing models relative to the CAPM market model in terms of 12-month-ahead forecasting ability. Further work is needed to investigate how the ZCAPM would perform in these tests.

In unreported results available upon request, we extended the cross-sectional tests by increasing the estimation window used to run time-series

[11]See Bansal and Yaron (2004) for discussion of persistence in the stochastic process of asset returns related to a long-run risk variable.

regression models with daily returns from 12-months to 36-months.[12] Different out-of-sample periods were again used (i.e., 1-, 3-, 6-, and 12-months). In all cases, *RD*'s estimated price of risk $\hat{\lambda}_{RD}$ was significant at the 5% level or lower and explanatory power was relatively high.

7.3.6 Other Four-Factor Models

As another robustness check, we conduct cross-sectional tests of two recently proposed four-factor models. The Hou et al. (2015) *q*-factor model contains four factors, including a market portfolio proxy (*m*), equity market capitalization (*ME*), investment to assets ratio (*IA*), and return on equity (*ROE*), which we obtained upon request from Professor Lu Zhang. The Stambaugh and Yuan (2017) model is also comprised of four factors, including a market portfolio proxy (*m*), size (*SMB*), management (*MGMT*), and performance (*PERF*), which we downloaded from Professor Robert Stambaugh's website. Their novel management and performance mispricing factors are developed from stocks' rankings for several well-known anomalies. They separate 11 anomalies into two clusters and use these clustered anomalies to compute two zero-investment portfolios as factors. Taking into account over 80 anomalies, their four-factor model outperformed the five-factor model of Fama and French (2015) as well as four-factor model of Hou et al. (2015). Other tests supported their model also. Hence, they concluded that a parsimonious model containing mispricing factors can help explain expected returns.[13]

We perform out-of-sample cross-sectional tests of these two models using different test asset portfolios in the sample periods January 1968 (due to data availability) to December 2015 for the Hou, Xue, and Zhang model and January 1965 to December 2015 for the Stambaugh and Yuan model. For comparison purposes, we report results for the empirical ZCAPM using the latter sample period also. Table 7.8 provides the findings.

[12] The distribution of stocks' daily volatilities changes over time, but their overall time-varying patterns are very similar for different estimation windows.

[13] A number of other multifactor models have been proposed in recent years but most utilize factors similar to those in the Fama and French six-factor model. For example, Hou et al. (2018) added a growth factor to the Hou, Zue, and Zhang *q*-factor model. Unlike these studies, Lettau and Pelger (2020) use Principal Component Analysis (PCA) methods to estimate five latent asset pricing factors. See Barillas and Shanken (2018) for comparisons of different models.

Panel A of Table 7.8 gives the results for the Hou, Xue, and Zhang model. We summarize the findings as follows: (1) the market portfolio proxy (*m*) and market capitalization (*ME*) factors are generally not priced; (2) the investment to assets (*IA*) and return on equity (*ROE*) factors are

Table 7.8 Out-of-sample Fama-MacBeth cross-sectional regressions for four-factor models proposed by Hou, Xue, and Zhang and Stambaugh and Yuan: 12-month rolling windows

Panel A: Hou, Xue, and Zhang four-factor model						
Test asset portfolios	$\hat{\alpha}$	$\hat{\lambda}_m$	$\hat{\lambda}_{ME}$	$\hat{\lambda}_{IA}$	$\hat{\lambda}_{ROE}$	R^2
25 size-B/M	1.63	−0.70	0.15	0.24	0.44	0.57
	(8.04)	(−3.26)	(1.01)	(1.77)	(2.41)	
47 industry	0.95	−0.01	−0.01	0.31	0.27	0.28
	(4.77)	(−0.06)	(−0.04)	(2.60)	(1.94)	
25 beta-zeta	1.09	−0.19	−0.26	0.18	0.12	0.77
	(5.55)	(−0.78)	(−1.28)	(1.24)	(0.69)	
25 size-B/M + 47 industry	1.13	−0.19	0.06	0.25	0.44	0.17
	(6.34)	(−0.89)	(0.44)	(2.89)	(1.75)	
25 size-B/M + 47 industry + 25 beta-zeta	1.10	−0.18	0.01	0.26	0.23	0.35
	(7.17)	(−0.89)	(0.08)	(2.34)	(1.71)	
96 size-B/M	1.32	−0.34	0.08	0.19	0.18	0.47
	(7.86)	(−1.99)	(0.53)	(1.72)	(1.36)	
Largest 500 stocks	0.92	0.05	0.02	0.10	0.09	n/a
	(6.73)	(0.02)	(0.21)	(1.25)	(1.05)	

Panel B: Stambaugh and Yuan four-factor model						
Test asset portfolios	$\hat{\alpha}$	$\hat{\lambda}_m$	$\hat{\lambda}_{SMB}$	$\hat{\lambda}_{MGMT}$	$\hat{\lambda}_{PERF}$	R^2
25 size-B/M	0.95	−0.43	0.34	0.31	0.60	0.63
	(4.51)	(−2.02)	(2.22)	(1.62)	(2.73)	
47 industry	0.10	0.44	0.20	0.33	0.44	0.15
	(0.52)	(1.96)	(1.29)	(2.44)	(2.64)	
25 beta-zeta	0.77	−0.22	−0.09	0.12	0.42	0.71
	(4.86)	(−1.01)	(−0.43)	(0.72)	(1.97)	
25 size-B/M + 47 industry	0.32	0.23	0.29	0.34	0.44	0.17
	(1.83)	(1.10)	(2.13)	(2.54)	(2.59)	
25 size-B/M + 47 industry + 25 beta-zeta	0.41	0.12	0.26	0.33	0.40	0.33
	(2.78)	(0.67)	(1.93)	(2.53)	(2.48)	
96 size-B/M	0.81	−0.24	0.26	0.28	0.34	0.49
	(4.86)	(−1.41)	(1.74)	(2.00)	(1.99)	
Largest 500 stocks	0.30	0.26	0.19	0.22	0.35	n/a
	(2.26)	(1.68)	(1.84)	(2.23)	(2.73)	

(continued)

Table 7.8 (continued)

Panel C: ZCAPM (see footnote 1)				
Test asset portfolios	$\hat{\alpha}$	$\hat{\lambda}_a$	$\hat{\lambda}_{RD}$	R^2
25 size-B/M	0.76	−0.18	0.49	0.97
	(3.08)	(−0.73)	(4.30)	
47 industry	0.44	0.16	0.35	0.73
	(2.39)	(0.77)	(4.37)	
25 beta-zeta	0.45	0.05	0.37	0.96
	(2.52)	(0.24)	(3.85)	
25 size-B/M + 47 industry	0.57	0.05	0.40	0.83
	(3.17)	(0.27)	(5.20)	
25 size-B/M + 47 industry + 25 beta-zeta	0.53	0.06	0.41	0.83
	(3.38)	(0.28)	(5.80)	
96 size-B/M	0.81	−0.15	0.31	0.93
	(4.04)	(−0.75)	(3.79)	
Largest 500 stocks	0.46	0.06	0.16	n/a
	(3.25)	(0.36)	(3.02)	

This table reports out-of-sample cross-sectional tests using the monthly rolling approach for four-factor models proposed by Hou et al. (2015) and Stambaugh and Yuan (2017). Daily return factors for the former study are defined as the value-weighted CRSP market index for the market portfolio proxy (m), equity market capitalization (ME), investment to assets ratio (IA), and return on equity (ROE). Data were obtained upon request from Lu Zhang. Daily return factors for the latter study are defined as the value-weighted CRSP index (m), size (SMB), management ($MGMT$), and performance ($PERF$). Data were downloaded from Robert Stambaugh's website. The two-step Fama and MacBeth (1973) procedure is used as described in the text and previous tables. The procedure is rolled forward one month at a time to enable cross-sectional regressions in each month from January 1968 (due to data availability) to December 2015 for the Hou, Xue, and Zhang model (Panel A) and from January 1965 to December 2015 for the Stambaugh and Yuan model (Panel B). For comparison purposes, we report results for the empirical ZCAPM (estimated via the EM algorithm) using the January 1965 to December 2015 sample period also (Panel C). For these models, the time-series average of $t = 1, \cdots, 576$ and $t = 1, \cdots, 612$ estimated factor prices, respectively, for the kth factor is denoted $\hat{\lambda}_k$ (t-statistics in parentheses). Results are shown for different sets of test asset portfolios as well as the largest 500 individual stocks

[1] In the ZCAPM, the price of beta risk associated with CRSP index excess returns is denoted $\hat{\lambda}_a$ rather than $\hat{\lambda}_m$ in the other models

significantly priced for several different test assets but their t-statistics do not surpass the 3 threshold; and (3) estimated R^2 values range widely from only 17% for the 25 size-BM and industry portfolios to 77% for the 25 beta-zeta portfolios.

Panel B of Table 7.8 reports the results for the Stambaugh and Yuan model. Again summarizing the results: (1) the market portfolio proxy (m) factor is generally not priced; (2) the size (SMB), management ($MGMT$), and performance (*PERF*) factors are significantly priced in different test assets but their t-statistics do not surpass the 3 threshold; and (3) estimated R^2 values range widely from only 15% for industry portfolios to 71% for beta-zeta sorted portfolios.

By comparison, using a Janaury 1965 to December 2015 sample period, the ZCAPM results in Panel C of Table 7.8 outperform both of the aforementioned models in terms of R^2 values ranging from 73% to 97% and highly significant $\hat{\lambda}_{RD}$ estimates with t-values from 3.25 for individual stocks to 4.04 for 96 size-B/M sorted portfolios. As in the case of the Fama and French models, the Hou, Xue, and Zhang as well as Stambaugh and Yuan models have difficulty with industry portfolios (e.g., R^2 values of only 28% and 15%, respectively). Given that previous researchers (e.g., Lewellen et al. 2010; Daniel and Titman 2012, and others) have recommended using industry portfolios as exogenous assets in asset pricing tests, this shortfall is troublesome. Overall, using similar test assets and sample periods, our results suggest that the ZCAPM outperforms these four-factor models in cross-sectional tests, especially when industry portfolios are included in the test assets.

7.4 Summary

Using standard out-of-sample Fama-MacBeth cross-sectional tests, we compared the asset pricing performance of the empirical ZCAPM to several popular models that are prominent in academic publications and investment practice. We conducted comprehensive tests based on a wide variety of test assets, including size-B/M sorted portfolios, beta-zeta coefficient sorted portfolios, industry portfolios, and combinations of these portfolios. Out-of-sample cross-sectional tests related previously estimated loadings for factors (using daily returns over one year) to one-month-ahead returns for test assets.

Our initial cross-sectional tests in Table 7.1 yielded economically meaningful market prices of zeta risk in the ZCAPM ranging from 0.32% to 0.46% per month for different test asset portfolios that were consistently significant at a high level with t-values from 4.0 to 5.4. Even for industry portfolios, in which previous studies have found it difficult to find priced factors, zeta risk associated with *RD* achieved a t-value of approximately 4.1. These cross-sectional t-values exceed the 3.0 t-statistic threshold proposed by Harvey et al. (2015) and Chordia et al. (2020) to evaluate the significance of asset pricing factors. By comparison, other factors, including the CAPM's market factor as well as popular multifactors in three-, four-, five-, and six-factor models—namely, *SMB* (size), *HML* (book-to-market equity or value), *MOM* (momentum), *RMW* (profit), and *CMA* (capital investment)—were less significant and priced in some but not all test assets. In these initial cross-sectional tests conducted using different portfolios, the popular multifactors never exceeded the 3.0 *t*-statistic threshold.

In addition to relatively high *t*-values associated with the estimated market prices of zeta risk, initial cross-sectional regression results for the empirical ZCAPM across a wide variety of test assets exhibited relatively high R^2 values ranging from a low of approximately 70% to a high of 96%. Interestingly, for Fama and French's often-used 25 size and B/M sorted portfolios, the ZCAPM achieved a cross-sectional R^2 equal to 94% that well exceeded the three-to-six-factor models, which is remarkable given that these test assets are exogenous to the ZCAPM's market and return dispersion factors. Apparently, there is little or no need for additional factors to price these test assets.

Numerous robustness checks of the results were performed. Results for split subsample periods confirmed that *RD* loadings (associated with zeta risk) were significantly priced across different test assets. The results in the subperiod 1965 to 1989 were very similar to the full sample period; by contrast, in the 1990 to 2018 subperiod, multifactors were generally insignificant, and *RD* loadings were significantly priced but less strongly than in the previous subperiod and full sample period.

Further analyses of microcap stocks and large market capitalization stocks showed that *RD* loadings were highly significant at the one percent level or lower with *t*-values equal to 4.2 and 3.1, respectively. We found that *HML* (i.e., value factor) was the most significant multifactor, especially among microcaps, but its *t*-values did not exceed those of *RD* in these two sample groups. Also, estimated R^2 values across all models were higher for microcaps compared to larger capitalization stocks. For microcaps the ZCAPM achieved an R^2 estimate of 98% which is outstanding.

Extending our tests to profit and capital investment sorted portfolios, the pattern of results was the same as in other test asset portfolios for the most part. *RD* loadings were significantly priced with *t*-values exceeding 4, and multifactors were occasionally significant but at lower levels below the *t*-value threshold of 3. Again cross-sectional R^2 values were relatively high ranging from 81% to 95%. The multifactor models had very good explanatory power for 25 value-profit sorted portfolios that exceeded the empirical ZCAPM, but our ZCAPM continued to outperform for 25 value-investment and 25 profit-investment sorted portfolios.

Analyses of the 500 largest individual stocks by market capitalization indicated that *RD* and *RMW* (profit) loadings were significantly priced with *t*-values of 2.8 and 2.4, respectively, but other factors were not priced.

Further analyses showed that zeta risk was significantly priced in different out-of-sample periods longer than one month (e.g., using a 3-month out-of-sample period in cross-sectional tests, *RD* loadings had a *t*-value equal to 3.7) as well as different estimation windows used to run time-series regressions to estimate factor loadings. Rarely were any multifactors significantly priced in these tests.

Lastly, different factors' loadings in four-factor models by Hou et al. (2015) and Stambaugh and Yuan (2017) were generally significant at the 5% level across different test assets, but their *t*-values did not exceed the 3 threshold, and estimated R^2 results for test assets including industry portfolios were well below those of the ZCAPM.

In sum, our empirical evidence suggests that: (1) zeta risk associated with cross-sectional dispersion is a salient asset pricing factor and (2) the empirical ZCAPM's market and return dispersion factors explain most of the cross-sectional variation in stock returns. As such, we conclude that the ZCAPM represents the next generation in asset pricing for academic research and investment practice. An important implication of the ZCAPM is that it helps to resolve the *factor zoo* problem observed by Cochrane (2011). In his Presidential Address to the American Finance Association, due to the growing list of contending multifactors in asset pricing models, Cochrane (2011, p. 1061) opined, "... the world would be much simpler if betas on only a few factors, important in the covariance matrix of returns, accounted for a larger number of mean characteristics." The evidence in this chapter bodes well for the ZCAPM in this respect. The plethora of proposed factors by many researchers, most of which are constructed as zero-investment portfolios (i.e., long stock returns minus short stock returns), are themselves different return dispersion measures. Each factor accounts for a portion or slice of the total cross-sectional standard deviation of returns among all stocks in the market. Hence, they can be dropped after taking into account *RD* per the ZCAPM.

To offer some evidence that zero-investment factors used in popular asset pricing models are in fact measures of return dispersion, we conducted some simple regression tests. We regressed *RD* on the Fama and French factors, including *SMB*, *HML*, *MOM*, *RMW*, and *CMA*. Using daily returns in the sample period January 1965 to December 2018, in unreported results, as multifactors were incrementally added to the regression, R^2 estimates gradually increased from 19% when regressing *RD* on *SMB* to 57% when regressing *RD* on all five multifactors. The *t*-statistics for these factors were all very high in the range of 25 to 75, which indicates a strong relationship between *RD* and these factors. Corroborating our earlier argument, multifactors based on long minus short portfolio returns represent different measures of return dispersion that are contained within the total return dispersion of stock returns.

Daniel et al. (2020) have argued that multifactors based on zero-investment portfolios are "... unlikely to span the mean variance efficient frontier of all assets, because they do not take into account the asset covariance structure" (Daniel et al. 2020, p. 1929).[14] According to the geometry of the ZCAPM, however, another way to span the investment parabola is with the average market return and cross-sectional return dispersion of asset returns. This geometry is important because, as covered in Chapter 3, it circumvents the need to compute the covariance matrix of all assets. Since multifactors are return dispersion measures, they help to span the investment parabola without the need for incorporating return covariances, albeit not as completely as total return dispersion in the ZCAPM.

Further research is recommended on other asset classes (e.g., bonds, commodities, real estate, etc.), other countries, and different test assets. Because our results have shown that the size, value, profit, and capital investment anomalies can be explained for the most part by the empirical ZCAPM, an interesting research question is the extent to which the empirical ZCAPM can explain other anomalies, including earnings accruals, return on equity, idiosyncratic volatility, net stock issuances, etc. And, the empirical ZCAPM can be applied to other finance areas of study—for example, event studies of abnormal returns defined as realized returns minus predicted returns computed from previously estimated beta and zeta risk coefficients. Lastly, models with a latent independent variable that take

[14] Using this shortfall as motivation, Daniel et al. constructed a hedge portfolio to eliminate unpriced (diversifiable) risk in each characteristic, zero-investment portfolio in Fama and French's (2015) five-factor model. They combined hedge portfolios with conventional multifactors to construct efficient-characteristic portfolios. The optimal combination of the latter portfolios had higher in-sample squared Sharpe ratios than those of conventional portfolios.

into account positive and negative predictor variable effects have potential applications to other academic disciplines (e.g., the applied, natural, and social sciences).

Bibliography

Adrian, T., Etula, E., & Muir, T. (2014). Financial intermediaries and the cross-section of asset returns. *Journal of Finance*, *69*, 2557–2596.

Ang, A., Liu, J., & Schwarz, K. (2020). Using stocks or portfolios in tests of factor models. *Journal of Financial and Quantitative Analysis*, *55*, 709–750.

Bansal, R., & Yaron, A. (2004). Risks for the long run: A potential resolution of asset pricing puzzles. *Journal of Finance*, *59*, 1481–1509.

Barillas, F., & Shanken, J. (2018). Comparing asset pricing models. *Journal of Finance*, *73*(2), 715–754.

Black, F. (1972). Capital market equilibrium with restricted borrowing. *Journal of Business*, *45*, 444–454.

Black, F., Jensen, M. C., & Scholes, M. (1972). The capital asset pricing model: Some empirical tests. In M. C. Jensen (Ed.), *Studies in the theory of capital markets*. New York, NY: Praeger.

Carhart, M. M. (1997). On persistence in mutual fund performance. *Journal of Finance*, *52*, 57–82.

Chordia, T., Goyal, A., & Saretto, A. (2020). Anomalies and false rejections. *Review of Financial Studies*, *33*, 2134–2179.

Chordia, T., Subrahmanyam, A., & Tong, Q. (2014). Have capital market anomalies attenuated in the recent era of high liquidity and trading activity? *Journal of Accounting and Economics*, *58*, 41–58.

Cochrane, J. H. (2011). Presidential address: Discount rates. *Journal of Finance*, *56*, 1047–1108.

Daniel, K., Mota, L., Rottke, S., & Santos, T. (2020). The cross-section of risk and returns. *Review of Financial Studies*, *33*, 1927–1979.

Daniel, K., & Titman, S. (2012). Testing factor-model explanations of market anomalies. *Critical Finance Review*, *1*, 103–139.

Dempster, A. P., Laird, N. M., & Rubin, D. B. (1977). Maximum likelihood from incomplete data via the EM algorithm. *Journal of the Royal Statistical Society*, *39*, 1–38.

Fama, E. F., & French, K. R. (1992). The cross-section of expected stock returns. *Journal of Finance*, *47*, 427–465.

Fama, E. F., & French, K. R. (1993). The cross-section of expected returns. *Journal of Financial Economics*, *33*, 3–56.

Fama, E. F., & French, K. R. (1995). Size and book-to-market factors in earnings and returns. *Journal of Finance*, *50*, 131–156.

Fama, E. F., & French, K. R. (1996). The CAPM is wanted, dead or alive. *Journal of Finance, 51*, 1947–1958.

Fama, E. F., & French, K. R. (2004). The capital asset pricing model: Theory and evidence. *Journal of Economic Perspectives, 18*, 25–46.

Fama, E. F., & French, K. R. (2015). A five-factor asset pricing model. *Journal of Financial Economics, 116*, 1–22.

Fama, E. F., & French, K. R. (2018). Choosing factors. *Journal of Financial Economics, 128*, 234–252.

Fama, E. F., & MacBeth, J. D. (1973). Risk, return, and equilibrium: Empirical tests. *Journal of Political Economy, 81*, 607–636.

Ferson, W. E., Nallareddy, S. K., & Xie, B. (2013). The "out-of-sample" performance of long-run risk models. *Journal of Financial Economics, 107*, 537–556.

Gagliardini, P., Ossola, E., & Scaillet, O. (2016). Time-varying risk premium in large cross-sectional data sets. *Econometrica, 84*, 985–1046.

Green, J., Hand, J. R. M., & Zhang, X. F. (2016). The characteristics that provide independent information about average U.S. monthly stock returns. *Review of Financial Studies, 30*, 1–80.

Harvey, C. (2017). The scientific outlook in financial economics. *Journal of Finance, 72*, 1399–1440.

Harvey, C. R., Liu, Y., & Zhu, H. (2015). and the cross-section of expected returns. *Review of Financial Studies, 29*, 5–68.

Hou, K., Mo, H., Xue, C., & Zhang, L. (2018). q^5 (Working Paper). Ohio State University.

Hou, K., Xue, C., & Zhang, L. (2015). Digesting anomalies: An investment approach. *Review of Financial Studies, 28*, 650–705.

Jagannathan, R., & Wang, Z. (1996). The conditional CAPM and the cross-section of asset returns. *Journal of Finance, 51*, 3–53.

Kim, D. (1995). The errors-in-the-variables problem in the cross-section of stock returns. *Journal of Finance, 50*, 1605–1634.

Lettau, M., & Ludvigson, S. (2001). Consumption, aggregate wealth, and expected stock returns. *Journal of Finance, 56*, 815–849.

Lettau, M., & Pelger, M. (2020). Factors that fit the time series and cross-section of stock returns. *Review of Financial Studies, 33*, 2274–2325.

Lewellen, J., Nagel, S., & Shanken, J. A. (2010). A skeptical appraisal of asset pricing tests. *Journal of Financial Economics, 96*, 175–194.

Linnainmaa, J., & Roberts, M. (2018). The history of the cross-section of stock returns. *Review of Financial Studies, 31*, 2606–2649.

Liu, W. (2013). *A new asset pricing model based on the zero-beta CAPM: Theory and evidence* (Doctoral dissertation). Texas A&M University.

Liu, W., Kolari, J. W., & Huang, J. Z. (2012, October). *A new asset pricing model based on the zero-beta CAPM*. Presentation at the annual meetings of the Financial Management Association, Atlanta, GA.

Liu, W., Kolari, J. W., & Huang, J. Z. (2020, October). *Return dispersion and the cross-section of stock returns*. Presentation at the annual meetings of the Southern Finance Association, Palm Springs, CA.

McLean, R. D., & Pontiff, J. (2016). Does academic publication destroy predictability? *Journal of Finance*, *71*, 5–32.

Roll, R. (1977). A critique of the asset pricing theory's tests, part I: On past and potential future testability of the theory. *Journal of Financial Economics*, *4*, 129–176.

Schwert, G. W. (2003). Anomalies and market efficiency. In G. M. Constantinides, R. M. Stulz, & M. Harris (Eds.), *Handbook of the economics of finance* (Vol. 1, Part B, pp. 939–974). North Holland and Amsterdam, Netherlands: Elsevier.

Sharpe, W. F. (1964). Capital asset prices: A theory of market equilibrium under conditions of risk. *Journal of Finance*, *19*, 425–442.

Stambaugh, R. F., & Yuan, Y. (2017). Mispricing factors. *Review of Financial Studies*, *30*, 1270–1315.

PART V

Applications of the ZCAPM

CHAPTER 8

The Momentum Mytery: An Application of the ZCAPM

Abstract This chapter employs the empirical ZCAPM to show that anomalous momentum returns are highly related to market zeta risk arising from return dispersion (*RD*). Using U.S. stock returns in the sample period January 1965 to December 2017, cross-sectional tests show that momentum risk loadings and *RD* risk loadings are similarly priced in momentum portfolios. Also, they are similarly priced in zeta risk sorted portfolios. Comparative analyses find that zero-investment momentum portfolios and zero-investment, return dispersion portfolios earn high returns relative to other risk factors. Further regression tests indicate that zero-investment momentum returns are very significantly related to zero-investment portfolios formed based on sensitivity to return dispersion in the ZCAPM. We conclude that the momentum is closely related to zeta risk associated with return dispersion.

Keywords Anomalous return · Asset pricing · Beta risk · CAPM · Cross-sectional regression tests · Empirical ZCAPM · Expectation-maximization (EM) algorithm · Fama and French · Jegadeesh and Titman · Market risk · Momentum factor · Momentum portfolios · Momentum returns · Momentum strategies · Multifactor models · Out-of-sample returns · Return dispersion · Risk-managed portfolios · Securities investment · Signal variable · Stock market · ZCAPM · Zero-beta CAPM · Zero-investment portfolios · Zeta risk

J. W. Kolari et al., *A New Model of Capital Asset Prices*,
https://doi.org/10.1007/978-3-030-65197-8_8

8.1 Preview of Momentum Results

Now famous work by Jegadeesh and Titman (1993) showed that abnormal trading profits can be earned on simple, relative-strength momentum strategies that buy (sell) recent winners (losers). For example, in the period 1965 to 1989, trading profits of about 1.49% per month are produced by constructing zero-investment momentum portfolios with long (short) positions in high (low) return stocks in the past 12 months and holding them for the next 3 months. Numerous studies have proven that this momentum effect is persistent in stock returns. The momentum literature is extensive—for example, see studies and citations therein by Conrad and Kaul (1998), Rouwenhorst (1998), Moskowitz and Grinblatt (1999), Grundy and Martin (2001), Jegadeesh and Titman (2001), Chordia and Shivakumar (2002), Lewellen (2002), Griffin et al. (2003), Cooper et al. (2004), Fama and French (2008), Gutierrez and Kelley (2008), Liu and Zhang (2008), Novy-Marx (2012), Asness et al. (2013), Kim and Choi (2014), Barroso and Santa-Clara (2015), Daniel and Moskowitz (2016), Li (2016), Andrei and Cujean (2017), Hou et al. (2017), Chang et al. (2018), Goyal and Jegadeesh (2018), Daniel et al. (2019), Kelly et al. (2019), and others. Other contrarian trading strategies investigate short-term reversal in a week or month (e.g., Jegadeesh 1990; Lehmann 1990; Lo and MacKinlay 1990, among others) as well as long-term reversals in three-to-five years (e.g., DeBondt and Thaler 1985, 1987; Andrei and Cujean 2017; Conrad and Yavuz 2017) that can yield significant abnormal returns.

As observed by Daniel (2014), momentum has been documented to exist for a wide variety of asset classes, including bonds, commodities, currencies, and exchange-traded funds. Moskowitz et al. (2012) found that momentum profits are pervasive across different futures and forwards contracts that span a broad spectrum of asset classes and markets. Also, professional managers commonly utilize momentum investment strategies. Due to its widespread recognition among academics and practitioners, in the context of various anomalous patterns in average stock returns, Fama and French (2008) have cited momentum as the premier puzzle in financial economics. Because momentum is so simple yet enables investors to outperform the general market, Subrahmanyam (2018) has named momentum as the biggest challenge to the efficient markets hypothesis (see Petruno 2018).

In an attempt to better understand the momentum anomaly, a growing body of research has sought to investigate behavioral theories (e.g., Barberis et al. 1998; Daniel et al. 1998; Hong and Stein 1999; Brav and Heaton 2002; George and Hwang 2004; Grinblatt and Han 2005; Da et al. 2014; Luo et al. 2020, and others) as well as rational explanations (e.g., Fama and French 1996; Johnson 2002; Sagi and Seasholes 2007, and others).[1] Subrahmanyam (2018) has written an excellent synthesis of the growing theoretical and empirical research on momentum and concluded that no consensus exists on its root cause. He recommended that future research should focus on empirical tests of potential drivers of momentum that help explain whether it emanates from behavioral versus rational phenomenon.

Contributing to previous literature, we hypothesize that momentum profits are rationally explained in large part by market zeta risk reflected in cross-sectional return dispersion. The ZCAPM asset pricing model in this book posits market risk is comprised of two components: (1) beta risk related to the average return of all assets in the market and (2) zeta risk associated with the cross-sectional standard deviation of returns, i.e., return dispersion (*RD*). Here we apply the ZCAPM to the problem of understanding what explains momentum profits. No previous studies investigate the relation between momentum profits and return dispersion.

To test our momentum hypothesis, we conduct three-related tests using U.S. stocks in the sample period 1965 to 2017. First, cross-sectional tests of momentum portfolios find that estimated loadings for *RD* and momentum returns are very similarly priced. For example, we initially conduct tests based on momentum portfolio returns downloaded from Kenneth French's online data library. Using 25 size-momentum portfolios with equal-weighted returns, the market prices of *RD* and momentum loadings have t-values of 6.65 and 6.39, respectively. Using value-weighted returns for these portfolios, their t-values are 5.54 and 3.20, respectively. Further analyses with stocks sorted into 25 momentum portfolios and 25 zeta risk portfolios corroborate these findings. Other popular factors, such as size, value, profit, and investment, have lower and less consistent significance in these asset pricing tests. We infer that *RD* and momentum loadings are similarly priced in the cross-section of stock returns among portfolios constructed from past returns and zeta risk levels.

[1] See also the excellent review of behavioral theory and evidence in Thaler (1999).

Second, we compare the returns and risks of zero-investment momentum portfolios to those of zero-investment, return dispersion portfolios based on zeta risk. A 12-month estimation period is used to sort stocks into zeta risk portfolios, and post-formation monthly returns are computed. The return dispersion portfolio based on high-decile/low-decile zeta risk returns earns on average 1.50% per month, which outperforms the traditional momentum zero-investment portfolio using high-decile/low-decile past returns at 0.94% per month. Combining these two zero-investment portfolios into a hybrid strategy, average returns in excess of 1.50% per month can be earned. Other zero-investment portfolios, including the size, value, profit, and capital investment factors of Fama and French (1992, 1993, 1995, 2015), earn at most 0.34% per month. Also, risk management of the hybrid strategy yields average returns as high as 2.03% per month, which is remarkable.

Third, and last, we regress zero-investment momentum portfolio returns on zero-investment, return dispersion portfolio returns in addition to the aforementioned multifactors. We find a very close relationship between momentum returns and return dispersion returns with an estimated t-value on their regression coefficient of 31.76 and adjusted R^2 value of 61%, whereas other factors have at most an estimated R^2 of 5%. Based on these findings, we conclude that momentum returns are closely related to market risk arising from return dispersion.

8.2 Empirical Tests

Our research hypothesis is that momentum profits are explained in large part by market zeta risk associated with return dispersion. All NYSE, AMEX, and NASDAQ stocks return from the Center for Research in Security Prices (CRSP) in the sample period January 1965 to December 2017 are used. Small firms with common stock prices below $5 are dropped. As described below, three empirical tests of this hypothesis are conducted.

8.2.1 *Cross-Sectional Asset Pricing Tests*

First, following the same procedures as in Chapter 7, we conduct standard out-of-sample Fama and MacBeth (1973) cross-sectional tests to investigate the relation between *RD* loadings (i.e., zeta risk) in the empirical ZCAPM and one-month-ahead (out-of-sample) momentum returns.

Extending the analyses in Chapter 7, we test the ZCAPM using a variety of different (1) momentum portfolios and (2) zeta risk sorted portfolios. Moreover, we compare ZCAPM results to Sharpe's (1964) CAPM market model, Fama and French's (1992, 1993, 1995) three-factor model, Carhart's (1997) four-factor model (containing a momentum factor), and Fama and French's (2015) five-factor model. We hypothesize that momentum is similarly priced in both momentum and zeta risk sorted portfolios. Likewise, zeta risk is priced similarly in both momentum and zeta risk sorted portfolios.

8.2.2 Comparative Returns

Second, in further comparative analyses of the relationship between momentum and return dispersion, we construct zero-investment momentum portfolios and zero-investment, return dispersion portfolios. We build momentum portfolios by ranking holding period returns in previous 12-month estimation periods that start with the period January to December 1964. Stocks are placed into deciles, and high to low return portfolios are formed denoted $M10$ to $M1$. Following convention, we use equal weights to compute average monthly returns in the post-formation month January 1965. This process is rolled forward one month at a time to develop time series of one-month-ahead holding period returns for $M10$ to $M1$ from January 1965 to December 2017. Next, momentum return series are computed for the following zero-investment portfolios: $M10 - M1$, $M9 - M2$, $M8 - M3$, $M7 - M4$, and $M6 - M5$. Like Jegadeesh and Titman (1993), we compute results for momentum portfolios using a 1-week lag (i.e., the last week of the 12-month period) between the estimation period and post-formation, one-month holding period.[2]

One-month-ahead returns for return dispersion portfolios are constructed by means of the ZCAPM. According to the *theoretical ZCAPM* derived in Chapter 3, which is a special case of Black's (1972) zero-beta CAPM, the expected return for the ith asset at time t is[3]:

$$E(R_{it}) - R_{ft} = \beta_{i,a}[E(R_{at}) - R_{ft}] + Z^*_{i,a}\sigma_{at}, \tag{8.1}$$

[2] We also computed post-formation returns using a 1-month lag to explore lag effects on momentum profits. However, because 1-week lag profits were higher than those using a 1-month lag, we only report the 1-week lag results.

[3] See also Liu et al. (2012) and Liu (2013).

where $E(R_{at})$ is the expected market return based on the average return of all assets (rather than a proxy m for the theoretical market portfolio M in Sharpe's [1964] CAPM), R_{ft} is the riskless rate, $\beta_{i,a}$ is the beta risk coefficient measuring sensitivity to expected excess market returns, σ_{at} is the cross-sectional standard deviation of all asset returns (or return dispersion denoted RD) at time t, and $Z^*_{i,a}$ is the zeta risk coefficient measuring dichotomous positive or negative sensitivity to return dispersion. The asterisk on the zeta risk coefficient indicates that it is theoretically related to orthogonal portfolios I^* and ZI^* on the mean-variance investment parabola. This pair of efficient and zero-beta portfolios is unique due to their equal return variances.

For the purpose of estimating the ZCAPM with real-world data, as covered in Chapter 4, the following novel *empirical ZCAPM* was specified[4]:

$$R_{it} - R_{ft} = \beta_{i,a}(R_{at} - R_{ft}) + Z_{i,a}D_{it}\sigma_{at} + u_{it}, \quad t = 1, \cdots, T \qquad (8.2)$$

where $R_{it} - R_{ft}$ is the excess return for the ith stock portfolio (or stock) over the Treasury bill rate, $\beta_{i,a}$ measures sensitivity of the ith stock portfolio (or stock) to excess average market returns based on the value-weighted CRSP index minus Treasury bill rate equal to $R_{at} - R_{ft}$, $Z_{i,a}$ measures sensitivity of the ith stock portfolio (or stock) to return dispersion σ_{at} (denoted RD), D_{it} is a signal variable with values +1 and −1 representing positive and negative RD effects, respectively, on stock returns, and $u_{it} \sim$ iid $N(0, \sigma_i^2)$.[5] Importantly, signal variable D_{it} is defined as an independent random variable with the following two-point distribution:

$$D_{it} = \begin{cases} +1 & \text{with probability } p_i \\ -1 & \text{with probability } 1 - p_i, \end{cases} \qquad (8.3)$$

where p_i (or $1 - p_i$) is the probability of a positive (or negative) return dispersion effect, and D_{it} are independent of u_{it}. To estimate the parameters of the empirical ZCAPM including the probability parameter p_i, we use the expectation-maximization (EM) algorithm (see Dempster et al. 1977).[6]

[4] See also Liu et al. (2020).

[5] As discussed in Chapter 4, we set the intercept parameter α_i to zero for several reasons. In the present case, our interest is in out-of-sample returns of zero-investment, return dispersion portfolios, rather than their in-sample returns in Eq. (8.2).

[6] See Chapter 4 for detailed instructions for estimating the empirical ZCAPM via the EM algorithm. Further citations to related finance and statistics literature are provided there also.

Since $E(D_{it}) = 2p_i - 1$, the marginal form of the empirical ZCAPM is[7]:

$$R_{it} - R_{ft} = \beta_{i,a}(R_{at} - R_{ft}) + Z^*_{i,a}\sigma_{at} + u^*_{it}, \quad t = 1, \cdots, T \tag{8.4}$$

where $\beta_{i,a}$ is the beta risk coefficient, $Z^*_{i,a} = Z_{i,a}(2p_i - 1)$ is the zeta risk coefficient, u^*_{it} is the error term with variance related to return dispersion (see Eq. (4.13) of Chapter 4), and other notation is as before. Whether the sign of zeta risk loading $Z^*_{i,a}$ is positive or negative is determined by the probability p_i associated with the expected value of signal variable D_{it} in period $t = 1, \cdots, T$.

To form return dispersion portfolios, we start by estimating empirical ZCAPM relation (8.4) in the 12-month period January to December 1964. All stocks are ranked in terms of their estimated zeta coefficient $\hat{Z}^*_i$. Stocks are placed in high to low deciles denoted Z10 to Z1. Using a 1-week lag between the estimation period and the post-formation period, equal-weighted returns for these portfolios are computed in the next month January 1965. The process is rolled forward one month at a time to rebalance the portfolios until the last post-formation holding period return is computed in December 2017. Zero-investment, return dispersion portfolio returns are computed for the following portfolios: Z10 – Z1, Z9 – Z2, Z8 – Z3, Z7 – Z4, and Z6 – Z5. We conjecture that momentum portfolio returns and returns-dispersion portfolio returns are similar to one another and diverge considerably from the returns of other zero-investment portfolios.

8.2.3 Regression Tests

Third, and last, we conduct regression tests to investigate the relationship between the returns from zero-investment momentum and zero-investment, return dispersion strategies. The following OLS regression is estimated:

$$MOM_T = \alpha_{MOM} + \beta_{MOM} FACTOR_T + \varepsilon_T, \tag{8.5}$$

[7] Matlab programs for estimating the empirical ZCAPM are available at the end of the book in the Compendium. Additionally, R programs for these analyses can be downloaded from GitHub (https://github.com/zcapm). Our R programs run faster than the Matlab programs. R is a free software environment available on the internet.

where MOM_T is the momentum return in month T, and $FACTOR_T$ is the factor return in the same month. We test alternative dependent variable MOM factors defined as: $M10 - M1, M9 - M2, M8 - M3, M7 - M4$, and $M6 - M5$. Alternative return dispersion portfolio returns are used as the independent variable $FACTOR$: $Z10 - Z1, Z9 - Z2, Z8 - Z3, Z7 - Z4$, and $Z6 - Z5$. Multifactor returns SMB, HML, RMW, and CMA are used as independent variable $FACTOR$ also. We conjecture that a highly significant relationship exists between momentum portfolio returns and return dispersion portfolio returns, which well exceeds their relationship with the returns of other zero-investment factors.

8.3 Empirical Results

This section presents the empirical results of cross-sectional tests of momentum portfolios, return comparisons of momentum and return dispersion portfolios, and regression analyses of momentum portfolio returns and return dispersion portfolio returns.

8.3.1 Cross-Sectional Test Results

Are momentum portfolio returns and zeta risk sorted portfolios priced similarly by momentum and return dispersion factor loadings? We downloaded momentum portfolio returns from Kenneth French's online data library.[8] These portfolios use quintiles of size and quintiles of past returns in the previous year (excluding the last month).

The test results are summarized in Table 8.1. Panels A and B show the results for 25 size-momentum portfolios using value- and equal-weighted returns, respectively. Not surprisingly, size and momentum are significantly priced in models containing these factors. Size is more significantly priced in Panel B with equal-weighted returns, which places more emphasis on small stocks than Panel A with value-weighted returns. The value (HML) and capital investment (CMA) factors are significant in some models but not the profit (RMW) factor. The market factor (M) is not priced using value-weighted returns but is highly significant for equal-weighted returns across most models. Unfortunately, it is negatively priced which is difficult to interpret.

[8] See https://mba.tuck.dartmouth.edu/pages/faculty/ken.french/data_library.

Table 8.1 Fama-MacBeth cross-sectional regression tests of momentum portfolios: January 1965 to December 2017

Panel A: 25 size-momentum value-weighted portfolios

Model	$\hat{\alpha}$	$\hat{\lambda}_m$	$\hat{\lambda}_{RD}$	$\hat{\lambda}_{SMB}$	$\hat{\lambda}_{HML}$	$\hat{\lambda}_{MOM}$	$\hat{\lambda}_{RMW}$	$\hat{\lambda}_{CMA}$	Adj R^2
CAPM	0.61	0.10							−0.01
	(2.61)	(0.41)							
ZCAPM	0.41	0.22	0.61						0.98
	(1.86)	(0.99)	(5.54)						
Three-factor	0.56	0.03		0.33	-0.05				0.51
	(2.16)	(0.12)		(2.39)	(−0.28)				
Four-factor		1.01	−0.41		0.32	−0.19	0.56		0.70
	(4.94)	(−1.83)		(2.32)	(−1.15)	(3.20)			
Five-factor	0.40	0.20		0.32	−0.35		0.27	−0.07	0.50
	(1.71)	(0.81)		(2.51)	(−1.83)		(1.55)	(−0.42)	

Panel B: 25 size-momentum equal-weighted portfolios

Model	$\hat{\alpha}$	$\hat{\lambda}_m$	$\hat{\lambda}_{RD}$	$\hat{\lambda}_{SMB}$	$\hat{\lambda}_{HML}$	$\hat{\lambda}_{MOM}$	$\hat{\lambda}_{RMW}$	$\hat{\lambda}_{CMA}$	Adj R^2
CAPM	1.47	−0.70							0.32
	(6.91)	(−3.34)							
ZCAPM	0.85	−0.19	0.74						0.96
	(4.14)	(−0.95)	(6.70)						
Three-factor	1.79	−1.22		0.72	−0.17				0.74
	(8.07)	(−5.69)		(4.86)	(−0.17)				
Four-factor		1.95	−1.39		0.64	−0.20	0.54		0.77
	(9.35)	(−6.79)		(4.35)	(−0.96)	(2.93)			
Five-factor	1.52	−0.95		0.51	−0.46		−0.28	0.47	0.82
	(7.35)	(−4.43)		(3.76)	(−2.11)		(−1.23)	(2.52)	

Panel C: 25 momentum equal-wt portfolios using all stocks

Model	$\hat{\alpha}$	$\hat{\lambda}_m$	$\hat{\lambda}_{RD}$	$\hat{\lambda}_{SMB}$	$\hat{\lambda}_{HML}$	$\hat{\lambda}_{MOM}$	$\hat{\lambda}_{RMW}$	$\hat{\lambda}_{CMA}$	Adj R^2
CAPM	−0.29	1.62							0.48
	(−1.06)	(3.40)							
ZCAPM	−0.17	1.26	0.60						0.82
	(−0.68)	(3.11)	(3.83)						
Three-factor	−0.21	1.75		−0.61	0.16				0.51
	(−0.72)	(3.27)		(−1.39)	(0.42)				
Four-factor		0.19	0.75		−0.14	0.13	1.01		0.82
	(0.68)	(1.46)		(−0.35)	(0.47)	(3.20)			
Five-factor	−0.18	1.65		−0.61	−0.25		0.34	−0.38	0.50
	(−0.74)	(3.29)		(−1.64)	(−0.80)		(0.98)	(−1.25)	

(continued)

Table 8.1 (continued)

Panel D: 25 momentum equal-wt portfolios 60% largest market capitalization stocks

Model	$\hat{\alpha}$	$\hat{\lambda}_m$	$\hat{\lambda}_{RD}$	$\hat{\lambda}_{SMB}$	$\hat{\lambda}_{HML}$	$\hat{\lambda}_{MOM}$	$\hat{\lambda}_{RMW}$	$\hat{\lambda}_{CMA}$	Adj R^2
CAPM	0.37	0.27							−0.01
	(1.77)	(0.80)							
ZCAPM	0.22	0.36	0.92						0.99
	(0.97)	(1.14)	(7.14)						
Three-factor	0.33	1.39		−1.32	−0.29				0.77
	(1.36)	(2.76)		(−3.15)	(−1.10)				
Four-factor		0.56	0.44		−0.60	0.45	1.41		0.97
	(2.49)	(1.12)		(−2.06)	(2.08)	(6.43)			
Five-factor	0.21	1.16		−0.92	−0.06		0.36	0.01	0.98
	(0.90)	(2.53)		(−2.57)	(−0.21)		(1.66)	(0.06)	

Panel E: 25 momentum equal-wt portfolios 40% smallest market capitalization stocks

Model	$\hat{\alpha}$	$\hat{\lambda}_m$	$\hat{\lambda}_{RD}$	$\hat{\lambda}_{SMB}$	$\hat{\lambda}_{HML}$	$\hat{\lambda}_{MOM}$	$\hat{\lambda}_{RMW}$	$\hat{\lambda}_{CMA}$	Adj R^2
CAPM	0.09	2.30							0.38
	(0.39)	(2.30)							
ZCAPM	0.03	1.93	0.65						0.76
	(0.14)	(3.61)	(4.71)						
Three-factor	0.41	1.40		−0.53	0.27				0.28
	(1.95)	(2.48)		(−1.48)	(0.54)				
Four-factor		0.41	1.22		−0.55	0.01	0.15		0.27
	(2.10)	(2.40)		(−1.63)	(0.01)	(0.37)			
Five-factor	0.48	1.35		−0.74	−0.11		−0.04	−0.28	0.34
	(2.32)	(2.48)		(−2.00)	(−0.26)		(−0.12)	(−0.91)	

Using value- and equal-weighted returns, this table contains results for the analysis period January 1965 to December 2017. We report out-of-sample (one-month-ahead) estimated prices of risk based on standard two-step Fama-MacBeth cross-sectional tests. Estimated prices of risk are denoted $\hat{\lambda}_k$ for the kth factor in monthly percent return terms (t-statistics in parentheses). Factors are denoted as m (CRSP index return minus Treasury bill rate, see footnote 1), *RD* (return dispersion), *SMB* (size), *HML* (value), *MOM* (momentum), *RMW* (profit), and *CMA* (investment). Results are shown for different sets of test asset portfolios constructed based on momentum

[1] In the ZCAPM, the price of beta risk associated with CRSP index excess returns is denoted $\hat{\lambda}_a$ rather than $\hat{\lambda}_m$ in the other models

Turning to our main focus, momentum is similarly priced for both value- and equal-weighted returns with $\hat{\lambda}_{MOM}$ = 0.56% per month (t = 3.20) and $\hat{\lambda}_{MOM}$ = 0.54% per month (t = 2.93), respectively, both significant at the one percent level. Importantly, for the ZCAPM in Panels A and B, the return dispersion (*RD*) factor is highly significant with $\hat{\lambda}_{RD}$ = 0.61% per month (t = 5.54) and $\hat{\lambda}_{RD}$ = 0.74% per month (t = 6.70), respectively. Hence, *RD* has noticeably higher t-values[9] than the momentum factor, and *RD* and momentum factors have similar magnitudes for the market prices of their respective risk loadings.

Next we construct equal-weighted returns for 25 momentum portfolios sorted on past returns. These portfolios are formed by sorting all CRSP stocks on their past holding period returns in a 12-month period (e.g., January 1964 to December 1964 excluding the last week). One-month-ahead returns are computed for portfolios in January 1965. This process is rolled forward monthly to construct time series of momentum returns from January 1965 to December 2017. Panel C of Table 8.1 reports the cross-sectional regression tests for these portfolios. There we see that return dispersion and momentum loadings are significantly priced: $\hat{\lambda}_{RD}$ = 0.60% (t = 3.83) and $\hat{\lambda}_{MOM}$ = 1.01% (t = 3.20), respectively. Market factor loadings are significantly priced in most models, but size loadings are not priced. Adjusted R^2 values equal 82% for both the ZCAPM and four-factor model with momentum, whereas other models have lower estimated values around 50%.

To examine size effects, we reform the 25 momentum portfolios using the 60% largest and 40% smallest stocks by market capitalization. Using these portfolios, panels D and E in Table 8.1 display the results. The most consistently significant loadings correspond to return dispersion (i.e., t = 7.14 and t = 4.71 in Panels D and E, respectively). Momentum loadings are highly significant for larger stocks in Panel D (i.e., t = 6.43) but not for smaller stocks in Panel E. Size and profit loadings exhibit some significance but are negatively signed. A notable difference related to size is that the adjusted R^2 values for all but the CAPM are markedly higher for larger stocks compared to smaller stocks, with the highest R^2 values coincident with the ZCAPM.

Since we hypothesize that momentum and zeta risk are related to one another, we formed 25 portfolios sorted by zeta coefficients from the empirical ZCAPM estimated in the prior year using daily returns. Again results are provided for all stocks as well as largest 60% and smallest 40% of stocks by market capitalization. In Panel A of Table 8.2 for all stocks, the results for return dispersion and momentum loadings are both very signifi-

[9] As cited in previous chapters, Harvey et al. (2015) and Chordia et al. (2020) document evidence that factors should have t-values of 3.0 or more to be recognized as statistically significant.

Table 8.2 Fama-MacBeth cross-sectional regression tests of zeta risk portfolios: January 1965 to December 2017

Panel A: 25 zeta risk equal-wt portfolios using all stocks

Model	$\hat{\alpha}$	$\hat{\lambda}_m$	$\hat{\lambda}_{RD}$	$\hat{\lambda}_{SMB}$	$\hat{\lambda}_{HML}$	$\hat{\lambda}_{MOM}$	$\hat{\lambda}_{RMW}$	$\hat{\lambda}_{CMA}$	Adj R^2
CAPM	0.58	0.52							0.23
	(2.14)	(1.08)							
ZCAPM	0.16	0.71	0.69						0.95
	(0.76)	(2.01)	(5.01)						
Three-factor	0.44	0.29		0.18	−0.16				0.77
	(2.02)	(0.66)		(0.50)	(−0.42)				
Four-factor		0.17	0.57		0.35	−0.45	1.42		0.96
	(0.96)	(1.68)		(1.08)	(−1.81)	(4.16)			
Five-factor	0.05	0.77		0.21	−0.77		0.40	−0.54	0.83
	(0.24)	(1.97)		(0.66)	(−2.62)		(1.41)	(1.64)	

Panel B: 25 zeta risk equal-wt portfolios 60% largest market capitalization stocks

Model	$\hat{\alpha}$	$\hat{\lambda}_m$	$\hat{\lambda}_{RD}$	$\hat{\lambda}_{SMB}$	$\hat{\lambda}_{HML}$	$\hat{\lambda}_{MOM}$	$\hat{\lambda}_{RMW}$	$\hat{\lambda}_{CMA}$	Adj R^2
CAPM	0.71	−0.12							−0.03
	(3.16)	(−0.33)							
ZCAPM	0.31	0.22	0.92						1.00
	(1.66)	(0.78)	(7.55)						
Three-factor	0.55	0.35		−0.38	−0.05				0.80
	(2.62)	(0.94)		(−1.23)	(−0.20)				
Four-factor		0.37	0.90		−0.74	−0.15	1.40		0.98
	(2.09)	(3.06)		(−2.99)	(−0.77)	(5.85)			
Five-factor	0.14	0.84		−0.24	−0.52		0.60	0.07	0.98
	(0.71)	(2.55)		(−0.88)	(−2.04)		(2.92)	(0.31)	

Panel C: 25 zeta risk equal-wt portfolios 40% smallest market capitalization stocks

Model	$\hat{\alpha}$	$\hat{\lambda}_m$	$\hat{\lambda}_{RD}$	$\hat{\lambda}_{SMB}$	$\hat{\lambda}_{HML}$	$\hat{\lambda}_{MOM}$	$\hat{\lambda}_{RMW}$	$\hat{\lambda}_{CMA}$	Adj R^2
CAPM	0.59	1.08							0.25
	(2.77)	(1.69)							
ZCAPM	0.42	0.89	0.57						0.93
	(1.86)	(1.72)	(4.37)						
Three-factor	0.52	−0.58		0.93	0.42				0.36
	(2.57)	(−1.10)		(3.12)	(0.87)				
Four-factor		0.50	−0.37		0.84	0.13	0.84		0.68
	(2.69)	(−0.85)		(2.82)	(0.44)	(2.08)			
Five-factor	0.66	−0.89		0.64	0.19		−0.38	0.08	0.65
	(3.38)	(−1.92)		(2.15)	(0.53)		(−1.13)	(0.25)	

Using value-weighted returns, this table contains results for the analysis period January 1965 to December 2017. We report out-of-sample (one-month-ahead) estimated prices of risk based on standard two-step Fama-MacBeth cross-sectional tests. Estimated prices of risk are denoted $\hat{\lambda}_k$ for the kth factor in monthly percent return terms (t-statistics in parentheses). Factors are denoted as m (CRSP index returns minus Treasury bill rate, see footnote 1), *RD* (return dispersion), *SMB* (size), *HML* (value), *MOM* (momentum), *RMW* (profit), and *CMA* (capital investment). Results are shown for different sets of test asset portfolios constructed based on zeta risk

[1]In the ZCAPM, the price of beta risk associated with CRSP index excess returns is denoted $\hat{\lambda}_a$ rather than $\hat{\lambda}_m$ in the other models

Table 8.3 Fama-MacBeth cross-sectional regression tests of momentum and zeta risk portfolios: January 1965 to December 2017

Model	$\hat{\alpha}$	$\hat{\lambda}_m$	$\hat{\lambda}_{RD}$	$\hat{\lambda}_{SMB}$	$\hat{\lambda}_{HML}$	$\hat{\lambda}_{MOM}$	$\hat{\lambda}_{RMW}$	$\hat{\lambda}_{CMA}$	Adj R^2
CAPM	0.68	0.14							−0.01
	(3.43)	(0.62)							
ZCAPM	0.35	0.33	0.73						0.88
	(0.76)	(2.01)	(5.01)						
Three-factor	0.76	−0.28		0.57	−0.12				0.37
	(3.89)	(−1.43)		(3.25)	(−0.44)				
Four-factor		0.83	−0.33		0.55	−0.17	0.85		0.47
	(5.35)	(−1.95)		(3.04)	(−0.82)	(4.00)			
Five-factor	0.54	−0.02		0.48	−0.47		0.10	−0.01	0.41
	(3.26)	(−0.11)		(3.25)	(−2.19)		(0.41)	(−0.08)	

Using value-weighted returns, this table contains results for the analysis period January 1965 to December 2017. We report out-of-sample (one-month-ahead) estimated prices of risk based on standard two-step Fama-MacBeth cross-sectional tests. Estimated prices of risk are denoted $\hat{\lambda}_k$ for the kth factor in monthly percent return terms (t-statistics in parentheses). Factors are denoted as m (CRSP index return minus Treasury bill rate, see footnote 1), *RD* (return dispersion), *SMB* (size), *HML* (value), *MOM* (momentum), *RMW* (profit), and *CMA* (capital investment). Results are shown for equal-weighted returns using 75 combined portfolios comprised of 25 size-momentum, 25 momentum, and 25 zeta risk portfolios

[1] In the ZCAPM, the price of beta risk associated with CRSP index excess returns is denoted $\hat{\lambda}_a$ rather than $\hat{\lambda}_m$ in the other models

cant: $\hat{\lambda}_{RD} = 0.69\%$ ($t = 5.01$) and $\hat{\lambda}_{MOM} = 1.42\%$ ($t = 4.16$), respectively. In some models the market factor and value factor loadings are significantly priced but value loadings negatively so. In Panels B and C, return dispersion and momentum loadings are the most significant and consistently priced factors. And, like momentum sorted portfolios in Panels D and E of Table 8.1, estimated R^2 values are generally higher for larger stocks than smaller stocks.

Finally, we combine the equal-weighted returns for the 25 size-momentum, 25 momentum, and 25 zeta risk portfolios for a total of 75 test asset portfolios. The cross-sectional regression results in Table 8.3 again show that return dispersion and momentum loadings are highly significant (i.e., $t = 5.01$ and $t = 4.00$, respectively). Also, market and size factor loadings are signficant in most cases. For this expanded set of test assets, the adjusted R^2 estimate for the ZCAPM at 88% is substantially higher than those for other models, which range from 37 to 47%.

This goodness-of-fit of the ZCAPM relative to the three-, four-, and five-factor models is illustrated in Figs. 8.1 and 8.2. There we plot the

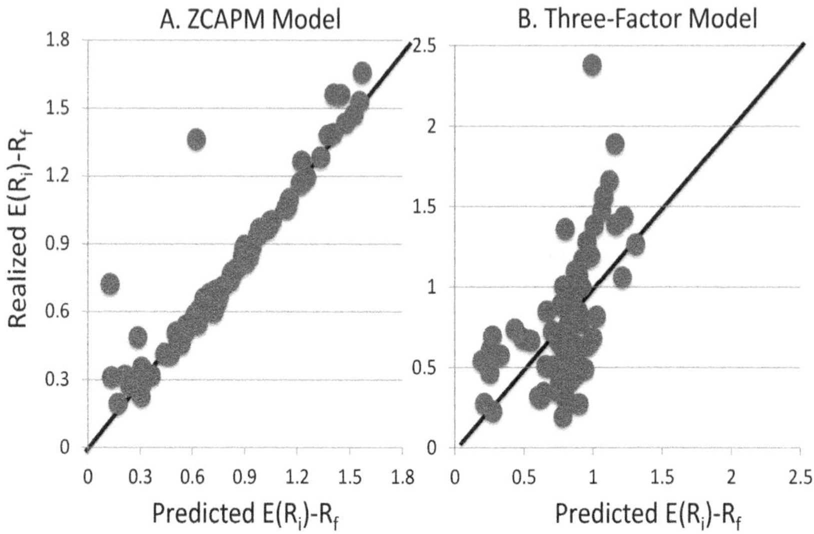

Fig. 8.1 Out-of-sample cross-sectional relationship between average one-month-ahead realized excess returns in percent and average one-month-ahead predicted excess returns in percent for 25 size-momentum, 25 momentum, and 25 zeta risk portfolios: empirical ZCAPM in Panel A and Fama and French three-factor model in Panel B. The analysis period is January 1965 to December 2017

one-month-ahead realized excess returns and one-month-ahead predicted excess returns (using the cross-sectional regression model estimates) for the aforementioned 75 test asset portfolios. Realized and predicted excess returns are averages of 632 cross-sectional monthly values. The graphs for three-, four-, and five-factor models are similar due to comparable R^2 values in Table 8.3. Compared to these models, the ZCAPM in Panel A of Fig. 8.1 has noticeably higher goodness-of-fit. With the exception of two portfolios,[10] most portfolios lie very close to the 45-degree line describing an almost perfect relation between realized and predicted returns. Relevant

[10] These two portfolios have the most extreme negative past returns among the 25 momentum portfolios. In one-month-ahead returns after the formation period, these portfolios sometimes have return reversals that account for their higher than predicted returns. Using the 60% highest market capitalization stocks, we found that all 25 portfolios lie very close to the 45-degree line.

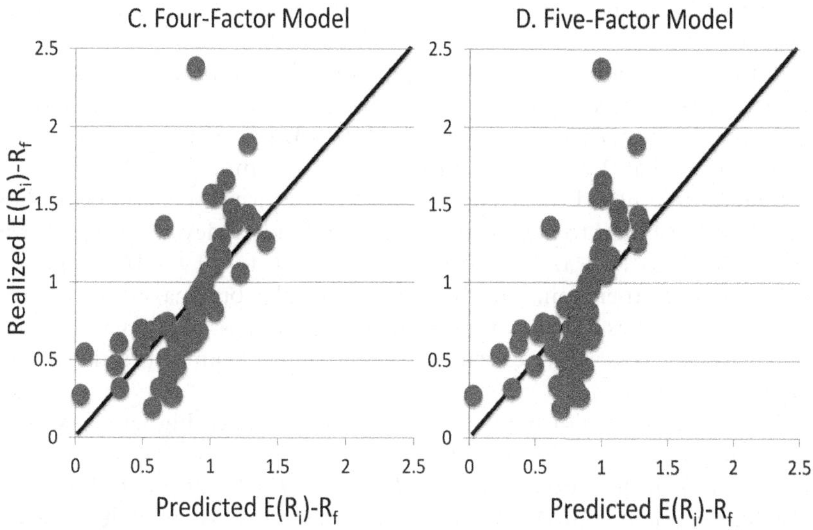

Fig. 8.2 Out-of-sample cross-sectional relationship between average one-month-ahead realized excess returns in percent and average one-month-ahead predicted excess returns in percent for 25 size-momentum, 25 momentum, and 25 zeta risk portfolios: Carhart four-factor model in Panel A and Fama and French five-factor model in Panel B. The analysis period is January 1965 to December 2017

to our research hypothesis, this graph shows that momentum and zeta risk portfolios are similarly priced by the empirical ZCAPM.

In sum, our cross-sectional test results support the hypothesis that momentum and return dispersion loadings are similarly priced using test asset portfolios related to momentum returns as well as zeta risk.

8.3.2 Comparative Return Results

Are zero-investment momentum and return dispersion portfolio returns similar? Descriptive return statistics for these portfolios are shown in Table 8.4. Here we focus attention on the decile 10 minus decile 1 and decile 9 minus decile 2 strategies. The highest momentum return is the traditional $M10 - M1$ strategy at 0.94% per month. Returns drop off markedly for the $M9 - M2$ strategy to 0.59% month. As the average return gap between winners and losers narrow further, momentum returns largely dissipate.

Return-dispersion portfolios outperform their momentum portfolio counterparts. For example, the $Z10 - Z1$ strategy earns 1.48% per month or about 57% more than the traditional $M10 - M1$ portfolio. Also, $Z9 - Z2$ does quite well at 0.80% per month or about 36% more than $M9 - M2$.

It should be noted that higher returns for return dispersion portfolios cannot be attributed to higher total risk. The standard deviations of returns are similar for $M10 - M1$ and $Z10 - Z1$ as well as for $M9 - M2$ and $Z9 - Z2$. Also, since their minimum returns are similar but maximum returns are higher for these return dispersion strategies, it is upside gains rather than downside losses that explain the higher gains from return dispersion relative to momentum.

An obvious return disparity in Table 8.4 is the much higher gains from the return dispersion and momentum portfolios compared to the average monthly returns for popular size (SMB), value (HML), profit (RMW), and capital investment (CMA) factors. The latter factors have much lower average returns in the range of 0.26%–0.34% per month. Their total risk as measured by the standard deviation of returns is about 50% less than the $M10 - M1$ and $Z10 - Z1$ portfolios but not much less than the $M9 - M2$ and $Z9 - Z2$ portfolios. Hence, the latter portfolios are clearly superior in return/risk terms compared to these popular factors.

The relatively high returns of momentum strategies compared to other zero-investment factors has led many authors to infer that they are anomalous. In the absence of a market-risk-based explanation of momentum, controversy has surrounded this factor. As mentioned earlier, Fama and French (2008) and Subrahmanyam (2018) have recognized momentum as the most vexing puzzle in the field of finance. Because our return dispersion portfolios likewise outperform popular factors by a wide margin, one might infer that they represent another anomaly. However, rather than being two separate anomalies, another possible explanation is that these two anomalies are closely related to one another via their common link to market risk associated with market return dispersion.

Assuming that momentum and return dispersion portfolios have a common market risk link, we should be able to combine them into a hybrid zero-investment portfolio strategy. Tables 8.5 and 8.6 report the performance results for hybrid momentum-zeta risk portfolios without and with risk management, respectively. In these analyses, we drop small stocks due to potential short-term reversals and use only the 80% largest stocks by

Table 8.4 Descriptive return statistics for zero-investment momentum and return-dispersion portfolios

Zero-Investment Factor	Mean	Std Dev	Min	Max	Max Loss
$M10 - M1$	0.94	6.24	−59.95	19.30	−82.24
$M9 - M2$	0.59	3.61	−28.78	13.69	−57.38
$M8 - M3$	0.32	2.50	−18.63	9.95	−40.67
$M7 - M4$	0.20	1.61	−8.42	4.91	−24.94
$M6 - M5$	0.03	1.01	−4.87	2.89	−18.04
$Z10 - Z1$	1.48	6.08	−42.57	52.14	−61.04
$Z9 - Z2$	0.80	3.56	−17.54	30.27	−37.84
$Z8 - Z3$	0.39	2.28	−9.55	15.38	−23.68
$Z7 - Z4$	0.21	1.44	−5.93	6.75	−14.23
$Z6 - Z5$	0.05	0.92	−2.96	3.54	−21.93
SMB	0.27	3.07	−14.94	18.38	−57.05
HML	0.34	2.84	−11.10	12.90	−40.89
RMW	0.26	2.19	−17.99	12.83	−38.99
CMA	0.29	2.02	−6.88	9.58	−17.30

This table provides descriptive statistics for the returns on zero-investment momentum and zero-investment, return dispersion portfolios in the analysis period January 1965 to December 2017
Momentum portfolios are formed by ranking holding period returns in previous 12-month estimation periods. Stocks are placed into deciles from low-to-high denoted $M1$-to-$M10$. The following zero-investment momentum portfolios are formed: $M10 - M1$, $M9 - M2$, $M8 - M3$, $M7 - M4$, and $M6 - M5$. Returns are computed in the post-formation, one-month-ahead period
Zero-investment, return dispersion are constructed by estimating times-series regressions for the empirical ZCAPM in Eq. (8.4) with daily returns for 12-month estimation periods. All stocks are ranked in terms of their estimated zeta coefficient $\hat{Z}_i^*$. The following zero-investment portfolios are formed. $Z10 - Z1$, $Z9 - Z2$, $Z8 - Z3$, $Z7 - Z4$, and $Z6 - Z5$. Returns are computed in the post-formation, one-month-ahead period

market capitalization (see footnote 4). Hybrid portfolios are formed by taking the intersection of stocks in the $M10$ and $Z10$ portfolios as well as the intersection of stocks in the $M1$ and $Z1$ portfolios. The equal-weighted hybrid zero-investment portfolio is denoted $MZ10 - MZ1$. Also, we weighted individual stocks based on their $|Z^*|$ proportions to form hybrid portfolio $MZ10^* - MZ1^*$.

Without risk management, due to dropping small stocks, Table 8.5 shows that the average return of the momentum portfolio $M10 - M1$ is boosted from 0.94% (in Table 8.4) to 1.74% per month. The hybrid portfolios $MZ10 - MZ1$ and $MZ10^* - MZ1^*$ further boost average returns to 1.81% and 1.91% per month, respectively. Hence, combining momentum and zeta risk portfolios tends to increase returns relative to traditional momentum.

Table 8.5 Hybrid zero-investment portfolios formed by combining momentum and zeta risk strategies

Zero-Investment Portfolio	Mean	Std Dev	Min	Max	Max Loss
$CRSP - R_f$	0.52	4,44	−23.24	16.10	−55.68
$M10 - M1$	1.74	7.18	−59.39	41.83	−76.47
$MZ10 - MZ1$	1.81	7.35	−62.07	46.82	−78.25
$MZ10^* - MZ1^*$	1.91	7.82	−67.62	50.04	−80.20

This table shows the average monthly return performance of zero-investment portfolios formed by combining momentum and zeta risk strategies in the analysis period from January 1965 to December 2017. Small stocks are dropped in these analyses due to potential short-term reversals. One-month-ahead, post-formation returns are computed for each zero-investment portfolio. Zeta coefficients are estimated for the empirical ZCAPM using the EM algorithm with one year of daily returns. CRSP excess returns over the Treasury bill are shown for comparison purposes. Zero-investment portfolios are formed as follows:

- $M10 - M1$: Form 10 past return equal-weighted portfolios using the 80% largest market capitalization stocks with high to low return portfolios denoted $M10$ to $M1$. The momentum portfolio is formed by longing the winner portfolio $M10$ and shorting the loser portfolio $M1$
- $MZ10 - MZ1$: Form 10 zeta risk equal-weighted portfolios using the 80% largest market capitalization stocks with high to low zeta risk portfolios denoted $Z10$ to $Z1$. The hybrid momentum-zeta risk portfolio is formed by longing the intersection of stocks in the $M10$ and $Z10$ portfolios and shorting the intersection of stocks in the $M1$ and $Z1$ portfolios
- $MZ10^* - MZ1^*$: Form portfolio $MZ10 - MZ1$ with weights for individual stocks based on their $|Z^*|$ proportions, rather than equal weights

In Table 8.6 we repeat the analyses in Table 8.5 but implement risk management. In any month, if the average zeta risk span between the $Z10$ and $Z1$ portfolios is within the smallest quintile of all previous months in the sample period (i.e., zeta risk spread), then this zero-investment portfolio is replaced by the market factor $CRSP - R_f$ for monthly rebalancing purposes. As shown in Table 8.6, the resultant risk-managed portfolios earn yet higher average monthly returns: $M10 - M1$ from 1.74% (in Table 8.5) to 1.87% (in Table 8.6); $MZ10 - MZ1$ from 1.81% (in Table 8.5) to 1.94% (in Table 8.6); and $MZ10^* - MZ1^*$ from 1.91% (in Table 8.5) to 2.03% (in Table 8.6). These results further support our hypothesis that momentum-based portfolio returns are related to zeta risk.

8.3.3 *Regression Test Results*

How closely related to one another are the returns of zero-investment momentum and return dispersion strategies? The regression results in Table 8.7 strongly support this relationship. In Panel A using momentum portfolio returns $M10 - M1$ as the dependent variable, the independent

Table 8.6 Risk-managed hybrid zero-investment portfolios formed by combining momentum and zeta risk strategies

Zero-Investment Portfolio	Mean	Std Dev	Min	Max	Max Loss
$CRSP - R_f$	0.52	4,44	−23.24	16.10	−55.68
$M10 - M1$	1.87	6.48	−59.39	41.83	−63.47
$MZ10 - MZ1$	1.94	6.71	−62.07	46.82	−65.88
$MZ10^* - MZ1^*$	2.03	7.22	−67.62	50.04	−70.88

This table shows the average monthly return performance of risk managed zero-investment portfolios formed by combining momentum and zeta risk strategies in the analysis period January 1965 to December 2017. Small stocks are dropped in these analyses due to potential short-term reversals. One-month-ahead, post-formation returns are computed for each zero-investment portfolio. Zeta coefficients are estimated for the empirical ZCAPM using the EM algorithm with one year of daily returns. CRSP excess returns over the Treasury bill are shown for comparison purposes. Zero-investment portfolios are formed as follows:

- $M10 - M1$: Form 10 past return equal-weighted portfolios using the 80% largest market capitalization stocks with high to low return portfolios denoted $M10$ to $M1$. The momentum portfolio is formed by longing the winner portfolio $M10$ and shorting the loser portfolio $M1$
- $MZ10 - MZ1$: Form 10 zeta risk equal-weighted portfolios using the 80% largest market capitalization stocks with high to low zeta risk portfolios denoted Z10 to Z1. The hybrid momentum-zeta risk portfolio is formed by longing the intersection of stocks in the $M10$ and $Z10$ portfolios and shorting the intersection of stocks in the $M1$ and $Z1$ portfolios
- $MZ10^* - MZ1^*$: Form portfolio $MZ10 - MZ1$ with weights for individual stocks based on their $|Z^*|$ proportions, rather than equal weights

We apply risk management to zero-investment portfolios. In any month, if the average zeta risk span between the Z10 and Z1 portfolios is within the smallest quintile of all previous months in the sample period, then the zero-investment portfolio is replaced by market portfolio $CRSP - R_f$ for monthly rebalancing purposes

variable defined as return dispersion portfolio returns $Z10 - Z1$ has a t-value of 31.76 and adjusted R^2 value of 61%. These results far exceed the statistical significance and goodness-of-fit associated with popular *SMB*, *HML*, *RMW*, and *CMA* factors at no more than 5%. Not surprisingly, in unreported results, the estimated correlation coefficient between $M10 - M1$ and $Z10 - Z1$ is fairly high at 0.78.

The Panel B results using $M9 - M2$ as the dependent variable are similar to those in Panel A, with a t-value of 27.03 associated with $Z9 - Z2$ and adjusted R^2 value of 53% (i.e., estimated correlation coefficient of 0.73). By contrast, other factors again have almost no explanatory power.

Even the results in Panel C for $M8 - M3$ and $Z8 - Z3$ exhibit a very strong relationship with t-value equal to 24.21 and adjusted R^2 of 48% (i.e., estimated correlation coefficient of 0.69). This relationship drops off in Panels D and E for portfolios with smaller return spreads.

The close relationship between momentum portfolio and return dispersion portfolio returns in Table 8.7 suggests that, as conjectured previously, these two phenomena can be attributed to a single underlying explanation. As discussed in Chapter 3, a large body of literature has shown that return dispersion is related to economic fundamentals indicative of general market risk. According to the ZCAPM, market return dispersion largely defines the width of the mean-variance parabola, which impacts stock returns as it changes over time. Thus, by transitive logic, we can infer that momentum is

Table 8.7 Time series OLS regression tests

Panel A: Momentum portfolio $M10 - M1$					
Factors	α	t-value	β	$t$value	Adj R^2
$Z10 - Z1$	−0.25	−1.57	0.80	31.76	0.61
SMB	1.03	4.20	−0.34	−4.29	0.03
HML	1.02	4.14	−0.25	−2.92	0.01
RMW	0.78	3.19	0.62	5.62	0.05
CMA	0.92	3.69	0.05	0.44	−0.00
Panel B: Momentum portfolio $M9 - M2$					
Factors	α	t-value	β	t-value	Adj R^2
$Z9 - Z2$	−0.00	−0.04	0.74	27.03	0.53
SMB	0.64	4.54	−0.20	−4.41	0.03
HML	0.62	4.35	−0.11	−2.15	0.01
RMW	0.49	3.50	0.36	4.12	0.05
CMA	0.57	3.92	0.08	1.11	0.00
Panel C: Momentum portfolio $M8 - M3$					
Factors	α	t-value	β	t-value	Adj R^2
$Z8 - Z3$	0.02	0.31	0.76	24.21	0.48
SMB	0.35	3.60	−0.14	−4.24	0.03
HML	0.36	3.60	−0.11	−3.27	0.02
RMW	0.27	2.73	0.18	4.12	0.02
CMA	0.31	3.10	0.03	0.52	−0.00
Panel D: Momentum portfolio $M7 - M4$					
Factors	α	t-value	β	t-value	Adj R^2
$Z7 - Z4$	0.09	1.54	0.52	13.28	0.22
SMB	0.22	3.40	−0.06	−3.02	0.01
HML	0.21	3.28	−0.03	−1.42	0.00
RMW	0.17	2.69	0.11	3.82	0.02
CMA	0.19	2.99	0.02	0.76	0.00

(continued)

Table 8.7 (continued)

Panel E: Momentum portfolio $M6 - M5$

Factors	α	t-value	β	t-value	Adj R^2
$Z6 - Z5$	0.02	0.41	0.16	3.74	0.02
SMB	0.04	0.88	−0.04	−3.04	0.01
HML	0.03	0.77	−0.02	−1.27	0.00
RMW	0.01	0.27	0.05	2.98	0.01
CMA	0.02	0.43	0.03	1.28	0.00

This table reports OLS regressions of zero-investment momentum returns on zero-investment factor returns in the analysis period January 1965 to December 2017. The following OLS regression is estimated:

$$MOM_T = \alpha_{MOM} + \beta_{MOM} FACTOR_T + \varepsilon_T, \tag{8.6}$$

where MOM_T is the momentum return in month T, and $FACTOR_T$ is the factor return in month T. The dependent variable MOM is defined in different panels as: $M10 - M1$, $M9 - M2$, $M8 - M3$, $M7 - M4$, and $M6 - M5$. The independent variable $FACTOR$ is defined as: $Z10 - Z1$, $Z9 - Z2$, $Z8 - Z3$, $Z7 - Z4$, and $Z6 - Z5$ in addition to SMB, HML, RMW, and CMA. All returns are equal-weighted for different investment portfolios

connected to market risk associated with return dispersion. Consistent with this inference, Chordia and Shivakumar (2002) have found that momentum profits adjusted for macroeconomic variables are much smaller than unadjusted profits.[11]

8.4 Summary

This chapter sought to provide empirical evidence on the long-standing momentum mystery. We hypothesized that a large portion of momentum profits arise rationally from market zeta risk associated with cross-sectional market volatility. In previous chapters, we developed a special case of the zero-beta CAPM dubbed the ZCAPM that posits market risk has two components: (1) beta risk related to average market returns and (2) zeta risk associated with cross-sectional market volatility (denoted RD). It is well known that momentum profits are not explained by market risk arising

[11] However, Griffin et al. (2003) found that momentum profits and the business cycle are only weakly related in international markets.

from the market factor; however, no previous studies consider their relation to market risk stemming from cross-sectional market volatility.

For U.S. stocks in the sample period 1965 to 2017, we conducted three different analyses of the relation between return dispersion and momentum returns: (1) cross-sectional asset pricing tests, (2) comparisons of historical returns, and (3) regression analyses. For cross-sectional tests, we estimated the empirical ZCAPM via the expectation-maximization (EM) algorithm. Based on test assets sorted on momentum and out-of-sample (one-month-ahead) cross-sectional regression tests, we found that the market prices of both return dispersion and momentum loadings were highly significant and more consistently priced than the loadings of other popular risk factors, including size, value, profit, and capital investment. Similar results were obtained for test assets sorted on zeta risk levels (i.e., sensitivity to return dispersion). Also, using momentum and zeta risk portfolios as test assets, the empirical ZCAPM provides a much closer fit between out-of-sample (one-month-ahead) realized excess returns and predicted excess returns than popular three-, four-, and five-factor models.

Comparatively, in our analysis period, zero-investment, return dispersion portfolios based on high-decile/low-decile zeta risk averaged approximately 1.50% compared to 0.94% for high-decile/low-decile zero-investment momentum portfolios. And, average monthly returns greater than 1.50% were possible by combining zero-investment momentum and return dispersion strategies into a hybrid portfolio. Other popular zero-investment factors earned at most 0.34% per month. Additionally, usng risk management, the hybrid portfolio earned as much as 2.03% per month.

Lastly, regression analyses indicated that momentum portfolio returns are very significantly related to return dispersion portfolio returns with much higher t-statistics and adjusted R^2 values compared to other factors.

In view of this evidence, we conclude that momentum profits are closely related to market risk associated with return dispersion. A number of possible areas of research are suggested by our findings. For example, future research is recommended to examine momentum profits and return dispersion in other asset classes, such as bonds, commodities, currencies, etc. Another area of interest is whether other anomalous patterns in average returns, including (for example) net stock issues, accruals, asset growth, etc., are largely captured by return dispersion. Most anomalies are measured with zero-investment portfolio returns which themselves proxy return dispersion. Finally, research is recommended on the relation between business cycle and macroeconomic variables and both zero-investment momentum and return dispersion profits.

Bibliography

Andrei, D., & Cujean, J. (2017). Information percolation, momentum and reversal. *Journal of Financial Economics*, *123*, 617–645.

Angelidis, T., Sakkas, A., & Tessaromatis, N. (2015). Stock market dispersion, the business cycle and expected factor returns. *Journal of Banking and Finance*, *59*, 256–279.

Asness, C., Moskowitz, T., & Pedersen, L. (2013). Value and momentum everywhere. *Journal of Finance*, *68*, 929–985.

Barberis, M., Shleifer, A., & Vishny, R. (1998). A model of investor sentiment. *Journal of Financial Economics*, *49*, 307–343.

Barroso, P., & Santa-Clara, P. (2015). Momentum has its moments. *Journal of Financial Economics*, *116*, 111–120.

Bekaert, G., & Harvey, C. (2000). Foreign speculators and emerging equity markets. *Journal of Finance*, *55*, 565–513.

Black, F. (1972). Capital market equilibrium with restricted borrowing. *Journal of Business*, *45*, 444–454.

Brav, A., & Heaton, J. B. (2002). Competing theories of financial anomalies. *Review of Financial Studies*, *15*, 575–606.

Carhart, M. M. (1997). On persistence in mutual fund performance. *Journal of Finance*, *52*, 57–82.

Chang, R., Ko, K., Nakano, S., & Rhee, G. (2018). Residual momentum in Japan. *Journal of Empirical Finance*, *45*, 283–299.

Chordia, T., Goyal, A., & Saretto, A. (2020). Anomalies and false rejections. *Review of Financial Studies*, *33*, 2134–2179.

Chordia, T., & Shivakumar, L. (2002). Momentum, business cycle, and time-varying expected returns. *Journal of Finance*, *57*, 985–1019.

Connolly, R., & Stivers, C. (2003). Momentum and reversals in equity index returns during periods of abnormal turnover and return dispersion. *Journal of Finance*, *58*, 1521–1556.

Conrad, J., & Kaul, G. (1998). An anatomy of trading strategies. *Review of Financial Studies*, *11*, 489–519.

Conrad, J., & Yavuz, D. (2017). Momentum and reversal: Does what goes up always come down? *Review of Finance*, *21*, 555–581.

Cooper, M. J., Gutierrez, R. C, Jr., & Hameed, A. (2004). Market states and momentum. *Journal of Finance*, *59*, 1345–1365.

Da, Z., Gurun, U., & Warachka, M. (2014). Frog in the pan: Continuous information and momentum. *Review of Financial Studies*, *27*, 2171–2218.

Daniel, K. (2014). *Momentum crashes* (Working Paper). Columbia University.

Daniel, K., Hirshleifer, D., & Subrahmanyam, A. (1998). Investor psychology and security market under- and overreactions. *Journal of Finance*, *53*, 1839–1885.

Daniel, K., Jagannathan, R., & Kim, S. (2019). *A hidden Markov model of momentum* (Working Paper). Columbia University, Northwestern University, and Georgia Institute of Technology.

Daniel, K., & Moskowitz, T. J. (2016). Momentum crashes. *Journal of Financial Economics, 12*, 221–247.

De Bondt, W. F. M., & Thaler, R. (1985). Does the stock market overreact? *Journal of Finance, 40*, 793–805.

DeBondt, W. F. M., & Thaler, R. (1987). Further evidence of stock market overreaction and seasonality. *Journal of Finance, 42*, 557–581.

Dempster, A. P., Laird, N. M., & Rubin, D. B. (1977). Maximum likelihood from incomplete data via the EM algorithm. *Journal of the Royal Statistical Society, 39*, 1–38.

Fama, E. F., & French, K. R. (1992). The cross-section of expected stock returns. *Journal of Finance, 47*, 427–465.

Fama, E. F., & French, K. R. (1993). Common risk factors in the returns on stocks and bonds. *Journal of Financial Economics, 33*, 3–56.

Fama, E. F., & French, K. R. (1995). Size and book-to-market factors in earnings and returns. *Journal of Finance, 50*, 131–156.

Fama, E. F., & French, K. R. (1996). Multifactor explanations of asset pricing anomalies. *Journal of Finance, 51*, 55–84.

Fama, E. F., & French, K. R. (2008). Dissecting anomalies. *Journal of Finance, 63*, 1653–1678.

Fama, E. F., & French, K. R. (2015). A five-factor asset pricing model. *Journal of Financial Economics, 116*, 1–22.

Fama, E. F., & MacBeth, J. D. (1973). Risk, return, and equilibrium: Empirical tests. *Journal of Political Economy, 81*, 607–636.

Garcia, R., Mantilla-Garcia, D., & Martellini, L. (2014). A model-free measure of aggregate idiosyncractic volatility and the prediction of market returns. *Journal of Financial and Quantitative Analysis, 49*, 1133–1165.

George, T. J., & Hwang, C.-Y. (2004). The 52-week high and momentum investing. *Journal of Finance, 59*, 2145–2176.

Goyal, A., & Jegadeesh, N. (2018). Cross-sectional and time-series tests of return predictability: What is the difference? *Review of Financial Studies, 31*, 1784–1824.

Griffin, J. M., Ji, X., & Martin, J. S. (2003). Momentum investing and business cycle risk: Evidence from pole to pole. *Journal of Finance, 58*, 2515–2547.

Grinblatt, M., & Han, B. (2005). Prospect theory, mental accounting and momentum. *Journal of Financial Economics, 78*, 311–339.

Grundy, B. D., & Martin, J. S. (2001). Understanding the nature of the risks and the source of the rewards to momentum investing. *Review of Financial Studies, 14*, 29–78.

Gutierrez, R. C., & Kelly, E. K. (2008). The long-lasting momentum in weekly returns. *Journal of Finance, 63*, 415–447.

Harvey, C. R., Liu, Y., & Zhu, H. (2015). ... and the cross-section of expected returns. *Review of Financial Studies, 29*, 5–68.

Hong, H., & Stein, J. C. (1999). A unified theory of underreaction, momentum trading, and overreaction in asset markets. *Journal of Finance, 54*, 2143–2184.

Hou, K., Xue, C., & Zhang, L. (2017). *Replicating anomalies* (Working Paper No. WP 2017-10). Ohio State University.

Jegadeesh, N. (1990). Evidence of predictable behavior of security returns. *Journal of Finance, 45*, 881–898.

Jegadeesh, N., & Titman, S. (1993). Returns to buying winners and selling losers: Implications for stock market efficiency. *Journal of Finance, 48*, 65–91.

Jegadeesh, N., & Titman, S. (2001). Profitability of momentum strategies: An evaluation of alternative explanations. *Journal of Finance, 56*, 699–720.

Johnson, T. C. (2002). Rational momentum effects. *Journal of Finance, 57*, 585–608.

Kelly, B., Moskowitz, T., & Pruitt, S. (2019). *Understanding momentum and reversal* (Working Paper). Arizona State University and Yale University.

Kim, H., & Choi, S. M. (2014). Momentum effect as part of a market equilibrium. *Journal of Financial and Quantitative Analysis, 49*, 107–130.

Lehmann, B. N. (1990). Fads, martingales, and market efficiency. *Quarterly Journal of Economics, 105*, 1–28.

Li, J. (2016). Explaining momentum and value simultaneously. *Management Science, 64*, 4239–4260.

Liu, W. (2013). *A new asset pricing model based on the Zero-Beta CAPM: Theory and evidence* (Doctoral dissertation). Texas A&M University.

Liu, W., Kolari, J. W., & Huang, J. Z. (2012, October). *A new asset pricing model based on the zero-beta CAPM*. Presentation at the annual meetings of the Financial Management Association, Atlanta, GA.

Liu, W., Kolari, J. W., & Huang, J. Z. (2020, October). *Return dispersion and the cross-section of stock returns*. Presentation at the annual meetings of the Southern Finance Association, Palm Springs, CA.

Liu, L. X., & Zhang, L. (2008). Momentum profits, factor pricing, and macroeconomic risk. *Review of Financial Studies, 21*, 2417–2448.

Lewellen, J. (2002). Momentum and autocorrelation in stock returns. *Review of Financial Studies, 15*, 533–563.

Lo, A. W., & MacKinlay, A. C. (1990). When are contrarian profits due to stock market overreaction? *Review of Financial Studies, 3*, 175–205.

Luo, J., Subrahmanyam, A., & Titman, S. (2020). Momentum and reversals when overconfident investors underestimate their competition. *Review of Financial Studies*. Forthcoming.

Moskowitz, T. J., & Grinblatt, M. (1999). Do industries explain momentum? *Journal of Finance*, *54*, 1249–1290.
Moskowitz, T. J., Ooi, Y. H., & Pedersen, L. H. (2012). Time series momentum. *Journal of Financial Economics*, *104*, 228–250.
Novy-Marx, R. (2012). Is momentum really momentum? *Journal of Financial Economics*, *103*, 429–453.
Pastor, L., & Veronesi, P. (2009). Technological revolutions and stock prices. *American Economic Review*, *99*, 1451–1483.
Petruno, T. (2018, October 31). Momentum investing: It works, but buy?, *UCLA Anderson Review*. Featured research by Avanidhar Subrahmanyam.
Rouwenhorst, K. G. (1998). International momentum strategies. *Journal of Finance*, *53*, 267–284.
Sagi, J. S., & Seasholes, M. S. (2007). Firm-specific attributes and the cross-section of momentum. *Journal of Financial Economics*, *84*, 389–434.
Sharpe, W. F. (1964). Capital asset prices: A theory of market equilibrium under conditions of risk. *Journal of Finance*, *19*, 425–442.
Subrahmanyam, A. (2018). Equity market equilibrium: A synthesis of the literature and suggestions for future work. *Pacific-Basin Finance Journal*, *51*, 291–296.
Thaler, R. H. (1999). The end of behavioral finance. *Financial Analysts Journal*, *55*, 12–17.

CHAPTER 9

Efficient Investment Portfolios: An Application of the ZCAPM

Abstract This chapter constructs aggregate stock market portfolios that outperform general market indexes in out-of-sample tests. Given that most mutual funds cannot consistently outperform general market indexes over time, the performance of our aggregate portfolios is impressive. To achieve these results, we apply the ZCAPM to develop weights for individual stocks in well-diversified portfolios. The analyses employ U.S. stock returns from 1965 to 2018. As in previous chapters, we estimate the empirical ZCAPM using one year of daily returns. Zeta risk coefficient estimates from the ZCAPM are employed to create 24 stock portfolios with different zeta risk levels. One-month-ahead (out-of-sample) returns are computed for these portfolios. Next, the 24 portfolios are formed into 12 long/short portfolios with increasing levels of zeta risk. These portfolios' average returns are shown to increase linearly with both zeta risk and total risk. Lastly, we add the long/short zeta risk portfolios to the CRSP index to form aggregate portfolios with different total risk levels. Average one-month-ahead returns in our sample period and their standard deviation of returns are plotted to trace out the shape of a mean-variance parabola. Further analyses utilize the empirical ZCAPM to estimate a proxy for the minimum variance portfolio (denoted g). When this portfolio is added to the long/short zeta risk portfolios, a more efficient frontier is obtained with higher returns per unit total risk than when using the CRSP index. Additionally, long only aggregate portfolios are formed using either the CRSP index or portfolio g in combination with long zeta risk portfolios. In general, our results show

J. W. Kolari et al., *A New Model of Capital Asset Prices*,
https://doi.org/10.1007/978-3-030-65197-8_9

that superior aggregate portfolios with higher Sharpe ratios than the CRSP index can be created using the empirical ZCAPM. Institutional investors could utilize these procedures and adaptations thereof to create diversified portfolios with relatively high average returns per unit total risk for individual, business, and government clients.

Keywords Aggregate portfolios · Asset pricing · Beta risk · CAPM · Diversified portfolios · Efficient portfolios · Empirical ZCAPM · Expectation–maximization (EM) algorithm · Fama and French · Global minimum variance portfolio · Investment parabola · Long only portfolios · Long/short portfolios · Markowitz · Multifactor models · Out-of-sample returns · Return dispersion · Securities investment · Signal variable · Stock market · Test assets · ZCAPM · Zero-beta CAPM · Zero-investment portfolios · Zeta risk

9.1 Preview of Portfolio Results

According to our previous mean-variance parabola findings in Chapters 3 and 4, the average market return lies approximately on the axis of symmetry in the middle of the parabola, and the width of the parabola is substantially shaped by return dispersion (*RD*). These new insights about the investment parabola are relevant to the ZCAPM, wherein average market returns and *RD* are return generating factors that explain asset returns. The geometry of the ZCAPM uses these two factors to specify a special case of Black's zero-beta CAPM based on efficient and inefficient (zero-beta) minimum variance portfolios. The ZCAPM approximates these portfolios by moving horizontally along the axis of symmetry of the parabola at the average market return and then vertically up or down within the parabola using zeta risk related to *RD* to locate portfolios I^* and ZI^* (see Chapter 3). Can this geometry be used to create efficient portfolios with relatively high returns per unit risk compared to general market indexes? In this section we preview our findings, which show that high performing portfolios can be created using the geometry of the ZCAPM.

We begin by estimating the empirical ZCAPM with one year of daily returns in 1964 for individual stocks in the U.S. stock market. Stocks are formed into 24 portfolios based on their ranked zeta coefficient estimates. Then 12 long/short portfolios are created that have different levels of zeta risk. Average stock returns in the next month (out-of-sample) of January

1965 are computed for these portfolios. This procedure is repeated month-by-month to obtain a time series of monthly returns for these portfolios from January 1965 to December 2018. Upon doing so, we find a strong linear relationship between these portfolios' returns and both zeta risk and total risk.

Next, to construct aggregate portfolios with different risk levels, we combine the CRSP index with our 12 long/short zeta risk portfolios. One-month-ahead returns are computed for these aggregate portfolios from January 1965 to December 2018. We find that our aggregate portfolios trace out an upward sloping frontier in mean-variance space that dominates the CRSP index in terms of Sharpe ratios (i.e., excess returns divided by total risk). For example, in our analysis period covering over 50 years, the average monthly returns for the CRSP index plus 12 long/short zeta risk portfolios range from 0.95% to 3.22% per month, which exceed the CRSP index itself at 0.88%. These returns are achieved across a broad range of total risk levels as measured by the standard deviation of monthly returns in the analysis period.

One problem with the above approach to constructing aggregate portfolios is that ZCAPM theory contends that the CRSP index lies on the axis of symmetry of the investment parabola at an interior location on the axis. To create efficient investment portfolios, a better approach is to add long/short zeta risk portfolios to a minimum variance portfolio that lies at the left-most vertex of the axis of symmetry. In Chapter 1 we plotted the theoretical minimum variance portfolio G in Figure 1.1 on the investment parabola. Our empirical proxy for G is hereafter denoted g. Using the empirical ZCAPM to estimate g, consistent with ZCAPM theory, minimum variance portfolio proxy g is more efficient than the CRSP index with comparable average returns but noticeably lower variance of returns. We then add our 12 long/short zeta risk portfolios to g to construct another set of aggregate portfolios. Remarkably, holding total risk similar to that of the CRSP index earning 0.88% per month on average in our analysis period, our new aggregate portfolio earns approximately 1.75% per month, which is about 100% higher than the CRSP index! At higher risk levels than the CRSP index, aggregate portfolios earn average monthly returns as high as 3.30% per month on an out-of-sample basis. This evidence corroborates ZCAPM theory that efficient portfolios can be created by moving horizontally along the axis of symmetry of the mean-variance parabola at approximately the average return in the market as a whole and then vertically using sensitivity to return dispersion (RD) via zeta risk.

Further results are produced that create long only aggregate portfolios combining either the CRSP index or our minimum variance portfolio proxy

g with 24 long only zeta risk portfolios. Again the aggregate portfolios using g are more efficient than those using the CRSP index. Interestingly, holding total risk constant, our aggregate portfolio with g has an average return of approximately 1.24% per month compared to 0.88% for the CRSP index. Hence, our ZCAPM investment technology can boost the market index return by more than 40%.

Our empirical results have direct implications to the global practice of investment management. First, using the empirical ZCAPM, risk can be controlled in forming large, well-diversified portfolios. Different portfolios can be constructed that have different levels of total risk. Investors can choose portfolios based on their risk preferences, and managers can reliably provide portfolios that earn returns commensurate with chosen risk levels. This risk control advantage is critical to prudent investment management. Second, given a risk level, aggregate portfolio returns can be generated that outperform common market indexes (e.g., CRSP index, S&P 500 index, etc.). Transactions costs are minimal in monthly rebalancing due to only marginal changes in the holdings of particular stocks in the aggregate portfolio. The authors have constructed similar long only portfolios in the real world and have found that transactions costs do not materially change investment performance. Third, and last, the portfolio formation techniques in this chapter are flexible in the sense that they can be adapted to constructing many different kinds of portfolios, including sector portfolios, style portfolios (e.g., size and value characteristics), international market indexes, exchange traded funds (ETFs) with different portfolio objectives, etc. While our analyses focus on stocks, the methods can be immediately extended to bonds, commodities, and other assets with available daily market prices. In general, institutional investors could use this investment technology to provide diversified portfolios with relatively high returns per unit risk for clients.

9.2 Background Discussion

To our knowledge, no previous studies apply an asset pricing model to the formation of investment portfolios. Unlike other models (as shown in forthcoming results), the empirical ZCAPM can be utilized to create investment portfolios that trace out a mean-variance parabola. Given average stock market returns, the ZCAPM predicts that stocks with positive (negative) sensitivity to RD should earn higher (lower) returns than the overall stock market. By forming portfolios with different zeta risk levels, portfolios with different risk/return profiles can be constructed. We next review the ZCAPM for ease of reference in the next section on building portfolios based on zeta risk.

As mathematically derived in Chapter 3, the *theoretical ZCAPM* is a special case of Black (1972) zero-beta CAPM. According to the ZCAPM, the expected return for the ith asset at time t is[1]:

$$E(R_{it}) - R_{ft} = \beta_{i,a}[E(R_{at}) - R_{ft}] + Z^*_{i,a}\sigma_{at}, \tag{9.1}$$

where $E(R_{at})$ is the expected market return based on the average return of all assets (rather than a proxy m for the theoretical market portfolio M in Sharpe (1964) CAPM), R_{ft} is the riskless rate, $\beta_{i,a}$ is the beta risk coefficient measuring sensitivity to expected excess market returns, σ_{at} is the cross-sectional standard deviation of all asset returns (or return dispersion denoted RD) at time t, and $Z^*_{i,a}$ is the zeta risk coefficient measuring dichotomous positive or negative sensitivity to return dispersion. The asterisk on $Z^*_{i,a}$ links zeta risk to theoretical orthogonal portfolios I^* and ZI^* on the mean-variance investment parabola. These efficient and zero-beta portfolios, respectively, are unique due to their equal return variances.

As proposed in Chapter 4, to estimate the ZCAPM, the following novel *empirical ZCAPM* is employed[2]:

$$R_{it} - R_{ft} = \beta_{i,a}(R_{at} - R_{ft}) + Z_{i,a}D_{it}\sigma_{at} + u_{it}, \quad t = 1, \cdots, T \tag{9.2}$$

where $R_{it} - R_{ft}$ is the excess return for the ith stock portfolio (or stock) over the Treasury bill rate, $\beta_{i,a}$ measures sensitivity of the ith stock portfolio (or stock) to excess average market returns based on the value-weighted CRSP index minus Treasury bill rate equal to $R_{at} - R_{ft}$, $Z_{i,a}$ measures sensitivity of the ith stock portfolio (or stock) to return dispersion σ_{at} (denoted RD), D_{it} is a signal variable with values +1 and −1 representing positive and negative RD effects, respectively, on stock returns, and $u_{it} \sim$ iid $N(0, \sigma_i^2)$.[3] Importantly, signal variable D_{it} is defined as an independent random variable with the following two-point distribution:

[1] See also Liu et al. (2012) and Liu (2013).

[2] See also Liu et al. (2020).

[3] As discussed in Chapter 4, we set the intercept parameter α_i to zero for several reasons. In the present case, our interest is in out-of-sample returns of zero-investment and aggregate portfolios based on zeta risk, rather than their in-sample returns in Eq. (9.2).

$$D_{it} = \begin{cases} +1 & \text{with probability } p_i \\ -1 & \text{with probability } 1 - p_i, \end{cases} \quad (9.3)$$

where p_i (or $1 - p_i$) is the probability of a positive (or negative) return dispersion effect, and D_{it} is independent of u_{it}.

We use the expectation–maximization (EM) algorithm (see Dempster et al. 1977) to estimate the parameters of the empirical ZCAPM including the probability parameter p_i.[4] Since $E(D_{it}) = 2p_i - 1$, the marginal form of the empirical ZCAPM is:

$$R_{it} - R_{ft} = \beta_{i,a}(R_{at} - R_{ft}) + Z^*_{i,a}\sigma_{at} + u^*_{it}, \quad t = 1, \cdots, T \quad (9.4)$$

where $\beta_{i,a}$ is the beta risk coefficient, $Z^*_{i,a} = Z_{i,a}(2p_i - 1)$ is the zeta risk coefficient, u^*_{it} is the error term with variance related to return dispersion (see Eq. (4.13) of Chapter 4), and other notation is as before. Whether the sign of zeta risk loading $Z^*_{i,a}$ is positive or negative is determined by the probability p_i associated with the expected value of signal variable D_{it} in period $t = 1, \cdots, T$.

Matlab programs for estimating the empirical ZCAPM are available at the end of the book in the Compendium. Additionally, R programs for these analyses can be downloaded from GitHub (https://github.com/zcapm). R is a free software environment available on the internet. Our R programs run faster than the Matlab programs.

9.3 Building Portfolios Based on Zeta Risk

We use all U.S. stocks in the intersection of the NYSE, AMEX, and NASDAQ return files from the Center for Research in Security Prices (CRSP) in the period January 1964 to December 2018. Relatively small firms with market capitalization in the bottom 10% at year-end are dropped in the next year. Daily CRSP value-weighted returns and Treasury bill rates are used to proxy mean market returns ($\widetilde{R}_{at}$) and riskless returns (R_{ft}), respectively. To proxy the cross-sectional standard deviation of assets' returns (i.e., RD), value-weighted returns for i = 1, ..., n assets on day t ($\widetilde{R}_{it}$) are used to compute

[4] See Chapter 4 for detailed instructions on how to estimate the empirical ZCAPM using the EM algorithm. Further citations to related finance and statistics literature are provided there also.

$$\widetilde{\sigma}_{at} = \sqrt{\frac{n}{n-1} \sum_{i=1}^{n} w_{it-1} (\widetilde{R}_{it} - \widetilde{R}_{at})^2}, \tag{9.5}$$

where w_{it} = the market value weight for asset i. Within our analysis period January 1965 to December 2018, the mean daily *RD* of stocks in the CRSP index equals 1.81%, and the mean daily CRSP return of 0.04%. Hence, cross-sectional market *RD* is large in magnitude relative to mean market returns on any given day t. Relevant to later evaluating the performance of aggregate portfolios constructed using the empirical ZCAPM, the mean monthly CRSP return and standard deviation of CRSP monthly returns throughout our analysis period equal 0.88% and 4.44%, respectively (see Table 5.1 in Chapter 5).

We begin by utilizing the sensitivity of stocks to *RD* movements (i.e., zeta risk) to construct zero-investment portfolios.[5] The following steps are used to build a variety of zero-investment (long/short) stock portfolios with different zeta risk levels.

(1) Times-series regressions are used to estimate empirical ZCAPM Eq. (9.4) via the expectation–maximization (EM) algorithm for all individual stocks with daily returns for the initial 12-month estimation period January to December 1964.
(2) All stocks are ranked in terms of their estimated zeta coefficient $\hat{Z}^*_{i,a}$.
(3) A total of 24 portfolios are formed from positive to negative zeta risk. Equal-weighted returns are computed for each portfolio in the next month January 1965 (i.e., out-of-sample returns).
(4) Using these portfolios, 12 zero-investment portfolios are formed with one long and one short portfolio.

    (a) Portfolios 1 and 2 are zero-investment portfolios that are long/short in stocks with high zeta market risk $\hat{Z}^*_{i,a}$s in the top +1%/bottom −1% and top +2%/bottom −2% of all sample stocks, respectively. We form these tail portfolios to better understand extreme risk/return profiles associated with *RD*.

[5] Related work by Ang et al. (2006) constructed a volatility mimicking factor based on innovations in the *VIX* (i.e., the Chicago Board Options Exchange's CBOE Volatility Index). The VIX attempts to measure the market's expectation of 30-day volatility, which is a time-series market volatility measure rather than cross-sectional return dispersion measure.

(b) Portfolios 3 to 12 are comprised of long/short stocks in incremental +5/−5% portfolios with respect to zeta risk $\hat{Z}^*_{i,a}$. More specifically, portfolio 3 contains the top +5/−5% stocks with relatively high zeta risk coefficients, portfolio 4 contains the next +5/−5% of stocks per their zeta risk coefficients, ..., portfolio 12 contains the bottom +5/−5% stocks with zeta risk coefficients near zero.

(5) For all stocks in each long/short zeta risk portfolio, we compute the one-month-ahead (out-of-sample), equal-weighted portfolio holding period return R_{pt+1} in January 1965.[6] This out-of-sample approach mimics actual investor behavior in terms of forming portfolios at time $t = T$ and then observing their performance in the next month $T + 1$.

(6) The above process is repeated by rolling the estimation period in step (1) forward one month at a time to rebalance the zero-investment, return dispersion portfolios until their last one-month-ahead holding period returns are computed in December 2018. The time-series standard deviation of these 648 out-of-sample portfolio returns in the analysis period January 1965 to December 2018 is computed also.

Our 12 zero-investment portfolios based on zeta risk span a wide range of market risk associated with cross-sectional *RD*. If there is a relation between one-month-ahead returns and zeta risk loadings, average returns should increase from low for portfolio 12 to high for portfolio 1.

We build aggregate zeta risk portfolios by combining the value-weighted CRSP index with each of the 12 zero-investment, zeta risk portfolios. Aggregate portfolios have weights for all CRSP stocks that add to one plus a positive weight for the long/short zeta risk portfolios. Post-formation, one-month-ahead returns are computed for these aggregate zeta risk portfolios from January 1965 to December 2018. As an example to clarify our assumptions, suppose that you have $100 dollars and buy the CRSP index that earns the average market return. At the same time, your brokerage firm allows you to buy $100 stocks (long) and sell $100 stocks (short) in a long/short portfolio (i.e., a positive constant 1 is assigned as the weight

[6] These returns should be primarily attributable to zeta risk, as the betas of diversified long and short portfolios will be near one and cancel out for the most part.

for the long/short zeta risk portfolio). After one month, the CRSP index generates \$2 and the long/short portfolio earns \$3, such that your total return is (\$2 + \$3)/\$100 = 5%. This aggregate portfolio is leveraged.[7]

Previous studies have shown that short positions are needed to create more efficient portfolios.[8] However, a criticism of this approach is that many investors only hold long portfolios (e.g., pension funds, mutual funds, etc.). Accordingly, we also examine the average performance of the 24 zeta risk portfolios with long only positions. Moreover, we build 24 long only aggregate portfolios by investing 50% of funds in the CRSP index and 50% in each long zeta risk portfolio, which enables insights into the effects of restricting aggregate portfolios to long only positions compared to allowing short positions.

Lastly, we build another set of aggregate portfolios based on a proxy for the theoretical minimum variance portfolio G denoted g. As discussed in Chapter 3, the CRSP index lies on the axis of symmety of the mean-variance parabola and therefore is not an efficient portfolio. A more efficient general market index is the portfolio G located at the vertex of the parabola. To develop a proxy g portfolio from the empirical ZCAPM, we reduce both idiosyncratic and zeta risks (i.e., g has little or no zeta risk as it is unaffected by return dispersion that defines the width of the investment parabola per our findings in Chapters 3 and 4). As in the case of the zeta risk portfolios, we drop the lowest 10% of stocks by market capitalization at year-end in the subsequent year. Also, we drop stocks with standard deviations of monthly returns in each one-year estimation period less than 20% of the CRSP index. This volatility filter eliminates stocks in each estimation window with volatility less than a highly diversified market index. These stocks are likely very illiquid or have other issues that are idiosyncratic (i.e.,

[7] Alternatively, what if the brokerage does not allow you to form the zero-investment, long/short portfolio without cash collateral? Now you can only buy \$50 of the CRSP index and another \$50 long/short, such that your monthly return is (\$1 + \$1.5)/\$100 = 2.5%. This portfolio is not leveraged. In forthcoming analyses we allow leveraged positions.

[8] Numerous studies have documented that efficient portfolios as proposed by Markowitz (1959) contain short positions (e.g., Pulley 1981; Levy 1983; Kallberg and Ziemba 1983; Kroll et al. 1984; Green and Hollifield 1992; Jagannathan and Ma 2003; Brennan and Lo 2010; Levy and Ritov 2010). Strong theoretical support for short positions in efficient portfolios is provided by Brennan and Lo (2010), who proved that mean-variance efficient frontiers with long only portfolios are virtually impossible. More generally, Kothari (1995) have argued that the equity portfolio most highly correlated with the market portfolio is efficient.

firm specific) in nature. To build portfolio g, we follow steps similar to the construction of the 24 zeta risk portfolios.

(1) Times-series regressions are used to estimate the empirical ZCAPM Eq. (9.4) via the expectation–maximization (EM) algorithm for all individual stocks with daily returns for the initial 12-month estimation period January to December 1964.
(2) To reduce idiosyncratic and zeta risks, all stocks are weighted as $w_i = 1/(0.01+|\hat{Z}^*_{i,a}|) \times 1/\text{var}(\widetilde{u}_{it})$, where idiosyncratic risk is measured by the variance of the residual error terms denoted $\text{var}(\widetilde{u}_{it})$, and 0.01 is added to the absolute value of the estimated zeta risk coefficient $\hat{Z}^*_{i,a}$ to avoid the case of singularity when $\hat{Z}^*_{i,a} = 0$.[9]
(3) For all stocks, we compute the one-month-ahead, weighted portfolio holding period return R_{gT+1} in January 1965.
(4) The above process is repeated by rolling the estimation period in step (1) forward one month at a time to rebalance portfolio g until the last one-month-ahead holding period return is computed in December 2018.

As in the case of the CRSP index, aggregate portfolios are formed by combining proxy minimum variance portfolio g with the 12 long/short zeta risk portfolios

9.4 Empirical Results

9.4.1 *Zero-Investment Portfolios Sensitive to Return Dispersion*

The average return and risk results for the 12 zero-investment, return dispersion portfolios created from 24 zeta risk portfolios are shown in Table 9.1. As discussed in the previous section, zeta risk coefficients $Z^*_{i,a}$ for individual stocks are estimated using a one-year period with daily returns. Stocks are sorted into 24 zeta risk portfolios which are used to construct 12 long/short portfolios. For each long, short, and long/short portfolio in the analysis period January 1965 to December 2018, the table reports the average estimated zeta risk coefficient for constituent stocks denoted

[9] As mentioned above, we drop low volatility stocks with less than 20% of the CRSP index in the one year estimation period. This filter eliminates stocks that would receive relatively large weights and bias our construction of proxy portfolio g.

Table 9.1 Construction details for long/short zeta risk portfolios

Zero-investment portfolios	Long $\bar{Z}^*_{pt}$	Short $\bar{Z}^*_{pt}$	$\bar{Z}^*_{pt}$	Long $\bar{R}_{pt+1}$	Short $\bar{R}_{pt+1}$	$\bar{R}_{pt+1}$	Sharpe ratio
Portfolio 1 – Top +1%/ – 1%	5.75	−4.99	10.73	1.86	−0.48	2.34	0.26
	(1.64)	(1.28)	(1.66)	(9.19)	(11.06)	(9.12)	
Portfolio 2 – Top +2%/ – 2%	5.15	−4.54	9.68	1.77	−0.39	2.16	0.28
	(1.47)	(1.17)	(1.42)	(7.56)	(10.30)	(7.67)	
Portfolio 3 – Top +5%/ – 5%	4.17	−3.74	7.91	1.80	−0.16	1.96	0.29
	(1.21)	(0.99)	(1.06)	(7.84)	(9.15)	(6.78)	
Portfolio 4	2.53	−2.30	4.82	1.69	0.41	1.29	0.26
	(0.80)	(0.71)	(0.59)	(6.49)	(7.38)	(4.98)	
Portfolio 5	1.87	−1.65	3.52	1.56	0.51	1.04	0.27
	(0.66)	(0.61)	(0.46)	(5.84)	(6.52)	(3.92)	
Portfolio 6	1.45	−1.23	2.68	1.47	0.72	0.75	0.22
	(0.58)	(0.55)	(0.38)	(5.36)	(5.96)	(3.35)	
Portfolio 7	1.13	-0.91	2.05	1.31	0.79	0.52	0.19
	(0.52)	(0.50)	(0.32)	(5.10)	(5.61)	(2.72)	
Portfolio 8	0.88	−0.66	1.54	1.24	0.81	0.43	0.20
	(0.48)	(0.46)	(0.27)	(4.84)	(5.29)	(2.18)	
Portfolio 9	0.66	−0.46	1.12	1.12	0.88	0.24	0.13
	(0.45)	(0.43)	(0.23)	(4.76)	(5.02)	(1.80)	
Portfolio 10	0.48	−0.28	0.76	1.11	0.96	0.15	0.10
	(0.42)	(0.40)	(0.18)	(4.64)	(4.82)	(1.54)	
Portfolio 11	0.31	−0.13	0.44	1.07	0.94	0.13	0.11
	(0.40)	(0.38)	(0.12)	(4.58)	(4.73)	(1.22)	
Portfolio 12 – Bottom +5%/ – 5%	0.16	0.02	0.14	1.00	0.93	0.07	0.07
	(0.38)	(0.37)	(0.05)	(4.59)	(4.68)	(1.05)	
CRSP index–R_f						0.50	0.11
						(4.44)	
Portfolio $g - R_f$						0.57	0.16
						(3.50)	

This table reports construction details for zero-investment, return dispersion (RD) portfolios. Individual stocks are sorted in the estimation period based on their estimated $Z^*_{i,a}$ coefficients in the empirical ZCAPM. Long/short portfolios are formed using stocks with high/low $Z^*_{i,a}$ coefficients. Average one-month-ahead portfolio returns in the analysis period January 1965 to December 2018 are shown (with time-series standard deviations in parentheses). Average $Z^*_{i,a}$ coefficients for portfolios are shown also. We report Sharpe ratios as well as descriptive statistics for long/short portfolios. For comparison purposes, information is shown for excess returns of the CRSP index minus Treasury bills (R_f) and the proxy minimum variance portfolio g (developed from the empirical ZCAPM) minus Treasury bills

$\bar{Z}^*_{pt}$ (i.e., 12-month zeta risk estimates are rolled forward one month at a time to yield 648 estimates for each portfolio ending in November 2018), their average one-month-ahead return denoted $\bar{R}_{pt+1}$ (for 648 months from January 1965 to December 2018), and the time-series standard deviation of these estimates in parentheses. Strikingly, for stocks in portfolios 1, 2, and 3 containing the top +1%/bottom −1%, top +2%/bottom −2%, and top +5%/bottom −5% of estimated zeta risk coefficients, portfolio returns average 2.34%, 2.16%, and 1.96%, respectively, in the post-formation month. These average one-month-ahead returns surpass published results in momentum studies that have attracted considerable attention for high zero-investment portfolio returns.[10]

As shown in Table 9.1, for stocks in zero-investment portfolios 1–12, average one-month-ahead holding period returns in our analysis period gradually decrease from 2.34% per month for portfolio 1 to 0.07% for portfolio 12. Also, the corresponding Sharpe ratios decline from 0.26 for portfolio 1 to 0.07 for portfolio 12, which can be compared to the CRSP index at 0.11. As average zeta risk decreases from 10.73 for portfolio 1 to 0.14 for portfolio 12, average monthly holding period returns and Sharpe ratios decline in step with diminishing market risk. Corroborating our evidence in Chapters 6 and 7, the close relation between one-month-ahead stock returns and zeta risk lends support for the empirical ZCAPM as an asset pricing model that captures common systematic market risk.

Turning to the construction details of the zero-investment portfolios in Table 9.1, the average values of $\bar{Z}^{*}_{i,a}$ for long and short stocks in portfolios 1–12 range from 5.75 to 0.16 and −4.99 to −0.13, respectively. Also, average one-month-ahead returns for long and short stocks in zero-investment portfolios 1 to 12 range from approximately 1.86 to 1.00% and 0.48 to 0.93%, respectively. For both long and short portfolios, total risk as measured by the time-series standard deviation of returns in the analysis period (shown in parentheses) gradually decreases from portfolio 1–12. Notice that long portfolios 1 and 2 earn approximately 1.86% and 1.77%, respectively, which are two times the average return on the CRSP index equal to 0.88%; however, their total risks as measured by the time-series standard

[10] For example, upon experimenting with different undiversified momentum strategies, Jegadeesh and Titman (1993, p. 70) obtained an abnormally high average monthly return of 1.49% per month on momentum portfolios created from 12 months of past returns and 3-month holding periods for U.S. stocks. In another paper, Jegadeesh and Titman (2001, p. 704) examined different subperiods for U.S. stocks and report relatively high 6-month momentum profits of 1.65% in the period 1990 to 1998 for small U.S. stocks. For the longer period 1965 to 1998, the highest momentum profit was 1.42%. Due to these strong return results, momentum strategies have attracted the attention of both academics and practitioners. It should be noted that Daniel (2011) found poor momentum performance in some months (known as "crashes") after the year 2000. In this regard, Barroso and Santa-Clara (2015) and Daniel and Moskowitz (2016) have shown that risk management strategies can mitigate momentum crashes to some extent.

deviation of monthly returns in parentheses are higher at 9.19% and 7.56% compared to 4.44% for the CRSP index. Holding total risk approximately constant, long portfolios 11–12 earn somewhat higher average returns of 1.07% and 1.00%, respectively, than the CRSP index (i.e., these portfolios have similar time-series standard deviations of returns of 4.58% and 4.59%, respectively). Also notice that short portfolios 1 and 2 have relatively high negative zeta risk that results in negative post-formation average portfolio returns of −0.48% and −0.39%, respectively.

Using results in Table 9.1, Fig. 9.1 graphs the relationship between average one-month-ahead returns, or $\bar{R}_{pt+1}$, and average zeta risk in the estimation period, or $\bar{Z}^*_{pt}$, for the 12 zero-investment long/short portfolios based on zeta risk. Further supporting our earlier inference that zeta risk levels are predictive of relative one-month-ahead holding period returns, a strong positive and linear relation is clearly evident among the 12 zero-investment portfolios.

Average one-month-ahead returns for the 12 zero-investment portfolios with respect to their time-series standard deviation of returns in the analysis period January 1965 to December 2019 are plotted in Fig. 9.2. Again, a strong positive and linear relation is obvious. We also show the locations in this risk/return space for the popular zero-investment portfolios *SMB*, *HML*, *RM W*, *CMA*, and *MOM* (i.e., the size, value, profit, and capital investment of Fama and French (1992, 1993, 1995, 2015, 2018) plus the momentum factor of Jegadeesh and Titman (1993)). The *SMB*, *HML*, *RM W*, and *MOM* portfolios are noticeably below our zero-investment portfolios with similar standard deviations of returns, but the *CMA* portfolio has an average risk return profile close to our zero-investment portfolios. Also, *MOM* has a higher average return and risk profile compared to the other multifactor portfolios.

It is noteworthy that previous researchers provide little or no explanation for these anomalous zero-investment factors. The evidence in Fig. 9.2 suggests that popular multifactors mimic long/short *RD* portfolios. That is, *SMB*, *HML*, *RM W*, *CMA*, and *MOM* are zero-investment portfolios that pick up market risk information related to cross-sectional *RD*. As mentioned in earlier chapters, because these multifactors are themselves rough measures of cross-sectional return dispersion (i.e., long higher return stocks and short lower return stocks), this inference is not surprising.

It is important to recognize that the 12 zero-investment portfolios in Fig. 9.2 are financially engineered by progressively adding zeta risk. In practice, an investment manager can control the amount of zeta risk and, in

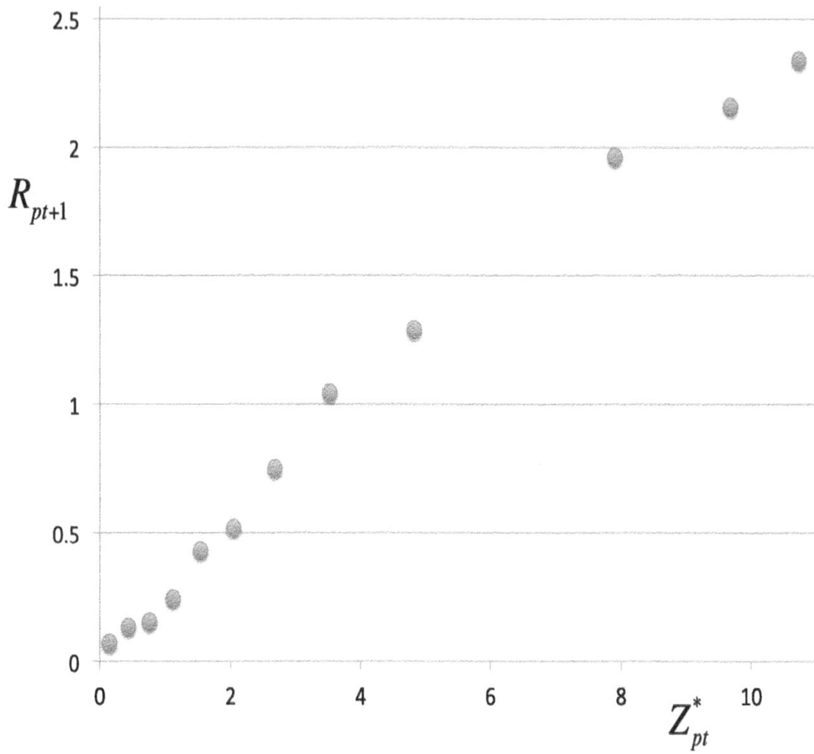

Fig. 9.1 A positive, linear relation is shown between average one-month-ahead (out-of-sample) returns for 12 long/short zeta risk portfolios formed based on zeta coefficient estimates in the previous year. The analysis period is January 1965 to December 2018

turn, the relative return compared to other portfolios that span different levels of zeta risk. By contrast, risk is not controlled in the *SMB*, *HML*, *RM W*, *CMA*, and *MOM* portfolios. As such, their relative returns and risks will move around over time in mean-return/standard-deviation-of-returns space in an unpredictable fashion. Hence, a major advantage of forming portfolios based on zeta risk is the ability to control their relative risks and returns over time.

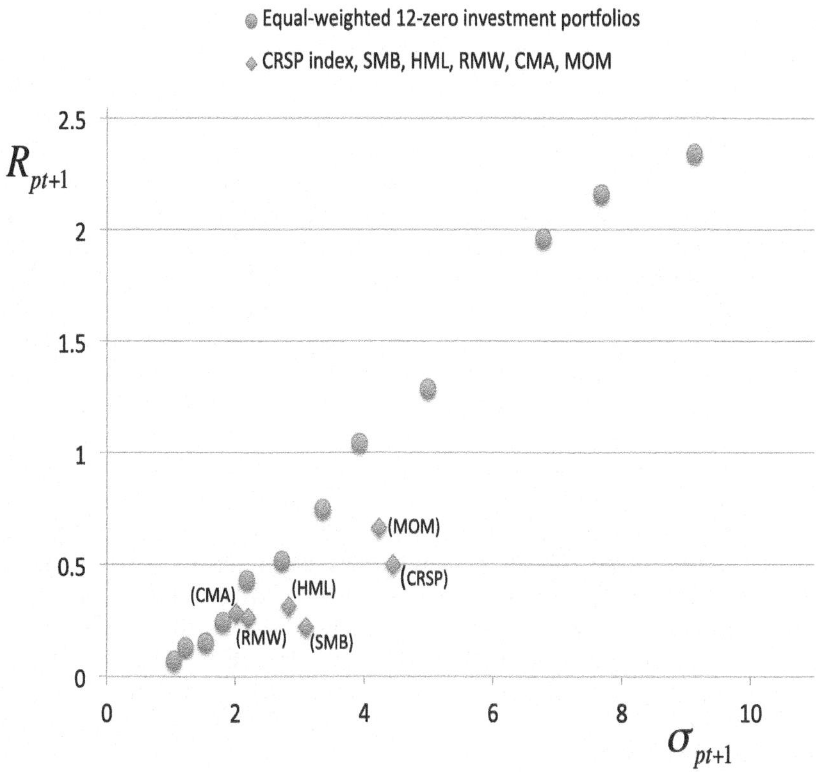

Fig. 9.2 A positive, linear relation is shown between average one-month-ahead (out-of-sample) returns and the time-series standard deviation of these returns for 12 long/short zeta risk portfolios. Visual comparisons can be made to the CRSP index as well as popular long/short multifactors size (*SMB*), value (*HML*), profit (*RMW*), capital investment (*CMA*), and momentum (*MOM*) from Kenneth French's website. The analysis period is January 1965 to December 2018

9.4.2 Aggregate Portfolios Sensitive to Return Dispersion

Here we report the results for aggregate stock portfolios based on combining either the CRSP value-weighted index or minimum variance portfolio *g* with each of the 12 zero-investment *RD* mimicking portfolios.Aggregate portfolios have aggregate weights for all stocks greater than one and therefore are leveraged due to inclusion of short positions in the zero-investment portfolios. One-month-ahead returns are computed for aggregate portfolios from January 1965 to December 2018.

Figure 9.3 shows the relationship between average one-month-ahead returns for our 12 aggregate portfolios using either the CRSP index (denoted a) or minimum variance portfolio g and their time-series standard deviations. As shown there, these aggregate portfolios trace out smooth frontiers in mean-return/standard-deviation-of-returns space. The resultant aggregate portfolio frontiers can be used to evaluate the relative performance of other portfolios. For example, an asterisk marks the location of the CRSP index, and the locations of different combinations of either the CRSP index or portfolio g plus zero-investment portfolios *SMB*, *HML*, *RM W*, *CMA*, and *MOM* are plotted. Tables 9.2 and 9.3 contain the average return and standard deviation of returns data used to construct Fig. 9.3.

Using the CRSP index in combination with 12 long/short zeta risk portfolios, and assuming that the time-series standard deviation of returns is similar to the CRSP index, a moderately higher average monthly return can be achieved in the range of 0.95%–1.02% per month compared to 0.88% for the CRSP index (see Table 9.2). The highest earning aggregate portfolios combine the highest long/short zeta risk portfolios 1 and 2 to the CRSP index to yield 3.22% and 3.04%, respectively; however, their total risks in terms of standard deviations of returns are relatively high at 9.76% and 8.12%, respectively. Conspicuously, these 12 aggregate portfolios (marked by round dots) in Fig. 9.3 trace out the shape of the upper frontier of an investment parabola.

Turning to aggregate portfolios created by combining proxy minimum variance portfolio g with the 12 long/short zeta risk portfolios, the frontier of aggregate portfolio returns (marked by diamond shapes) dominates those using the CRSP index (marked by round dots). The results in Fig. 9.3 based on data in Table 9.3 show that using g in place of the CRSP index enables higher average returns per unit risk. For example, holding total risk approximately the same as the CRSP index at a standard deviation of returns of 4.44%, aggregate portfolios earn about 1.75% compared to the CRSP index at 0.88% per month. Hence, our aggregate portfolio with g outperforms the average return of the CRSP index by approximately 100%! Overall, combining g with the 12 long/short zeta risk portfolios, a range of average returns from 1.03% to 3.30% is earned across the full range of aggregate portfolios.

The empirical evidence for aggregate portfolios formed by combining the CRSP index or proxy minimum variance portfolio g with long/short

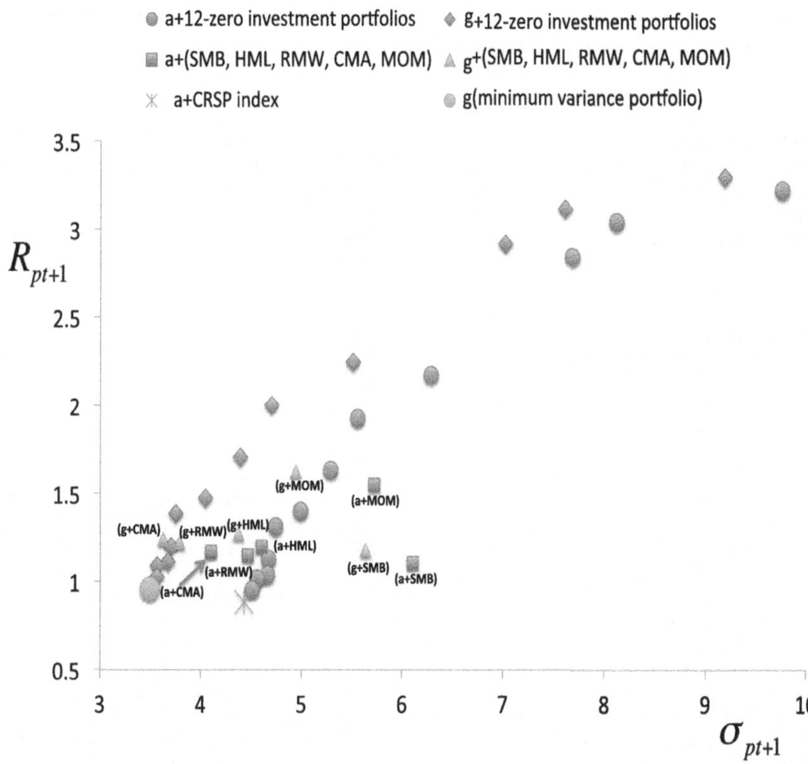

Fig. 9.3 Frontier estimates are shown based on average one-month-ahead (out-of-sample) returns and the time-series standard deviation of these returns for aggregate portfolios with different levels of zeta risk. Aggregate portfolios are constructed by adding either the CRSP market index (denoted a) or the proxy minimum variance portfolio g to 12 long/short zeta risk portfolios. Visual comparisons can be made to the CRSP market index, portfolio g, and aggregate portfolios combining either the CRSP index or portfolio g with popular long/short multifactors size (*SMB*), value (*HML*), profit (*RMW*), capital investment (*CMA*), and momentum (*MOM*) from Kenneth French's website. The analysis period is January 1965 to December 2015

Table 9.2 Construction details for aggregate portfolios composed of the CRSP index plus long/short zeta risk portfolios

Aggregate portfolios	$\bar{R}_{CRSPt+1} + \bar{R}_{pt+1}$	$\sigma_{CRSP+p,t+1}$	Sharpe ratio
CRSP + portfolio 1	3.22	9.76	0.29
CRSP + portfolio 2	3.04	8.12	0.33
CRSP + portfolio 3	2.84	7.69	0.32
CRSP + portfolio 4	2.17	6.28	0.28
CRSP + portfolio 5	1.93	5.56	0.28
CRSP + portfolio 6	1.63	5.29	0.24
CRSP + portfolio 7	1.40	4.99	0.20
CRSP + portfolio 8	1.31	4.74	0.20
CRSP + portfolio 9	1.13	4.67	0.16
CRSP + portfolio 10	1.04	4.66	0.14
CRSP + portfolio 11	1.02	4.56	0.14
CRSP + portfolio 12	0.95	4.51	0.13
CRSP + SMB	1.10	6.10	0.12
CRSP + HML	1.20	4.60	0.18
CRSP + RMW	1.15	4.46	0.17
CRSP + CMA	1.17	4.10	0.19
CRSP + MOM	1.55	5.72	0.20
CRSP index	0.88	4.44	0.11

This table reports construction details for aggregate portfolios formed by combining the CRSP index with 12 zero-investment, return dispersion (*RD*) portfolios formed on slices of zeta risk associated with cross-sectional *RD* in the empirical ZCAPM. Individual stocks are sorted in the one-year estimation period based on their estimated $Z^*_{i,a}$ coefficients. Long/short portfolios are formed using stocks in the top +1%/bottom −1% and top +2%/bottom −2% of estimated $Z^*_{i,a}$ coefficients (i.e., portfolios 1 and 2, respectively), in addition to 10 zero-investment portfolios based on stocks in progressive +5/ − 5% slices of estimated $Z^*_{i,a}$ coefficients (i.e., portfolios 3 to 12). Using 648 months in the analysis period January 1965 to December 2018, we report for each aggregate portfolio the average one-month-ahead return denoted as $\bar{R}_{CRSPt+1}$ + $\bar{R}_{pt+1}$, time-series standard deviation of this aggregate monthly return series denoted as $\sigma_{CRSP+p,t+1}$, and Sharpe ratio. For comparison purposes, results for the CRSP index are shown as well as combinations of the CRSP index with zero-investment multifactors size (*SMB*), value (*HML*), profit (*RMW*), capital investment (*CMA*), and momentum (*MOM*) from Kenneth French's website

zeta risk portfolios supports our new geometric findings in Chapters 3 and 4 concerning the mean-variance investment parabola. There we proposed that the average return of all assets in the market lies approximately on the axis of symmetry at an interior location and cross-sectional return dispersion defines the span of the parabola. Relevant to the former proposition, using the frontier traced out by the 12 aggregate portfolios incorporate portfolio *g* in Fig. 9.3, the CRSP index lies at an interior position along the axis of symmetry as previously conjectured. Thus, our out-of-sample aggregate

Table 9.3 Construction details for aggregate portfolios composed of the proxy minimum variance portfolio g plus long/short zeta risk portfolios

Aggregate portfolios	$\bar{R}_{gt+1} + \bar{R}_{pt+1}$	$\sigma_{g+p,t+1}$	Sharpe ratio
Min var portfolio g + portfolio 1	3.30	9.19	0.32
Min var portfolio g + portfolio 2	3.12	7.61	0.36
Min var portfolio g + portfolio 3	2.92	7.02	0.36
Min var portfolio g + portfolio 4	2.25	5.51	0.34
Min var portfolio g + portfolio 5	2.00	4.70	0.34
Min var portfolio g + portfolio 6	1.71	4.39	0.30
Min var portfolio g + portfolio 7	1.48	4.04	0.27
Min var portfolio g + portfolio 8	1.39	3.75	0.27
Min var portfolio g + portfolio 9	1.20	3.71	0.22
Min var portfolio g + portfolio 10	1.11	3.67	0.20
Min var portfolio g + portfolio 11	1.09	3.57	0.20
Min var portfolio g + portfolio 12	1.03	3.56	0.18
Min var portfolio g + SMB	1.18	5.63	0.14
Min var portfolio g + HML	1.27	4.37	0.20
Min var portfolio g + RMW	1.22	3.78	0.22
Min var portfolio g + CMA	1.24	3.63	0.24
Min var portfolio g + MOM	1.62	4.94	0.25
Min var portfolio g	0.96	3.49	0.16

This table reports construction details for aggregate portfolios formed by combining the proxy minimum variance portfolio g with 12 zero-investment, return-dispersion (RD) portfolios formed on slices of zeta risk associated with cross-sectional RD in the empirical ZCAPM. Portfolio g is developed from the empirical ZCAPM as described in the text. Individual stocks are sorted in the estimation period based on their estimated $Z^*_{i,a}$ coefficients. Long/short portfolios are formed using stocks in the top +1%/bottom −1% and top +2%/bottom −2% of estimated $Z^*_{i,a}$ coefficients (i.e., portfolios 1 and 2, respectively), in addition to 10 zero-investment portfolios based on stocks in progressive +5/ − 5% slices of estimated $Z^*_{i,a}$ coefficients (i.e., portfolios 3 to 12). Using 648 months in the analysis period January 1965 to December 2018, we report for each aggregate portfolio the average one-month-ahead return denoted as $\bar{R}_{gt+1} + \bar{R}_{pt+1}$, time-series standard deviation of this aggregate monthly return series denoted as $\sigma_{g+p,t+1}$, and Sharpe ratio. For comparison purposes, results for proxy minimum variance portfolio g are shown as well as combinations of portfolio g with the zero-investment multifactors size (*SMB*), value (*HML*), profit (*RMW*), capital investment (*CMA*), and momentum (*MOM*) from Kenneth French's website

portfolios corroborate earlier insights about the shape of the investment parabola.

The Sharpe ratio, defined as the average excess return divided by the standard deviation of returns over time, is commonly used to compare the relative performance of investment portfolios. In terms of this risk-adjusted metric, the results in Tables 9.2 and 9.3 for aggregate portfolios formed using the CRSP index and g, respectively, are impressive. For aggregate portfolios based on the CRSP index, Sharpe ratios range from 0.13 to 0.33 compared to the CRSP index itself at 0.11. For aggregate portfolios based on proxy minimum variance portfolio g, Sharpe ratios have an even higher range from 0.18 to 0.36. Thus, our aggregate portfolios substantially outperform the CRSP index in terms of average excess return per unit total risk.

We next apply the well-known Gibbons et al. (1989) test for the efficiency of a portfolio to our aggregate portfolios. Are they efficient relative to the CRSP index? Can they be explained by other asset pricing models? First, we test the efficiency of our 12 aggregate zeta risk portfolios based on the CRSP index plus 12 long/short zeta risk portfolios relative to the CRSP stock index. Given $N = 12$ test assets and $T = 648$ months, the F statistic is 5.96, which is highly significant at less than the 1% level. Thus, the GRS test fails to accept the null hypothesis that the CRSP index is efficient, which means that our aggregate CRSP-based portfolios are relatively more efficient. We also compute the GRS test for whether the Fama and French (2018) six-factor model explains our 12 aggregate portfolios' returns. Given $N = 12$ test assets, $L = 6$ factors, and $T = 648$ months, the F statistic is 5.42, which is highly significant at less than the 1% level. Thus, the GRS test fails to accept the null hypothesis that the six-factor model explains these portfolios. Second, using proxy minimum variance portfolio g in combination with our 12 aggregate zeta risk portfolios, the corresponding F-statistics are 8.09 and 5.57, respectively. Again, aggregate portfolios engineered using the zeta risk significantly outperform the CRSP index and are not explained by the six-factor model.

The outsized performance of our aggregate portfolios is exceptional in view of published studies. Empirical evidence has shown that most actively managed equity mutual funds cannot consistently outperform broad stock market averages such as the S&P 500 index, CRSP index, etc., over periods of five years or more. Early studies in this area by Jensen (1968), Malkiel (1995), and Carhart Carhart (1997) documented this professional management shortfall. More recent studies by Bollen and Busse (2004), Barras et al. (2010), Fama and French (2010), and others have continued to find little or no evidence of persistently high performance in most actively managed mutual funds. In an article summarizing the evidence, Malkiel (2005) concluded that over 80% of investment professionals cannot beat passive general equity indexes after fees and expenses. In this respect it is important to emphasize that our optimized aggregate portfolios are not based on stock picking ability but rather risk measurement via the empirical ZCAPM asset pricing model. Thus, they are consistent with the efficient market hypothesis.

We also report the results of aggregate portfolios combining the CRSP index and portfolio g with the Fama and French multifactor long/short portfolios *SMB*, *HML*, *RMW*, *CMA*, and *MOM*. In general, as evidenced by Sharpe ratios in Tables 9.2 and 9.3, these aggregate portfolios outperform the CRSP index also. Like our aggregate portfolios using 12 long/short zeta risk portfolios, combinations with g yield higher Sharpe ratios. Also, in Fig. 9.3 we see that combinations of g with *RMW* and *CMA* yield aggregate portfolios with performance similar to our aggregate portfolios with long/short zeta risk portfolios. This finding is again not surprising because, as mentioned earlier, these multifactors are themselves rough measures of cross-sectional dispersion and therefore capture some amount of zeta risk associated with cross-sectional *RD*.

9.4.3 Long Only Aggregate Portfolios Sensitive to Return Dispersion

The average performances of the 24 long only zeta risk portfolios are displayed in mean-return/standard-deviation-of-returns space in Fig. 9.4. A return/risk investment parabola shape is traced by these portfolios. The CRSP index lies below the frontier and approximately represents the average performance of all stocks in the 24 portfolios.

When we combine the CRSP index (i.e., 50% weight) with each of these 24 long only zeta risk portfolios (i.e., 50% weight), the results in Fig. 9.5 are obtained. These aggregate portfolios are entirely long portfolios with no short positions (i.e., the aggregate weight of all stocks in the portfolios sum to one).

Based on combining the CRSP index with the 24 long only zeta risk portfolios, Table 9.4 documents the 24 long only aggregate portfolio results in Fig. 9.5. Combining the CRSP index with long portfolios 16 to 24 yields Sharpe ratios between 0.14 and 0.17 compared to 0.11 for the CRSP index (i.e., in the range of 35%–45% improvement). Portfolios combining CRSP with portfolios 22, 23, and 24 earn average monthly returns of 1.34%, 1.33%, and 1.37% per month, respectively, which well exceeds the CRSP index at 0.88% per month. Long only aggregate portfolios combining the CRSP index with long portfolios 15 and 16 have similar return volatility as the CRSP index but somewhat higher returns at 1.00% per month.[11]

[11] Polson and Tew (2000) used a Bayesian approach in combination with hierarchical models to estimate predicted expected returns and variance-covariance matrices for stocks. These

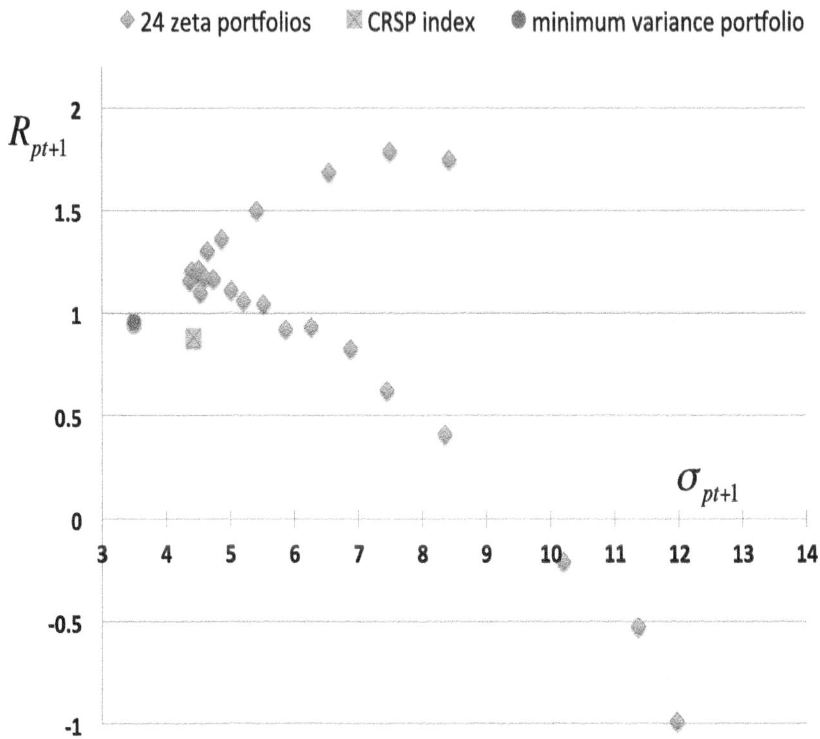

Fig. 9.4 Frontier estimates are shown based on average one-month-ahead (out-of-sample) returns and the time-series standard deviation of these returns for 24 long only zeta risk portfolios. Visual comparisons can be made to the CRSP market index and proxy minimum variance portfolio g. The analysis period is January 1965 to December 2018

estimates were used to optimize portfolio weights in the S&P 500 index from January 1970 to December 1996. In their study, the value-weighted S&P 500 index earned on average 1.02% per month compared to 1.17% for their optimized portfolio containing S&P 500 index stocks. They did not provide information on the return volatility or Sharpe ratios of different aggregate portfolios. See also related work on estimation risk and portfolio selection by Klein and Bawa (1976) and Jorion (1986). Moreover, Levy and Roll (2010) have shown that small variations in the mean-variance parameters of assets within a typical market proxy portfolio can yield more efficient market indexes.

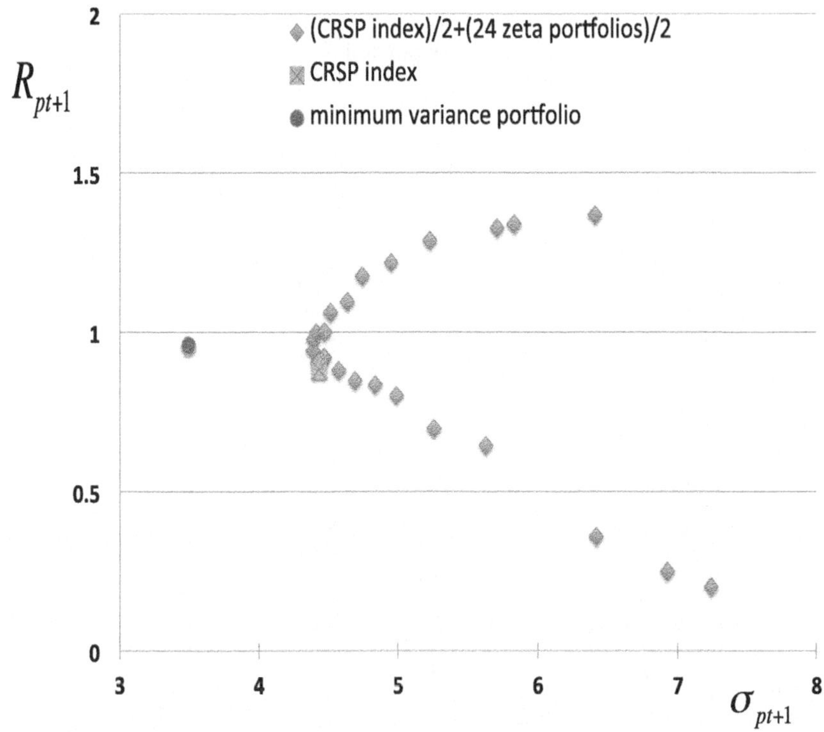

Fig. 9.5 Frontier estimates are shown based on average one-month-ahead (out-of-sample) returns and the time-series standard deviation of these returns for 24 long only aggregate portfolios. These long aggregate portfolios are formed by investing 50% of funds in the CRSP market index and 50% of funds in 24 long zeta risk portfolios. Visual comparisons can be made to the CRSP market index and proxy minimum variance portfolio g. The analysis period is January 1965 to December 2018

Comparing the frontiers based on aggregate portfolios formed with the CRSP index in Figs. 9.3 and 9.5 allows some insight into the effects of short positions on aggregate portfolio efficiency. Consistent with the literature cited earlier, short positions visibly increase efficiency, especially for higher total risk portfolios. As such, our U.S. stock market evidence does not support the CAPM assumption that a positive-by-definition market portfolio is efficient (see Brennan and Lo 2010; Levy and Roll 2010). Short posi-

Table 9.4 Construction details for long only aggregate portfolios composed of the CRSP index plus long only zeta risk portfolios

Long aggregate portfolios	$\bar{R}_{CRSPt+1} + \bar{R}_{pt+1}$	$\sigma_{CRSP+p,t+1}$	Sharpe ratio
CRSP + portfolio 1	0.20	7.24	-0.03
CRSP + portfolio 2	0.25	6.92	-0.02
CRSP + portfolio 3	0.36	6.42	-0.00
CRSP + portfolio 4	0.64	5.63	0.05
CRSP + portfolio 5	0.70	5.26	0.06
CRSP + portfolio 6	0.80	4.99	0.08
CRSP + portfolio 7	0.84	4.83	0.09
CRSP + portfolio 8	0.85	4.69	0.10
CRSP + portfolio 9	0.88	4.57	0.11
CRSP + portfolio 10	0.92	4.47	0.12
CRSP + portfolio 11	0.91	4.44	0.12
CRSP + portfolio 12	0.91	4.42	0.12
CRSP + portfolio 13	0.94	4.39	0.13
CRSP + portfolio 14	0.98	4.39	0.14
CRSP + portfolio 15	1.00	4.41	0.14
CRSP + portfolio 16	1.00	4.47	0.14
CRSP + portfolio 17	1.06	4.51	0.15
CRSP + portfolio 18	1.10	4.63	0.15
CRSP + portfolio 19	1.18	4.74	0.17
CRSP + portfolio 20	1.22	4.95	0.17
CRSP + portfolio 21	1.29	5.23	0.17
CRSP + portfolio 22	1.34	5.83	0.16
CRSP + portfolio 23	1.33	5.71	0.17
CRSP + portfolio 24	1.37	6.41	0.15
CRSP index	0.88	4.43	0.11

This table reports construction details for long only aggregate portfolios formed by combining the CRSP index with long only zeta risk portfolios formed on $Z^*_{i,a}$ coefficients estimated in the empirical ZCAPM. A total of 24 long zeta risk portfolios are formed. Long aggregate portfolios are created using a 50% weight for the CRSP index and 50% weight for each long zeta risk portfolio. For 648 months in the analysis period January 1965 to December 2018, we report for each long aggregate portfolio the average one-month-ahead return denoted as $\bar{R}_{CRSPt+1} + \bar{R}_{pt+1}$, time-series standard deviation of this aggregate monthly return series denoted as $\sigma_{CRSP+p,t+1}$, and the Sharpe ratio. For comparison purposes, results for the CRSP index are shown

tions enable the formation of more efficient portfolios in the investment opportunity set (see footnote 5 citations).

Table 9.5 gives results for the 24 long only aggregate portfolios formed by combining the proxy minimum variance portfolio g with the 24 long only zeta risk portfolios. Combining g with portfolios 8 to 24 yields Sharpe ratios between 0.12 and 0.20, which are higher than the CRSP index at 0.11 as well as the corresponding aggregate portfolios formed using the

Table 9.5 Construction details for long only aggregate portfolios composed of the proxy minimum variance portfolio g plus long only zeta risk portfolio

Long aggregate portfolios	$\bar{R}_{gt+1} + \bar{R}_{pt+1}$	$\sigma_{g+p,t+1}$	Sharpe ratio
Min var portfolio g + portfolio 1	0.24	6.88	-0.02
Min var portfolio g + portfolio 2	0.29	6.56	-0.02
Min var portfolio g + portfolio 3	0.40	6.04	0.00
Min var portfolio g + portfolio 4	0.68	5.24	0.06
Min var portfolio g + portfolio 5	0.74	4.88	0.07
Min var portfolio g + portfolio 6	0.84	4.62	0.10
Min var portfolio g + portfolio 7	0.87	4.47	0.11
Min var portfolio g + portfolio 8	0.89	4.33	0.12
Min var portfolio g + portfolio 9	0.92	4.20	0.13
Min var portfolio g + portfolio 10	0.96	4.11	0.14
Min var portfolio g + portfolio 11	0.95	4.07	0.14
Min var portfolio g + portfolio 12	0.95	4.05	0.14
Min var portfolio g + portfolio 13	0.98	4.00	0.15
Min var portfolio g + portfolio 14	1.02	4.00	0.16
Min var portfolio g + portfolio 15	1.04	4.02	0.16
Min var portfolio g + portfolio 16	1.04	4.07	0.16
Min var portfolio g + portfolio 17	1.10	4.11	0.17
Min var portfolio g + portfolio 18	1.13	4.22	0.18
Min var portfolio g + portfolio 19	1.21	4.31	0.19
Min var portfolio g + portfolio 20	1.26	4.51	0.19
Min var portfolio g + portfolio 21	1.33	4.77	0.20
Min var portfolio g + portfolio 22	1.38	5.35	0.19
Min var portfolio g + portfolio 23	1.37	5.24	0.19
Min var portfolio g + portfolio 24	1.41	5.94	0.17
Min var portfolio g	0.96	3.49	0.16

This table reports construction details for long only aggregate portfolios formed by combining the proxy minimum variance portfolio g with long only zeta risk portfolios formed on $Z^*_{i,a}$ coefficients estimated in the empirical ZCAPM. Portfolio g is developed from the empirical ZCAPM. A total of 24 long zeta risk portfolios are formed. Long aggregate portfolios are created using a 50% weight for portfolio g and 50% weight for each long zeta risk portfolio. For 648 months in the analysis period January 1965 to December 2018, we report for each long aggregate portfolio the average one-month-ahead return denoted as $\bar{R}_{gt+1} + \bar{R}_{pt+1}$, time-series standard deviation of this aggregate monthly return series denoted as $\sigma_{g+p,t+1}$, and Sharpe ratio. For comparison purposes, results for portfolio g are shown

CRSP index in Table 9.4. Among high risk portfolios, combining g with long only portfolios 22, 23, and 24 earns relatively high average returns of 1.38%, 1.37%, and 1.41%, respectively, which again exceed average returns for the CRSP index as well as corresponding aggregate portfolios containing the CRSP index. Notice that the following portfolios are better proxies for market returns than the CRSP index: portfolio g plus long only portfolios 13 and 14. These two portfolios have the lowest total risk at 4.00%

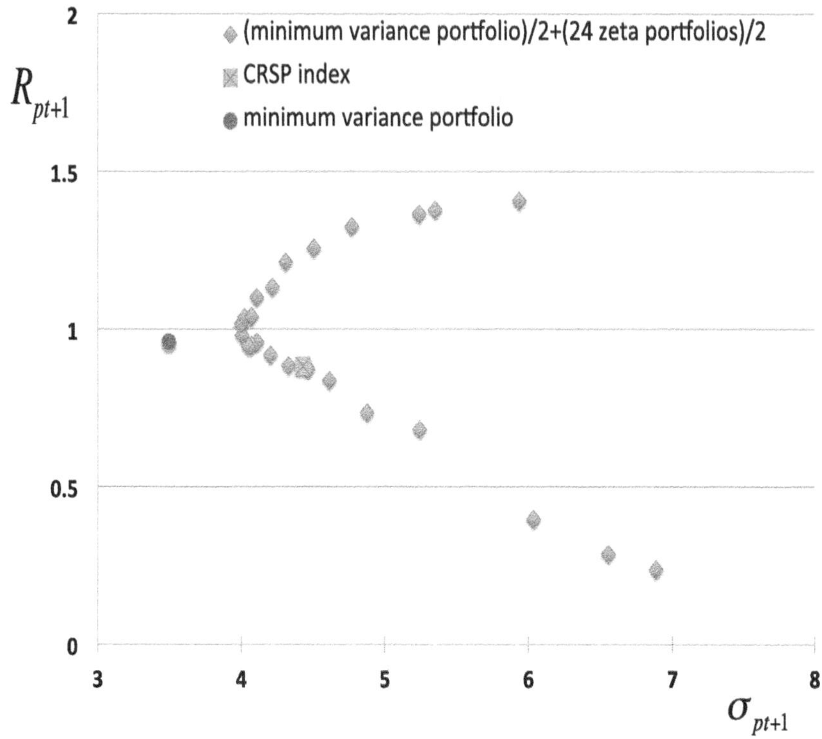

Fig. 9.6 Frontier estimates are shown based on average one-month-ahead (out-of-sample) returns and the time-series standard deviation of these returns for 24 long only aggregate portfolios. These long aggregate portfolios are formed by investing 50% of funds in the proxy minimum variance portfolio g and 50% of funds in 24 long zeta risk portfolios. Visual comparisons can be made to the CRSP market index and proxy minimum variance portfolio g. The analysis period is January 1965 to December 2018

(or 4.39% in Table 9.4 using the CRSP index) but earn from 0.98% and 1.02%(or 0.94 and 0.98% in Table 9.4 based on the CRSP index), respectively, which exceeds the CRSP index at 0.88%. Of course, they have higher Sharpe ratios than the CRSP index also.

Figures 9.5 and 9.6 visually summarize our long only aggregate portfolio findings. By combining market indexes with long only zeta risk portfolios, we can create aggregate portfolios with only long positions that outperform the CRSP index. Also, these long only aggregate portfolios trace out a mean-variance investment parabola as predicted by our earlier theoretical results on the parabola in Chapters 3 and 4—namely, average market returns lie approximately on the axis of symmetry and return dispersion defines the width of the parabola. Based on these insights, we can construct aggregate portfolios that depict a parabola.

Importantly, using zeta risk, we can control the relative risks of different aggregate portfolios. An array of aggregate portfolios with different risk levels can be created by investment professionals that meet a wide variety of client risk preferences. The out-of-sample relative performance of these portfolios will match their financially engineered risk levels. This kind of investment process was originally a dream of the CAPM. Using market model estimates of beta, different risk portfolios over a spectrum of beta risks could be constructed. However, as we know from out-of-sample cross-sectional results in Chapters 6 and 7 as well as published findings of many other authors, the subsequent performance of these portfolios did not provide lower risk investors lower returns and higher risk investors higher returns. It is not possible to use the CAPM as an investment tool to manage risk and return for clients.

What about other asset pricing models based on popular multifactors? Can they be used to construct different risk/return aggregate portfolios similar to the empirical ZCAPM? To test this possibility, we repeat the above analyses by forming zero-investment long/short portfolios based on beta coefficient estimates for the size and value factors of Fama and French (1992, 1993, 1995) in addition to the momentum factor of Jegadeesh and Titman (1993). Using daily data for one year in each estimation period downloaded from Kenneth French's website, we estimated the Carhart (1997) four-factor model, which contains market, size (*SMB*), value (*HML*), and momentum (*MOM*) factors. Similar to our earlier analyses using zeta risk, stocks are sorted to form 12 risk slices based on their estimated size beta coefficients denoted $\beta(SMB)$. Likewise, 12 risk slices are formed based on value beta coefficients denoted $\beta(HML)$ as well as momentum beta coefficients denoted $\beta(MOM)$. Equal weights for each stock in any given beta slice are used as before to compute one-month-ahead returns.

The results are summarized in Fig. 9.7. It is obvious from this figure that there is no relation between average one-month-ahead stock returns and zero-investment portfolios sensitive to factor loadings for $\beta(SMB)$, $\beta(HML)$, and $\beta(MOM)$. Aggregate portfolios formed by combining the CRSP index with each of these long/short beta risk portfolios trace out flat

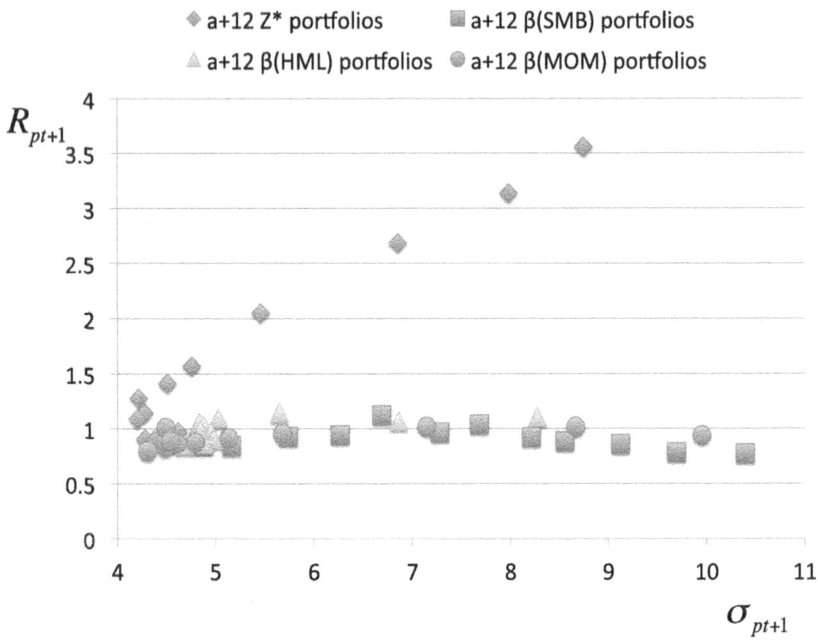

Fig. 9.7 The graph compares average one-month-ahead (out-of-sample) returns and the time-series standard deviation of these returns for: (1) aggregate portfolios comprised of the CRSP market index (denoted *a*) plus 12 long/short zeta risk portfolios, and (2) aggregate portfolios comprised of the CRSP market index (denoted *a*) plus 12 long/short beta risk portfolios based on sensitivity to the popular multifactors size (*SMB*), value (*HML*), and momentum (*MOM*). The analysis period is January 1965 to December 2018

lines well below the frontier produced by combining the CRSP index with long/short portfolios based on zeta risk. Thus, these multifactors are not useful in constructing superior aggregate portfolios. A likely reason for this failure is that it is not possible to control the relative risk of *SMB*, *HML*, and *MOM* over time. These long/short portfolios are not constructed based on risk levels as in the case of our long/short zeta risk portfolios.

9.5 Summary

This chapter applied the ZCAPM asset pricing model to the problem of constructing superior performing stock portfolios. According to the ZCAPM, expected asset returns are a function of beta risk related to average market returns and zeta risk associated with cross-sectional return dispersion (*RD*). Given beta-adjusted market returns, as *RD* increases, assets with positive (negative) sensitivity to *RD* will tend to have increasing (decreasing) returns, and vice versa as *RD* decreases. In this regard, as previously proven in Chapters 3 and 4 but previously unknown, the mean-variance investment parabola of Markowitz (1959) is defined by the average market return (e.g., CRSP index return) on the axis of symmetry and *RD* related to its width. In view of these new insights about the investment parabola, to earn stock portfolio returns greater than a general market index return, we added portfolios with different levels of sensitivity to *RD* to the CRSP market index. No precedent exists in the literature for this investment portfolio strategy, which is motivated by our previously unknown findings about the parabola and related ZCAPM asset pricing model.

Applying the expectation–maximization (EM) algorithm to estimate the empirical ZCAPM for U.S. stocks, zeta risk coefficients (i.e., sensitivity to return dispersion) were estimated for all stocks in a one year period with daily returns. Stocks were ranked on their zeta risk estimates and formed into 24 portfolios. These portfolios were used to construct 12 long/short portfolios that stratify zeta risk into slices ranging from high to low. One-month-ahead (out-of-sample) returns for the portfolios were computed. This process was repeated over time to generate a monthly series of returns for all portfolios from January 1965 to December 2018. Strikingly, for stocks in the top +1%/bottom −1%, top +2%/bottom −2%, and top +5%/bottom −5% of estimated zeta risk coefficients, average returns in the post-formation month equaled 2.34%, 2.16%, and 1.96%, respectively, which are exceptional for long/short portfolios. More generally, supporting the ZCAPM's ability to capture market risk, a strong positive and linear relation between one-month-ahead returns and zeta risk was documented.

Next, we combined the CRSP value-weighted index with our 12 zero-investment *RD* portfolios to form 12 aggregate zeta risk portfolios. The latter aggregate portfolios' post-formation, one-month-ahead returns traced out an upward sloping frontier earning one-month-ahead returns in the range of 0.95% to 3.22% per month as zeta risk increases. Additionally, we constructed long only aggregate portfolios by combining the CRSP index with portfolios containing different levels of zeta risk. These aggregate portfolios earned average returns in the analysis period from 0.20% to 1.37% per month depending on different levels of zeta risk.

We conjectured that more efficient aggregate portfolios could be created by combining minimum variance portfolio *G* with zeta risk portfolios. For this purpose, we used the empirical ZCAPM to estimate a proxy for the theoretical *G* denoted *g* that contains most stocks in the U.S. stock market. Portfolio *g* was constructed to have both low zeta risk and low idiosyncratic risk. Out-of-sample returns for portfolio *g* were computed from January 1965 to December 2018. Substituting our *g* portfolio for the CRSP index, another set of aggregate portfolios was formed by adding the 12 long/short zeta risk portfolios. As anticipated, these aggregate portfolios were more efficient than those based on the CRSP index. For example, holding total risk similar to the CRSP index, an average monthly return of 1.75% was earned. This exceptional return performance is approximately 100% higher than the CRSP index at 0.88%. The highest earning aggregate portfolio achieved an average monthly return of 3.30% but at the cost of higher total risk.

Related to these tests, average Sharpe ratios ranged from 0.13 to 0.33 across our 12 aggregate portfolios based on the CRSP index and 0.18 to 0.36 across 12 aggregate portfolio with the *g* portfolio. These average Sharpe ratios clearly dominated the CRSP index at 0.11 in our analysis period. Gibbons et al. (1989) test statistics based on Sharpe ratios indicated that both of our aggregate zeta risk portfolios—namely, those based on the CRSP index plus 12 long/short zeta portfolios as well as proxy portfolio *g* plus the 12 long/short zeta risk portfolios—are highly significant. By inference, the CRSP index is relatively inefficient compared to our aggregate portfolios. Also, GRS tests showed that our aggregate portfolios could not be explained by the Fama and French six-factor model.

Further robustness tests found that different levels of beta risk associated with popular size, value, and momentum factors were not useful in creating aggregate portfolios that outperform the CRSP index.

We conclude that the sensitivity of stock returns to cross-sectional return dispersion in the stock market enables the creation of superior performing diversified portfolios. Further research is recommended on international stocks as well as other asset classes, including bonds, commodities, real estate, etc., to replicate our findings in other samples.

An important implication of our findings is that practitioners can use our methods to develop zeta risk portfolios and aggregate portfolios. Prudence would advise paper trading tests incorporating trading costs of rebalancing portfolios from month to month. Also, experiments with long only and long/short portfolios should be conducted. Assuming these tests were successful, new investment products could be created for customers. Products that span a wide array of total risk levels would enable customers to choose products that best fit their risk preferences. As shown by our results, lower (higher) risk portfolios earn lower (higher) returns on average over time, thus enabling managers to control relative risk and return outcomes available to customers. A caveat here is that our portfolio methods require investment horizons of at least three-to-five years. In earlier paper trading tests performed by the authors in cooperation with the Teachers Retirement System of Texas, based on backtesting over about 20 years, we found that aggregate long only portfolios using the same stocks as in the S&P 500 index outperformed this index in almost all three-year periods of time. Hence, our ZCAPM approach to building stock portfolios is a long-run investment strategy.

Lastly, we would like to emphasize that the investment technology presented in this chapter is more practitioner than academic oriented. Much academic research is devoted to various anomalous portfolio returns not explained by asset pricing models. For example, as discussed in the previous Chapter 8, many studies have documented anomalous returns associated with momentum. Little or no theory helps to explain abnormally high momentum returns. Most momentum studies form long/short portfolios using the top/bottom deciles of stocks in terms of average return performance over the past year. More consistent with prudential investment practices, we form a wide variety of long/short portfolios that span different risk levels (rather than choosing portfolios based solely on returns with little or no consideration of risk). We subsequently add our long/short zeta risk portfolios to an aggregate index (such as the CRSP index or minimum variance *g* portfolio) to form new aggregate portfolios with different risk levels. In both long/short zeta risk portfolios and aggregate portfolios incorporating these zero-investment portfolios, our methods are more consistent with the practice of prudent risk management in professional investment services than the search for anomalous returns in academic literature.

Bibliography

Ang, A., Hodrick, R. J., Xing, Y., & Zhang, X. (2006). The cross-section of volatility and expected returns. *Journal of Finance, 61*, 259–299.

Barras, L., Scaillet, O., & Wermers, R. (2010). False discoveries in mutual fund performance: Measuring luck in estimated alphas. *Journal of Finance, 65*, 179–216.

Barroso, P., & Santa-Clara, P. (2015). Momentum has its moments. *Journal of Financial Economics, 116*, 111–120.

Black, F. (1972). Capital market equilibrium with restricted borrowing. *Journal of Business, 45*, 444–454.

Bollen, N., & Busse, J. (2004). Short-term persistence in mutual fund performance. *Review of Financial Studies, 18*, 569–597.

Brennan, T. J., & Lo, W. W. (2010). Impossible frontiers. *Management Science, 56*, 905–923.

Carhart, M. M. (1997). On persistence in mutual fund performance. *Journal of Finance, 52*, 57–82.

Daniel, K. (2011). *Momentum crashes* (Working Paper). Columbia University.

Daniel, K., & Moskowitz, T. (2016). Momentum crashes. *Journal of Financial Economics, 122*, 221–247.

Dempster, A. P., Laird, N. M., & Rubin, D. B. (1977). Maximum likelihood from incomplete data via the EM algorithm. *Journal of the Royal Statistical Society, 39*, 1–38.

Fama, E. F., & French, K. R. (1992). The cross-section of expected stock returns. *Journal of Finance, 47*, 427–465.

Fama, E. F., & French, K. R. (1993). The cross-section of expected returns. *Journal of Financial Economics, 33*, 3–56.

Fama, E. F., & French, K. R. (1995). Size and book-to-market factors in earnings and returns. *Journal of Finance, 50*, 131–156.

Fama, E. F., & French, K. R. (2010). Luck versus skill in the cross-section of mutual fund returns. *Journal of Finance, 65*, 131–156.

Fama, E. F., & French, K. R. (2015). A five-factor asset pricing model. *Journal of Financial Economics, 116*, 1–22.

Fama, E. F., & French, K. R. (2018). Choosing factors. *Journal of Financial Economics, 128*, 234–252.

Fama, E. F., & MacBeth, J. D. (1973). Risk, return, and equilibrium: Empirical tests. *Journal of Political Economy, 81*, 607–636.

Gibbons, M. R., Ross, S. A., & Shanken, J. (1989). A test of the efficiency of a given portfolio. *Econometrica, 57*, 1121–1152.

Green, R. C., & Hollifield, B. (1992). When will mean-variance efficient portfolios be well diversified? *Journal of Finance, 47*, 1785–1809.

Jagannathan, R., & Ma, T. (2003). Risk reduction in large portfolios: A role for portfolio weight constraints. *Journal of Finance*, *58*, 1651–1684.

Jegadeesh, N., & Titman, S. (1993). Returns to buying winners and selling losers: Implications for stock market efficiency. *Journal of Finance*, *48*, 65–91.

Jegadeesh, N., & Titman, S. (2001). Profitability of momentum strategies: An evaluation of alternative explanations. *Journal of Finance*, *56*, 699–720.

Jensen, M. C. (1968). The performance of mutual funds in the period 1945–1964. *Journal of Finance*, *23*, 389–416.

Jorion, P. (1986). Bayes-Stein estimation for portfolio analysis. *Journal of Financial and Quantitative Analysis*, *21*, 279–292.

Kallberg, J. G., & Ziemba, W. T. (1983). Comparison of alternative utility functions in portfolio selection problems. *Management Science*, *29*, 1257–1276.

Klein, R. W., & Bawa, B. S. (1976). The effect of estimation risk on optimal portfolio choice. *Journal of Financial Economics*, *3*, 215–231.

Kothari, S. P., Shanken, J., & Sloan, R. G. (1995). Another look at the cross-section of expected stock returns. *Journal of Finance*, *50*, 185–224.

Kroll, Y., Levy, H., & Markowitz, H. (1984). Mean-variance versus direct utility maximization. *Journal of Finance*, *39*, 47–61.

Levy, H. (1983). The capital asset pricing model: Theory and empiricism. *Economic Journal*, *93*, 145–165.

Levy, M., & Ritov, Y. (2010). Mean-variance efficient portfolios with many assets: 50% short. *Quantitative Finance*, *11*, 1461–1471.

Levy, M., & Roll, R. (2010). The market portfolio may be mean/variance efficient after all. *Review of Financial Studies*, *23*, 2464–2491.

Liu, W. (2013). *A new asset pricing model based on the zero-beta CAPM: Theory and evidence*. Doctoral dissertation, Texas A&M University.

Liu, W., Kolari, J. W., & Huang, J. Z. (2012, October). *A new asset pricing model based on the zero-beta CAPM*. Presentation at the annual meetings of the Financial Management Association, Atlanta, GA.

Liu, W., Kolari, J. W., & Huang, J. Z. (2020, October). *Return dispersion and the cross-section of stock returns*. Presentation at the annual meetings of the Southern Finance Association, Palm Springs, CA.

Malkiel, B. G. (1995). Returns from investing in equity mutual funds 1971 to 1991. *Journal of Finance*, *50*, 549–572.

Malkiel, B. G. (2005). Reflections on the efficient market hypotheses: 30 years later. *The Financial Review*, *40*, 1–9.

Markowitz, H. M. (1959). *Portfolio selection: Efficient diversification of investments*. New York, NY: Wiley.

Polson, N. G., & Tew, B. V. (2000). Bayesian portfolio selection: An empirical analysis of the S&P 5000 index 1970–1996. *Journal of Business and Economic Statistics*, *18*, 164–173.

Pulley, L. B. (1981). General mean-variance approximation to expected utility for short holding periods. *Journal of Financial and Quantitative Analysis*, *16*, 361–373.

Sharpe, W. F. (1964). Capital asset prices: A theory of market equilibrium under conditions of risk. *Journal of Finance*, *19*, 425–442.

PART VI

Conclusion

CHAPTER 10

Synopsis of Asset Pricing and the ZCAPM

Abstract During the period from the 1960s to early 1990s, the *Capital Asset Pricing Model* (CAPM) of John Lintner, Jan Mossin, William Sharpe, and Jack Treynor developed into the main branch of asset pricing. A path-breaking theoretical masterpiece, the CAPM was derived from equilibrium pricing conditions as well as seminal portfolio theory by Harry Markowitz. However, early empirical evidence suggested that CAPM relation between beta risk associated with the market portfolio and stock returns was weaker than predicted. In an effort to take into account this evidence, Fischer Black proposed the *zero-beta CAPM*. Extending the CAPM to continuous time, Robert Merton advanced the *intertemporal CAPM* (ICAPM). Other forms of the CAPM were derived also. In recognition of the CAPM's worldwide prominence, Professors Markowitz and Sharpe shared the Nobel Prize in Economics in 1990. Immediately thereafter in the early 1990s, Eugene Fama and Kenneth French published a series of papers that overturned the CAPM. Using U.S. stock returns over many years, they documented evidence against the relation between beta risk and the cross section of U.S. stock returns. Creating a new branch of asset pricing, they proposed a *three-factor model* comprised of market, size, and value factors to better fit stock return data. The latter so-called *multifactors* are zero-investment portfolios based on stocks with different firm characteristics. This long-minus-short portfolio method of specifying factors motivated many researchers to propose new multifactors based on other firm characteristics and stock return anomalies. A growing number of contender models evolved with

J. W. Kolari et al., *A New Model of Capital Asset Prices*,
https://doi.org/10.1007/978-3-030-65197-8_10

different zero-investment factors. The resultant ***multifactor model*** competition has raised questions about the most important factors and models to use. A major problem with this branch of literature is that there is little or no theoretical foundation for zero-investment factors. In defense, some researchers loosely tie multifactor models to the *Arbitrage Pricing Theory* (APT) of Stephen Ross or the ICAPM of Robert Merton. In this book we developed a new theoretical CAPM that is a special case of Black's zero-beta CAPM dubbed the *ZCAPM*. Our new asset pricing model departs from the multifactor model branch of literature by returning to the main CAPM branch. Based on the same mean-variance portfolio theory and equilibrium conditions of the CAPM and zero-beta CAPM, the ZCAPM hypothesizes that expected returns are a function of beta risk associated with average market returns and zeta risk related to return dispersion. Unlike previous asset pricing models, assets can have asymmetric positive and negative sensitivity to return dispersion (*RD*) in any given time period (e.g., one day). To estimate the theoretical ZCAPM with stock return data, we specified the ***empirical** ZCAPM* as a novel regression model containing a dummy signal variable to capture positive versus negative sensitivity to *RD*. The probability that this latent (or hidden) signal variable is positive or negative was estimated using the well-known expectation–maximization (EM) algorithm. This marginal form of the ZCAPM is a probabilistic mixture of two-factor models that take into account positive versus negative sensitivity to *RD*. Using over 50 years of U.S. common stock returns, comparative graphical analyses and batteries of cross-sectional tests strongly favored the empirical ZCAPM over popular multifactor models. In repeated out-of-sample cross-sectional tests with different portfolios, individual stocks, and sample periods, the ZCAPM dominated popular multifactor models. Also, we found that a number of prominent anomalies, including size, value, momentum, profit, and capital investment, are explained by the empirical ZCAPM. It is important to recognize that zero-investment portfolios themselves are rough measures of return dispersion that capture slices of the total dispersion. Taken together, they proxy total return dispersion. In this sense, multifactor models bear some relation to the ZCAPM and thereby the CAPM.

Keywords Arbitrage pricing theory (APT) · Asset pricing · Beta risk · CAPM · Cross-sectional regression tests · Dualism · Empirical ZCAPM · Expectation-maximization (EM) algorithm · Eugene Fama · Fischer Black · Kenneth French · Harry Markowitz · Industry portfolios ·

Multifactor models · Out-of-sample returns · Return dispersion · Securities investment · Signal variable · Stock market · Test assets · Theoretial ZCAPM · William Sharpe · ZCAPM · Zero-beta CAPM · Zeta risk

10.1 The CAPM Lives

Asset pricing has evolved into two branches of literature. The main branch of research is rooted in the Capital Asset Pricing Model (CAPM) of Treynor (1961, 1962), Sharpe (1964), Lintner (1965), Mossin (1966), and Black (1972). The CAPM represented a major theoretical advance due to the use of the mean-variance investment parabola of Markowitz (1959) and equilibrium financial market conditions. Derivative models, such as the consumption CAPM (CCAPM) of Lucas (1978) and Breeden (1979) as well as intertemporal CAPM (ICAPM) of Merton (1973), showed promise along this evolutionary path. Other variants of the CAPM made further contributions, including the conditional CAPM of Ferson and Harvey (1991, 1996), production-based asset pricing model (PAPM) of Cochrane (1991), and international CAPM of Stulz (1981, 1995). In 1990 Professors Markowitz and Sharpe shared the Nobel Prize in Economics, a strong endorsement of the CAPM and its portfolio theory underpinnings as a tour de force in the asset pricing world.[1]

However, early CAPM tests by Black et al. (1972) found that the relation between average U.S. stock returns and beta was flatter than predicted. Many studies confirmed this weaker than expected CAPM relation. In response to this evidence, Black (1972) derived a more general form of the CAPM known as the *zero-beta CAPM*. Unfortunately, he did not provide a proxy for the zero-beta portfolio for empirically estimating the zero-beta CAPM. Also, Roll (1977) has argued that the CAPM cannot be empirically tested without a suitable proxy for the market portfolio.

In the 1970s another branch of literature emerged known as the *arbitrage pricing theory* (APT) of Ross (1976). Rather than defining market equilibrium based on Markowitz's mean-variance portfolio theory, the APT posits that equilibrium is reached when no arbitrage possibilities exist. After taking into account all risk factors, which are orthogonal to one another,

[1] Merton Miller also shared the Nobel Prize with these authors for his important contributions to corporate valuation.

investors earn zero arbitrage profits. Assuming zero arbitrage opportunities and a linear factor structure, Ross showed that the unconditional form of Merton's ICAPM holds. Even so, it is important to distinguish between the APT's relative pricing of each asset against one another and the ICAPM's absolute pricing of each asset with respect to fundamental risk factors.[2] While the APT and ICAPM take into account many different risk factors in pricing assets, they do not specify the factors for empirical estimation purposes. Thus, even though the APT and ICAPM are theoretically attractive models, they are difficult to operationalize with actual data.

In the 1990s, just after the Nobel Prize Awards for the CAPM, Fama and French (1992, 1993, 1995) documented U.S. stock return evidence against the CAPM. As summarized by Fama and French (2004), based on many years of stock return data and numerous tests, the empirical evidence did not support the CAPM relation between average stock returns and beta risk associated with the market factor. Given their findings and those of others, Fama and French (1996) declared the beloved CAPM *dead*. In its place, they augmented the market factor with zero-investment size and value factors based on firm characteristics to create a three-factor model that better explained the cross section of average stock returns. Their atheoretical (or ad hoc) approach to model building relied upon the empirical success of potential contender factors.[3]

Following Fama and French, many researchers proposed zero-investment factors with some significance in the cross section of average stock returns. For example, Carhart (1997) added a momentum factor to the three-factor model. Building on their three-factor model, Fama and French (2015, 2018, 2020) added profit, capital investment, and momentum factors. Other researchers, such as Hou et al. (2015, 2018), Stambaugh and Yuan (2017), and Lettau and Pelger (2020), proposed alternative multifactor models containing various empirically justified, zero-investment multifactors. At the time of this writing, considerable confusion prevails about the most important factors and models to use in asset pricing. It is likely that this confusion will continue to grow due to the *factor zoo* problem (Cochrane 1991) and, as perceived by the present authors, related

[2] See Cochrane (2005, Chapter 9, pp. 182–183) for further discussion. For example, as pointed out there, the APT assumes risk factors are orthogonal to another but the ICAPM does not.

[3] Black (1993) believed that the Fama and French models were the product of data mining and therefore suspect due to the lack of theoretical foundations.

model mall problem. Karolyi and Nieuwerburgh (2020) have forecasted that thousands of new factors are possible that take into account conditioning variables, nonlinear functions, and combinations of multiple factors. In our opinion, these multifactor models are consistent to some extent with Ross' APT branch of asset pricing, in which unspecified factors must be analytically determined.[4]

Returning to the main branch of asset pricing, this book proposed a new capital asset pricing model. Extending the CAPM branch of literature, we derived our model from Markowitz (1959) portfolio theory, Sharpe (1964) equilibrium conditions, and Black (1972) more general zero-beta CAPM. Our research began a decade ago with an inquiry into the possibility of an empirically estimable form of the zero-beta CAPM. Assuming an efficient portfolio and zero-beta counterpart portfolio with the same total risk denoted I^* and ZI^*, respectively, we obtained an alternative form of the zero-beta CAPM dubbed the *ZCAPM*.

A crucial step in our theoretical model development was the discovery of new properties of Markowitz's mean-variance investment parabola: (1) the average market return lies on the axis of symmetry of the parabola at an interior location, and (2) the width of the investment parabola is defined in large part by cross-sectional return dispersion (*RD*). These two properties are inextricably linked—if *RD* is a major determinant of the parabola's width, then logically the average market return must lie approximately in the middle of the parabola on its axis of symmetry.

Armed with these new insights, we proposed a new geometric approach to locating efficient and zero-beta (orthogonal) portfolios in Black's zero-beta CAPM. Using this approach, we derived the ZCAPM as a special case of Black's model. The ZCAPM consists of: (1) beta risk (β) associated with the average market return factor, and (2) zeta risk (Z^*) related to the cross-sectional return dispersion factor (i.e., the cross-sectional standard deviation of all assets in the market). Unlike other models that incorporate return dispersion (*RD*) as a multifactor, our inclusion of *RD* as an asset pricing factor was grounded in mean-variance portfolio and general equilibrium CAPM theories. Also, different from other models, we posit dichotomous positive and negative effects of *D* on asset prices.

A geometric proposition of the ZCAPM is that Sharpe's market portfolio *M* can be reached in a different manner than in the CAPM. The CAPM

[4] Also, see Cochrane (2005, p. 183), who similarly classified these models as closer to Ross' APT.

uses the Capital Market Line (CML) to locate M at the tangent point on the efficient frontier of the mean-variance parabola (i.e., the highest-slope, most efficient line extending from the riskless rate to the frontier). By contrast, the ZCAPM moves horizontally via the average market return along the axis of symmetry of the parabola and then vertically up or down via positive or negative RD, respectively, to two orthogonal portfolios located on the efficient and inefficient boundaries of the parabola. Together, as proven by Black, these two portfolios can be used to locate the market portfolio M.

With ZCAPM theory in hand, a major hurdle arose. How can an empirical model be specified that captures opposing RD sensitivity effects at any given time? No previous models in the asset pricing literature were suitable for this purpose. To tackle this problem, we introduced a signal dummy variable D_{it} that equals $+1(-1)$ at any time t (e.g., one day) when the ith asset's return increases (decreases) in response to an increase in RD, or vice versa in response to a decrease in RD, all else the same. Assuming that D_{it} is a latent or unobservable variable, we utilized the widely accepted expectation–maximization (EM) algorithm of Dempster et al. (1977) to estimate the probability p that $D_{it} = +1$ or probability $1-p$ that $D_{it} = -1$.[5] This empirical ZCAPM provides estimates of beta risk (β) and zeta risk (Z^*) coefficients using a mixture model. Crucially, it takes into account the dualistic nature of return dispersion with both positive and negative RD effects on stock returns.

Based on the empirical ZCAPM, we conducted a large number of out-of-sample cross-sectional tests using over 50 years of U.S. stock returns from January 1965 to December 2018.[6] The evidence was surprising in terms of both the consistency and significance of our findings. In test-after-test, our ZCAPM consistently outperformed not only the CAPM market model but popular multifactor models that augment the market model

[5] See also Wu (1983), Rudd (1991), and McLachlan and Krishnan (2008).

[6] Matlab programs for estimating the empirical ZCAPM and conducting cross-sectional regression tests are available at the end of the book in the Compendium. Additionally, R programs for these analyses can be downloaded from GitHub (https://github.com/zcapm). Our R programs run faster in terms of estimating the empirical ZCAPM than our Matlab programs. R is a free software environment available on the internet. At the time of this writing, we contemplate that our Matlab programs as well as Python coding will be available on Github also.

with a number of different zero-investment portfolios.[7] Also, using stock portfolios associated with various anomalies (i.e., size, value, momentum, profit, and investment portfolios), a strong relation between one-month-ahead predicted returns by the empirical ZCAPM and realized returns was found, which clearly outperformed multifactor models. Hence, the empirical ZCAPM explains these previously anomalous factors for the most part. In these predicted/realized returns graphical analyses, multifactor models performed poorly using industry portfolios, but the empirical ZCAPM continued to do a good job. Hence, many anomalies in the literature that are not explained by the CAPM or other models are explained by the empirical ZCAPM. The anomalies no longer can be attributed to market inefficiency. They were due to an incorrect equilibrium model. It is important to recognize that the ZCAPM is another form of the CAPM in general and zero-beta CAPM in particular. By implication, the CAPM is reborn in the form of the theoretical ZCAPM and lives again through evidence based on the empirical ZCAPM.

Our out-of-sample cross-sectional ZCAPM tests of estimated zeta risk loadings (Z^*) associated with return dispersion generated very significant t-values in the range of 3 to 6. After surveying the vast asset pricing literature, Harvey et al. (2015) recommended that factor loadings should have t-values of 3 or more to be considered legitimate. Similarly, to avoid data-snooping biases in the proliferation of proposed asset pricing factors, Chordia et al. (2020) have estimated the appropriate t-statistic threshold at 3.4. Both of these studies have argued that, because many reported discoveries in asset pricing later turn out to be false, high statistical thresholds need to be used in evaluating factors. The fact that the empirical ZCAPM can pass these statistical hurdles in cross-sectional tests (but not popular multifactor models) is testimony to the wisdom contained in Sharpe's CAPM, its equilibrium conditions, and Markowitz portfolio foundations.

An important implication of our ZCAPM research concerns Fama (1970) famous efficient market hypothesis (EMH). The idea that security prices reflect all available information was one of the pillars of modern finance for many years, for which (among other contributions) Fama received the Nobel Prize in Economics. However, according to Brown (2000), the stock market crash of 1987, dot-com bubble in March 2000, growing acceptance of behavioral theories as elucidated by Thaler (1999),

[7] See also corroborating evidence in Liu et al. (2012, 2020) and Liu (2013) based on different sample periods.

and other reasons have seriously challenged the EMH. Additionally, given that tests of asset pricing models are joint tests of the EMH and the models themselves, rejection of the CAPM in the 1990s was a partial rejection of the EMH that was consistent with the increasingly accepted behavioral story of potentially irrational investors. By supporting the CAPM, our empirical ZCAPM evidence bodes well for the EMH. As originally hypothesized by the co-creators of the CAPM, average returns are significantly related to systematic market risk.

Due to new higher threshold standards for the statistical significance of factors, Harvey (2017) has conjectured that increased data mining might occur. A telltale sign that this is not true of the ZCAPM is our earlier quotation in Chapter 2 of Fischer Black: "Lack of theory is a tipoff: watch out for data mining!" (Black 1993, p. 75). In this respect, the ZCAPM stands on the theoretical shoulders of its CAPM predecessors as an equilibrium asset pricing model with empirical support that satisfies the latest efficacy standards. Looking back at our research path over the past decade, we first developed the theoretical ZCAPM and, subsequently, specified an empirical ZCAPM. In our view, ZCAPM theory and evidence presented in this book cannot be attributed to luck, false positives, or other potential explanations of false discovery.

10.2 The ZCAPM and Multifactor Models

Fama and French (1992) invented the long/short, zero-investment factor. This factor design became very widespread over time. Many researchers proposed hundreds of different multifactors based on various firm characteristics and stock return anomalies in the literature. The upswelling of contender factors proposed by researchers has been a phenomenon in its own right. As we have mentioned before, these factors have little or no theoretical support. Yet they have demonstrated their empirical success in stock return tests. Are they proof that Ross' APT holds in the real world? Are many common factors needed to reach zero arbitrage profits? Could they be proxies for state variables in the spirit of Merton's ICAPM? Do they have any redeeming value beyond empirical success?

Exemplary for its lack of theoretical justification, momentum is emerging as a relatively strong zero-investment factor in multifactor models. In Chapter 8 we focused our attention on what has become known as the *momentum mystery*. There we saw that long-winner/short-loser momentum returns are highly correlated with long/short zeta risk factors developed from the empirical ZCAPM. The main takeaway was that the momentum factor is a proxy for return dispersion and therefore is related to the width of the mean-variance investment parabola. Ipso facto, momentum is closely related to zeta risk in the ZCAPM.

Given our momentum findings, there is another explanation for the empirical success of many multifactors. Because long/short portfolios are themselves measures of return dispersion, they have some connection to the ZCAPM and its return dispersion factor. From this perspective, multifactor models do not represent an entirely different branch of asset pricing. Each long-minus-short return factor picks up a slice of the total dispersion in cross-sectional returns at any time t. Since return dispersion plays a major role in defining the width of the mean-variance investment parabola, the multifactors do so also. For example, in the Fama and French six-factor model, the five multifactors of size, value, profit, capital investment, and momentum encompass some share of total return dispersion. It is interesting to note that, in cross-sectional tests of the Fama and French three-, five-, and six-factor models in previous chapters, size factor loadings had a negative price of risk in a number of different test asset portfolios. Given that average small stock returns were greater than average big stock returns in our analysis period from January 1965 to December 2018, this negative price of risk is difficult to explain in the context of previous asset pricing models. However, in view of the ZCAPM, a plausible interpretation is that the size factor loadings were picking up negative zeta risk associated with some test assets.

Yet another explanation for flipping market prices of risk related to the size factor is that it can become negative in different periods of time. In our analysis period from 1965 to 2018, the size, value, profit, and capital investment factors had positive average monthly returns (see Table 5.1 in Chapter 5). However, in a recent paper, Blitz (2020) documented that the Fama-French factors had negative average returns in the 2010 to 2019 period, which was similar to the 1990s and some earlier periods such as the 1950s. These changing time-series patterns in the difference between small stock returns and big stock returns implies that this spread is not a good measure of market risk.[8] By contrast, the cross-sectional standard deviation

[8] It should be noted that the difference between the average market return and the Treasury bill rate intermittantly becomes negative for short periods of time but is positive most of the time. Also, momentum returns are normally positive but occasionally negative returns occur (known as *momentum crashes*).

of returns in the empirical ZCAPM is always positive. This property is consistent with Sharpe's notion of systematic risk, which is always present, affects all assets, and has a positive risk premium.

Following this line of reasoning, the ZCAPM grafts the multifactor model branch of asset pricing literature onto the main CAPM branch. Paraphrasing an often-quoted saying by Milton Freidman about Keynesian economics: "We are all Sharpians now." The empirical market model form of the CAPM is incomplete due to relying solely upon the average market return to proxy Sharpe's market portfolio M. To reach optimal portfolio M, according to the mean-variance parabola geometry of the ZCAPM, it is important to include return dispersion RD in the model. Multifactor models add return dispersion slices to the average market return in an attempt to reach the efficient frontier and market portfolio M.[9] As such, multifactor models are a more complete representation of the CAPM than the market model alone, albeit inferior to the ZCAPM. The empirical ZCAPM supplants multifactor models by explaining their previously anomalous factor returns. More generally, all of these models are related to one another with a common market portfolio heritage.

10.3 Future Research

If we could create an efficient proxy portfolio m for market portfolio M, there would be no need for the empirical ZCAPM or multifactor models. This single efficient portfolio in the proximity of M would be very significantly priced in the cross section of average stock returns due to capturing both changes in average market returns and return dispersion effects as the mean-variance parabola changes over time. In Chapter 9 we combined the CRSP index with long/short zeta risk portfolios to create more efficient aggregate portfolios. Results using a proxy g for the minimum variance portfolio G in combination with zeta risk portfolios further boosted the aggregate portfolios' efficiency. Extending this analysis, we could form efficient/inefficient pairs of portfolios to be used in a two factor zero-beta CAPM. By adding zeta risk portfolios to proxy g, efficient aggregate portfolios could be constructed. Subtracting zeta risk portfolios

[9] Daniel et al. (2020) have argued that long/short portfolio multifactors do not span the mean variance efficient frontier due to unpriced sources of common variation. They proposed a hedging method of removing unpriced risk to develop characteristic-efficient portfolios (CEPs).

from proxy g would construct inefficient aggregate portfolios. Orthogonal pairs of efficient/inefficient aggregate portfolios would be candidates for approximating Black's zero-beta CAPM.

Another possibility is to use portfolio g in place of the CRSP index to estimate the empirical ZCAPM. We next describe some preliminary evidence along this line of inquiry but recommend further study. Using CRSP common stocks in the period from 1963 to 2018, we drop stocks in the bottom 10% of market capitalization on the last day of each 12-month estimation window. We also drop stocks with a variance of daily returns in the one-year estimation window less than one-fourth of the CRSP index return variance (due to potential illiquidity). Starting in 1964, the empirical ZCAPM is estimated for all remaining CRSP stocks. Following procedures in Chapter 9, we construct a proxy minimum variance portfolio g in January 1965. In this out-of-sample month, daily portfolio g returns are computed by using individual stock returns on each day weighted by their zeta risk and residual error variance in the previously estimated empirical ZCAPM.[10] By rolling forward one month at a time, a daily series of g portfolio returns is constructed from January 1965 to December 2018.

Replacing daily CRSP index returns with daily portfolio g returns, we next create beta-zeta sorted portfolios. To do this, we estimate the empirical ZCAPM in 1964 for all CRSP stocks (after the aforementioned filters) and then sort stocks by their beta and zeta risk coefficients. A total of 25 beta-zeta sorted portfolios are formed by sorting on beta quintiles and then zeta quintiles within each beta quintile. One-month-ahead returns for each portfolio are computed in January 1965. For these out-of-sample returns, individual stocks are weighted by the inverse of their residual variance in the empirical ZCAPM estimated in 1964 (i.e., we do not weight using zeta risk to avoid adding or removing zeta risk from these already beta-zeta sorted portfolios). This process is rolled forward one month at a time to generate monthly series of beta, zeta, and one-month-ahead returns for each portfolio from January 1965 to December 2018. The standard deviation of monthly returns in this analysis period is computed for each portfolio. It should be noted that all portfolios are long only with no short positions.

[10] As defined in Chapter 9, the weight for each stock is computed as: $w_i = 1/(0.01+|\hat{Z}^*_{i,a}|) \times 1/\mathrm{var}(\widetilde{u}_{it})$, where $\hat{Z}^*_{i,a}$ is the estimated zeta risk coefficient, and idiosyncratic risk is measured by the variance of the residual error terms in the estimation of the empirical ZCAPM denoted $\mathrm{var}(\widetilde{u}_{it})$.

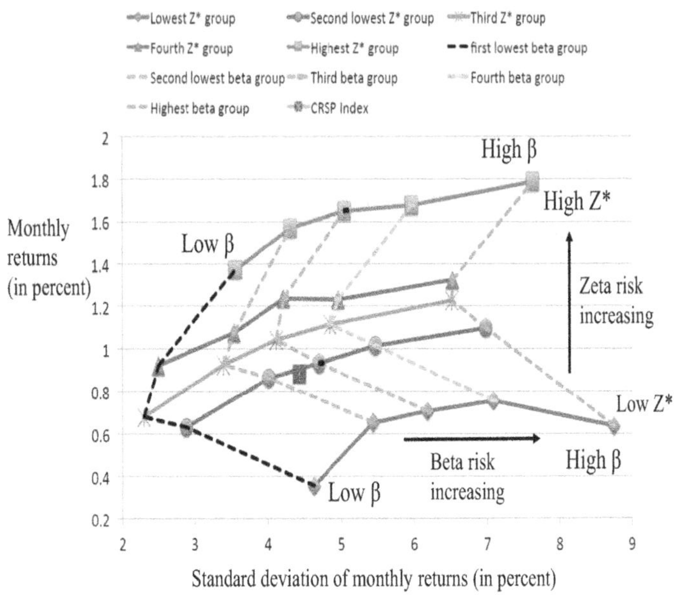

Fig. 10.1 This graph shows the average beta risk, zeta risk, and one-month-ahead returns for 25 beta-zeta sorted portfolios. These long only portfolios approximate the shape of an investment parabola. In each one-year estimation window, the empirical ZCAPM is estimated using daily returns for proxy *g* minimum variance portfolio in place of the CRSP market index. The analysis period is from January 1965 to December 2018

Using these results, we constructed Fig. 10.1. The top horizontal frontier contains the five stock portfolios with the highest average zeta risk in the analysis period. The frontier has an upward tilt due to increasing levels of beta risk among these five portfolios. The bottom boundary is composed of five stock portfolios with the lowest zeta risk but varying levels of beta risk from low to high. With the exception of the bottom boundary, the upward slope of each zeta risk curve (i.e., represented by a solid line) is due to increasing beta risk within each zeta risk level. Also, at each beta risk level, there is a vertical beta risk curve (i.e., represented by a dashed line) that intersects different zeta risk curves. Altogether, the intersecting latticework of orthogonal beta risk and zeta risk levels in the graph takes on the general form of a mean-variance parabola. These results strongly support our theoretical ZCAPM derived in Chapter 3.

Figure 10.1 shows that stock portfolios within the parabola have beta and zeta risk characteristics that jointly determine their expected returns. Rather than being randomly distributed within the parabola, these portfolios are ordered by their systematic risks related to average market returns and market return dispersion. Hence, equilibrium prices are established within the architecture of the parabola due to these two market forces.

Lastly, repeating methods detailed in Chapter 5 and applied in Chapter 7, we conducted out-of-sample Fama and MacBeth (1973) cross-sectional regression tests of the empirical ZCAPM estimated with portfolio g in place of the CRSP market index. Appendix A provides a review of the empirical ZCAPM and cross-sectional test methods. For the 25 beta-zeta sorted portfolios described above, the following cross-sectional regression model estimates are obtained: (1) $\hat{\alpha} = 0.21$ ($t = 2.13$), (2) $\hat{\lambda}_g = 0.38$ ($t = 2.01$), $\hat{\lambda}_{RD} = 0.51$ ($t = 6.45$), and $R^2 = 99\%$. These findings are extraordinary. The goodness-of-fit is near 100% perfect, which says that these portfolios' one-month-ahead returns are fully explained by their previously estimated beta risk and zeta risk loadings. Notice that, unlike our earlier results using the CRSP index, beta risk loadings are significantly priced at the five percent level. This finding agrees with the zeta risk curves in Fig. 10.1 that show portfolio returns increasing with beta risk. And, zeta risk loadings are very significantly priced with a t-statistic exceeding 6.

While these cross-sectional results are impressive, a word of caution is that endogeneity exists between our empirical ZCAPM factors of g portfolio returns and their return dispersion with respect to the 25 beta-zeta sorted portfolio returns. This issue was discussed in Chapters 5 and 7 in the context of cross-sectional tests using 25 size-B M sorted portfolios to test the Fama and French (1992, 1993, 1995) three-factor model with size and value multifactors. Repeating the cross-sectional tests with 47 exogenous industry portfolios, we get the following results: (1) $\hat{\alpha} = 0.46$ ($t = 2.54$), (2) $\hat{\lambda}_g = 0.15$ ($t = 0.71$), $\hat{\lambda}_{RD} = 0.27$ ($t = 4.57$), and $R^2 = 62\%$. And, using 25 size-BM portfolios, which are exogenous to the empirical ZCAPM, we obtain: (1) $\hat{\alpha} = 0.76$ ($t = 3.20$), (2) $\hat{\lambda}_g = -0.16$ ($t = -0.69$), $\hat{\lambda}_{RD} = 0.37$ ($t = 4.66$), and $R^2 = 88\%$. These results are similar to those using the CRSP index (instead of portfolio g) in Chapter 7 and therefore further support the empirical ZCAPM. This similarity is not surprising in view of the fact that, in our analysis period from 1965 to 2018, the average daily market returns of portfolio *g* and the CRSP index are close to one another (viz., 0.0446% per day and 0.0413%, respectively) and share a high correlation coefficient equal to 0.87.

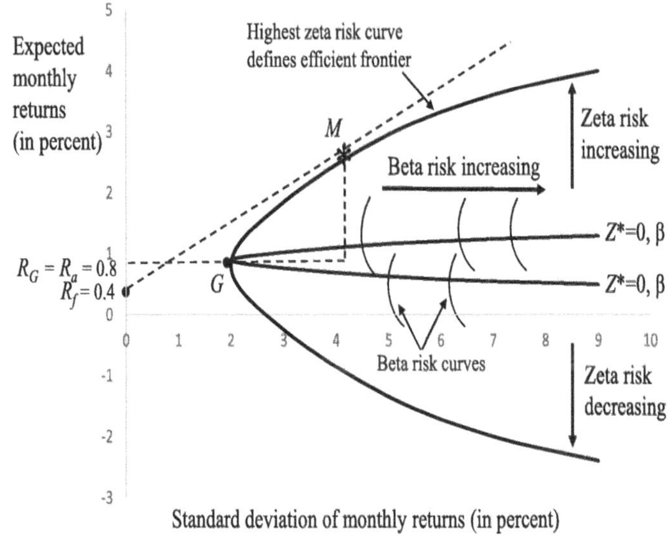

Fig. 10.2 This graph illustrates the effects of beta and zeta risks in the theoretical ZCAPM on the investment parabola with short positions allowed. Here we assume that minimum variance portfolio G is used as the market index. Beta risk and zeta risk are based on expected *G* returns and the total return dispersion of individual stock returns in portfolio *G*, respectively. Zeta risk curves share a common vertex at portfolio *G* and plot from left to right in the graph. Zeta risk increases from the lower to upper boundaries of the parabola. Beta risk curves plot vertically and intersect zeta risk curves. Beta risk imparts an upward or downward slope to each zeta risk curve depending on if beta is greater or less than one. The latticework of interlocking beta risk and zeta risk curves determine the expected returns of stocks within the parabola. The CAPM market portfolio *M* can be reached via a tangent ray from the riskless rate R_f (only if the location of the parabola is known) or the combination of moving horizontally along the axis of symmetry of the parabola at the expected return R_G and then upward based on zeta risk associated with market return dispersion (which shapes the width of the parabola) as well as beta risk related to portfolio *G*

Figure 10.2 is a theoretical depiction of the beta risk and zeta risk structure of the investment parabola. These two risks are orthogonal to one another and therefore take the form of a lattice. In the theoretical ZCAPM, the minimum variance portfolio G has beta $\beta_{G,G} = 1$ by definition and $Z^*_{G,G} = 0$. Here we allow short positions which result in two zeta risk curves with $Z^*_{i,G} = 0$: (1) one curve has beta risk for the ith asset greater than one (i.e., as $\beta_{i,G}$ associated with portfolio G increases, the zeta risk curve slopes upward), and (2) a second curve has beta risk for the ith asset less than one (i.e., as $\beta_{i,G}$ associated with portfolio G becomes more negative, the zeta risk curve slopes downward). The CAPM's market portfolio M can be reached via the tangent line from the riskless rate (i.e., $R_f = 0.4\%$ per month) to the efficient frontier of the parabola; however, this geometry assumes that the location of the parabola is known, which is not possible in the real world. Another way to reach market portfolio M is the combination of moving horizontally along the axis of symmetry at the average market return (i.e., $R_G = R_a = 0.8\%$ per month) and then upward based on increasing zeta risk levels associated with market return dispersion. Market portfolio M lies on the highest zeta risk curve on the efficient frontier. If M's expected return is used in the CAPM, it has $\beta_{M,M} = 1$ by definition; however, M's beta in the ZCAPM ($\beta_{M,G}$) is greater than one according to the theoretical graph in Fig. 10.2. Certainly these new ideas about the investment parabola and how beta and zeta risks affect asset returns within the parabola are deserving of further research.

As proven in Chapter 3, the theoretical ZCAPM is a special case of Black's zero-beta CAPM. Empirical specifications of theoretical models are always less than perfect representations. A major advantage of our ZCAPM is that the independent variables—namely, average market returns and their cross-sectional return dispersion—are readily estimable from available daily return series in financial markets. Using these data series, we employed the EM algorithm to estimate the statistical parameters in the empirical ZCAPM. For various reasons, we set the intercept (alpha) term equal to zero empirical ZCAPM.[11] In this regard, research is suggested to develop

[11] Some researchers compare different asset pricing models using in-sample tests of estimated in the coefficients in time-series multifactor models. As observed by Ferson et al. (2019), the well-known Gibbons et al. (1989) test compares the maximum squared Sharpe ratios of a set of test assets, or $S^2(r)$, and a portfolio of factors, or $S^2(f)$. The difference

a time-series regression specification of the empirical ZCAPM model that optimizes the EM algorithm and contains a nonzero intercept, in addition to statistical tests of beta and zeta parameters as well as a goodness-of-fit measure.

Empirical ZCAPM estimates of beta and zeta coefficients based on the EM algorithm are good measures of systematic market risks among stocks as evidenced by their success in predicting their relative future returns. Repeating the earlier citation of Fama and MacBeth (1973, p. 613) in Chapter 6: "As a normative theory the model only has content if there is some relation between future returns and estimates of risk that can be made on the basis of current information." In terms of out-of-sample stock return evidence documented in this book, the empirical ZCAPM outshines extant asset pricing models. Given the ZCAPM's strong performance in out-of-sample tests, more work is warranted in the following areas:

- Investigations of the ZCAPM in explaining other anomalous long/short return factors would extend our results on dispelling the size, value, profit, capital investment, and momentum anomalies.
- Replication of our analyses would be worthwhile using other samples of stock returns (including stocks in other countries) in addition to different asset classes, such as bonds, commodities, currencies, and real estate.
- Development of an industry factor to supplement the ZCAPM's average market return and return dispersion factors for usage with industry portfolios or portfolios with substantial sector weights.
- Applications of the ZCAPM to the cost of equity (and capital), event study analyses, and other finance topics that benefit from an asset pricing model are recommended.
- Further work on practical applications of the ZCAPM to portfolio investments and securities trading is possible.

$S^2(r) - S^2(f)$ equals a quadratic form of a multifactor model's alpha and therefore measures mispricing error. This modified GRS test approach has been used by researchers to compare asset pricing models (e.g., see MacKinlay 1995; Barillas and Shanken 2017, 2018; Barillas et al. 2018; Fama and French 2018). In a recent working paper, Ferson et al. (2019) extended previous GRS tests to provide asymptotic standard errors for asset pricing tests and model comparisons with conditioning information. An area of future study is the development of similar methods for estimating and testing mispricing error in the empirical ZCAPM.

Regarding practical applications, we believe that the greatest potential future contribution of our ZCAPM lies in the area of professional investment management. A major problem exists with unfunded pension liabilities in the U.S., Europe, and other countries. Millions of retirees depend on pensions for financial security in their golden years. One way to mitigate looming shortfalls affecting pensioners is to earn higher returns per unit risk on their savings. Pension funds, mutual funds, and other institutional investors could use ZCAPM technology to boost diversified investment performance. Likewise, exchange traded funds (ETFs) could be developed based on ZCAPM principles. In any of these applications, we recommend that risk be controlled by managers to offer products spanning a spectrum of risk preferences that earn commensurate returns.

10.4 Final Remarks

Dualism is an important concept in many philosophies, including *epistemology* (e.g., being and thought, subject and object, etc.), *metaphysics* (e.g., matter and spirit, body and mind, etc.), and *theology* (e.g., God and matter, good and evil, etc.). Aristotle used dualisms such as matter and form, immaterial and material substance, and body and soul. The ancient Chinese concept of *yin and yang* balances opposite natural forces. Some examples of this dualistic principle are dark–bright, fire–water, expanding–contracting, winter–summer, north–south, disorder–order, negative–positive, etc. It is thought that the mixture of two opposites interacts simultaneously in a dynamic system. Because they complement one another, the whole is greater than the sum of its parts.

Analogously, our ZCAPM has dualistic roots that take into account both negative and positive sensitivity to return dispersion (*RD*). Depending on this sensitivity, return dispersion can have opposite return effects on different assets, all else the same. To capture these dual market forces, we specify the empirical ZCAPM estimated via the expectation–maximization (EM) algorithm. Our empirical ZCAPM is a mixture model of two models with an average market return factor plus either positive or negative sensitivity to the *RD* factor. Together, the two models produce zeta risk, which combines the probability p of positive sensitivity and probability $1-p$ of negative sensitivity to *RD*. These opposite *RD* sensitivities, in addition to beta risk associated with sensitivity to average market returns, create the architecture of the mean-variance investment parabola at any given time and thereby influence equilibrium asset prices.

As discussed in Chapter 7, researchers have found that cross-sectional return anomalies, such as size, value, momentum, etc., tend to dissipate after their publication in academic literature.[12] Is this true for return dispersion in the empirical ZCAPM? Will publication of this book diminish the significance of *RD* loadings? Is the empirical ZCAPM a false discovery? We encourage researchers to address these questions. Our sincere hope is that researchers will make use of the ZCAPM in their academic and professional finance activities. Certainly tests of time and widespread usage are the ultimate challenges for any asset pricing model. In our opinion, given that the average market return and market return dispersion characterize the level and shape of the mean-variance investment parabola, these ZCAPM factors have as little chance of disappearing as the parabola itself.

In closing, the Preface of the book recounted that our initial research goal was to find out what Fischer Black may have learned about the zero-beta ZCAPM during his days at Goldman Sachs but did not publish for proprietary reasons. After the Fama and French (1992, 1993) papers on the failure of the CAPM and proposed three-factor model were published, Black (1993) openly criticized the size and value factors in their model as the result of data mining. Was his criticism so overt due to a deep understanding of the zero-beta CAPM? It is not a great stretch of the imagination to contemplate the difference in returns between efficient portfolios and zero-beta portfolio counterparts on the mean-variance parabola and conjecture that this difference was related to return dispersion in the population of stock returns in the market. And, he may well have viewed the size and value factors in the three-factor model as rough measures of return dispersion that had some empirical merit but were far from adequate measures of the cross-sectional standard deviation of returns that shapes the width of the parabola. Even though these possibilities are intriguing, we must leave unanswered the question of whether Black had discovered our empirical ZCAPM or close approximation thereof. Whatever the case may be, he motivated us to take a closer look at the zero-beta CAPM, derive the special case of the ZCAPM based on market return dispersion, and develop the empirical ZCAPM for estimation and testing purposes.

[12] See Schwert (2003), Chordia et al. (2014), Hou et al. (2015), McLean and Pontiff (2016), Green et al. (2016), Harvey (2017), Linnainmaa and Roberts (2018), and others.

Appendix A: Review of the Empirical ZCAPM and Cross-Sectional Test Methods

The *theoretical ZCAPM* was mathematically derived as a special case of Black (1972) zero-beta CAPM in Chapter 3.[13] According to the ZCAPM, the expected return on the ith asset can be defined as:

$$E(R_{it}) - R_{ft} = \beta_{i,a}[E(R_{at}) - R_{ft}] + Z^{*}_{i,a}\sigma_{at}, \qquad \text{(A10.1)}$$

where $E(R_{at})$ is the expected market return based on the average return of all assets at time t (rather than a proxy m for the theoretical market portfolio M in Sharpe [1964] CAPM), R_{ft} is the riskless rate, $\beta_{i,a}$ is the beta risk coefficient measuring sensitivity to expected excess market returns, σ_{at} is the cross-sectional standard deviation of all asset returns (or return dispersion denoted RD) at time t, and $Z^{*}_{i,a}$ is the zeta risk coefficient measuring dichotomous positive or negative sensitivity to return dispersion.[14] An asterisk is added, or $Z^{*}_{i,a}$, to indicate that zeta risk is linked to orthogonal portfolios I^{*} and ZI^{*} on the mean-variance investment parabola. These two portfolios correspond to portfolio I^{*} on the efficient frontier and its orthogonal counterpart zero-beta portfolio ZI^{*} on the lower boundary of the parabola. They represent a unique pair of portfolios with equal return variances.

To take into account the dual opposing effects of RD on asset returns in the theoretical ZCAPM , in Chapter 4 we proposed a novel regression model for estimation purposes. More specifically, we allow the sign of the zeta risk coefficient in ZCAPM relation (A10.1) to change over time. The following *empirical ZCAPM* is specified as a time-series regression model[15]:

$$R_{it} - R_{ft} = \beta_{i,a}(R_{at} - R_{ft}) + Z_{i,a}D_{it}\sigma_{at} + u_{it}, \quad t = 1, \cdots, T \qquad \text{(A10.2)}$$

where $R_{it} - R_{ft}$ is the excess return for the ith stock portfolio (or stock) over the riskless rate at time t, $\beta_{i,a}$ measures sensitivity to excess average market returns equal to $R_{at} - R_{ft}$, $Z_{i,a}$ measures sensitivity to return dispersion

[13] See also earlier work in Liu et al. (2012) and Liu (2013).

[14] Because RD is not a traded factor, its factor loading is denoted as Z rather than β to distinguish it from commonly-used zero-investment factors that are tradeable.

[15] See also Liu et al. (2020).

σ_{at} (or RD), D_{it} is a signal variable with values +1 and −1 representing positive and negative RD effects on stock returns, respectively, and $u_{it} \sim$ iid $N(0, \sigma_i^2)$. Note that no mispricing error (i.e., $\alpha_i = 0$) is included in empirical ZCAPM Eq. (A10.2) due to: (1) no error term in theoretical ZCAPM relation (A10.1); (2) our empirical tests of the empirical ZCAPM are based on out-of-sample or one-month-ahead returns and, therefore, α_i is not needed to improve in-sample data fitting; and (3) experiments with an α_i terms did not improve in-sample data fitting (i.e., lower residual variance in the regression model).

The value of signal variable D_{it} is unknown and therefore is a latent or hidden variable. However, D_{it} can be defined as an independent random variable with the following two-point distribution:

$$D_{it} = \begin{cases} +1 & \text{with probability } p_i \\ -1 & \text{with probability } 1 - p_i, \end{cases} \tag{A10.3}$$

where p_i (or $1 - p_i$) is the probability of a positive (or negative) return dispersion effect, and D_{it} is independent of u_{it}. To estimate parameters $\theta_i = (\beta_{i,a}, Z_{i,a}, p_i)$ in the empirical ZCAPM, we utilize an expectation–maximization (EM) algorithm (see Dempster et al. 1977).[16]

Given that $E(D_{it}) = 2p_i - 1$, we can write the marginal form of the empirical ZCAPM as follows:

$$R_{it} - R_{ft} = \beta_{i,a}(R_{at} - R_{ft}) + Z^*_{i,a}\sigma_{at} + u^*_{it}, \quad t = 1, \cdots, T, \tag{A10.4}$$

where $\beta_{i,a}$ is the beta risk coefficient, $Z_i^* = Z_i(2p_i - 1)$ is the zeta risk coefficient, u^*_{it} is the error term, and other notation is as before. Here the variance of the error term u^*_{it} depends on return dispersion as follows:

$$\text{Var}(u^*_{it}) = 4\,p_i(1 - p_i)\,Z^2_{i,a}\,\sigma^2_{at} + \text{Var}(u_{it}). \tag{A10.5}$$

For purposes of Fama and MacBeth (1973) cross-sectional tests of the empirical ZCAPM, we incorporate estimates of beta and zeta risk coeffi-

[16] For further statistical studies on EM, see Jones and McLachlan (1990), McLachlan and Peel (2000), McLachlan and Krishnan (2008), among others. Wikipedia provides a good overview of the EM algorithm and additional literature citations. For finance studies that utilize EM in their analyses, see Wu (1983), Kon (1984), Rudd (1991), Asquith et al. (1998), McLachlan and Krishnan (2008), Harvey and Liu (2016), Chen et al. (2017), and citations therein.

cients from time-series regression (A10.4) above into the following cross-sectional OLS regression:

$$R_{iT+1} - R_{fT+1} = \lambda_0 + \lambda_a \hat{\beta}_{i,a} + \lambda_{RD} \hat{Z}^*_{i,a} + u_{it}, i = 1, ..., N, \quad (A10.6)$$

where the coefficients denoted λ_a and λ_{RD} provide estimates of the market prices of the beta and zeta risk factors in percent terms, respectively, and other notation is as before. The estimated risk premium λ_a (λ_{RD}) approximates a mimicking portfolio return that is long stocks with higher betas (zetas) and short stocks with lower betas (zetas).

Beta risk loadings are benchmarked to one on average for the average market index. Also, beta loadings are largely time invariant with similar values using daily or monthly returns. By comparison, zeta risk loadings are not benchmarked to one, and the holding period can affect their estimated values. The market price $\hat{\lambda}_{RD}$ associated with RD can be interpreted as the risk premium per unit zeta risk. Because zeta loadings are estimated in a time-series regression (A10.4) with daily returns, and one-month-ahead excess returns are used as the dependent variable in cross-sectional regression equation (A10.6), we rescale $\hat{Z}^*_{i,a}$ from a daily to monthly basis as follows:

$$R_{iT+1} - R_{fT+1} = \lambda_0 + \lambda_a \hat{\beta}_{i,a} + \lambda_{RD} \hat{Z}^*_{i,a} N_{T+1} + +u_{it}, i = 1, ..., N, \quad (A10.7)$$

where N_{T+1} is the number of trading days in a month $T + 1$ (i.e., 21 days), $Z^*_{i,T} N_{T+1}$ is the monthly estimated zeta risk, and λ_{RD} is the monthly risk premium associated with zeta risk. The risk premium $\hat{\lambda}_{RD}$ per unit zeta risk is unchanged by this rescaling. Without rescaling $Z^*_{i,T}$ up to a monthly basis, much larger λ_{RD} estimates would not be comparable to λ_a estimates associated with beta loadings.

We provide Matlab programs for estimating the empirical ZCAPM and conducting cross-sectional regression tests at the end of the book in the Compendium. Also, R programs can be downloaded from GitHub (https://github.com/zcapm). R is a free software environment available on the internet. Our R programs run faster in terms of estimating the empirical ZCAPM than the Matlab programs. Also, the GitHub website provides Matlab programs as well as Python programs.

Bibliography

Asquith, D., Jones, J., & Kieschnick, R. (1998). Evidence on price stabilization and underpricing in early IPO returns. *Journal of Finance*, *53*, 1759–1773.

Barillas, F., & Shanken, J. (2017). Which alpha? *Review of Financial Studies*, *30*, 1316–1338.

Barillas, F., & Shanken, J. (2018). Comparing asset pricing models. *Journal of Finance*, *73*, 715–754.

Barillas, F., Kan, R., Robotti, C., & Shanken, J. (2018). *Model comparison with Sharpe ratios* (Working Paper). Emory University, University of Toronto, and University of Georgia.

Black, F. (1972). Capital market equilibrium with restricted borrowing. *Journal of Business*, *45*, 444–454.

Black, F. (1993). Beta and return. *Journal of Portfolio Management*, *20*, 8–18.

Black, F., Jensen, M. C., & Scholes, M. (1972). The capital asset pricing model: Some empirical tests. In M. C. Jensen (Ed.), *Studies in the Theory of Capital Markets*. New York, NY: Praeger.

Blitz, D. (2020). Factor performance 2010–2019: A lost decade? *The Journal of Index Investing*, *12*, forthcoming.

Breeden, N. D. (1979). An intertemporal asset pricing model with stochastic consumption and investment opportunities. *Journal of Financial Economics*, *7*, 265–296.

Brown, S. J. (2000). The efficient market hypothesis, the Financial Analysts Journal, and the professional status of investment management. *Financial Analysts Journal*, *76*, 5–14.

Carhart, M. M. (1997). On persistence in mutual fund performance. *Review of Financial Studies*, *33*, 2134–2179.

Chen, Y., Cliff, M., & Zhao, H. (2017). Hedge funds: The good, the bad, and the lucky. *Journal of Financial and Quantitative Analysis*, *52*, 1081–1109.

Chordia, T., Goyal, A., & Saretto, A. (2020). Anomalies and false rejections. *Review of Financial Studies*, *33*, 2134–2179.

Chordia, T., Subrahmanyam, A., & Tong, Q. (2014). Have capital market anomalies attenuated in the recent era of high liquidity and trading activity? *Journal of Accounting Economics*, *58*, 41–58.

Cochrane, J. H. (1991). Production-based asset pricing and the link between stock returns and economic fluctuations. *Journal of Finance*, *46*, 209–237.

Cochrane, J. H. (2005). *Asset Pricing* (Rev. ed.). Princeton, NJ: Princeton University Press.

Daniel, K., Mota, L., Rottke, S., & Santos, T. (2020). The cross-section of risk and returns. *Review of Financial Studies*, *33*, 1927–1979.

Dempster, A. P., Laird, N. M., & Rubin, D. B. (1977). Maximum likelihood from incomplete data via the EM algorithm. *Journal of the Royal Statistical Society*, *39*, 1–38.

Fama, E. F. (1970). Efficient capital markets: A review of theory and empirical work. *Journal of Finance, 25*, 383–417.
Fama, E. F., & French, K. R. (1992). The cross-section of expected stock returns. *Journal of Finance, 47*, 427–465.
Fama, E. F., & French, K. R. (1993). The cross-section of expected returns. *Journal of Financial Economics, 33*, 3–56.
Fama, E. F., & French, K. R. (1995). Size and book-to-market factors in earnings and returns. *Journal of Finance, 50*, 131–156.
Fama, E. F., & French, K. R. (1996). The CAPM is wanted, dead or alive. *Journal of Finance, 51*, 1947–1958.
Fama, E. F., & French, K. R. (2004). The capital asset pricing model: Theory and evidence. *Journal of Economic Perspectives, 18*, 25–46.
Fama, E. F., & French, K. R. (2015). A five-factor asset pricing model. *Journal of Financial Economics, 116*, 1–22.
Fama, E. F., & French, K. R. (2018). Choosing factors. *Journal of Financial Economics, 128*, 234–252.
Fama, E. F., & French, K. R. (2020). Comparing cross-section and time-series factor models. *Review of Financial Studies, 33*, 1892–1926.
Fama, E. F., & MacBeth, J. D. (1973). Risk, return, and equilibrium: Empirical tests. *Journal of Political Economy, 81*, 607–636.
Ferson, W. E., & Harvey, C. R. (1991). The variation of economic risk premiums. *Journal of Political Economy, 99*, 385–415.
Ferson, W. E., & Harvey, C. R. (1996). *Conditioning variables and the cross-section of stock returns* (Working Paper). Duke University.
Ferson, W., Siegel, A. F., & Wang, J. L. (2019). *Asymptotic distributions of tests of portfolio efficiency and factor model comparisons with conditioning information* (Working Paper). University of Southern California and University of Washington.
Gibbons, M. R., Ross, S. A., & Shanken, J. (1989). A test of the efficiency of a given portfolio. *Econometrica, 57*, 1121–1152.
Green, J., Hand, J. R. M., & Zhang, X. F. (2016). The characteristics that provide independent information about average U.S. monthly stock returns. *Review of Financial Studies, 30*, 1–80.
Harvey, C. (2017). The scientific outlook in financial economics. *Journal of Finance, 72*, 1399–1440.
Harvey, C. R., & Liu, Y. (2016). *Rethinking performance evaluation* (Working Paper No. 22134). Cambridge, MA: National Bureau of Economic Research.
Harvey, C. R., Liu, Y., & Zhu, H. (2015). ... and the cross-section of expected returns. *Review of Financial Studies, 29*, 5–68.
Hou, K., Mo, H., Xue, C., & Zhang, L. (2018). q^5 (Working Paper). Ohio State University.

Hou, K., Xue, C., & Zhang, L. (2015). Digesting anomalies: An investment approach. *Review of Financial Studies, 28*, 650–705.

Jones, P. N., & McLachlan, G. J. (1990). Algorithm AS 254: Maximum likelihood estimation from grouped and truncated data with finite normal mixture models. *Applied Statistics, 39*, 273–282.

Karolyi, G. A., & Nieuwerburgh, S. V. (2020). New methods for the cross-zection of returns. *Review of Financial Studies, 33*, 1879–1890.

Kon, S. (1984). Models of stock returns: A comparison. *Journal of Finance, 39*, 147–165.

Lettau, M., & Pelger, M. (2020). Factors that fit the time series and cross-section of stock returns. *Review of Financial Studies, 33*, 2274–2325.

Linnainmaa, J., & Roberts, M. (2018). The history of the cross-section of stock returns. *Review of Financial Studies, 31*, 2606–2649.

Lintner, J. (1965). The valuation of risk assets and the selection of risky investments in stock portfolios and capital budgets. *Review of Economics and Statistics, 47*, 13–37.

Liu, W. (2013). *A new asset pricing model based on the zero-beta CAPM: Theory and evidence* (Doctoral dissertation). Texas A&M University.

Liu, W., Kolari, J. W., & Huang, J. Z. (2012, October). *A new asset pricing model based on the zero-beta CAPM*. Presentation at the annual meetings of the Financial Management Association, Atlanta, GA.

Liu, W., Kolari, J. W., & Huang, J. Z. (2020, October). *Return dispersion and the cross-section of stock returns*. Presentation at the annual meetings of the Southern Finance Association, Palm Springs, CA.

Lucas, R. E. (1978). Asset prices in an exchange economy. *Econometrica, 46*, 1429–1445.

MacKinlay, A. C. (1995). Multifactor models do not explain deviations from the CAPM. *Journal of Financial Economics, 38*, 3–28.

MacKinlay, A. C., & Richardson, M. P. (1991). Using generalized method of moments to test mean/variance efficiency. *Journal of Finance, 46*, 511–527.

Markowitz, H. M. (1959). *Portfolio selection: Efficient diversification of investments*. New York, NY: Wiley.

McLachlan, G., & Peel, D. (2000). *Finite Mixture Models*. New York, NY: Wiley-Interscience.

McLachlan, G. J., & Krishnan, T. (2008). *The EM algorithm and extensions* (2nd ed.). New York, NY: Wiley.

McLean, D. R., & Pontiff, J. (2016). Does academic research destroy stock return predictability? *Journal of Finance, 71*, 5–32.

Merton, R. C. (1973). An intertemporal capital asset pricing model. *Econometrica, 41*, 867–887.

Mossin, J. (1966). Equilibrium in a capital asset market. *Econometrica, 34*, 768–783.

Prono, T. (2015). Market proxies as factors in linear asset pricing models: Still living with the Roll critique. *Journal of Empirical Finance, 31*, 36–53.

Roll, R. (1977). A critique of the asset pricing theory's tests, part I: On past and potential future testability of the theory. *Journal of Financial Economics, 4*, 129–176.

Ross, S. A. (1976). The arbitrage theory of capital asset pricing. *Journal of Economic Theory, 13*, 341–360.

Rudd, P. (1991). Extensions of estimation methods using the EM algorithm. *Journal of Econometrics, 49*, 305–341.

Schwert, G. W. (2003). Anomalies and market efficiency. In G. M. Constantinides, R. M. Stulz, & M. Harris (Eds.), *Handbook of the economics of finance* (Vol. 1, Part B, pp. 939–974). North Holland and Amsterdam, Netherlands: Elsevier.

Sharpe, W. F. (1964). Capital asset prices: A theory of market equilibrium under conditions of risk. *Journal of Finance, 19*, 425–442.

Stambaugh, R. F., & Yuan, Y. (2017). Mispricing factors. *Review of Financial Studies, 30*, 1270–1315.

Stulz, R. M. (1981). A model of international asset pricing. *Journal of Financial Economics, 9*, 383–406.

Stulz, R. M. (1995). International portfolio choice and asset pricing: An Integrative Survey, Chapter 6. In R. A. Jarrow, V. Maksimovic, & W. T. Ziemba, *Handbooks in operations research and management science* (Vol. 9, pp. 201–223). North-Holland, Amsterdam.

Thaler, R. H. (1999). The end of behavioral finance. *Financial Analysts Journal, 55*, 12–17.

Treynor, J. L. (1961). *Market value, time, and risk*. Unpublished manuscript.

Treynor, J. L. (1962). *Toward a theory of market value of risky assets*. Unpublished manuscript.

Wu, J. (1983). On the convergence properties of the EM algorithm. *Annals of Statistics, 11*, 95–103.

A New Model of Capital Asset Prices: Theory and Evidence

Compendium: Matlab Programs

This compendium provides Matlab programs for analyses in this book. The programs are used to: (1) estimate the empirical ZCAPM, and (2) conduct cross-sectional regression tests of the empirical ZCAPM. The expectation-maximization (EM) algorithm is employed to estimate ZCAPM regression model parameters.

If the cross-sectional tests are not needed, you can output the empirical ZCAPM regression results. To do this, uncomment code in the main.m file by removing the percentage symbol: %xlswrite('ts_coeff',ts_coeff). The results will be stored in an excel file called *ts_coeff*. In this file, the first column is beta (β), second column is zeta (Z), and third column is the probability (p) that Z is positive in sign. To get Z^*, simply calculate $Z(2p-1)$. The scale of Z^* is for daily returns. To convert to a monthly return scale, simply multiply Z^* by 21 as used in our codes (see Eq. (5.5) in Chapter 5).

J. W. Kolari et al., *A New Model of Capital Asset Prices*,
https://doi.org/10.1007/978-3-030-65197-8

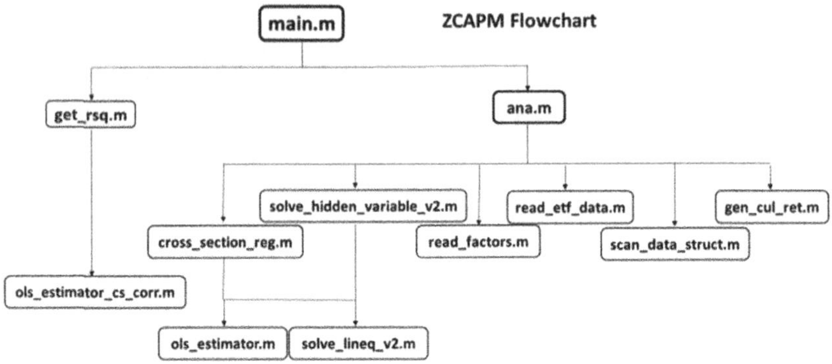

main.m

- The main function of the program, which assigns the start date and prediction window, calculates cross-sectional regression estimates for λ_a and λ_{RD} and their t-statistics in the second step of the Fama and MacBeth procedure, and outputs results (i.e., the filename is named *results*). Run this file to start all codes.
- Called by: n/a
- Calls: ana.m, get_rsq.m
- The % symbol comments out code or wording from being run in the Matlab program. Code can be uncommented by removing this symbol.

```
function main()

date_start=196501;
%date_start=199001;           %%%% second half for split data results

holding_unit=[1,3,6,9,12,24];  %%%% number of months rolled forward each time

num_roll_window=[6,12];       %%%% number of months used to estimate beta and zeta
for ii=2:2
roll_window_mon=num_roll_window(ii);
for j=1:1
holding_mon=holding_unit(j);
[ts_coeff, ts_coeff1,cs_coeff,ret_mon,factors_a]...
        =ana(date_start,roll_window_mon,holding_mon);
  %%%%% rolling month approach
dim=size(cs_coeff);
[rsq,beta,t_stat,t1]=get_rsq(ts_coeff1,ret_mon,factors_a);  %%%% single regression to get R²

%%%% The following codes calculate the average estimates of λa and λRD, their t-statistics, and
other outputs that appear in the results file %%%%
num_para=(dim(2)-1)/2;
results=NaN(2*num_para+1,2+1);
for i=1:num_para
  results(i,1)=mean(cs_coeff(:,2*i-1));
  results(i,2)=results(i,1)/std(cs_coeff(:,2*i-1))*sqrt(dim(1)-1);
end
%output shanken test
        results(5,3)=t1(1);
        results(6,3)=t1(2);
        results(7,3)=t1(3);
results(num_para+1,1)=rsq;
results(num_para+2,1:2)=[beta(1),t_stat(1)];
results(num_para+3,1:2)=[beta(2),t_stat(2)];
results(num_para+4,1:2)=[beta(3),t_stat(3)];
xlswrite('results',results);
%xlswrite('ts_coeff',ts_coeff); %%% output time-series regression results for empirical ZCAPM
%xlswrite('cs_coeff',cs_coeff);
%xlswrite('ret_mon',ret_mon)
end
end
```

ana.m

- The workhorse of the program, this subroutine generates coefficients which are then used in both main.m and get_rsq.m to output the final beta, zeta, and t-statistic outputs.
- Called by: main.m

- Calls: read_etf_data.m, read_factors.m, scan_data_struct.m, solve_hidden_variable_v2.m, cross_section_reg.m, and gen_cul_ret.m

```
function [ts_coeff, ts_coeff1,cs_coeff,ret_mon,factors_a]...
   =ana(date_start,roll_window,holding_mon)

[ff25,ind47,own25,bm100,bmop25,bminv25,opinv25]=read_etf_data;
%%%% Read Excel data files containing daily returns of test asset portfolios %%%%

%%%% Choose different test assets, change as your data structure changes %%%%
%%%% Only one stock_ret= should be uncommented at a time %%%%
stock_ret=ff25;
%stock_ret=ind47;
%stock_ret=own25;
%stock_ret=[ff25,ind47(:,2:48)];
%stock_ret=[ff25,ind47(:,2:48),own25(:,2:26)];

%stock_ret=bm100;
%stock_ret=bm100(:,1:21);                    %%%% bottom 20
%stock_ret=[bm100(:,1),bm100(:,22:end)];     %%%%% top 80
%stock_ret=bm100(:,1:51);                    %%%% bottom 50
%stock_ret=[bm100(:,1),bm100(:,52:end)];     %%%% bottom 50

%stock_ret=bmop25;
%stock_ret=bminv25;
%stock_ret=opinv25;

%%%% Split data in half (as robustness check using subperiods) %%%%
%stock_ret=ff25(1:6538,:);
%stock_ret=ff25(6287:end,:);

%stock_ret=ind47(1:6538,:);
%stock_ret=ind47(6287:end,:);

%stock_ret=own25(1:6538,:);
%stock_ret=own25(6287:end,:);
```

```
%stock_ret=[ff25(1:6538,:),ind47(1:6538,2:48)];
%stock_ret=[ff25(6287:end,:),ind47(6287:end,2:48)];

%stock_ret=[ff25(1:6538,:),ind47(1:6538,2:48),own25(1:6538,2:26)];
%stock_ret=[ff25(6287:end,:),ind47(6287:end,2:48),own25(6287:end,2:26)]; %%%% using the
above codes, choose different test assets or their combinations %%%%

dim_ret=size(stock_ret);
factors=read_factors;                    %%%% read factors from data file
%%%% Factors for split data (optional) %%%%
%factors=factors(1:6538,:);              %%%% first half
%factors=factors(6287:end,:);            %%%% second half


%%%% Get row numbers in daily data for each calendar month %%%%
[data_nm,data_str]=scan_data_struct(int32(factors(:,1)/100));
dim=size(data_nm);
for i=1:dim(1)
   if (date_start==data_nm(i,1))
      pos_i=i;
      break;
   end
end

%%%% All factors used for Shanken t-statistic if needed %%%%
factors_a=factors(data_str(pos_i-roll_window,1):data_str(dim(1)-1,2),2:4);

cs_coeff=[]; %%%% empty dataset to store results later
ts_coeff=[];
ret_mon=[];
ts_coeff1=[];

for itr_pd=pos_i:holding_mon:dim(1)
   factors_pr=factors(data_str(itr_pd-roll_window,1):data_str(itr_pd-1,2),2:4); % factors for time
series regression
   regress_ret=stock_ret(data_str(itr_pd-roll_window,1):data_str(itr_pd-1,2),2:dim_ret(2));
   % return for time series regression

   out_sampl_ret_pr=stock_ret(data_str(itr_pd,1):data_str(itr_pd+holding_mon-
1,2),2:dim_ret(2))...
      -factors(data_str(itr_pd,1):data_str(itr_pd+holding_mon-1,2),4)...
      *ones(1,dim_ret(2)-1); %%%% return for out-of-sample month in cross-sectional regression

   coeff=solve_hidden_variable_v2(regress_ret,factors_pr);%%%% time-series ZCAPM regression
   coeff_pr=[coeff(:,1),coeff(:,2).*(2*coeff(:,3)-1)*21];     %%%% 21 trading days per month
ts_coeff_i=[ts_coeff;coeff_pr];            %%%% output results for time-series regression only
```

```
    ts_coeff=ts_coeff_i;
    ts_coeffl_i=[ts_coeffl;coeff_pr];  %%%% time-series results used later in cross-sectional test
    ts_coeffl=ts_coeffl_i;

    out_sample_ret=gen_cul_ret(out_sampl_ret_pr);
    out_sample_mon=out_sample_ret(end,:)/holding_mon;
    %out_sample_mon=((1+out_sample_ret(end,:)/100).^(1/holding_mon)-1)*100;
    cs_coeff_pr=cross_section_reg(out_sample_mon,coeff_pr);%%%% cross-sectional regression
    ret_mon_i=[ret_mon;out_sample_mon(end,:)];
    ret_mon=ret_mon_i;
    cs_coeff_i=[cs_coeff;cs_coeff_pr];
    cs_coeff=cs_coeff_i;
end
```

get_rsq.m

The rolling cross-sectional regression approach does not generate an R^2 value. In this program, time-series for λ_a and λ_{RD} coefficients and out-of-sample monthly returns are averaged for each stock. One cross-sectional regression is estimated to generate an R^2 value. Coefficients for beta and alpha are stored and output in the main.m file also. To adjust for the cross-correlation problem, ols_estimator_cs_cor is used, in which the Shanken *t*-statistic is computed to adjust estimation errors in betas.

- Calculates the R^2 value, a goodness-of-fit measure of the cross-sectional regression model.
- Called by: main.m
- Calls: ols_estimator_cs_corr.m

```
function [rsq,beta_hat,t_stat,t1]=get_rsq(coeff,ret_mon,factors_a)

mean_ret=mean(ret_mon);
dim=size(ret_mon);
dim_cff=size(coeff);

mean_cff=zeros(dim(2),dim_cff(2));

for j=1:dim_cff(2)
   for i=1:dim(1)
      mean_cff(:,j)=mean_cff(:,j)+coeff((i-1)*dim(2)+1:i*dim(2),j);
   end
end

mean_cff=mean_cff/dim(1);

X=[ones(dim(2),1),mean_cff];
Y=mean_ret';
factors=factors_a(:,1:2);  %%%% for Shanken t-statistic

[beta_hat,rs,t_stat,t1,u_hat]=ols_estimator_cs_corr(X,Y,ret_mon,coeff,factors);

rsq=rs;
```

ols_estimator_cs_corr.m

- This function takes the data and calculates estimates of beta_hat, rsqr, t_stat, t1, and u_hat after adjusting for cross-correlation in the single regression approach. Note that t1 computes the Shanken *t*-statistics to adjust errors in beta estimations.
- Called by: get_rsq.m
- Calls: n/a

```
function [beta_hat,rsqr,t_stat,t1,u_hat]=ols_estimator_cs_corr(X,Y,ret,coeff,factors)

%%%% OLS estimation %%%%
dim_r=size(ret);
dim=size(Y);
beta_hat = inv(X'*X)*X'*Y;                 %%%% OLS estimation of beta
u_hat = Y - X*beta_hat;                    %%%% estimated residual
s = (u_hat'*u_hat)/(dim(1)-1)*inv(X'*X);  %%%% estimated covariance matrix
se = sqrt(diag(s));

%%%% define variables needed for Shanken test
beta_no_cons=beta_hat(2:end,:);
sig_f=cov(factors)*21;
c=beta_no_cons'*inv(sig_f)*beta_no_cons;
dim_s=size(sig_f);
sig_f_hat=zeros(dim_s(1)+1,dim_s(2)+1);
sig_f_hat(2:end,2:end)=sig_f;

%%%% variance matrix %%%%
ss=inv(X'*X)*X'*(cov(ret)/dim_r(1))*X*inv(X'*X);  %%%% adjust for correlation
ss=inv(X'*X)*X'*(cov(ret)/dim_r(1))*X*inv(X'*X)*(1+c)+sig_f_hat/dim_f(1); %%%% for
Shanken t-statistic

sse= sqrt(diag(ss));                       %%%% standard errors of beta_hat
sse1= sqrt(diag(ss1));                     %%%% Shanken standard errors of beta_hat


t_stat = beta_hat./sse;                    %%%% t-statistic for beta_hat
t1=beta_hat./sse1;                         %%%% Shanken t-statistic for beta_hat

%p = 2*(1-tcdf(abs(t),dim(1)-1));          %%%% p-value for the t-statistic

y_av=0;

for i=1:dim(1)
   y_av=y_av+Y(i);
end
y_av=y_av/dim(1);

err_y=0;
for i=1:dim(1)
   err_y=err_y+(Y(i)-y_av)^2;
end
rsqr=1.0-(dim(1)-1)/(dim(1)-dim(2))*(u_hat'*u_hat)/err_y;
```

ols_estimator.m

- This function takes the data and calculates estimates of beta_hat, rsqr, t_stat, and u_hat (simple OLS regression).
- Called by: cross_section_reg.m, solve_hidden_variable_v2.m
- Calls: n/a

```
%%%% OLS estimation %%%%
dim=size(Y);
beta_hat = inv(X'*X)*X'*Y;                    %%%% OLS estimation of beta
u_hat = Y - X*beta_hat;                       %%%% estimated residual
s = (u_hat'*u_hat)/(dim(1)-1)*inv(X'*X);      %%%% estimated covariance matrix
se = sqrt(diag(s));                           %%%% standard errors of beta_hat
t_stat = beta_hat./se;                        %%%% t-statistic for beta_hat
%p = 2*(1-tcdf(abs(t),dim(1)-1));              %%%% p-value for the t-statistic

y_av=0;
for i=1:dim(1)
   y_av=y_av+Y(i);
end
y_av=y_av/dim(1);

err_y=0;
for i=1:dim(1)
   err_y=err_y+(Y(i)-y_av)^2;
end
rsqr=1.0-(dim(1)-1)/(dim(1)-dim(2))*(u_hat'*u_hat)/err_y;
```

cross_section_reg.m

- This function manipulates two data sets within ana.m to create a row of data with 7 values, consisting of beta_hat, t_stat, and rs values. It estimates the cross-sectional OLS regression in the second step of the Fama and MacBeth procedure after reading parameters from the time-series empirical ZCAPM regression.
- Called by: ana.m
- Calls: ols_estimator.m

```
function coeff=cross_section_reg(assets,factors_pr)

dim=size(assets);
dim_f=size(factors_pr);

%%%% Cross-sectional regression %%%%
coeff=zeros(1,2*dim_f(2)+3);

X=[ones(dim(2),1),factors_pr];
Y=assets';
[beta_hat,rs,t_stat,u_hat]=ols_estimator(X,Y);

for i=1:dim_f(2)+1
   coeff(1,2*i-1)=beta_hat(i);
   coeff(1,2*i)=t_stat(i);
end
coeff(1,2*dim_f(2)+3)=rs;
```

solve_hidden_variable_v2.m

- This function is called in ana.m within a *for loop*. The function selects a slice of data to be processed through this function. Once this data is processed, output is continually stacked in a column in ana.m for final data matrix output to go to main.m. The output is a 3 element row of data, where the first two elements are the beta_hat values, and the third element is a probability element. It utilizes the EM algorithm to estimate the time-series empirical ZCAPM regression.
- Called by: ana.m
- Calls: ols_estimator.m, solve_lineq_v2.m

```
function coeff=solve_hidden_variable_v2(assets,mu_sigma)

dim=size(assets);
factors=mu_sigma(:,1:2);

num_factor=2;
%%%% ZCAPM regression (EM) %%%%
hat_pt=zeros(dim(1),1);
eta_p=zeros(dim(1),1);
eta_n=zeros(dim(1),1);
coeff=zeros(dim(2),num_factor+1);
for j=1:dim(2)
   X=factors(:,1);
   Y=assets(:,j)-mu_sigma(:,3);
   [beta_hat,rs,t_stat,u_hat]=ols_estimator(X,Y);
```

```
    Z=factors;
    for kk=1:dim(1)
      if (u_hat(kk)>=0)
        Z(kk,2)=factors(kk,2);
        hat_pt(kk,1)=1;
      else
        Z(kk,2)=-factors(kk,2);
        hat_pt(kk,1)=0;
      end
    end
    [beta_hat,rs,t_stat,u_hat]=ols_estimator(Z,Y);
    p_0=0;
    for kk=1:dim(1)
      if (hat_pt(kk,1)==1)
        p_0=p_0+hat_pt(kk,1);
      end
    end
    p_0=p_0/dim(1);
    sigma_0=mean(u_hat(:,1).*u_hat(:,1));

    delta=1;
    while (delta>0.001)
      for kk=1:dim(1)
        eta_p(kk,1)=exp(-(Y(kk,1)-beta_hat(1)*factors(kk,1)-beta_hat(2)*factors(kk,2))^2....
          /2/sigma_0);
        eta_n(kk,1)=exp(-(Y(kk,1)-beta_hat(1)*factors(kk,1)+beta_hat(2)*factors(kk,2))^2....
          /2/sigma_0);
        hat_pt(kk,1)=eta_p(kk,1)*p_0/(eta_p(kk,1)*p_0+eta_n(kk,1)*(1-p_0));
      end

      [beta_itr,hat_sigma,p]=solve_lineq_v2(Y,hat_pt,factors);

      diff=[abs((beta_itr(1)-beta_hat(1))/beta_hat(1)),abs((beta_itr(2)-beta_hat(2))/beta_hat(2)),...
        abs((p-p_0)/p_0),abs((hat_sigma-sigma_0)/sigma_0)];
      delta=max(diff);

      p_0=p;
      sigma_0=hat_sigma;
      beta_hat=beta_itr;
    end

    for i=1:num_factor
      coeff(j,i)=beta_hat(i);
    end
    coeff(j,num_factor+1)=p_0;
end
```

read_factors.m

- Loads the data for asset pricing factors input files into the program. Here the data set mu_sigma.xlsx contains both value-weighted market mean return and value-weighted market daily sigma (or cross-sectional return dispersion or *RD*). Only sigma is stored in factors and used later. The data set ff_factors_day.xlsx contains the three factors in the Fama and French three-factor model downloaded from Kenneth French's dataset. The market factor and riskless rate are stored in factors and used later. Our data starts from 1960, but our sample period starts from 1964. Therefore, factors only read rows starting from 1005 or 1006 in the original excel file. Users should change this row number based on their own data sources and structure. The data file must be stored within the same folder as Matlab codes – otherwise, a new path will need to be defined. Variable names appear in the first row of the data set.
- Called by: ana.m
- Calls: n/a

```
function factors=read_factors()

filename='mu_sigma.xlsx';
data1 = xlsread(filename);

filename='ff_factors_day.xlsx';
data2 = xlsread(filename);

factors=[data1(1005:end,1),data2(1006:end,2),...
   data1(1005:end,3)*100,data2(1006:end,6)]; %%%% combines the RD (sigma) and market
factor together
```

read_etf_data.m

- Loads data set files of daily stock returns for test asset portfolios into the program. The xlsx files starting with ff and ind47 are data downloaded from Kenneth French's website. Like factor data, all Excel data files need to be stored in the same folder as the codes. Users need to redefine which data and which row that Matlab reads based own their own data structure. Variable names appear in the first row.

- Called by: ana.m
- Calls: n/a

```
function [ff25,ind47,own25,bm100,bmop25,bminv25,opinv25]=read_etf_data()

filename='ff25_day_vw.xlsx';    %%%% 25 size-BM portfolios from Kenneth French website
ff25 = xlsread(filename);
ff25=ff25(1006:end,:);          %%%% row (date) that daily returns begin

filename='ind47_day_vw.xlsx';  %%%% 47 industry portfolios from Kenneth French website
ind47 = xlsread(filename);
ind47=ind47(1006:end,:);

filename='beta_zstar_assets.xlsx';
own25 = xlsread(filename);
own25=[own25(:,1),own25(:,2:end)*100]; %%%% 25 beta-zeta portfolios created by the authors

filename='ff_bm_100.xlsx';
bm100 = xlsread(filename);
bm100=bm100(1006:end,:);

filename='ff_bmop_25.xlsx';
bmop25 = xlsread(filename);
bmop25=bmop25(127:end,:);

filename='ff_bminv_25.xlsx';
bminv25 = xlsread(filename);
bminv25=bminv25(127:end,:);

filename='ff_opinv_25.xlsx';
opinv25 = xlsread(filename);
opinv25=opinv25(127:end,:);  %%%% other test asset portfolios from Kenneth French website
```

scan_data_struct.m

- Daily data in Matlab only contains rows instead of calendar date. Because our regression uses daily data within calendar time, this function gets the starting and ending row numbers for each corresponding calendar time. (e.g., rows from 1 to 22 in daily data files are days in January 1964)
- Called by: ana.m
- Calls: n/a

```
function [data_nm,data_str]=scan_data_struct(data)

dim=size(data);

data_ini=data(1,1);
data_inf=data_ini;
data_ps=zeros(1000,2);
data_ps(1,1)=1;
count=1;
for i=2:dim(1)
   if (data(i,1)~=data_ini)
      count=count+1;
      data_ps(count-1,2)=i-1;
      data_ps(count,1)=i;
      temp=[data_inf;data(i,1)];
      data_ini=data(i,1);
      data_inf=temp;
   end
end
data_ps(count,2)=dim(1);
data_str=data_ps(1:count,:);
data_nm=data_inf;
```

gen_cul_ret.m

- Compounding daily returns to get monthly returns. For each out-of-sample month, the monthly return is calculated by compounding all daily returns within the month.
- Called by: ana.m
- Calls: n/a

```
function cul_ret=gen_cul_ret(data)

dim=size(data);
cul_ret=zeros(dim(1),dim(2));
for i=1:dim(1)
   if (i>=2)
      cul_ret(i,:)=(1+data(i,:)/100).*(1+cul_ret(i-1,:))-1;
   else
      cul_ret(i,:)=data(i,:)/100;
   end
end
cul_ret=cul_ret*100;
```

solve_lineq_v2.m

- Solves linear equations for the empirical ZCAPM.
- Called by: solve_hidden_variable_v2.m
- Calls: n/a

```
function [hat_beta,hat_sigma,p]=solve_lineq_v2(Y,hat_pt,factors)

dim=size(Y);

a=zeros(2,2);
b=zeros(2,1);
hat_dt=2*hat_pt-1;

a(1,1)=sum(factors(:,1).*factors(:,1));
a(1,2)=sum(hat_dt(:,1).*factors(:,1).*factors(:,2));
a(2,1)=sum(hat_dt(:,1).*factors(:,1).*factors(:,2));
a(2,2)=sum(factors(:,2).*factors(:,2));

b(1,1)=sum(Y(:,1).*factors(:,1));
b(2,1)=sum(hat_dt(:,1).*Y(:,1).*factors(:,2));

hat_beta=linsolve(a,b);
p=mean(hat_pt(:,1));

sigma_t=zeros(dim(1),1);

for i=1:dim(1)
   sigma_t(i,1)=(Y(i,1)-hat_beta(1,1)*factors(i,1))^2 ...
      -2*(Y(i,1)-hat_beta(1,1)*factors(i,1))* ...
      hat_beta(2,1)*hat_dt(i,1)*factors(i,2)...
      +hat_beta(2,1)^2*factors(i,2)^2;
end
hat_sigma=mean(sigma_t(:,1));
```

Excel Data Set Formating

Test asset portfolios (e.g., the 25 size-BM portfolios from Kenneth French website). Returns are in percentage terms.

Date	SMALL LoBM	ME1 BM2	ME1 BM3	ME1 BM4	SMALL HiBM	ME2 BM1	ME2 BM2
19600104	−0.45	−0.13	1.52	0.59	1.30	0.88	0.22
19600105	3.05	0.30	−0.18	0.29	1.10	0.24	0.17
19600106	−0.50	0.05	−0.05	−0.22	0.31	−0.79	−0.46
19600107	−1.44	−0.24	−0.04	0.25	0.25	−0.58	0.06

Factors in the Fama and French three-factor model plus momentum factor (from Kenneth French website). Returns are in percentage terms.

Date	Mkt-RF	SMB	HML	MOM	RF
19600104	−0.03	0.6	0.68	−0.79	0.017
19600105	0.78	−0.4	0.55	−0.5	0.017
19600106	−0.47	0.12	0.35	0.08	0.017
19600107	−0.65	0.36	0.09	−0.31	0.017

Factors in the ZCAPM. Here mu is Mkt-RF (or excess average market return over the Treasury rate) and sigma is cross-sectional return dispersion (*RD*). Data are in raw terms.

	mu	sigma
19600105	0.007798	0.013337
19600106	−0.00439	0.010727
19600107	−0.0063	0.012206
19600108	−0.00318	0.011563

Excel Output in File Named Results

Empirical ZCAPM estimation outputs. Each row is a test asset stock portfolio or stock.

beta	zeta	p
1.099748	0.115203	0.42717
1.002184	0.216142	0.476845
0.771063	0.066483	0.67937
0.710273	0.092007	0.501039

Cross-sectional regression outputs. Single regression results are shown also, including Shanken t-statistics for this single (one) regression approach.

	lambda	t-stat	Shanken t
alpha	0.759312	3.084977	
market	−0.17832	−0.72595	
zeta*	0.488589	4.296504	
r-square	0.969062		
alpha(one regression)	0.446998	1.180255	
market(one regression)	0.08308	0.187951	−0.714536
zeta*(one regression)	1.515916	4.795311	3.3367293

Index

J. W. Kolari et al., *A New Model of Capital Asset Prices*,
https://doi.org/10.1007/978-3-030-65197-8

The manufacturer's authorised representative in the EU is Springer Nature Customer Service Centre GmbH, Europaplatz 3, 69115 Heidelberg, Germany. If you have any concerns regarding our products, please contact ProductSafety@springernature.com

Printed and bound by CPI Group (UK) Ltd, Croydon, CR0 4YY

30/09/2026

02225326-0015